Beware of False Religions
&
Pagan Traditions
Part 2

Other Books by Apostle Hèlèné Fulton

Witchcraft in the Church

Only a Born-Again will make it into Heaven. Are you ready?

Beware of False Religions & Pagan Traditions Part 1

Beware of False Religions & Pagan Traditions Part 3

The Complete Deliverance Manual

Get Sanctified in 365 days. The Ultimate Devotional for men and women.

Beware of Pagan Healing & Exercises!

Did you sell your soul to the devil? There is a way out!

Beware of False Religions & Pagan Traditions
Part 2

Hélèné Fulton

Light the World Publishers
2014

Copyright © 2014 by Hélèné Fulton

All rights reserved. This book or any portion thereof may not be reproduced or used in any manner whatsoever without the express written permission of the publisher.

First Printing: 2014

ISBN 978-0-620-60890-9

Light the World Publishers

www.lighttheworldpublishers.com

For any help or orders e-mail our office:
admin@lighttheworldpublishers.com

Ordering Information:
Special discounts are available on quantity purchases by corporations, associations, educators, and others. For details, contact the publisher at the above listed e-mail address.

U.S. trade bookstores and wholesalers:

Please contact Light the World Publishers on e-mail address below.
admin@lighttheworldpublishers.com

Dedication

For all the unconditional love, guidance and teachings, all glory goes to:

God the Father
God the Son
God the Holy Spirit

To my loving husband Robert. Thank you for all the love and support. You truly have a servants heart and a love for God.

A special thanks to all my spiritual children & spiritual brothers and sisters who not only assisted with writing this book but who prays for me daily.

Tanja Davey – Thank you for allowing the Holy Spirit to guide you in the design of the cover for this book. You are a true daughter of the King of kings.

Contents

Acknowledgements	xiii
Foreword	xv
Preface	xvi
Introduction	20
Chapter 1: Lutheran	43
Chapter 2: Hinduism	94
Chapter 3: Witchcraft	161
Chapter 4: Kabbalah	256
Chapter 5: Zion Christian Church (ZCC)	277
Chapter 6: William Marrion Branahm	303
Chapter 7: Freemasonry	386
Chapter 8: United Church of Christ	413
Chapter 9: Church of Christ	415
Chapter 10: Buddhism	424
Chapter 11: Amish	442
Chapter 12: Seventh-Day Adventist	461
Chapter 13: Roman Catholicism	495
Chapter 14: Father and Father's day	586
Annexure A - Babylon	596
Annexure B - Testimony of Daniel M Phaladi	621
Annexure C - Sevenfold Glory of His Person	628
Annexure D	643
References	671

Acknowledgements

I would like to thank my Spiritual brothers & sisters and spiritual children who wrote some of the Chapters in this book.

Without your dedication and hard work it would not have been possible to get this book written and published in such a short time.

By helping to write this book, you are helping to inform the world about the false teachings out there and our prayer is that those people and the people that they are teaching a false doctrine will be saved.

Foreword

My people are destroyed for lack of knowledge: because thou hast rejected knowledge, I will also reject thee, that thou shalt be no priest to me: seeing thou hast forgotten the law of thy God, I will also forget thy children.
Hosea 4:6

4 Now the Spirit speaketh expressly, that in the latter times some shall depart from the faith, giving heed to seducing spirits, and doctrines of devils
1 Timothy 4:1

Even today it still shocks me when I listen to a Television channel or hear a preacher teach God's children the wrong doctrine. Every time I think I have heard it all just to be shocked even more.

God gave me the two scriptures above to make me understand why some are teaching false doctrines and why some people will keep listening to these false teachings.

When God gave me the title of this book I had no idea that this book will be in a 3 part series because of the amount of False Religions there are in the world.

Why this book? To tell the people the truth according to God's word the Holy Bible.

If you have a problem with this book take it up with our Father in Heaven and read His Word from the King James Bible. I can only pray that your eyes will be opened then.

Preface

There are only two roads; one leads to heaven and one leads to hell. This is a spiritual fact, without change or compromise; there is no middle road and no chance to "sit on the fence".

"Wide is the gate and broad is the way that leads to destruction, and there are many who go in by it."

Matthew 7:13

[19] "I call heaven and earth as witnesses today against you, that I have set before you life and death, blessing and cursing; therefore choose life, that both you and your descendants may live"

Deuteronomy 30:19

There are numerous false religions operating in the world today, falsely broadcasting themselves as truth or as God's truth for that matter. These religions may, on the contrary, be the foundation of lifelong poverty, family breakdown, mental derangement, physical illness or varying manifestations of bizarre behaviour in the lives of people.

In a world where the motto is that "all roads lead to Rome" and suggests that everyone serves the same god, this book not only exposes these lies but also seeks to convey the truth to the many deceived individuals. These individuals have either turned their back on the true God completely or, by their actions, have allowed some of these pagan and false religious practises to creep into there every day lives. By clinging to these pagan traditions, we inadvertently give Satan a foothold in our lives.

In these books these false religions have been measured up against the word, wisdom and knowledge of God. The word of God says that His word is like fire and is a hammer that breaks rocks into pieces.

"Is not My word like a fire?" says the Lord, "And like a hammer that breaks the rock in pieces?"
Jeremiah 23:29

The false religions have been measured up and are left wanting.

"Casting down arguments and every high thing that exalts itself against the knowledge of God, bringing every thought into captivity to the obedience of Christ,"
2 Corinthians 10:5

Hell was not made for humans, but for the devil and the demons. God never intended for humans to go to hell. By humans denying and turning their backs on the precious blood of His only begotten Son (who gave His life freely), they will find themselves ending up in this place of burning fire, where there is no ease to their pain.

"There shall be weeping and gnashing of teeth, when ye shall see Abraham, and Isaac, and Jacob, and all the prophets, in the kingdom of God, and you yourselves thrust out".
Luke 13:28

God has no interest in leaving anyone out. His heart is for all to be saved. God is "not willing that any should perish but that all should come to repentance."

[9] "The Lord is not slack concerning His promise, as some count slackness, but is longsuffering toward us, not willing that any should perish but that all should come to repentance."
2 Peter: 3:9

The last days are nearing and God is preparing His bride. He is bringing to light the lies that has been believed for so many years.

When the light of God shines on darkness, darkness has to flee and the enemy has no more power or place to hide. He can only operate in darkness and where he cannot be seen.

"He shall be driven from light into darkness, and chased out of the world".
John 18:18

Knowledge is power and the intention of this book is not to condemn, but rather equip believers and bring those who are in darkness into the light, so that everyone may come to know the truth….as it is the truth that sets one free.

"Yea, though I walk through the valley of the shadow of death, I will fear no evil; For You are with me; Your rod and Your staff, they comfort me"
Psalm 23:4

[31] "So Jesus said to the Jews who had believed him, "If you abide in my word, you are truly my disciples, [32] and you will know the truth, and the truth will set you free."

John 8:31-32

Scott Davey

Introduction

The Introduction is very important in this book as it will give you the foundation complete with scripture on how to make sure you are not part of a False or Pagan Religion.

What it means to be Born Again

The New Birth
3 There was a man of the Pharisees named Nicodemus, a ruler of the Jews. 2 This man came to Jesus by night and said to Him, "Rabbi, we know that You are a teacher come from God; for no one can do these signs that You do unless God is with him." ³ Jesus answered and said to him, **"Most assuredly, I say to you, unless one is born again, he cannot see the kingdom of God."** ⁴ Nicodemus said to Him, "How can a man be born when he is old? Can he enter a second time into his mother's womb and be born?" ⁵ Jesus answered, **"Most assuredly, I say to you, unless one is born of water and the Spirit, he cannot enter the kingdom of God.** ⁶ That which is born of the flesh is flesh, and that which is born of the Spirit is spirit. ⁷ Do not marvel that I said to you, 'You must be born again.' ⁸ The wind blows where it wishes, and you hear the sound of it, but cannot tell where it comes from and where it goes. So is everyone who is born of the Spirit." ⁹ Nicodemus answered and said to Him, "How can these things be?" ¹⁰ Jesus answered and said to him, "Are you the teacher of Israel, and do not know these things? ¹¹ Most assuredly, I say to you, We speak what We know and testify what We have seen, and you do not receive Our witness. ¹² If I have told you earthly things and you do not believe, how will you believe if I tell you heavenly things? ¹³ No one has ascended to heaven but He who came down from heaven, *that is,* the Son of Man who is in heaven. ¹⁴ And as Moses lifted up the serpent in the wilderness, even so must the Son of Man be lifted up, ¹⁵ that

whoever believes in Him should not perish but have eternal life.
¹⁶ For God so loved the world that He gave His only begotten Son, that whoever believes in Him should not perish but have everlasting life.
¹⁷ For God did not send His Son into the world to condemn the world, but that the world through Him might be saved.
¹⁸ "He who believes in Him is not condemned; but he who does not believe is condemned already, because he has not believed in the name of the only begotten Son of God. ¹⁹ And this is the condemnation, **that the light has come into the world, and men loved darkness rather than light, because their deeds were evil.**
²⁰ For everyone practicing evil hates the light and does not come to the light, lest his deeds should be exposed. ²¹ But he who does the truth comes to the light, that his deeds may be clearly seen, that they have been done in God."

John 3:1-21

Nicodemus was a theological professor and a member in parliament, he paid his tithe from all his income, he fasted two days a week, he prayed two hours a day. But look at what Jesus is asking Nicodemus in verse 10. *"Are you the teacher of Israel, and do not know these things?*

Even in today's modern world with millions of preachers about 95% of them are not born again and probably does not even know what it means. This is scary as they are the teachers of the gospel.

It is very easy to say that I believe the Bible. It is very easy to say I know the Bible. It is even easier to say I'm a Christian but are you really a Christian? Are you 100% sure that you will enter the kingdom of God (Heaven) when your physical body dies.

You might be a very good person doing wonderful deeds for your fellow man but have you really been born again!

Are you a new person in Jesus Christ?

Are you willing to deny yourself and give yourself completely over to Jesus Christ? Are you willing to let Jesus Christ control your life?

Jesus did not say you ought to be born again He said **you have to be** born again if you want to enter the kingdom of God.

What Jesus was saying is that it is easy to say I'm a Christian but it is different matter to really know Jesus Christ.

You cannot just do the things to show people you're a Christian; you need to know Jesus Christ Himself. Jesus said this because he knows your heart. Yes Jesus Christ knows every person's heart. He knows you say you love Him but He knows that your heart belongs to business or pleasure or even to Satan.

All the sins you're doing each day comes from within. It starts from the heart and once it reaches the mind you're already making plans to fulfill that desire. That is why God said guard your heart in His word (the Bible).

[23] Keep thy heart with all diligence; for out of it are the issues of life.

Proverbs 4:23 (KJ)

There's a lot of good people supporting the under privilege, but some people are doing it to be seen by others. God looks at what's inside your heart. Even if man lived in paradise, he'll still have an evil heart.
You can only change this if you give your heart to God to control completely.

Never please people please God.
Born again means to be "born from above."
Nicodemus had a real need. He was hungry to change and he needed a change of his heart - a spiritual transformation.
New birth, being born again, is an act of God whereby eternal life is imparted to the person who believes indicates that "born again" also carries the idea "to become children of God" through trust in the name of Jesus Christ.

^{17} Therefore, if anyone *is* in Christ, *he is* a new creation; old things have passed away; behold, all things have become new.
2 Corinthians 5:17

^{5} not by works of righteousness which we have done, but according to His mercy He saved us, through the washing of regeneration and renewing of the Holy Spirit,
Titus 3:5

^{3} Blessed *be* the God and Father of our Lord Jesus Christ, who according to His abundant mercy has begotten us again to a living hope through the resurrection of Jesus Christ from the dead
1 Peter 1:3

^{29} If you know that He is righteous, you know that everyone who practices righteousness is born of Him.
1 John 2:29

⁹ Whoever has been born of God does not sin, for His seed remains in him; and he cannot sin, because he has been born of God.

1 John 3:9

⁷ Beloved, let us love one another, for love is of God; and everyone who loves is born of God and knows God.

1 John 4:7

5 Whoever believes that Jesus is the Christ is born of God, and everyone who loves Him who begot also loves him who is begotten of Him. ² By this we know that we love the children of God, when we love God and keep His commandments. ³ For this is the love of God, that we keep His commandments. And His commandments are not burdensome. ⁴ For **whatever is born of God overcomes the world. And this is the victory that has overcome the world—our faith.**

1 John 5:1-4

¹⁸ We know that whoever is born of God does not sin; but he who has been born of God keeps himself, and the wicked one does not touch him.

1 John 5:18

¹² But as many as received Him, to them He gave the right to become children of God, to those who believe in His name: ¹³ who were born, not of blood, nor of the will of the flesh, nor of the will of man, but of God.

John 1:12-13

Why do you need to be born again?

2 And you *He made alive,* who were dead in trespasses and sins,

Ephesians 2:1

To the Romans in Romans 3:23, the Apostle wrote, *for all have sinned and fall short of the glory of God,* So, a person needs to be born again in order to have their sins forgiven and have a relationship with God.

²³ for all have sinned and fall short of the glory of God
Romans 3:23

How does that come to be?

⁸ For by grace you have been saved through faith, and that not of yourselves; *it is* the gift of God, ⁹ not of works, lest anyone should boast.
Ephesians 2:8-9

When a person is "saved," he/she has been born again, spiritually renewed, and is now a child of God by right of new birth. Trusting in Jesus Christ, the One who paid the penalty of sin when He died on the cross, is what it means to be "born again" spiritually.

¹⁷ Therefore, if anyone *is* in Christ, *he is* a new creation; old things have passed away; behold, all things have become new.
2 Corinthians 5:17

If you have never trusted in the Lord Jesus Christ as your Savior, how can you hear the Holy Spirit as He speaks to you? How will you hear the Holy Spirit when He warns you of danger?

Do you have what it takes to be a born again Christian?

Do you want a personal relationship with Jesus?

Don't say the prayer just you want "fire protection".

Become born again because you want to with all your heart.

Will you pray the prayer of repentance and become a new creation in Jesus Christ today?

[12] But as many as received Him, to them He gave the right to become children of God, to those who believe in His name: [13] who were born, not of blood, nor of the will of the flesh, nor of the will of man, but of God.

John 1:12-13

If you are tired of living a life without meaning in a materialistic world that lacks compassion and love, a world that has chosen mammon as it's god and that will sacrifice anything and anybody to achieve its ultimate goal: "financial freedom", then please consider the alternative.

Jesus Christ is waiting for you every single day to open up your heart to Him and to invite Him into your life. If you prayed this prayer with a sincere and a true heart - then you can be assured that the Lord has prepared a place for you in heaven.

Once you are ready to take the next step the following prayer will be your ticket to Eternity:

The Prayer that will change Your Eternal Destiny

"Father, I thank You that Jesus died for me. I confess I have broken Your laws. Forgive my sins. I receive the pardon right now. Lord Jesus, come into my life. Give

me a new heart with new desires. And by Your Spirit, give me the power to live a life that is pleasing to You. Father please fill me with the Holy Spirit. Thank you for forgiving me as You have promised. Thank You for the gift of eternal Life."

Congratulations and welcome to the family of God. No matter what you've done in your life, you've received a full pardon in God's eyes. That's how easy it is for you. But it was not free - it cost God the life of His beloved Son, Jesus Christ in your place. Just thank Him for loving you so much.

Write this date in your Bible as this is the date the new you were born.

Why do we get Baptized

The English word "Baptism" comes from the Greek word "Baptizo", which means to, dip under, immerse, and whelm that is, to cover wholly with fluid. So this cannot include sprinkling a few drops of water on a baby's forehead.
You need to get baptised because Jesus was baptised and He **left an example for us to follow** in His steps.

John Baptizes Jesus
[13] Then Jesus came from Galilee to John at the Jordan to be baptized by him. [14] And John *tried to* prevent Him, saying, "I need to be baptized by You, and are You coming to me?" [15] But Jesus answered and said to him, "Permit *it to be so* now, for thus it is fitting for us to fulfill all righteousness." Then he allowed Him.
[16] When He had been baptized, Jesus came up immediately from the water; and behold, the heavens were opened to Him, and He

saw the Spirit of God descending like a dove and alighting upon Him. ¹⁷ And suddenly a voice *came* from heaven, saying, "This is My beloved Son, in whom I am well pleased."

Matthew 3:13-17

Jesus was baptised to "fulfil" or "complete" all righteousness by being **obedient** to His Father's (God) will. He was not baptised because He was a forgiven sinner, for He had no sin. He was always righteous. If Jesus was not baptised, He would have disobeyed His Father's will and would no longer have been righteous.

Obedience pleases God and brings the blessing of God.

²¹ For He made Him who knew no sin *to be* sin for us, that we might become the righteousness of God in Him.

2 Corinthians 5:21

Christians are also righteous and so like Christ are baptised to fulfil or complete all righteousness, by an act of obedience.

It is a commandment of God in scripture and children of God desire to obey God.

¹⁵ And He said to them, "Go into all the world and preach the gospel to every creature. ¹⁶ He who believes and is baptized will be saved; but he who does not believe will be condemned.

Mark 16:15-16

Do you love God? Look what the Bible tells us.

¹⁵ "If you love Me, keep My commandments.

John 14:15

Are there any special conditions you need to fulfil before you can be baptised?

³⁵ Then Philip opened his mouth, and beginning at this Scripture, preached Jesus to him. ³⁶ Now as they went down the road, they came to some water. And the eunuch said, "See, *here is* water. What hinders me from being baptized?"
³⁷ Then Philip said, "If you believe with all your heart, you may." And he answered and said, "I believe that Jesus Christ is the Son of God."
³⁸ So he commanded the chariot to stand still. And both Philip and the eunuch went down into the water, and he baptized him.
³⁹ Now when they came up out of the water, the Spirit of the Lord caught Philip away, so that the eunuch saw him no more; and he went on his way rejoicing.

Acts 8:35-39

When the Ethiopian eunuch asked the evangelist Phillip: "What hinders me from being baptized?" "

The Evangelist answered and said: "If you believe with all your heart, you may."

And he answered and said, "I believe that Jesus Christ is the Son of God."

⁹ that if you confess with your mouth the Lord Jesus and believe in your heart that God has raised Him from the dead, you will be saved.

Romans 10:9

Once you are saved, you are ready for baptism. There is no special spiritual level you have to reach to prepare yourself for baptism. When you are saved you are re-born with God's righteousness and there is nothing else you can do to prepare yourself for baptism.

Water baptism is a symbolic burial, by which the new born again Christian publicly declares they have died, and are now beginning a new life, in Christ.

Water baptism outwardly demonstrates what has happened inwardly. Water baptism helps you to grasp the reality of the spiritual truth that the old "you" has died.

Water baptism is only as important as the person being baptized believes it to be. Water baptism is their confession, and a public commitment.

You die to the old you when you accept Jesus Christ as your Lord and Savior. So some people see baptism as a burial to that old self. When they come out from under the water they come out as a new person.

But unless the person really believes they died, there is no need for a burial.

It is not something you do to impress God or your pastor, but something to impress on our mind what happened to us inwardly. Water baptism is for your benefit not God's.

[38] Then Peter said to them, "Repent, and let every one of you be baptized in the name of Jesus Christ for the remission of sins; and you shall receive the gift of the Holy Spirit.

Acts 2:38

Peter is not giving a new way for water baptism but is instructing these disciples in the authority of the name of Jesus Christ that since they have repented and been forgiven of their sins, they must now obey God and get baptised.

⁴¹ Then those who gladly received his word were baptized; and that day about three thousand souls were added *to them.*
Acts 2:41

Some Christians have struggled to receive the infilling of the Holy Spirit, because in their hearts they have determined to disobey God and not get baptised by immersion.

⁴⁷ "Can anyone forbid water, that these should not be baptized who have received the Holy Spirit just as we *have?*" ⁴⁸ And he commanded them to be baptized in the name of the Lord. Then they asked him to stay a few days.
Acts 10:47-48

Peter used his authority in the name of Jesus Christ to order them to be baptised and was not giving new instructions for water baptism.

We baptize people through our authority in Jesus Christ in the name of the Father and the Son and the Holy Spirit.

Why was Jesus baptized in water? He was, and is, our pattern. And, in a sense, He was, at that point, dying to His past life.

He was beginning His public ministry.

Jesus was declaring that He was dead to any selfishness and existed solely to do the will of Father God.

Must you be baptized to be saved? No. Once you have accepted Jesus Christ as your Lord and Saviour, you are saved.

^{43} And Jesus said to him, "Assuredly, I say to you, today you will be with Me in Paradise."

Luke 23:43

Jesus told this criminal that he will be with Him. This man was not baptized.

^{38} He who believes in Me, as the Scripture has said, out of his heart will flow rivers of living water." ^{39} But this He spoke concerning the Spirit, whom those believing in Him would receive; for the Holy Spirit was not yet *given,* because Jesus was not yet glorified.

John 7:38-39

^{17} And these signs will follow those who believe: In My name they will cast out demons; they will speak with new tongues

Mark 16:17

The household of Cornelius became believers, received the Holy Spirit, and began speaking in tongues, *before* being baptized in water.

According to Jesus receiving the Holy Spirit happens *only* to those who are believers, and they are therefore saved.
So, these believers were born again and ready for Heaven, before they were baptized in water.
If any of you want to be baptized and you are staying in Gauteng feel free to contact us on the e-mail provided in the front of this book.

The Doctrine of Christ

⁹ Whosoever transgresseth, and abideth not in the doctrine of Christ, hath not God. He that abideth in the doctrine of Christ, he hath both the Father and the Son.

2 John 1:9

There is nothing more important to Christianity than the fundamentals of the Bible - the Doctrine of Christ.

A "doctrine" is simply a teaching. Doctrines are composed of words. Thus words are critically important. The great theological battles and debates of our generation are being fought over the meaning of words, whether it is the word "repentance" or the word "inspired," the spiritual battle is raging.

God deliver us from deeper-life theologians who can quote the Bible, dissect it and expound upon it, but they never share the gospel with their neighbors and let the world die and go to Hell.

We aim to encourage everyone to be a soul-winner.

³⁰ The fruit of the righteous is a tree of life; and he that winneth souls is wise.

Proverbs 11:30

This is one Scripture that you won't hear often from the "intelligence" crowd.

Granted, it is "God that giveth the increase"

⁷ So then neither is he that planteth any thing, neither he that watereth; but God that giveth the increase.

1 Corinthians 3:7

Our part is to preach the gospel, sharing the good news of Jesus Christ Who died, was buried and rose again three days later for our sins.

15 Moreover, brethren, I declare unto you the gospel which I preached unto you, which also ye have received, and wherein ye stand;
² By which also ye are saved, if ye keep in memory what I preached unto you, unless ye have believed in vain.
³ For I delivered unto you first of all that which I also received, how that Christ died for our sins according to the scriptures;
⁴ And that he was buried, and that he rose again the third day according to the scriptures:

1 Corinthians 15:1-4

Thus, it is critically important that we never stop ringing the bell of the fundamental doctrines of the Christian faith, including the deity of Jesus, the virgin birth of Christ and His bodily, literal, resurrection from the dead. In an age when psychology is replacing Bible-preaching in our churches, and entertainment is replacing the power of God, the Doctrine of Christ cannot be stressed enough.

What is the Doctrine of Christ? It is THE TRUTH about Jesus Christ, as taught in the Word of God. The Doctrine of Christ includes, but is not limited to (as taught in the King James Bible):

- ➢ The Godhead, often called the "Trinity" one God

⁴ Hear, O Israel: The LORD our God is one LORD
Deuteronomy 6:4

Composed of the 3 literal Persons of God the Father, God the Son, and God the Holy Spirit.

¹⁹ Go ye therefore, and teach all nations, baptizing them in the name of the Father, and of the Son, and of the Holy Ghost:
²⁰ Teaching them to observe all things whatsoever I have commanded you: and, lo, I am with you always, even unto the end of the world. Amen.
Matthew 28:19-20

⁷ Go to, let us go down, and there confound their language, that they may not understand one another's speech.
Genesis 11:7

⁹ For in him dwelleth all the fulness of the Godhead bodily.
Colossians 2:9

¹⁶ And Jesus, when he was baptized, went up straightway out of the water: and, lo, the heavens were opened unto him, and he saw the Spirit of God descending like a dove, and lighting upon him:
¹⁷ And lo a voice from heaven, saying, This is my beloved Son, in whom I am well pleased.
Matthew 3:16-17

➢ The Godhead became FLESH in Jesus Christ

1 In the beginning was the Word, and the Word was with God, and the Word was God.
² The same was in the beginning with God.
³ All things were made by him; and without him was not any thing made that was made.

¹⁴ And the Word was made flesh, and dwelt among us, (and we beheld his glory, the glory as of the only begotten of the Father,) full of grace and truth.

John 1:14

¹⁶ And without controversy great is the mystery of godliness: God was manifest in the flesh, justified in the Spirit, seen of angels, preached unto the Gentiles, believed on in the world, received up into glory.

1 Timothy 3:16

⁹ For in him dwelleth all the fulness of the Godhead bodily.

Colossians 2:9

- ➢ **Jesus is the only BEGOTTEN Son of God**

¹⁶ For God so loved the world, that he gave his only begotten Son, that whosoever believeth in him should not perish, but have everlasting life.

John 3:16

- ➢ **Jesus is God Almighty**

1 In the beginning was the Word, and the Word was with God, and the Word was God.
² The same was in the beginning with God.
³ All things were made by him; and without him was not any thing made that was made.

John 1:1-3

¹⁴ And the Word was made flesh, and dwelt among us, (and we beheld his glory, the glory as of the only begotten of the Father,) full of grace and truth.

John 1:14

¹⁶ And without controversy great is the mystery of godliness: God was manifest in the flesh, justified in the Spirit, seen of angels, preached unto the Gentiles, believed on in the world, received up into glory.

1 Timothy 3:16

⁹ For in him dwelleth all the fulness of the Godhead bodily.
Colossians 2:9

⁸ I am Alpha and Omega, the beginning and the ending, saith the Lord, which is, and which was, and which is to come, the Almighty.

Revelation 1:8

➢ Christ's death, burial and bodily resurrection

15 Moreover, brethren, I declare unto you the gospel which I preached unto you, which also ye have received, and wherein ye stand;
² By which also ye are saved, if ye keep in memory what I preached unto you, unless ye have believed in vain.
³ For I delivered unto you first of all that which I also received, how that Christ died for our sins according to the scriptures;
⁴ And that he was buried, and that he rose again the third day according to the scriptures

1 Corinthians 15:1-4

➢ Jesus' sinless life and perfection

²¹ For he hath made him to be sin for us, who knew no sin; that we might be made the righteousness of God in him.

2 Corinthians 5:21

²¹ For even hereunto were ye called: because Christ also suffered for us, leaving us an example, that ye should follow his steps:
²² Who did no sin, neither was guile found in his mouth

1 Peter 2:21-22

¹⁵ For we have not an high priest which cannot be touched with the feeling of our infirmities; but was in all points tempted like as we are, yet without sin.

Hebrews 4:15

- ## Jesus' literal, physical, blood sacrifice for our sins

¹⁸ Forasmuch as ye know that ye were not redeemed with corruptible things, as silver and gold, from your vain conversation received by tradition from your fathers;
¹⁹ But with the precious blood of Christ, as of a lamb without blemish and without spot

1 Peter 1:18-19

¹² Neither by the blood of goats and calves, but by his own blood he entered in once into the holy place, having obtained eternal redemption for us.

Hebrews 9:12

²² And almost all things are by the law purged with blood; and without shedding of blood is no remission.
²³ It was therefore necessary that the patterns of things in the heavens should be purified with these; but the heavenly things themselves with better sacrifices than these.
²⁴ For Christ is not entered into the holy places made with hands, which are the figures of the true; but into heaven itself, now to appear in the presence of God for us:

Hebrews 9:22-24

- ➢ **Jesus Christ's virgin birth**

    [14] Therefore the Lord himself shall give you a sign; Behold, a virgin shall conceive, and bear a son, and shall call his name Immanuel.

    Isaiah 7:14

    [23] Behold, a virgin shall be with child, and shall bring forth a son, and they shall call his name Emmanuel, which being interpreted is, God with us.

    Matthew 1:23

- ➢ **Jesus' bodily ascension into Heaven**

    [11] Which also said, Ye men of Galilee, why stand ye gazing up into heaven? this same Jesus, which is taken up from you into heaven, shall so come in like manner as ye have seen him go into heaven.

    Acts 1:11

- ➢ **Jesus' bodily return at the Second Coming**

    [11] Which also said, Ye men of Galilee, why stand ye gazing up into heaven? this same Jesus, which is taken up from you into heaven, shall so come in like manner as ye have seen him go into heaven.

    Acts 1:11

    [7] Behold, he cometh with clouds; and every eye shall see him, and they also which pierced him: and all kindreds of the earth shall wail because of him. Even so, Amen.

    Revelation 1:7

These are all fundamental doctrines of the Bible-believing, Christian faith.
Please understand that I didn't know any of these doctrines when I got saved as a young girl. All I knew

was that I was a sinner and Jesus was the Savior. That's all I knew for years to come, until I gradually learned the Doctrine of Christ. You don't need to know all this to be saved; but if a person is taught these doctrines from the Bible, and they still deny them, then something is wrong. A saved person will not deny the Virgin Birth of Jesus if they've been taught so from the Scriptures.

I was saved at age 9. I had never heard of these doctrines, except that Jesus was the only Savior in Whom I needed to trust for salvation, to be forgiven of my sins. But years later when I was first taught these doctrines, I immediately knew they were true and accepted them as facts, because I was already saved and had the Holy Spirit dwelling within. I NEVER denied any of these Biblical fundamentals as a Christian, because the Bible teacher who first taught them to me used the Scriptures to prove them. A true believer will accept Biblical teachings; not strongly deny them.

If you would have asked me if Jesus was God when I got saved, I wouldn't have known, because I hadn't been taught that yet from the Bible. But when someone showed me in the Bible that Jesus was God, I got excited and wanted to learn all I could about my Savior. The Holy Spirit bears witness in my heart and said, that's true, Jesus is God almighty! I knew it was true because I saw it in the Word of God and the Holy Spirit said, that is correct.

I once spoke with a Catholic man about the deity of Jesus Christ. He immediately told me that he did not believe that Jesus was God. I quoted him some

Scriptures as evidence of the deity of Christ; but he didn't care, he still maintained that Jesus could not possibly be God. I knew right there that he was as unsaved as the Devil. So you see, if you are truly saved, then you will receive THE TRUTH.

²⁷ My sheep hear my voice, and I know them, and they follow me:

John 10:27

The King James Bible translators were very honest and scholarly in their work, even putting words in italics that they added to clarify the meaning in the original languages of Hebrew and Greek. In John 8:24, the masculine pronoun "he" is in italics, which means the literal translation is...

²⁴ I said therefore unto you, that ye shall die in your sins: for if ye believe not that **I am** he, ye shall die in your sins.

John 8:24

If you still want absolute solid proof of Christ's claim of deity, then read:

⁵⁷ Then said the Jews unto him, Thou art not yet fifty years old, and hast thou seen Abraham?
⁵⁸ Jesus said unto them, Verily, verily, I say unto you, Before Abraham was, **I am**.

John 8:57-58

¹⁴ And God said unto Moses, **I AM THAT I AM**: and he said, Thus shalt thou say unto the children of Israel, I AM hath sent me unto you.

Exodus 3:14

Here again we see that Jesus professed to be the "I AM" of Exodus 3:14. Jesus is almighty God!!!

Any Religion that denies Jesus Christ is a False Religion!

Chapter 1: Lutheran

What's wrong with the Lutheran religion?

To get right to the point, the Lutheran "religion" came out of the Catholic religion (often falsely so called a "church"). By the end of this chapter, you will also see that Martin Luther himself was a heretic. The Lutheran religion is a child of the parent Catholic monstrosity.

⁵ And on her forehead a name *was* written:
MYSTERY, BABYLON THE GREAT,
THE MOTHER OF HARLOTS
AND OF THE ABOMINATIONS
OF THE EARTH.

Revelation 17:5

The Catholic church is in no way a church. It is a false religion! For those of you who don't know, a church is not the same as a religion. A "church" is simply the assembling of two or more born-again believers in Jesus' name

²⁰ For where two or three are gathered together in My name, I am there in the midst of them."

Matthew 18:20

We foolishly tend to believe that to be in a "church" that one must be in some type of building.

This is simply NOT true. You can meet with other believers in an open field or in someone's home and still be just as much a local church. The persecuted

Christians during the brutal days of Rome met underground in the catacombs. "Religion" is all of man's traditions, lies, ceremonies, rituals and superstitions that imposters use in God's name as a crutch to take advantage of the masses (and they sure do). Religion is the worst thing that ever happened to this dark and sinful world. You see my friend, you need God, not religion. Religion is a sure road to hell and destruction.

The Narrow Way
¹³ "Enter by the narrow gate; for wide *is* the gate and broad *is* the way that leads to destruction, and there are many who go in by it. ¹⁴ Because narrow *is* the gate and difficult *is* the way which leads to life, and there are few who find it.

You Will Know Them by Their Fruits
¹⁵ "Beware of false prophets, who come to you in sheep's clothing, but inwardly they are ravenous wolves.
Matthew 7:13-15

You need the Lord Jesus Christ, not sacraments and rituals.

⁵ not by works of righteousness which we have done, but according to His mercy He saved us, through the washing of regeneration and renewing of the Holy Spirit,
Titus 3:5

Apart from simple faith in the loving Saviour, Jesus Christ, there can be no salvation.

⁶ Jesus said to him, "I am the way, the truth, and the life. No one comes to the Father except through Me.

John 14:6

The Lutheran religion is just that. **Religion!** It is more religion than God, more ritualistic tradition than truth. Every false religion on the planet is cloaked with some degree of truth. Too many sincere people have churchianity without Christianity. I definitely include the Lutheran religion here. The average person today is utterly confused concerning what the truth really is. Baptism is a prime example. The Bible clearly teaches that baptism is NOT a sacrament (i.e., necessary for one's salvation).

2 (though Jesus Himself did not baptize, but His disciples)
John 4:2

The verse above clearly informs us that Jesus did not baptize, the disciples did.

[17] For Christ did not send me to baptize, but to preach the gospel, not with wisdom of words, lest the cross of Christ should be made of no effect.
1 Corinthians 1:17

Paul did NOT come to baptize anybody, but he did come to *preach the gospel* of Jesus Christ.

I'm now going to share with you a few teachings from the "Small Catechism of Martin Luther" featured on many Lutheran church websites. Of course, these writings are authored by Martin Luther himself. I had always heard that Martin Luther became a believer after reading that "the just shall live by faith;" however, I simply have to question the genuine salvation of any man who believed and taught baptismal regeneration.

Q. What does Baptism give? What good is it?

A. It gives the forgiveness of sins, redeems from death and the Devil, gives eternal salvation to all who believe this, just as God's words and promises declare." Martin Luther

This is heresy! The thief on the cross was never baptized, yet Jesus promised him paradise that day. Nobody in the Old Testament was ever baptized, but we read that Abraham "believed God" and it was counted unto him for righteousness.

[3] For what does the Scripture say? "Abraham believed God, and it was accounted to him for righteousness.

Romans 4:3

You get your sins forgiven by placing your personal trust (faith) upon the Lord Jesus Christ to forgive your sins, NOT by getting wet through baptism. If you are a Lutheran who has been trusting in your baptism as the experience which forgive your sins, then you need to ask Jesus to forgive you immediately because you are not saved. As best you know how, simply ask the Lord Jesus to come into your heart as your personal Saviour. If you rely upon baptism as a DOOR to salvation, then you are going to end up in hell when you die.

The Catholic Church teaches in their Vatican II doctrines that baptism is "the door" into the Catholic church (and they teach the heresy that the Catholic church is Christ in the world). So according to the Vatican, only those who are baptized into the Catholic church will ever go to Heaven. That's a bunch of lies and damnable heresies!   You do NOT need to belong to any church to be saved. You do NOT need to go to church to be saved. You do NOT have to be baptized, pasteurized or homogenized to go to Heaven...you just need God (Jesus Christ, Who came into this wicked world to die on the cross for the sins of all mankind). Won't you trust Jesus Christ as your own Saviour right now before it's too late?

As I mentioned, the Lutheran religion came out of Catholicism, but Catholicism did NOT come out of the Lutheran movement. Proof of what I am saying is that Lutherans still practice infant baptism and the sacraments, just as the Catholic religion does.

As a side note, I'm going to jump on all churches here. Anybody can buy a building and hang a church sign in front. Does this make the building a church? Of course not! What makes a building a church? Nothing! A building can NEVER be a church. A true local church is when born-again believers congregate together in Jesus' name (building or no building). So if a bunch of unsaved people get together, they are just playing church.

If a so-called "church" has deteriorated to the place where all that matters is the offering plate being passed, it is no longer a church but a den of thieves (I speak of ALL churches and denominations here). All too common these days, the congregation goes through the motions, sings a few old hymns, the pastor tells a joke or two, announcements are read, etc, etc...like clock work...then the money collection! Though the church prides itself that it is not a "dead church" like others, it is in denial of its own dying and backslidden condition (if not dead itself). It seems that MONEY is the biggest concern in our Christian colleges and churches these days. Money, money, money...give us more money. I have grown to the point where I greatly detest nearly all of what we call churches and religion today. It's at the point nowadays where one needs to actually leave church to grow in the Lord.

Believers are so carnal that money has become the big issue. Listen carefully! Anyone who claims to be of God and speaks about money more than other things, get away from that person!

Getting back to the Lutheran religion, the following is another quote from the "Small Catechism of Martin Luther."

Q. What is confession?

A. Confession has two parts:

First, a person admits his or her sin

Second, a person receives absolution or forgiveness from the confessor, as if from God Himself, without doubting it, but believing firmly that his or her sins are forgiven by God in Heaven through it." Martin Luther

What a lie! This is heresy! No one can forgive your sins except Jesus Christ, God Almighty! It is the height of arrogance for any priest or pastor to claim the ability to absolve sins, this is totally unscriptural. We are advised to confess our "faults" one to another in James 5:16, but NEVER in the Bible are we told to confess our sins to anyone other than God alone.

[16] Confess *your* trespasses to one another, and pray for one another, that you may be healed. The effective, fervent prayer of a righteous man avails much.

James 5:16

It is no one's business what sins you have committed. Who is your pastor or priest going to confess to? God? Then why can't you do the same. Read the following Scripture...

[5] For *there is* one God and one Mediator between God and men, *the* Man Christ Jesus

1 Timothy 2:5

There is to be no one between you and God the Father other than the Lord Jesus Christ (the Son of God). This is 100% Bible, so NEVER confess your sins to any pastor (or any other human being for that matter). Only Jesus has the nail-scarred hands and feet, ONLY Jesus can forgive. Your minister or elder didn't die for your sins, he cannot absolve your sins or anybody else's. Catholics and Lutherans will readily admit that don't consider Mary a "mediator" yet then why do they pray to her? Their words contradict their actions. They pray to Mary and say their "Hail Marys" and yet have the audacity to say that they worship God only.

No Lutheran would ever exalt Mary to the level of deity as the Catholic do, yet the Lutherans idolize Mary in their prayers and commit a more subtle form of idolatry. The bottom line is that what they are doing is totally unbiblical and it originated in the heathen

Catholic religion. They are a confused bunch! In addition, the whole doctrine and practice of last rites is Satanic (the belief that a minister can forgive your sins on your death bed). If you have not accepted the Lord Jesus Christ as your personal Saviour to forgive your sins, then all the priests and pastors in the world cannot keep your soul out of the fires of hell. It's turn or burn, it's Jesus or hell my friend. Which will it be?

Q. What good does this eating and drinking do?

A. These words tell us: ``Given for you'' and ``Shed for you to forgive sins." Namely, that the forgiveness of sins, life, and salvation are given to us through these words in the Sacrament. Because, where sins are forgiven, there is life and salvation as well. Martin Luther

Again, more lies of the devil. There are NO words of any Sacrament that can forgive sin. This is the ritualistic mumbo-jumbo that God hates. Do you really think that by reading certain words audibly that you can get your sins forgiven? I understand that the Lutherans stress the importance of believing these words in your heart, but where in the Bible does it teach that we MUST recite ANY words at all? It does not! Martin Luther was very ignorant of theology. If you call upon the name of the Lord in your sincerest attempt, you will be saved.

[13] For "whoever calls on the name of the Lord shall be saved."
Romans 10:13

According to Martin Luther's "Large Catechism," a person MUST practice the Sacrament of Baptism and

Holy Communion in order to become a Christian. Remember, the Lutherans (as do the Catholics) believe that the Lord's Supper is a Sacrament (i.e., essential to one's salvation).

This is foolishness, not founded upon the Word of God. The Lutheran church prefers to call it the "Sacrament of the Alter" (holy communion) and the Catholics refer to it as the "Mass" or "Holy Eucharist." The Bible simply refers to it as the Lord's supper. So what is the Lord's supper? Scripturally, it is simply a time for us to stop everything and to reflect upon Christ's sacrifice of Himself upon the cross for our sins. It is a time of remembrance. To represent the body and shed blood of our Saviour, ONLY unleavened bread and unfermented grape juice should ever be used for the Lord's supper. Leaven and fermentation are decaying processing and certainly are not appropriate to represent the perfect sinless Lamb of God, Our Saviour Jesus Christ.

As with many false prophets, the writer of the "Small Catechism of Martin Luther" makes a deliberate effort to avoid taking any firm positions. Of course, the writer is Martin Luther himself. He "beats around the bush" (so-to-speak) without making any concrete points to argue. However, for the Bible-believing Christian who is skilled in the Word of God, the subtly of the author cannot hide his true intent. Martin Luther taught that water baptism and the Sacrament of the alter (Holy Communion) are necessary to salvation. Nothing could be further from the truth.

⁶ And if by grace, then *it is* no longer of works; otherwise grace is no longer grace. But **if *it is* of works, it is no longer grace**; otherwise work is no longer work.

Romans 11:6

You can't have it both ways. It's either by grace or by works! Either you are trying to work your way into heaven (which is a sure road to hell), or else you are trusting upon God's grace by placing your faith in the crucified Lord Jesus Christ.

Martin Luther was a Mary worshipper. Luther's many writings more than clearly reveal his Catholic allegiance to Mary. Listen people, Mary was a SINNER! Mary was not born of a virgin, nor were any of her other children besides Jesus. The only human being to ever be born into this world by a virgin birth conceived by the Holy Spirit was Jesus Christ, the ONLY begotten Son of God. Listen to the unscriptural ramblings of Luther...

"Our prayer should include the Mother of God...What the Hail Mary says is that all glory should be given to God, using these words: "Hail Mary, full of grace. The Lord is with thee; blessed art thou among women and blessed is the fruit of thy womb, Jesus Christ. Amen!" You see that these words are not concerned with prayer but purely with giving praise and honor... We can use the Hail Mary as a meditation in which we recite what grace God has given her. Second, we should add a wish that everyone may know and respect her... He who has no faith is advised to refrain from saying the Hail Mary." (Personal Prayer Book, 1522). Martin Luther

This is Satanic heresy, plain and simple! I've never said a "hail Mary" in my life and don't plan to start either. How silly and foolish for anyone to believe and practice such idolatry. I have nothing against the lady named Mary in heaven which gave birth to our earthly Saviour. I do have a problem with praising, adoring or even mentioning her in our prayers. Why? Because the first of the ten commandments forbids us to worship anyone other than God.

For a Catholic or Lutheran to claim to worship God only THROUGH Mary is heresy, a lie of the devil. We are clearly warned in

[5] For *there is* one God and one Mediator between God and men, *the* Man Christ Jesus

1 Timothy 2:5

that there is only ONE Mediator between God and man, the Lord Jesus Christ. Mary CANNOT mediate for you! And by the way, neither can the pope or your pastor. I speak the truth, you must decide for yourself. Most people make light of the truth and could care less about God or His TRUTH. Is your doctrine of God? Is it grounded firmly in the Bible? Can you back up what you believe with God's Word? Show me ONE, just one verse in the entire Bible that even remotely indicates that we should recognize Mary in ANY way. You cannot! On the contrary, Mary magnified Christ.

[5] His mother said to the servants, "Whatever He says to you, do *it.*"

John 2:5

Mary was a godly woman, no more...no less. It is wicked idolatry to say "hail Mary." It is a horrible, horrible sin to bow to Mary in any manner (statue or no statue). The Lutherans are committing sin if they "hail Mary." Even if the sincere intention is to indirectly worship God THROUGH Mary, it is wicked and wrong to do such a thing. It is idolatry. Mary worship is a sin.

I am proud to say I am NOT a Lutheran or a Catholic. I am a born again Christian, plain and simple. I do not pride myself in being part of any denomination or religious camp. I am a born again Christian! Why do nearly all religious people have a need to wear a label of some sort? Are we afraid to stand alone? I have faith in God, end of statement. I have no allegiance for any man-made organization or religious authority. I serve the Lord Jesus Christ and Him alone will I answer to. I've seen too many believers become saint worshippers. Meaning, they follow a human being instead of God.

Of course they know it's wrong to do so, so they live in denial of what they are doing. This is why you'll often see religious people following a man who is going down spiritually. When a preacher are exposed in the news for his extra-marital affairs and child out of wedlock, his religious followers will stand strong by his side. Though I admire their willingness to forgive their leader, where does holiness and being a true man of God come into place? It appears that anything goes nowadays. Do those people care about what God thinks? I'll let you answer for yourself, I condemn no one.

Who are you following? Who are you giving your offering money to? What is your church doing with that money? All I am saying is that you had better learn to THINK FOR YOURSELF. Start asking questions. Crooked ministers live high and mighty because of dumb religious people. It's sad but true. Why do you give them your money? To ease your religious guilt? To make you feel better? To stay on good terms with the leadership at your church? To impress others? You do not need to go to church to be spiritual, and anyone who says otherwise is a liar. I am not criticizing going to church, not at all. I am simply saying that it's about time that people start caring more about THE TRUTH and what God wants from us, instead of trying to figure out what our church wants from us (money mostly). God wants your heart, most churches want your wallet.

[1]Martin Luther's Small Catechism (1529)

---

[1] PROJECT WITTENBERG

Luther's Little Instruction Book
(The Small Catechism of Martin Luther)
Translated by Robert E. Smith
May 22, 1994
(Version 1.1 -- December 22, 1994)
PW# 001-003-002Ea

This text was translated in 1994 for Project Wittenberg by Robert E. Smith and is in the public domain. You may freely distribute, copy or print this text. Please direct any comments or suggestions to:

Rev. Robert E. Smith
Walther Library
Concordia Theological Seminary.

Surface Mail: 6600 N. Clinton St., Ft. Wayne, IN 46825 USA

THE TEN COMMANDMENTS

The Ten Commandments: The Simple Way a Father Should Present Them to His Household

A. The First Commandment

You must not have other gods.

Q. What does this mean?

A. We must fear, love, and trust God more than anything else.

B. The Second Commandment

You must not misuse your God's name.

Q. What does this mean?

A. We must fear and love God, so that we will not use His name to curse, swear, cast a spell, lie or deceive, but will use it to call upon Him, pray to Him, praise Him and thank Him in all times of trouble.

C. The Third Commandment

You must keep the Sabbath holy.

Q. What does this mean?

A. We must fear and love God, so that we will not look down on preaching or God's Word, but consider it holy, listen to it willingly, and learn it.

D. The Fourth Commandment

You must honor your father and mother. [So that things will go well for you and you will live long on earth].

Q. What does this mean?

A. We must fear and love God, so that we will neither look down on our parents or superiors nor irritate them, but will honor them, serve them, obey them, love them and value them.

E. The Fifth Commandment

You must not kill.

Q. What does this mean?

A. We must fear and love God, so that we will neither harm nor hurt our neighbor's body, but help him and care for him when he is ill.

F. The Sixth Commandment

You must not commit adultery.

Q. What does this mean?

A. We must fear and love God, so that our words and actions will be clean and decent and so that everyone will love and honor their spouses.

G. The Seventh Commandment

You must not steal.

Q. What does this mean?

A. We must fear and love God, so that we will neither take our neighbor's money or property, nor acquire it by fraud or by selling him poorly made products, but will help him improve and protect his property and career.

H. The Eighth Commandment

You must not tell lies about your neighbor.

Q. What does this mean?

A. We must fear and love God, so that we will not deceive by lying, betraying, slandering or ruining our neighbor's reputation, but will defend him, say good things about him, and see the best side of everything he does.

I. The Ninth Commandment

You must not desire your neighbor's house.

Q. What does this mean?

A. We must fear and love God, so that we will not attempt to trick our neighbor out of his inheritance or house, take it by pretending to have a right to it, etc. but help him to keep & improve it.

J. The Tenth Commandment

You must not desire your neighbor's wife, servant, maid, animals or anything that belongs to him.

Q. What does this mean?

A. We must fear and love God, so that we will not release his cattle, take his employees from him or seduce his wife, but urge them to stay and do what they ought to do.

K. The Conclusion to the Commandments

Q. What does God say to us about all these commandments?

A. This is what He says:

"I am the Lord Your God. I am a jealous God. I plague the grandchildren and great-grandchildren of those who hate me with their ancestor's sin. But I make whole those who love me for a thousand generations."

Q. What does it mean?

A. God threatens to punish everyone who breaks these commandments. We should be afraid of His anger because of this and not violate such commandments. But He promises grace and all good things to those who keep such commandments. Because of this, we, too, should love Him, trust Him, and willingly do what His commandments require.

[2]The Creed

---

[2] This text was translated in 1994 for Project Wittenberg by Robert E. Smith and is in the public domain. You may freely distribute, copy or

The Creed: The Simple Way a Father Should Present it to His Household

I. The First Article: On Creation

I believe in God the Almighty Father, Creator of Heaven and Earth.

Q. What does this mean?

A. I believe that God created me, along with all creatures. He gave to me: body and soul, eyes, ears and all the other parts of my body, my mind and all my senses and preserves them as well. He gives me clothing and shoes, food and drink, house and land, wife and children, fields, animals and all I own. Every day He abundantly provides everything I need to nourish this body and life. He protects me against all danger, shields and defends me from all evil. He does all this because of His pure, fatherly and divine goodness and His mercy, not because I've earned it or desrved it. For all of this, I must thank Him, praise Him, serve Him and obey Him. Yes, this is true!

II. The Second Article: On Redemption

And in Jesus Christ, His only Son, our Lord, Who was conceived by the Holy Spirit, born of the Virgin Mary, suffered under Pontius Pilate, was crucified, died and

---

print this text. Please direct any comments or suggestions to:

Rev. Robert E. Smith
Walther Library
Concordia Theological Seminary.

was buried, descended to Hell, on the third day rose again from the dead, ascended to Heaven and sat down at the right hand of God the Almighty Father. From there He will come to judge the living and the dead.

Q. What does this mean?

A. I believe that Jesus Christ is truly God, born of the Father in eternity and also truly man, born of the Virgin Mary. He is my Lord! He redeemed me, a lost and condemned person, bought and won me from all sins, death and the authority of the Devil. It did not cost Him gold or silver, but His holy, precious blood, His innocent body -- His death! Because of this, I am His very own, will live under Him in His kingdom and serve Him righteously, innocently and blessedly forever, just as He is risen from death, lives and reigns forever. Yes, this is true.

III. The Third Article: On Becoming Holy

I believe in the Holy Spirit, the holy Christian Church, the community of the saints, the forgiveness of sins, the resurrection of the body, and an everlasting life. Amen.

Q. What does this mean?

A. I believe that I cannot come to my Lord Jesus Christ by my own intellegence or power. But the Holy Spirit call me by the Gospel, enlightened me with His gifts, made me holy and kept me in the true faith, just as He calls, gathers together, enlightens and makes holy the whole Church on earth and keeps it with

Jesus in the one, true faith. In this Church, He generously forgives each day every sin committed by me and by every believer. On the last day, He will raise me and all the dead from the grave. He will give eternal life to me and to all who believe in Christ. Yes, this is true!

[3]The Lord's Prayer

The Our Father
The Simple Way a Father Should Present it to His Household

I. Introduction

Our Father, Who is in Heaven.

Q. What does this mean?

A. In this introduction, God invites us to believe that He is our real Father and we are His real children, so that we will pray with trust and complete confidence, in the same way beloved children approach their beloved Father with their requests.

II. The First Request

May Your name be holy.

---

[3] This text was translated in 1994 for Project Wittenberg by Robert E. Smith and is in the public domain. You may freely distribute, copy or print this text. Please direct any comments or suggestions to:

Rev. Robert E. Smith
Walther Library
Concordia Theological Seminary.

Q. What does this mean?

A. Of course, God's name is holy in and of itself, but by this request, we pray that He will make it holy among us, too.

Q. How does this take place?

A. When God's Word is taught clearly and purely, and when we live holy lives as God's children based upon it. Help us, Heavenly Father, to do this! But anyone who teaches and lives by something other than God's Word defiles God's name among us. Protect us from this, Heavenly Father!

III. The Second Request

Your Kingdom come.

Q. What does this mean?

A. Truly God's Kingdom comes by itself, without our prayer. But we pray in this request that it come to us as well.

Q. How does this happen?

A. When the Heavenly Father gives us His Holy Spirit, so that we believe His holy Word by His grace and live godly lives here in this age and there in eternal life.

IV. The Third Request

May Your will be accomplished, as it is Heaven, so may it be on Earth.

Q. What does this mean?

A. Truly, God's good and gracious will is accomplished without our prayer. But we pray in this request that is be accomplished among us as well.

Q. How does this happen?

A. When God destroys and interferes with every evil will and all evil advice, which will not allow God's Kingdom to come, such as the Devil's will, the world's will and will of our bodily desires. It also happens when God strengthens us by faith and by His Word and keeps living by them faithfully until the end of our lives. This is His will, good and full of grace.

V. The Fourth Request

Give us our daily bread today.

Q. What does this mean?

A. Truly, God gives daily bread to evil people, even without our prayer. But we pray in this request that He will help us realize this and receive our daily bread with thanksgiving.

Q. What does ``Daily Bread'' mean?

A. Everything that nourishes our body and meets its needs, such as: Food, drink, clothing, shoes, house, yard, fields, cattle, money, possessions, a devout spouse, devout children, devout employees, devout and faithful rulers, good government, good weather, peace, health, discipline, honor, good friends, faithful neighbors and other things like these.

VI. The Fifth Request

And forgive our guilt, as we forgive those guilty of sinning against us.

Q. What does this mean?

A. We pray in this request that our Heavenly Father will neither pay attention to our sins nor refuse requests such as these because of our sins and because we are neither worthy nor deserve the things for which we pray. Yet He wants to give them all to us by His grace, because many times each day we sin and truly deserve only punishment. Because God does this, we will, of course, want to forgive from our hearts and willingly do good to those who sin against us.

VII. The Sixth Request

And lead us not into temptation.

Q. What does this mean?

A. God tempts no one, of course, but we pray in this request that God will protect us and save us, so that the Devil, the world and our bodily desires will neither deceive us nor seduce us into heresy, despair or other serious shame or vice, and so that we will win and be victorious in the end, even if they attack us.

VIII. The Seventh Request

But set us free from the Evil One.

Q. What does this mean?

A. We pray in this request, as a summary, that our Father in Heaven will save us from every kind of evil that threatens body, soul, property and honor. We pray that when at last our final hour has come, He will grant us a blessed death, and, in His grace, bring us to Himself from this valley of tears.

IX. Amen.

Q. What does this mean?

A. That I should be certain that such prayers are acceptable to the Father in Heaven and will be granted, that He Himself has commanded us to pray in this way and that He promises to answer us. Amen. Amen. This means: Yes, yes it will happen this way.

[4]Holy Baptism

Q. What is Baptism?

---

[4] This text was translated in 1994 for Project Wittenberg by Robert E. Smith and is in the public domain. You may freely distribute, copy or print this text. Please direct any comments or suggestions to:

Rev. Robert E. Smith
Walther Library
Concordia Theological Seminary.

A. Baptism is not just plain water, but it is water contained within God's command and united with God's Word.

Q. Which Word of God is this?

A. The one which our Lord Christ spoke in the last chapter of Matthew:

Go into all the world, teaching all heathen nations, and baptizing them in the name of the Father, the Son and of the Holy Spirit.

Q. What does Baptism give? What good is it?

A. It gives the forgiveness of sins, redeems from death and the Devil, gives eternal salvation to all who believe this, just as God's words and promises declare.

Q. What are these words and promises of God?

A. Our Lord Christ spoke one of them in the last chapter of Mark:

Whoever believes and is baptized will be saved; but whoever does not believe will be damned.

Q. How can water do such great things?

A. Water doesn't make these things happen, of course. It is God's Word, which is with and in the water. Because, without God's Word, the water is plain water and not baptism. But with God's Word it is a Baptism, a grace-filled water of life, a bath of new birth in the Holy Spirit, as St. Paul said to Titus in the third chapter:

Through this bath of rebirth and renewal of the Holy Spirit, which He poured out on us abundantly through Jesus Christ, our Savior, that we, justified by the same grace are made heirs according to the hope of eternal life. This is a faithful saying.

Q. What is the meaning of such a water Baptism?

A. It means that the old Adam in us should be drowned by daily sorrow and repentance, and die with all sins and evil lusts, and, in turn, a new person daily come forth and rise from death again. He will live forever before God in righteousness and purity.

Q. Where is this written?

A. St. Paul says to the Romans in chapter six:

We are buried with Christ through Baptism into death, so that, in the same way Christ is risen from the dead by the glory of the Father, thus also must we walk in a new life.

[5]Confession
How One Should Teach the Uneducated to Confess

---

[5] This text was translated in 1994 for Project Wittenberg by Robert E. Smith and is in the public domain. You may freely distribute, copy or print this text. Please direct any comments or suggestions to:

Rev. Robert E. Smith
Walther Library
Concordia Theological Seminary.

Q. What is confession?

A. Confession has two parts:

First, a person admits his sin
Second, a person receives absolution or forgiveness from the confessor, as if from God Himself, without doubting it, but believing firmly that his sins are forgiven by God in Heaven through it.

Q. Which sins should people confess?

A. When speaking to God, we should plead guilty to all sins, even those we don't know about, just as we do in the "Our Father," but when speaking to the confessor, only the sins we know about, which we know about and feel in our hearts.

Q. Which are these?

A. Consider here your place in life according to the Ten Commandments. Are you a father? A mother? A son? A daughter? A husband? A wife? A servant? Are you disobedient, unfaithful or lazy? Have you hurt anyone with your words or actions? Have you stolen, neglected your duty, let things go or injured someone?

[6]The Sacrament of the Altar (Holy Communion)

---

[6] This text was translated in 1994 for Project Wittenberg by Robert E. Smith and is in the public domain. You may freely distribute, copy or print this text. Please direct any comments or suggestions to:

Rev. Robert E. Smith
Walther Library
Concordia Theological Seminary

The Simple Way a Father Should Present it to His Household

Q. What is the Sacrament of the Altar?

A. It is the true body and blood of our Lord Jesus Christ under bread and wine for us Christians to eat and to drink, established by Christ Himself.

Q. Where is that written?

A. The holy apostles Matthew, Mark and Luke and St. Paul write this:

Our Lord Jesus Christ, in the night on which He was betrayed, took bread, gave thanks, broke it, gave it to His disciples and said: "Take! Eat! This is My body, which is given for you. Do this to remember Me!" In the same way He also took the cup after supper, gave thanks, gave it to them, and said: "Take and drink from it, all of you! This cup is the New Testament in my blood, which is shed for you to forgive sins. This do, as often as you drink it, to remember Me!"

Q. What good does this eating and drinking do?

A. These words tell us: "Given for you" and "Shed for you to forgive sins." Namely, that the forgiveness of sins, life and salvation are given to us through these words in the sacrament. Because, where sins are forgiven, there is life and salvation as well.

Q. How can physical eating and drinking do such great things?

A. Of course, eating and drinking do not do these things. These words, written here, do them: "given for you" and "shed for you to forgive sins." These words, along with physical eating and drinking are the important part of the sacrament. Anyone who believes these words has what they say and what they record, namely, the forgiveness of sins.

Q. Who, then, receives such a sacrament in a worthy way?

A. Of course, fasting and other physical preparations are excellent disciplines for the body. But anyone who believes these words, "Given for you," and "Shed for you to forgive sins," is really worthy and well prepared. But whoever doubts or does not believe these words is not worthy and is unprepared, because the words, "for you" demand a heart that fully believes.

The Lutheran religion is based upon the writings of Martin Luther. Reading Luther's "Small Catechism" was enough to convince me he was way out of line with what God said in His Word the Bible. Lest any Lutherans today should try to separate themselves from Luther, simply do a web search for "small catechism Lutheran churches." You'll find a zillion Lutheran church websites that all echo Luther's writings in their statements of faith. The Lutheran religion is a child of the Catholic religion, the MOTHER of harlots, Revelation 17:5.)

Lutheran Doctrines

The Lutheran religion is nothing less than diet Catholicism, i.e., you get the same poison of Catholicism, just less of it. The Lutheran religion is straight from Satan himself. Jesus never commanded us to follow any man's teachings over the Word of God.

The damnable heresies which were taught by Martin Luther are still followed by the Lutheran Church today; but to their own destruction...

⁹ The Lord is not slack concerning his promise, as some men count slackness; but is longsuffering to us-ward, not willing that any should perish, but that all should come to repentance.
2 Peter 3:9

The following quote is from Luther's Small Catechism, as promoted by the Wisconsin Evangelical Lutheran Synod (WELS). The quote is found under the section, "THE SACRAMENT OF HOLY COMMUNION"; and then under the subheading, "THE BLESSINGS OF HOLY COMMUNION":

"*Second: What blessing do we receive through this eating and drinking and drinking?*
That is shown us by these words, 'Given and poured out for you for the forgiveness of sins.' **Through these words we receive forgiveness of sins, life, and salvation in this sacrament**. For where there is forgiveness of sins, there is also life and salvation."
(**underline bold** added)

What blasphemy!!! There is not one single Verse in the entire Word of God which teaches that salvation comes through "Holy Communion." In fact, the phrase

"Holy Communion" is NOT found in the Bible at all. The Bible speaks of "[7]communion" in

ⁱ⁶ The cup of blessing which we bless, is it not the **communion** of the blood of Christ? The bread which we break, is it not the **communion** of the body of Christ?

1 Corinthians 10:16

Thus, a person "participates" in the sin-cleansing blood of Jesus Christ through faith in Christ alone; and not, by works or the Lord's Supper. Paul was simply teaching the believers at Corinth that they were saved by the blood of Jesus, and were being hypocritical to partake of the Lord's supper while also eating meats offered to idols (partaking of idolatry). Paul told them that it was impossible to eat at God's table and the Devil's, **"Ye cannot drink the cup of the Lord, and the cup of devils: ye cannot be partakers of the Lord's table, and of the table of devils."**

Tragically, this is exactly what the Catholic and Lutheran religions are doing today when they RECOGNIZE Mary in ANY capacity.

The following quote is from Luther's Small Catechism, as promoted by the Wisconsin Evangelical Lutheran Synod (WELS). The quote is also found under the section, "THE MINISTRY OF THE KEYS AND CONFESSION"; and then under the subheading, "THE KEYS":

"First: What is the use of the Keys?

---

[7] The Greek word for "communion" is "koinonia," which means, "partnership. i.e. participation."

The use of the Keys is that special power and right which Christ gave to his church on earth, to forgive the sins of penitent sinners but to refuse forgiveness to the impenitent as long as they do not repent.
Where is this written?
The holy Evangelist John writes in chapter 20, "Jesus breathed on his disciples and said, 'Receive the Holy Spirit. If you forgive anyone his sins, they are forgiven; if you do not forgive them, they are not forgiven."

How arrogant!, How blasphemous!, How damnable!, for any human being to claim the power to forgive sins. Not one Verse in the entire Word of God records anyone forgiving sin apart from Jesus Christ alone. If the Lord had given this power to the Apostles, then why isn't it recorded? No, Jesus never gave such power to the church.

The Lutheran minister and the Catholic priest arrogantly and sinfully proclaim that they have the "special power and right" to forgive sins; but they certainly do NOT. They also claim the "special power and right" to deny forgiveness of sins to the impenitent; but, again, they certainly do NOT. This is clear from the words of Jesus in Matthew 6:15.

15 But if you do not forgive men their trespasses, neither will your Father forgive your trespasses.

Matthew 6:15

Who would be so arrogant as to deny someone forgiveness in lieu of such clear teachings of Scripture? If you'll follow me carefully, and think this through, you'll come to the ONLY conclusion that is possible--Forgiveness of sins can only come through faith in Jesus Christ. In other words, even if a minister or priest wants to forgive someone, they CANNOT if that person has no faith in Christ as Saviour. And likewise, no Lutheran minister or Catholic priest can deny forgiveness to someone who is trusting upon the blood of Jesus to forgive them. I'm simply saying that forgiveness is out of the minister's or priest's hand. Romans 1:16 tells us that the Gospel is the POWER unto salvation.

[16] For I am not ashamed of the gospel of Christ, for it is the power of God to salvation for everyone who believes, for the Jew first and also for the Greek.

Romans 1:16

Listen my friend, you can confess sins to your Lutheran minister or Catholic priest 'til the cows come home if you want, but that won't get you forgiven. Romans 1:16 declares that forgiveness comes through the power of the GOSPEL, and nothing else. The Gospel being Jesus' death, burial, and resurrection.

In so doing, Christ shed His precious blood for our sins. If we simply believe upon Jesus Christ as our personal Saviour, trusting upon the finished work of Christ to take away our sins with His blood, our sins will be forgiven. How dare any stiff-necked minister or priest teach differently. You can't be fooled if you'll follow the Word of God my friend.

²³ If you forgive the sins of any, they are forgiven them; if you retain the *sins* of any, they are retained."

John 20:23

¹² And forgive us our debts,
As we forgive our debtors.

Matthew 6:12

John 20:23 is used by the Lutheran minister and the Catholic priest to claim they have power to forgive your sins. I want you to notice carefully here that the EXACT same Greek word "aphiemi," which is used in John 20:23, is also used in Matthew 6:12, "And forgive us our debts, **as we forgive our debtors**."

The word literally means, "to send forth" (i.e., to "let go"). When we forgive our debtors, we "let it go." Again, in Matthew 6:14 and 15 we read, "For if ye **forgive** men their trespasses, your heavenly Father will also forgive you: But if ye **forgive** not men their trespasses, neither will your Father **forgive your trespasses.**" These are from the EXACT same Greek word, "aphiemi," found in John 20:23. Hence, ministers and priests have no more ability to pardon other people's sins than laymen do. Clearly, we have been lied to by Lutheran ministers and Catholic Priests!

Every believer is commanded by God to "forgive" (aphiemi) other's sins (Ephesians 4:30-32). Please understand that no human can cleanse another human's sins away. No minister or priest can make you right with God. If you commit a sin against me, and then make restitution, asking for my forgiveness. I am commanded by God to forgive (aphiemi) you; but that doesn't mean you're now saved and on your way to Heaven.

I cannot save you or make you right with God, you MUST go through Jesus Christ, Who is the ONLY Mediator between God and men, "For there is one God, and ONE MEDIATOR between God and men, the man **Christ Jesus**." Clearly, the forgiveness offered from one human to another CANNOT substitute one's need for forgiveness from God.

[7] "Why does this *Man* speak blasphemies like this? Who can forgive sins but **God alone**?"

Mark 2:7

The Word of God is clear that ONLY God can forgive sin.

So what was Jesus saying to the Apostles in John 20:23? Since Jesus spoke about people NOT being forgiven, there is only **one thing** He could have been talking about, the Gospel. The same is true of Matthew 16:19 concerning the word "key," and again in Matthew 18:18 concerning the word "bind."

[23] If you forgive the sins of any, they are forgiven them; if you retain the sins of any, they are retained."

John 20:23

[19] And I will give you the keys of the kingdom of heaven, and whatever you bind on earth will be bound in heaven, and whatever you loose on earth will be loosed in heaven."

Matthew 16:19

[18] "Assuredly, I say to you, whatever you bind on earth will be bound in heaven, and whatever you loose on earth will be loosed in heaven.

Matthew 18:18

The ONLY "key" to Heaven is the Gospel of Christ Jesus; hence, the preaching of the Gospel distributes the keys which allow men to become saved and enter Heaven. VINE'S EXPOSITORY DICTIONARY OF GREEK NEW TESTAMENT WORDS says concerning the word "key in Matthew 16:19...

" 'a key,' is used metaphorically (a) of "the keys of the kingdom of heaven," which the Lord committed to Peter, Matt. 16:19, by which he would open the door of faith, as he did to the Jews at Pentecost, and to Gentiles in the person of Cornelius, acting as one commissioned by Christ, through the power of the Holy Spirit; he had precedence over his fellow disciples, not in authority, but in the matter of time, on the ground of his confession of Christ (v. 16); equal authority was committed to them (18:18); (b) of "the keys of knowledge," Luke 11:52, i.e., knowledge of the revealed will of God, by which men entered into the life that pleases God; this the religious leaders of the Jews had presumptuously "taken away," so that they neither entered in themselves, nor permitted their hearers to do so..."

Clearly, the "key" which Jesus spoke of is, the Gospel. The POWER of the Gospel in Romans 1:16 is the key that frees us from the bondage of sin, the condemnation of the Law, the fires of Hell, and the lies of false religions which lay burdens "grievous to be borne" upon men's shoulders (Matthew 23:4).

But again, there is no reference to ministers or priests being given the "special power and right" to forgive sin. To teach such nonsense is to neglect hundreds of Scriptures which do NOT agree. We can forgive other's their debts, foolishness, wrongs, trespasses, and evil's against us; but only God alone can forgive SIN. Come down off your pedestal Mr. Lutheran minister.   Only Jesus can forgive sin.

[5] For *there is* one God and one Mediator between God and men, *the* Man Christ Jesus,

1 Timothy 2:5

[23] If you forgive the sins of any, they are forgiven them; if you retain the sins of any, they are retained."

John 20:23

The Bible commands us to forgive those who seek our forgiveness (Matthew 6:14 and 15), so Jesus couldn't have been speaking about personal forgiveness in John 20:23. Furthermore, it wasn't the "special power and right" of the disciples to decide whether a man was forgiven or not, that POWER is clearly stated in Romans 1:16 to be THE GOSPEL.

Listen to the frightening words of the Apostle Paul to all Christ-rejecters.

[8] in flaming fire taking vengeance on those who do not know God, and on those who do not obey the gospel of our Lord Jesus Christ.

2 Thessalonians 1:8

[9] These shall be punished with everlasting destruction from the presence of the Lord and from the glory of His power

2 Thessalonians 1:9

Clearly, the determination of whether a person is forgiven or not is based upon his or her acceptance or rejection of the Gospel of Jesus Christ; and not, upon the whims of some earthly pompous Lutheran minister or Catholic priest. You had better obey the Gospel, and not the Lutheran religion.

Mr. Luther made the error of ADDING to God's simple plan of salvation, which is faith alone in Jesus the Christ.

The following quote is from *Luther's Small Catechism*, as promoted by the *Wisconsin Evangelical Lutheran Synod* (WELS). The quote is also found under the section, "THE MINISTRY OF THE KEYS AND CONFESSION"; and then under the subheading, "WHAT IS CONFESSION?":

First: What is Confession?

Confession has two parts. The one is that we confess our sins; the other, that we receive absolution or forgiveness from the pastor* as from God himself, not doubting but firmly believing that our sins are thus forgiven before God in heaven.

Fourth: How will the pastor assure a penitent sinner of forgiveness?
He will say, "By the authority of Christ, I forgive you your sins in the name of the Father and of the Son and of the Holy Spirit. Amen." (underline added)

*The German term is best translated as 'confessor," that is, the person who hears the confession.

I've included this last section of the Lutheran Catechism to show how arrogant their ministers are, to actually claim that they have the power to forgive sins. How wicked! Mr. Luther, you are an imposter! You won't fool me with your damnable teachings, no Sir! I'm going to follow the Word of God, and not a man.

[4] Certainly not! Indeed, let God be true but every man a liar. As it is written:
"That You may be justified in Your words,
And may overcome when You are judged."

Romans 3:4

[8] *It is* better to trust in the LORD
Than to put confidence in man.

Psalm 118:8

EVERY Lutheran minister is required and expected by headquarters to TEACH that they (ministers) have the power to forgive sin. To teach such a lie is a damnable heresy!!!

Notice Luther's Catechism above states, "we receive absolution or forgiveness from the pastor." You've got to be kidding me! Only a child of the Devil would claim to have the power and right to forgive another person's sin. I have a few questions for you. Who does the Lutheran minister go to, to get his sins forgiven? Who does his wife and children go to, to get their sins forgiven?

¹³ And the tax collector, standing afar off, would not so much as raise *his* eyes to heaven, but beat his breast, saying, 'God, be merciful to me a sinner!'

Luke 18:13

Why can't we go directly to God like the publican in Luke 18:13 who cried, "God be merciful to me a sinner."

Are you so foolish to buy into Satan's lie that another sinful man can forgive your sins?

Do a little homework and I'm certain you'll find that EVERY Lutheran minister and Catholic priest which lived 150 years ago are DEAD today. Do you know why? Because Romans 6:23 proclaims "**for the wages of sin is death...**" They died because they were SINNERS, just like you and me. Listen friend, I don't know about you, but I feel a lot more secure trusting in the Perfect Lamb of God, Who died upon the cross for me; than in some sinful minister, who never did anything for me, nor could do anything for me.

Are you going to place all your faith in the hopes that some Lutheran minister has the self-proclaimed power to forgive your sins? Would you feel safer hearing a sinful minister say, "I forgive your sins"; or the words of...

¹⁶ Let us therefore come boldly to the throne of grace, that we may obtain mercy and find grace to help in time of need.

Hebrews 4:16

The Damnable Heresy of Salvation Through Holy Baptism

The following quote is from Luther's Small Catechism, as promoted by the Wisconsin Evangelical Lutheran Synod (WELS). The quote is also found under the section, "THE SACRAMENT OF HOLY BAPTISM"; and then under the subheading, "THE BLESSING OF BAPTISM":

Second: What does Baptism do for us?
<u>Baptism works forgiveness of sin</u>, delivers from death and the devil, and <u>gives eternal salvation to all who believe this</u>, as the words and promises of God declare. What are these words and promises of God? Christ our Lord says in the last chapter of Mark, "Whoever believes and is baptized will be saved, but whoever does not believe will be condemned." (underline added)

What a damnable lie of Satan!!! Not one verse in the entire Bible teaches that "Baptism works forgiveness of sin."
The following quote is from *Luther's Small Catechism*, as promoted by the *Wisconsin Evangelical Lutheran Synod* (WELS). The quote is also found under the section, "THE SACRAMENT OF HOLY BAPTISM"; and then under the subheading, "THE POWER OF BAPTISM":

"*Third: How can water do such great things?*
It is certainly not the water that does such things, but God's Word which is <u>in and with the water</u>, and faith which trusts this Word used <u>with the water</u>. For without God's Word the water is just plain water and not

baptism. But with this Word it is baptism, that is, <u>a gracious water of life and a washing of rebirth</u> by the Holy Spirit.

Where is this written?
St. Paul says in Titus, chapter 3, "God saved us through the washing of rebirth and renewal by the Holy Spirit, whom he poured out on us generously through Jesus Christ our Savior, so that, having been justified by his grace, we might become heirs having the hope of eternal life. This is a trustworthy saying." (underline added)

[5] not by works of righteousness which we have done, but according to His mercy He saved us, through the washing of regeneration and renewing of the Holy Spirit
Titus 3:5

Martin Luther was definitely out of line with God. The Scriptures quoted above are being taken out of context. A standard rule in interpreting the Word of God is that you NEVER base a doctrine upon one Scripture by itself. You COMPARE it to all the other Scriptures in the Bible.

Titus 3:5 clearly speaks of the "washing of regeneration," not the washing by Baptism.

[5] and from Jesus Christ, the faithful witness, the firstborn from the dead, and the ruler over the kings of the earth.
To Him who loved us and washed us from our sins in His own blood
Revelation 1:5

¹⁴ And I said to him, "Sir, you know."
So he said to me, "These are the ones who come out of the great tribulation, and washed their robes and made them white in the blood of the Lamb.

Revelation 7:14

It is clear from the Scriptures above that "washing" is speaking about Jesus' blood, and not baptism. It may be convenient for Lutherans to "claim" that Titus 3:5 is speaking about baptism, but a simple comparison of Titus 3:5 with other Scriptures in the Bible denies their foolish claim.

Just as false prophets always do, Lutherans target Scriptures that, by themselves, can be easily taken out of context. Well they can't pervert Revelation 1:5 or 7:14 because they clearly speak of the Blood of Jesus which WASHES our sins away.

Notice in Luther's Catechism above that he also tries to justify Baptismal Regeneration by quoting Mark 16:16, "**He that believeth and is baptized shall be saved; but he that believeth not shall be damned.**"

⁹ that if you confess with your mouth the Lord Jesus and believe in your heart that God has raised Him from the dead, you will be saved. ¹⁰ **For with the heart one believes unto righteousness**, and with the mouth confession is made unto salvation. ¹¹ For the Scripture says, "Whoever believes on Him will not be put to shame." ¹² For there is no distinction between Jew and Greek, for the same Lord over all is rich to all who call upon Him. ¹³ For "whoever calls on the name of the LORD shall be saved."

Romans 10:9-13

A simple comparison with Romans 10:9-13 refutes such an idea.

Salvation is of the heart; and not, through the ceremonial act of baptism. More on why we get baptized in my book Only a born again will enter Heaven. Are you ready?

[16] He who believes and is baptized will be saved; but he who does not believe will be condemned.
Mark 16:16

[3] For what does the Scripture say? "Abraham believed God, and it was accounted to him for righteousness."
Romans 4:3

[9] I am the door. If anyone enters by Me, he will be saved, and will go in and out and find pasture.
John 10:9

[10] Jesus answered and said to her, "If you knew the gift of God, and who it is who says to you, 'Give Me a drink,' you would have asked Him, and He would have given you living water."
John 4:10

The necessary thing to be saved is BELIEF; and not, baptism. There is NO reference to baptism; but only, faith. Jesus NEVER told anyone to be baptized to go to Heaven. Jesus claimed that He is the Door, by which men can be saved if they'll enter (John 10:9). Jesus claimed that He is the Living Water, by which men can be saved if they'll drink (John 4:10).

[35] And Jesus said to them, "I am the bread of life. He who comes to Me shall never hunger, and he who believes in Me shall never thirst.
John 6:35

⁶ Jesus said to him, "I am the way, the truth, and the life. No one comes to the Father except through Me.

John 14:6

³ Jesus answered and said to him, "Most assuredly, I say to you, unless one is born again, he cannot see the kingdom of God."

John 3:3

Jesus claimed that He is the Bread of Life, by which men can be saved if they'll eat (John 6:35). Jesus claimed that He is the Way, the Truth, and the Life (John 14:6). Yet, Jesus never ADDED anything about being Baptized in all these Scriptures. The "washing of Regeneration" in Titus 3:5 is nothing more than our sins being washed away by Jesus blood, and the Holy Spirit indwelling our body. We are "regened" when we are BORN-AGAIN (John 3:3).

2 And you *He made alive,* who were dead in trespasses and sins

Ephesians 2:1

¹⁷ Therefore, if anyone *is* in Christ, *he is* a new creation; old things have passed away; behold, all things have become new.

2 Corinthians 5:17

Our spirit which was dead in trespasses and sins, is quickened (made alive) by the Holy Spirit of God (Ephesians 2:1). The regeneration is the "new creature" (Christ) which comes to dwell within us (2nd Corinthians 5:17). The regeneration is the Holy Spirit of God; thus, we become a new creature in Christ.

³ Or do you not know that as many of us as were baptized into Christ Jesus were baptized into His death? ⁴ Therefore we were buried with Him through baptism into death, that just as Christ

was raised from the dead by the glory of the Father, even so we also should walk in newness of life.

Romans 6:3-4

In the entire book of Romans, Paul only mentions "baptized" or "baptism" TWICE.

Clearly, baptism is NOT necessary for salvation or else the Apostle would have mentioned it much more.

Carefully notice the word "like." Hence, baptism is only symbolic of the Gospel of Christ. It is simply a way for us to identify ourselves with Christ in His crucifixion, for others to witness. Just as Jesus died, was buried, and rose again, so do we identify with Him, showing forth our faith, through baptism.

BUT, please notice, baptism ALWAYS come AFTER a person is already saved. No one in the Word of God was ever baptized to get saved; but rather, were baptized because they were already saved. Though there are several passages in the New Testament which mention baptism with faith, there are umpteen more which only mention faith, and baptism is NOT mentioned at all. The diligent Bible student must "rightly divide" the Word of Truth. If baptism were as necessary for salvation as the cults all claim, than surely baptism would have been mentioned much more throughout the Word of God. Baptism is not even mentioned in the Book of revelation, yet faith is mentioned 11 times.

The Apostle Paul declares...

⁵ Examine yourselves *as to* whether you are in the faith. Test yourselves. Do you not know yourselves, that Jesus Christ is in you?—unless indeed you are disqualified.

2 Corinthians 13:5

Interestingly again, Paul does not mention baptism. In fact, baptism is not even mentioned in 2 Corinthians; but faith is mentioned 6 times. The Book of Hebrews mentions faith 34 times; but baptism once ONCE.

And let me also say that "baptism" in the Bible often refers to the baptism of the Holy Spirit (salvation) and NOT water baptism.

¹³ For by one Spirit we were all baptized into one body—whether Jews or Greeks, whether slaves or free—and have all been made to drink into one Spirit.

1 Corinthians 12:13

The word "baptized" here is NOT referring to water baptism, but to the baptism of the Holy Spirit which occurs the moment we accept Christ as our Saviour.

¹¹ I indeed baptize you with water unto repentance, but He who is coming after me is mightier than I, whose sandals I am not worthy to carry. He will baptize you with the Holy Spirit and fire.

Matthew 3:11

⁴ John came baptizing in the wilderness and preaching a baptism of repentance for the remission of sins.

Mark 1:4

It is clear from Scriptures that John the Baptist didn't teach baptismal Regeneration. It wasn't water baptism that saved those people under John's preaching; but rather, their repentance and faith in Christ.

⁴ Then Paul said, "John indeed baptized with a baptism of repentance, saying to the people that they should believe on Him who would come after him, that is, on Christ Jesus."
Acts 19:4

⁴⁷ "Can anyone forbid water, that these should not be baptized who have received the Holy Spirit just as we *have?*"
Acts 10:47

Please notice, they had already received the Holy Ghost (salvation, Romans 8:9), but they had not yet been baptized. How can any honest student of the Bible claim that baptism is required for salvation in lieu of such overwhelming evidence to the contrary?

In conclusion, these are but a few of the damnable doctrines of the Lutheran religion. Martin Luther didn't like the Book of Revelation because he couldn't understand it. He didn't believe it belonged in the Bible. He denied the Biblical teaching that Christ would one day reign from Jerusalem. He denied the Millennium altogether, in spite of clear Biblical prophecy supporting it. Luther denied the ⁸rapture

---

⁸ The Bible speaks about being caught up as per the verse below.

¹⁵ According to the Lord's word, we tell you that we who are still alive, who are left until the coming of the Lord, will certainly not precede those who have fallen asleep. ¹⁶ For the Lord himself will come down from heaven, with a loud command, with the voice of the archangel and with the trumpet call of God, and the dead in Christ will rise first. ¹⁷ After that, we who are still alive and are left will be **caught up** together with them in the clouds to meet the Lord in the air. And so we will be with the Lord

(caught up). Martin Luther was a heretic by all counts. Sadly, even professed Independent Fundamental Baptists ignorantly praise Martin Luther as a man of faith.

What many people fail to realize, as I once did, is that Luther's faith was not SOLELY in Christ, but in his own perverted theology which ADDED "holy baptism" and "holy communion" to his faith. Thus, there's not a dime's difference between Catholics are Lutherans. The following quote if from The Lutheran World Federation, and states:

"The dialogue between the Lutheran World Federation (LWF) and the Roman Catholic Church began soon after the end of the Second Vatican Council in 1965. [9] The Joint Declaration on the Doctrine of Justification is so far the high point of the more than 30-year process. The two dialogue partners confirm that they have reached 'a consensus on basic truths of the doctrine of justification' and 'that the mutual condemnations of former times do not apply to the Catholic and Lutheran doctrines of justification as they are presented in the Joint Declaration.'"

What a hoax! The Catholics and Lutherans sat down together and drew up an agreement, stating that they BOTH believed that justification by faith in Christ was necessary for salvation. They called this agreement,

---

forever.

1 Thessalonians 4:15-17

[9] The Joint Declaration on the Doctrine of Justification can be found by typing the following url or you can just do a google search.
http://www.vatican.va/roman_curia/pontifical_councils/chrstuni/documents/rc_pc_chrstuni_doc_31101999_cath-luth-joint-declaration_en.html

The Joint Declaration on the Doctrine of Justification. But the problem is that they BOTH ADD the sacraments to that faith. They BOTH require their congregations to seek forgiveness from the minister or priest, instead of from Jesus Christ as the Word of God teaches (1 John 1:9). Who's kidding who?

[9] If we confess our sins, He is faithful and just to forgive us *our* sins and to cleanse us from all unrighteousness.
1 John 1:9

There's a fine line between faith and foolishness friend, and it's the difference between Heaven or Hell when you die. You'd better forsake your false religion, and turn to the Lord Jesus Christ instead. Martin Luther was a heretic who taught Satanic lies. Let every Christian who names the name of Jesus Christ, EXPOSE this worker of darkness.

In conclusion, the Lutheran religion is BAD NEWS! It is a hybrid of Catholicism and Christian doctrine. The Catholic religion itself is a hybrid of all kinds of false religions, Vatican traditions and Christian teachings. This of course is tragic! Untold billions of people have gone to hell because of the damnable heresies of the Catholic religion. More on the Catholic religion in Part 3 of this book. The Lutheran teachings of baptismal regeneration (teaching baptism as a Sacrament), the Sacrament of holy communion and Mary worship (though they won't admit it) are more than enough to define them as a false religion in light of the Word of God. Though many profess to be saved Christians, we are clearly warned in the Scriptures that adding anything to simple faith in Christ is no faith at all. I've witnesses to Jehovah Witnesses who declared their acceptance of Christ as Saviour (the wrong Saviour of course because they deny the deity of Christ). More on Jehovah Witnesses in Part 1 of this book.

Just as the Jehovah Witnesses are false prophets, so are the Lutherans who teach that one is "normally" saved through a Sacrament of baptism. In addition, to teach the the Sacrament of Alter (the holy communion) can forgive sin by reciting a bunch of ceremonial and ritualistic prayers is bogus. What's with the "Hail Mary, full of grace...?" This is a wicked practice and should NEVER be practiced by anyone who truly loves the Lord Jesus Christ.

The bottom line is that the Lutherans are still very much Catholic in their beliefs and practices. Don't be deceived. Even the Catholics will claim that salvation is by faith, and works. They believe BOTH are essential to salvation.

Of course, Titus 3:5 and Ephesians 2:8-9 blow that lie right out of the water. No one can be saved through works, it is absolutely impossible. Only though child-like faith in the gospel of Jesus Christ (His death, burial and resurrection) can we be saved. This is a one-time happening. Once we accept Jesus into our heart, He comes in to stay forever and ever. We must be born-again.

Chapter 2: Hinduism

Written By: Leeanne Panday-Naicker

1. Belief

Hinduism is a collective term applied to the many philosophical and religious traditions native to India. It is unique among the world religions in that it has no founder or date of origin. It represents several traditions, each of which can be considered a religion in itself.

Hinduism is made up of many divisions with sub-divisions. Hinduism is rooted in the doctrines of **samsara** (the cycle of rebirth) or reincarnation and **karma** (universal law of cause and effect) or "you reap what you sow" as a result astrology is at the heart of hinduism. Astrology is considered a respectable science in India, and texts eulogise authentic astrologers as the most learned brahmanas *(any of the lengthy commentaries on the Vedas, composed in Sanskrit)*.

It has approximately 1billion followers worldwide with the majority believing that the universe contains deities and spiritual beings — gods and goddesses (or devas) and that these deities actively influence the world and interact with humans.

Hinduism is typically divided into four major sects: Shaiva (devotees of the god Shiva), Vaishnava (devotees of the god Vishnu), Shakta (devotees of the goddess), and Smarta (those who understand the ultimate form of the divine to be abstract and all encompassing, Brahman) with a highly ritualized form of worship. The many manifestations of Hinduism go from highly intellectual philosophies concerning numerous and puzzling metaphysical concerns, many rituals, mental and physical exercises such as Yoga to simple, almost childlike, tales and legends. Hinduism begins simply by differentiating between matter and spirit. Spirit is understood within two main categories, namely the individual self, or soul (the atman), the Supreme Self, or God (the paramatman). This simple diagram shows the three basic concepts that form the basis for Hindu thought. Different schools present various opinions on the nature of each "concept" and the relationships between them.

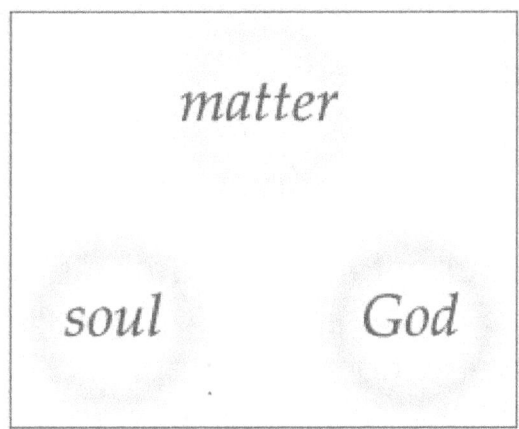

Well if we really want to know how the world has so many different cultures and languages then we need to turn to the bible where it tells us

And the whole earth was of one language, and of one speech

Genesis 11:1

It angered God when man decided to build the tower to reach heaven. He then decided to scatter men throughout all the earth and confuse their languages

⁶ And the Lord said, Behold, the people is one, and they have all one language; and this they begin to do: and now nothing will be restrained from them, which they have imagined to do.
⁷ Go to, let us go down, and there confound their language, that they may not understand one another's speech.
⁸ So the Lord scattered them abroad from thence upon the face of all the earth: and they left off to build the city.
⁹ Therefore is the name of it called Babel; because the Lord did there confound the language of all the earth: and from thence did the Lord scatter them abroad upon the face of all the earth.

Genesis 11:6-9

Therefore today we live in a world with multiple cultures, languages with their own belief systems and religions. As believers in Christ, we know that all of these belief systems, ideologies and religions are false because there is only one way to heaven, to eternal life, to our Father God and that is through His only begotten son, Jesus Christ.
Throughout this chapter you will come to learn about hinduism as a false religion and how millions of people on this earth are living in bondage and are born into bondage through the lies and deceit of the enemy.

2. When it Started - Origins

Hinduism is a complex religion. It has developed over 1000's of years originating in the Indian Continent. Some devout worshippers believe that it is the oldest religion in the world with prehistoric roots. It represents several traditions, each of which can be considered a religion in itself. It is generally believed to have originated around 2000 BC to 1500 BC; though archaeological evidence in the form of religious artefacts may point to an earlier era according to scholars.

The most ancient sacred texts of the Hindu religion are written in Sanskrit and called the Vedas (vedah means "knowledge"). The texts range from Epics about the lives and loves of the Gods, philosophical treatises on metaphysical questions, and law books. The Hindu religion has provided the roots of Jainism, Sikhism, and Buddhism. In the West it can be found in the Hare Krishna movement. Hinduism is the majority religion of India, Nepal, and Mauritius and a significant minority religion in Fiji, Suriname, Bhutan, Sri Lanka, Bangladesh, Malaysia, and Singapore.

Many hindu believers can and will debate the topic of hinduism being the oldest religion in the world whereas God the Father clearly shows us in the bible that He is creator of the Heavens and the Earth and creator of Man. Hinduism is a man-made religion through the work of the enemy, Christianity is a religion too but we cannot get caught up in the question of religion since it can be anything, instead we need to believe in what the word of God says, there is only one God and one way to Him which is through His son Jesus Christ.

Jesus saith unto him, I am the way, the truth, and the life: no man cometh unto the Father, but by me.

John 14:6

3. Traditions

There are literally thousands of traditions that are followed/observed in hinduism. People who live in the rural areas of India are much stauncher when it comes to observing tradition as opposed to those in more modern suburbs. In our modern day many are much less staunch when it comes to observing the traditions compared to past generations.

- When Hindus meet each other, they greet each other by saying 'Namaste' or 'Namaskar' whilst placing together the palms of both hands. Some other religious words are also used at times.
- Before the start of any good work and social and religious ceremonies, Hindus worship the god Ganesha and chant a mantra.
- Hindus do not wear any footwear inside homes, temples, and other holy places. They do not enter the temples after consuming alcohol and/or non-vegetarian food.
- They do not eat non-vegetarian food on Mondays, Thursdays, Fridays, Saturdays and many other festival or ceremonious days
- Respect for elders is an integral part of Hindu culture. Younger people always sit to the left of their elders, do not sit whilst elders are standing, not yawning or stretching or speaking excessively as it is considered very disrespectful to the elders.
- It is an unsaid rule that a person cannot answer back to elders and more so, when he/she is at fault. It is deemed disrespectful in India to refer to an elder by his / her name. Instead people prefer calling them uncle and aunt, especially if the person is very elderly.

- Elders must be given their food first before anyone else; men are given their food first before any others whilst women and children are last and generally sit separately from the men.
- Children prostrate and touch the feet of their parents at festivals and special occasions such as birthdays, before going on a journey.
- A son must take care of his parents in their old age. Younger people touch the feet of their elders to show respect and take blessings from them. Mother, Father, and Teacher are considered as next to god and are highly respected.
- All babies, children and adults use khol/kajal (black eye liner) to protect their eyes from ailments as well as the "evil eye" curse. Babies also wear black beaded bracelets on each hand to keep evil away.
- When babies are born, their ear/s are pulled and if the baby cries out loud then it really is healthy and shows that all organs work fine for a new born baby.
- Most of the marriages are arranged between families with the consent of bride and groom. Marrying outside the caste is considered as a bad practice. Arranged marriages generally take place within the respective castes only. However the practice of arranged marriages has lost momentum in this generation and is seldom practiced.
- Indian culture and tradition forbids unnecessary touching or any form of physical contact, especially between a man and a woman, in public.

- Gifts of sweets must be given to the family members of the future groom upon entering the home of the future bride. The future bride must serve her future in-laws beverages to show that she has been domesticated.
- As per the lifestyle of the Indian people, it is the duty of a woman to take care of her home. As such, from her very childhood, a girl child is taught to cook, clean her mother and other ladies in her family. She is also taught to attend to guests and strangers politely and elegantly because it is thought to greatly reflect upon her upbringing. Hers is a 24x7 job, yet she manages to execute it smoothly and is respected for this quality
- As soon as the guest arrives, the women of the house serve them water and then ask any preferences for food or drink
- A dowry (*an amount of property or money brought by a bride to her husband on their marriage*) is given by the bride's family to the groom's family.
- A married Hindu woman traditionally wears a Mangalsutra (*sacred necklace that a Hindu groom ties around the bride's neck during marriage ceremony*) around her neck, bangles in her hand and toe rings, which indicates that she is married. She also applies a Kumkum (*a red pigment used by Hindu women to make a round spot on the forehead*) spot or sticks a bindi (*a decorative mark worn in the middle of the forehead by Indian women*) between her two eyebrows.

- An elder priest always conducts or presides over all ceremonies.
- A dakshina – monetary fee or gift is given to a priest at the completion of any rite.
- Newly married couples have to live with their in-laws and families after their marriage. It is frowned upon to do differently however this is no longer followed in our modern day.
- Generally, Hindu women and girls wear clothes that would cover the entiree body except the face such as Saree, Lehengas, Salwar Kameez, Ghagra choli, etc.
- Whenever there is any happy occasion or festivity, the Indian women celebrate it by applying henna, also called mendhi, designs on their hands and feet. Application on the hair, hands and feet of a bride before the marriage ceremony is mandatory and is believed to bring good luck.
- The idols or pictures of hindu deities are positioned in such a way that they do not face South. The practice is observed in temples as well as homes as it is believed that hell is located at South and paradise at North
- Every household keeps an altar/shrine which contains miniature idols of many hindu deities. These are cleaned and worshipped daily.
- At the passing away of relatives especially parents, men shave their heads. All family members are not supposed to attend religious functions, eat certain

foods like sweets, wear new clothes or participate in any cultural activity or festivity.
- After attending a funeral both men and women stay outside the house. Then they go to the well and have a bath, wash all their clothes and then only enter the house. This is preventing any infection from the funeral house; this is more prevalent in villages.
- Widows are not allowed to attend certain functions or wear brightly coloured clothing.
- Widows are generally required to live with their in-laws and are not allowed to remarry.
- The left hand is primarily used for personal hygiene purposes and hence using left hand to receive or hand over anything from anyone is considered as an insult.
- If anyone in the house suffers from an infectious disease like chicken pox, measles etc. a bundle of neem or margosa leaves are hung at the gates of the house indicating there is an infection a brilliant method of isolation.
- Mango and neem leaves are tied to the doors of houses to prevent evil powers from entering the house.

What is tradition really? Simply put it is values, customs and beliefs that are passed on from one generation to another. It is very important in a believers walk with the Lord that we do not fall prey to the traditions or belief systems of the world or of our ancestors especially when the bible clearly tells us to heed the word of God. It is Gods will that we live a righteous life and honour the 10 commandments that He gave to us through Moses. Jesus also slated the Pharisees when they questioned Him about breaking tradition when He performed miracles on the Sabbath day since man twisted the meaning of the Sabbath for man's own convenience.

Beware lest any man spoil you through philosophy and vain deceit, after the tradition of men, after the rudiments of the world, and not after Christ.
Colossians 2:8

Neither give heed to fables and endless genealogies, which minister questions, rather than godly edifying which is in faith: so do.
1 Timothy 1:8

4. Rituals

Hindu culture is full of rituals and daily routines. The religious life of many Hindus is focused on devotion to God (perceived as Brahman, Shiva, Vishnu, or Shakti) or several gods. This devotion usually takes the form of rituals and practices associated with sculptures and images of gods in home shrines.
The rituals are usually very orderly, and are believed to move the individual from one stage of life to another. This personal movement, known as *samskara*, is ultimately to help the individual obtain liberation or moksa (*release from the cycle of rebirth impelled by the law of karma.*), and become free from the birth, death, and re-birth cycle.

4.1 Stages of rituals throughout life

Hindu religious practices centre on the importance of fulfilling the duties associated both with one's social position and one's stage of life. With regard to the latter, traditional Hindus are expected to pass through four stages *(ashramas)* over the course of their life:

- *Brahmacharga:* which takes place during the school years, is focused on acquiring knowledge and developing character;
- *Grastha:* the middle years, is focused on worldly pursuits and pleasures such as marriage, family and career;
- *Vanaprastha*: when one's children reach adulthood, is a time of increased focus on spiritual things; and
- *Sanngasu:* in the last years of life, one may abandon the world entirely for a life of contemplation.

All stages of life for the Hindu, however, involve religious rituals and practices. The ritual world of Hinduism, manifestations of which differ greatly among regions, villages, and individuals, offers a number of common features that link all Hindus into a greater Indian religious system.

4.2 Pregnancy & Birth

From the time of pregnancy until the child is born, people near the new born perform many rituals and rites for the benefit the infant since it is not able to do so for itself - the upanayana ritual (*initiation ritual by which initiates are invested with a sacred thread, to symbolize the transference of spiritual knowledge*). Observance to these rituals plays a key part in an individual's life. The birth has many rituals surrounding it, as parents, extended family, and those involved with a new born would want to provide the best possible conditions for a baby to progress in life and achieve moksa.

The pregnant women is not to be our after dark, is not supposed to walk past babul trees (since they are supposed to house evil spirits), and should always keep a piece of iron/metal with her to ward off any spirits. Once a women is pregnant the arathi ritual is perform that serves the purpose of removing the evil eye, and is similar to a western baby shower, since it primarily centres on the pregnant mother receiving gifts of good fortune, as well as special foods to eat. When the she enters into the seventh month of pregnancy, arathi is again preformed, and further attention is given to prepare for the coming of the child.

Once the baby has been delivered, attention is given to what time the birth took place, as this determines an accurate horoscope for the child, which, to a certain extent, will determine when other samskara rituals are performed. Also, the position of the moon at the birth of a child plays a key role when choosing a baby's name. Most Indian families still request a local brahmana to cast a chart for the new-born baby. The first syllable of the name is determined by the position of the moon at birth. After birth the baby is cleansed by being rubbed with a ball of turmeric and dough, and receives an oil message. In the case of a boy being born family and friends are invited to celebrate the birth; however in some instances the birth of a girl has limited celebration or none at all. This is based on the fact that a boy is seen as being able to perpetuate the family line and be a provider, whereas the girl's role is traditionally less dominant.

4.3 Domestic/Household Worship

For many households, the day begins when the women in the house draw auspicious geometric designs in chalk or rice flour on the floor or the doorstep.

Puja or worship is a religious ritual which some Hindus perform every morning after bathing and dressing but prior to taking any food or drink. Puja is seen as a way of relating humans to the domain and actions of the divine, and can be performed for anything considered divine. After bathing there is personal worship of the gods at a family shrine/altar, which typically includes lighting a lamp and offering food items before the images, while prayers in Sanskrit or a regional language are recited.

In the evenings, especially in rural areas, mostly female devotees may gather together for long sessions of singing hymns in praise of one or more of the gods.

Puja (worship) of the gods consists of a range of ritual offerings and prayers typically performed either daily or on special days before an image of the deity, which may be in the form of a person or a symbol of the sacred presence. In its more developed forms, puja consists of a series of ritual stages beginning with personal purification and invocation of the god, followed by offerings of flowers, food, or other objects such as clothing, accompanied by fervent prayers. Sacred ash or saffron powder, for example, is often distributed after puja and smeared on the foreheads of devotees. Hindus make an offering of food and later partake of it as *prasaada* - a holy gift from the respective deities.

In almost every Indian home a lamp is lit daily before the altar/shrine. In some houses it is lit at dawn, in some, twice a day – at dawn and dusk – and in a few it is maintained continuously (*akhanda deepa*). All auspicious functions commence with the lighting of the lamp, which is often maintained right throughout the occasion.

An oil lamp is always used as opposed to a light bulb as it has more spiritual significance. The oil or ghee in the lamp symbolizes the *vaasanas* or negative tendencies and the wick of the lamp, the ego. The flame of a lamp must always burns upwards. The prayer room or room where the altar/shrine is kept is the master room of the house.

Fasting in Sanskrit is called *upavaasa*. *Upa* means "near" + *vaasa* means "to stay". *Upavaasa* therefore means staying near god. Most devout hindus fast regularly or on special occasions like festivals. On such days they do not eat at all, eat once or make do with fruits or a special diet of simple food.

4.4 Temple Worship

Most hindus worship in their homes and some prefer to go to a temple (*mandir*) or do both. Others go to temples on special festival days and occasions that call for it. A characteristic of most temples is the presence of murtis (*idols*) of the Hindu deity to whom the temple is dedicated. They are usually dedicated to one primary deity, the presiding deity, and other deities associated with the main deity. However, some temples are dedicated to several deities, and others are dedicated to idols in an iconic form. Many temples are in key geographical points, such as a hill top, near waterfalls, caves and rivers, as these are, according to Hinduism, worship places and make it easier to contemplate God.

Hindus are supposed to be clean and without shoes when entering a temple.

There is always a bell placed on or above the deities in the temple. The bell is always rung during prayers. The ringing of the bell produces what is regarded as an auspicious sound. It produces the sound Om, the universal name of god. *Shaanti*, meaning "peace", is a natural state of being and is chanted three times at the end of all prayers. The hindus chant prayers to invoke peace, troubles end and peace is experienced internally, irrespective of the external disturbances. Some of the rites include a ritual bath, called *abhishekam*, in which water, sesame oil, turmeric water, saffron, milk, yogurt, ghee, honey, lime juice, sandalwood paste, *panchamritam* (mixture of five fruits), coconut water and rosewater are poured over the deities. Devotees are seated usually on the floor. Deities are usually dressed in new clothes and decorated with flowers. Devotees sing devotional songs after decorations are complete, incense is lit, oil lamps are burnt and food is offered. A conch or horn is also blown at temples during ceremonies, it is said to emanate the sound of om, an auspicious sound that was chanted by the gods before creating the world. It is said to represent the world and the Truth behind it. Animals are also sacrificed at temples during certain ceremonies and festivals. Some temples also have fountains where devotees or worshippers turn their backs away from the fountain and throw coins in specific method over their shoulders into the water, similar to "wishing wells". It is common to find lotus flowers in these fountains as the hindus believe they are the symbol of truth, auspiciousness and beauty (*satyam, shivam, sundaram*). They believe the god and his various aspects are compared to the lotus (i.e. lotus-eyes, lotus feet, lotus hands, the lotus of the heart etc.). The lotus blooms open with the rising sun and closes at night. The lotus leaf never gets wet even though it is always in water thereby symbolizing the man of wisdom.

4.4.1 The Coconut

The coconut (*Sriphala = god's fruit*) alone is also used to symbolize 'god'. In India one of the most common offerings in a temple is a coconut. The coconut plays a vital role in all ritual prayers, even in home worship. The coconut is a satvic fruit and is seen as sacred, pure, clean, and health giving, endowed with several properties. It is also offered on occasions like weddings, festivals, the purchase and use of a new vehicle, a new house etc.
It is offered in the sacrificial fire whilst performing ritual prayers. The coconut is broken and placed before the altar and is later distributed to worshippers. Three striped parallel lines using sacred ash is placed on the coconut to represent the three-eyed Lord Shiva. The coconut is also associated with Lord Ganesha. At the beginning of any auspicious task or a journey, people smash coconuts to propitiate Ganesha – the remover of all obstacles. They also break coconuts in temples or in front of idols in fulfilment of their vows made to

god. In all **sacrificial** rites, the coconut is offered as an offering to the sacred fire. Some people believe that this ritual as well as the customary breaking of coconuts on the altar of deities is associated with the fact that the coconut fruit resembles a human head. The shapes of the coconut once it is broken also signify good fortune or a bad omen for the person/s on behalf for which it is being offered.

4.5 Sun Worship

Sun worship is a predominant feature of the Hindu religion. All the myths prove that the combat between light and darkness, waged daily around us, is of solar origin. As with the Osiris, the Sun-God of the Egyptians, triumphing over the demons of darkness, so in India we find Indra, the great solar deity of the Hindus, successful in his combat with Vritra the serpent of night.
Every morning the Brahmans may be seen facing the east, standing on one foot, and stretching out their hands to the sun as they repeat a prayer which passed down through the ages.

4.6 Rites of Passage

A central part of every Hindu's life, are sacred rites of passage, such as coming of age and marriage, and childhood rites, including name-giving, first feeding, ear-piercing and head-shaving. They are held in temples, homes or halls. These rites usually include a prayer and/or a fire ceremony. The priest usually sets an auspicious time and date and presides over the ceremony, the priest also explains how to prepare, what to bring, and what to do during the ceremony. When hindus fall ill, certain rites are performed by priests. When death is imminent, family are notified. The person is placed in a room or in the entryway of the house, with the head facing east. A lamp is lit near the head, and is urged to concentrate on a mantra. Family keep vigil until death by singing hymns, praying and reading scripture. At the moment of death Holy ash or sandal paste is applied to the forehead, Vedic verses are chanted, and a few drops of milk, or other holy water are trickled into the mouth.

After death, the body is laid in the home's entryway, with the head facing south, on a cot or the ground, reflecting a return to the lap of Mother Earth. The lamp is kept lit near the head and incense burnt. A cloth is tied under the chin and over the top of the head. The thumbs are tied together, as are the large toes. Under no circumstances should the body be embalmed or organs removed for use by others. Religious pictures are turned to the wall, and in some traditions mirrors are covered. Relatives are asked to bid farewell and sing sacred songs at the side of the body. A fire ritual is then performed either by a priest or chief mourner. The chief mourner is usually the eldest son in the case of the father's death, and the youngest son in the case of the mother's. In some traditions, the eldest son serves for both, or the wife, son-in-law or nearest male relative.

The chief mourner then performs prayer, passing an oil lamp over the remains and offering flowers. The male (or female, depending on the gender of the deceased) relatives carry the body to the back area of the house (where possible), remove the clothes and drape it with a white cloth. The women walk around the body and offer puffed rice into the mouth to nourish the deceased for the journey ahead. A widow will place her wedding pendant (*managlsutra*) around her husband's neck, signifying her enduring tie to him. The coffin is then closed. The body is then cremated where only men are allowed to enter. The chief mourner circles the pyre and then, without turning to face the body, he lights the pyre and leaves the cremation grounds. The others follow. At a gas-fuelled crematorium, sacred wood and ghee are placed inside the coffin with the body. About 12 hours after cremation, family men return to collect the remains. The ashes are then either deposited into a river or the sea where more prayers are performed.

On the 3rd, 5th, 7th or 9th day, relatives gather for a meal of the deceased's favourite foods. A portion is offered before a photo of the deceased and later ceremonially left at an abandoned place, along with some lit camphor. A memorial ceremony is usually also held on the 31st, 40th days and a year after the day of passing.

5. Festivals and Holidays

Many annual festivals are celebrated in Hinduism. These are considered auspicious days when the veil between the worlds is thin and the various gods can touch the human world. Festivals provide the opportunity to go on pilgrimage, journeying to a far-off temple for blessings and renewal. As Professor Dr. Shiva Bajpai remarked, "Festivals, pilgrimages and temple worship are the faith armor of Hindus." Below are some of the more popular festivals.

5.1 Makara Sankranti/Pongal

This is a harvest festival also known by other various names and is the only hindu festival which is based on the Solar calendar rather than the Lunar calendar. The festival is celebrated by taking dips in the Ganges River or any river and offering water to the Sun god. In Tamil Nadu this is popularly called Pongal, and special prayers and offerings are given the Sun to thank it for the harvest.

5.2 Navaratri

"Nava-ratri" literally means "nine nights." This festival is observed twice a year, once in the beginning of summer and again at the onset of winter. During Navaratri, hindus invoke the energy aspect of god in the form of the universal mother, commonly referred to as "Durga," which literally means the remover of miseries of life. She is also referred to as "Devi" (goddess) or "Shakti" (energy or power). People usually dance and worship in this festival.
On the first three days, the mother is invoked as a powerful force called Durga in order to destroy all impurities, vices and defects. The next three days, the mother is adored as a giver of spiritual wealth, Lakshmi, who is considered to have the power of bestowing on her devotees inexhaustible wealth. The final set of three days is spent in worshipping the mother as the goddess of wisdom, Saraswati. In order have all-round success in life, hindus need the blessings of all three aspects of the divine mother; hence, the worship for nine nights.

5.3 Vasant Panchami/Saraswati Puja

This festival is observed on the fifth day of the waxing moon of Magh. The festival is is celebrated for the blessing of Saraswati, goddess of wisdom music, arts and nature. She is a part of the trinity of Saraswati, Lakshmi and Parvati. All the three forms help the trinity of Brahma, Vishnu and Shiva in the creation, maintenance and destruction of the Universe. The festival is celebrated in early February marking the start of spring for India and the Holi season.

5.4 Holi

Holi is a popular spring festival also known as the festival of colours and the festival of love. It is an ancient Hindu religious festival which has become popular with non-Hindus in many parts of South Asia, as well as people of other communities. Holi celebrations start with a Holika bonfire on the night before Holi where people gather, sing and dance. The next morning is a free-for-all carnival of colours where everyone plays, chases and colours each other with dry powder and coloured water, with some carrying water guns and coloured water-filled balloons for their water fight. The festival signifies the victory of good over evil, the arrival of spring, end of winter, and for many a festive day to meet others, play and laugh, forget and forgive, and repair ruptured relationships. The festival commemorates the slaying of the female demon Holika by Lord Vishnu's devotee Prahlad. Thus, the festival's name is derived from the Sanskrit words "Holika Dahanam", which literally mean "Holika's slaying".

5.5 Hanuman Jayanti

This festival is celebrated to commemorate the birth of Hanuman, the hindu monkey god, widely venerated throughout India. Hanuman is known for its great strength, power and immortal devotion towards Lord Rama. He is considered to be a greatest follower of Lord Rama and played a crucial role in his life. He is considered to be as one of the most powerful Hindu gods in India. The festival is an occasion to remember Lord Hanuman's unbridled devotion to Lord Rama and his feats their quest to fight against Ravana, Lord Hanuman led a monkey army and built a bridge to Lanka. He also carried a whole mountain of magic herbs on his shoulders to restore the life of Lakshman. Thus, the ubiquitous standing statue of Lord Hanuman with his heart stretched out open is at once a metaphoric as well as literal illustration of his infinite devotion to Lord Ram, his wife Sita and brother Lakshman. Also invoked as 'Sankat Mochan', Lord Hanuman can avert any ill-effects posed by the nine planets to one's life as well as save one from the influence of evil spirits. In India, Tuesdays and Saturdays are dedicated to the worship of Lord Hanuman to get his blessings for progress, wisdom and fearlessness.

5.6 Raksha Bandhan

Raksha Bandhan is a celebration of relationships specifically that of a brother and a sister. This relationship is nowhere so celebrated as in India. Raksha Bandhan is a festival which celebrates the bond of affection between brothers and sisters. It is a day when siblings pray for each other's' wellbeing and wish for each other's happiness and goodwill. The name 'Raksha Bandhan' suggests 'a bond of protection'. On this day, brothers make a promise to their sisters to protect them from all harms and troubles and the sisters pray to god to protect their brother from all evil. The festival falls generally in the month of August. Sisters tie the silk thread called rakhi on their brother's wrist and pray for their wellbeing and brothers promise to take care of their sisters and usually give their sisters a gift (money, sweets, clothing etc.) after the rakhi is tied.

5.7 Krishna Janmashtami

It is an annual commemoration of the birth of the hindu deity Krishna, the eighth avatar of Vishnu. Hindus celebrate Janmashtami by fasting and staying up until midnight, the time when Krishna is believed to have been born. Images of Krishna's infancy are placed in swings and cradles in temples and homes. At midnight, devotees gather around for devotional songs, dance and exchange gifts. Some temples also conduct readings of the Hindu religious scripture Bhagavad Gita (*the song of the Bhagavan, often referred to as simply the Gita, is a 700-verse scripture that is part of the Hindu epic Mahabharata. It is a sacred text of the Hindu*).

5.8 Deepavali/Diwali

Diwali is the abbreviation of the Sanskrit word "Deepavwali", which means "row of lights". It is also called the festival of lights. The festival celebrates the return of Rama and Sita to the kingdom Ayodhya after fourteen years of exile. The festival signifies the victory of light over darkness, knowledge over ignorance, good over evil, and hope over despair. The festival preparations and rituals typically extend over a five day period. Before Diwali night, people clean, renovate and decorate their homes. On Diwali night, Hindus dress up in new clothes or their best outfit, light up diyas (*lamps and candles*) inside and outside their homes, participate in family prayers typically to Lakshmi - the goddess of wealth and prosperity. Fireworks follow thereafter and a family feast including sweets and an exchange of gifts/sweets between family members and close friends.

5.9 Thaipusam or Kavadi

Thaipusam is a Hindu festival celebrated mostly by the Tamil community. The word Thaipusam is derived from the Tamil month name Thai and Pusam, which refers to a star near the location of the moon during the festival. The festival commemorates the occasion when Parvati gave Murugan a spear so he could vanquish the evil demon Soorapadman. The most potent rite that a devotee undertakes to perform is what is known as the "Kavadi". The benefits that the devotee gains from offering a Kavadi to the god are believed to be a million fold greater than the little pain that he inflicts upon himself.
Generally, people take a vow to offer the god a kavadi for the sake of tiding over a great calamity. After the ceremony the devotee gets so god-intoxicated that it is believed that their inner spiritual chamber is opened. The 'kavadi' varies in shape and size from the simple shape of a street hawker's storehouse (a wooden stick

with two baskets at each end, slung across the shoulder) to the costly palanquin structure, covered with flowers and interwoven with peacock feathers. In all cases the kavadi has brass bells adorning it, with brass containers filled with a concoction of milk and banana. The kavadi bearer observes silence as the priests lead a procession from a temple to an appointed area and journey back to the temple to fulfil the vow he/she has taken. In some cases the bearer is a carrier on behalf of someone for whom a vow has been made. The procession is led by large chariots covered with flowers, idols, pictures of deities that are pulled/drawn by men who are in a trance. The chariot puller has sharp metal hooks pierced into their backs with lines going back to the chariot thus allowing them to pull the chariot. Little to no blood is shed during this process. The procession is also led by women who are in a trance and dance hypnotically to the rhythm of drums, cymbals and singing.

Devotees go to the temple with their kavadis, milk pots, coconuts, rooster and goats. The animals are sacrificed to the gods and the coconuts split open to determine each devotee's fortune. Devotees also drink sweetened milk and are not allowed to consume any meat or anything containing meat including eggs, a month before the actual festival. At the end of the festival, the head priest or lead chariot puller climbs to the top of the temple – this devotee usually is in a trance of the god hanuman and imitates a monkey climbing to the top of the temple post to retrieve the flag on the temple. The many men and women who are already in a hypnotic trance then call out devotees and tell them their fortunes, also critically calling out their bad habits.

For most it is an auspicious occasion and for others it is also a fearful experience.

5.10 Maha Shivaratri

This festival is also known as the birthday of lord Shiva. The festival is principally celebrated by offerings of Bael or golden apple or Bilva/Vilvam leaves to Lord Shiva, all-day fasting and an all-night-long vigil (*jagarana*). All through the day, devotees chant a sacred mantra dedicated to the god. In accordance with scriptural and discipleship traditions, penances are performed in order to gain benefits in the practice of yoga and meditation. On this day, the planetary positions in the Northern hemisphere is said to act as catalysts to help a person raise his or her spiritual energy more easily.

5.11 Tamil New Year/Puthanda

This is the celebration of the first day of the Tamil New Year in mid-April. 14 April marks the first day of the traditional Tamil calendar and is a public holiday in both Tamil Nadu and Sri Lanka. Tropical vernal equinox fall around 22 March, and adding 23 degrees of oscillation to it, gives the Hindu sidereal or Nirayana Mesha Sankranti (*Sun's transition into Nirayana Aries*). Again alluding to the significant role of astrology in hinduism.

5.12 Karva Chauth

It is a one-day festival celebrated by Hindu women in North India in which married women fast from sunrise to moonrise for the safety and longevity of their husbands. Sometimes, unmarried women observe the fast for their fiancés or desired husbands. Karva is another word for 'pot' (*a small earthen pot of water*) and chauth means 'fourth' in Hindi (*a reference to the fact that the festival falls on the fourth day of the dark-fortnight of the month of Kartik*). Women begin preparing a few days in advance, by buying cosmetics, traditional jewellery, and prayer items, such as the Karva lamps, henna and the decorated prayer plate (*thali*).

The fast begins at dawn with fasting, women do not eat during the day, and some do not drink any water either. In traditional observances of the fast, the fasting woman does not perform any domestic chores. Women apply henna and other cosmetics to themselves and each other. In the evening, a community women-only ceremony is held. Participants dress in fine clothing and wear jewellery and henna and (in some regions) dress in the complete finery of their wedding dresses. The ceremony concludes and the women await the rising of the moon. Once the moon is visible, depending on the region and community, it is customary for a fasting woman, with her husband nearby, to view its reflection in a vessel filled with water, through a sieve, or through the cloth of a scarf (*dupatta*). Water is offered to the moon (*som or chandra, the lunar deity*) to secure its blessings. She then turns to her husband and views his face indirectly in the same manner. In some regions, the woman says a brief prayer asking for her husband's life. It is believed that at this stage, spiritually strengthened by her fast, the woman can successfully confront and defeat death. The husband then takes the water from the plate and gives his wife her first sip and feeds her with the first morsel of the day (usually something sweet). The fast is now broken, and the woman has a complete meal.

5.13 Draupadi

Traditional temples in KwaZulu Natal usually host fire walking during March, April or May to celebrate and honour the goddess Draupadi. Devotees take a vow to test their faith. They walk over a 10m long fire pit. Amazingly their feet are unburned and this is seen as proof of their faith and devotion to God. Various rituals and dramas are performed to remember the trials of Draupadi and the highlight is reached when the devotees walk across the fire pit. An image of Draupadi is placed at the end of the fire pit to guide and protect the faithful devotees as they walk across. It also blesses them and gives new life and health to the whole community.

5.14 Katha and Jhunda

The Katha is a prayer that precedes the hoisting of the flag. A priest performs the ritual prayers with the family of the home. The family fasts the entire day and are only allowed to consume food once the prayer is complete. Mantras are recited by the priest and the family members are required to repeat each mantra. The mantras are performed over a fire, each time a mantra is recited, the family members toss a little of a concoction of ghee and other items into the fire. The mantras involve cleansing the family and thanking the gods for obstacles that were overcome and for prosperity in the future. When the prayer is over, food is served to the people who have gathered to witness the prayer. The food is vegetarian and is usually puri (ghee bread) and vegetable curries. Sweet doughy bread called roth is specifically prepared only for this ceremony. The family eats a bit of the sweet bread and other sweets, usually feeding each other, before they sit to dine a full meal with the rest of the people. The sweet bread is also bread served to all who are present including the priest.

The principal element in the Jhunda prayer is the hoisting of a red flag on a very high bamboo pole on the premises of the devotee or at a temple/shrine. This is done in glorification of Hanuman. The Jhunda ceremony is performed by many. In hoisting the flag one indicates to the public and the world their willingness to follow in the footsteps of the Lord and by the rules and ethics of Sanathan Dharma. The flag also symbolizes Hanuman as the flag bearer. Hanuman is therefore accepted as the spiritual guide and mentor and the devotee thereafter follows the direct principles of devotional service. When one erects a Jhunda one is symbolizing that one has conquered the elements around oneself and it also signifies victory and another reason is to signify one is a Hindu.

What does the bible say about rituals? Here are a few verses that clearly show that we are to honour and abide in God's word which simple and straight forward. We no longer need to perform any sacrifice to the Lord because Jesus was the ultimate sacrifice; that through the shedding of His blood we are saved and redeemed and made blameless. We are to honour God by leading a righteous life, abiding in Him as His word abides in us and obeying His commandments. The Lord does not require us to keep any special days for him either, nor does he require any special fasting. He wants us to worship Him in spirit and in truth, anywhere and at any time. There are no boundaries or limits on how we worship Him as long as it is through the Holy Spirit. If and when we choose to fast, it is out of our own free will and it can be whether we are ill, have specific needs or wanting to further develop our relationship with God. Regardless, God looks at our hearts and He already knows what we need before we even take it to Him through prayer and fasting.

To do justice and judgment is more acceptable to the Lord than sacrifice.
Psalm 21:3

[16] For thou desirest not sacrifice; else would I give it: thou delightest not in burnt offering. [17] The sacrifices of God are a broken spirit: a broken and a contrite heart, O God, thou wilt not despise.
Psalm 51:16-17

[1] Him that is weak in the faith receive ye, but not to doubtful disputations. [2] For one believeth that he may eat all things: another, who is weak, eateth herbs. [3] Let not him that eateth despise him that eateth not; and let not him which eateth not judge him that eateth: for God hath received him. [4] Who art thou that judgest another man's servant? to his own master he standeth or falleth. Yea, he shall be holden up: for God is able to make him stand.
Romans 8:1-4

[16] Let no man therefore judge you in meat, or in drink, or in respect of an holyday, or of the new moon, or of the sabbath days: [17] Which are a shadow of things to come; but the body is of Christ.
Colossians 2:16-17

He that sacrificeth unto any god, save unto the Lord only, he shall be utterly destroyed.

Exodus 22:20

[1] And the Lord spake unto Moses, saying, [2] Speak unto the children of Israel, and say unto them, I am the Lord your God. [3] After the doings of the land of Egypt, wherein ye dwelt, shall ye not do: and after the doings of the land of Canaan, whither I bring you, shall ye not do: neither shall ye walk in their ordinances. [4] Ye shall do my judgments, and keep mine ordinances, to walk therein: I am the Lord your God.

Leviticus 18:1-4

6. Wedding Ceremonies

The Indian culture celebrates marriage as a sacrament (*Sanskara*), a rite enabling two individuals to start their journey in life together. Hindu marriages are the most lavish and extensive. They extend over a period of four to five days. They are highly traditional and strongly adhere to the ancient customs and traditions. Moreover, wedding is considered an important religious practice in Hindu religion. The Hindu marriage is primarily divided into three segments, pre wedding rituals, wedding rituals, and post wedding rituals. The Hindu wedding places emphasis on three essential values: happiness, harmony, and growth. The institution of marriage can be traced back to Vedic times. The ceremony should be held on a day in the "bright half" of the northern course of the sun. Months before the wedding an engagement ceremony known as Mangni is held. This is to bless the couple, who are then given gifts of jewellery and clothing by their new family.

Indian weddings, also called 'Vivaah', are best known for the grandeur, traditions, grace, colours and almost carnival-type celebration associated with the event. Hindu marriage is solemnised in accordance with an approved ritual instructed by the Vedas, the holy scriptures of the Hindus. It is the firm uniting of two souls such that after marriage the individual bodies remain as separate entities but the souls merge into one harmonious whole. According to Hindu traditions, the engagement ceremony is done a few months before the marriage. This ceremony is a formal announcement of the impending marriage and the start of the planning for the big event.

6.1 Pre-Wedding Ceremonies

The pre wedding rituals comprise of engagement, tilak, sagai, sangeet and mehendi-haldi ceremonies.

- The Engagement can also be called the ring ceremony, wherein the prospective couple exchanges rings. The father of the groom requests the father of the bride for the bride's hand in marriage with his son. The bride's father wants to make sure that the groom has no skeletons in his closet. Having confirmed that, the bride's father also tells the groom's father to make sure that his daughter is also as good, if not better than the groom! The couple exchanges the wedding rings and the ceremony ends with best wishes and blessings from all the attendees. The engaged couple is then referred to as bride and groom, although they do not become so until the pre-

wedding ceremony a day or two before the actual wedding.
- Next is the Tilak ceremony, in which the bride's brother applies tilak (*a mark worn by a Hindu on the forehead to indicate caste, status, or sect, or as an ornament*) to the groom and gives him gifts. The ceremony is held in different styles according to different culture and caste. Mostly the ceremony is held at the groom's residence or at any temple.
- Thereafter is the Sagai ceremony in which both the parties exchange gifts. Sagai ceremonies are always vibrant and fun. In sagai, the bride is given jewellery, clothes, make-up and baby toys, by the mother of the groom. On the other hand, the groom is given gifts by the family of the bride.
- Then comes the Sangeet ceremony, wherein the female members sing and dance to rejoice the occasion. It is one of the most enjoyable ceremonies before the wedding and is exclusively for women. Initially, the sangeet party was organized only by the bride's family but with changing times it is now observed by the groom's family as well. Also, it was a ritual which was only seen in North Indian weddings, but nowadays it is conducted in Bengali and South Indian marriages as well.
- Just before the wedding, the mehndi ceremony is organized, in which mehndi-is applied on bride's hands and feet. Indian people are ardent lovers of beauty and elegance. This is what reflects in the

mehndi ceremony before marriage. The ceremony has been prevalent since ages and forms an integral part of the wedding ceremony, furthermore, mehndi is one of the sixteen adornments of the bride and her beauty is incomplete without it.

- The groom and bride goes through the haldi or pithi ceremony. Pithi is the paste that is made out of chickpea flour, turmeric, rose water and a few other ingredients. Since ancient times, in Hindu weddings the Pithi ceremony is celebrated separately in both the bride's and the groom's houses. The family members apply "haldi" (turmeric paste) on their faces, hands and legs to cleanse, purify and prepare them for holy matrimony. The paste also has medicinal properties – when rubbed on, it is excellent for the skin and evens out the skin tone.

6.2 Wedding Rituals

Also called the mandap ceremony holds utmost importance on the day of the wedding. This is because all the significant rituals are performed during the ceremony. In India, weddings take place in accordance with the age old customs and traditions. It is a very meticulous process and is fulfilled with the feeling that it is a one-time affair.

- The groom's procession (*baraat*): Accompanied by his family and friends in a festive procession known as the baraat, the groom arrives at the entrance of the wedding venue on a horse, sometimes even an elephant. The procession consists of his family and friends singing and dancing around him to music. The baraat is met by the bride's family at the entrance to the wedding venue. It symbolizes the pleasure and happiness of the groom's family in accepting the bride as a part of their family; as their very own.

- Meeting of the two families (*milni*): The bride's mother greets the groom with a welcoming ritual. Relatives of the bride and groom embrace and greet each other with garlands of flowers. The bride's family then escorts the groom to the mandap, a canopied altar where the ceremony is performed. The mandap represents the home that the bride and groom will make together.
- Prayer to lord Ganesh (*Ganesh puja*): The ceremony begins with a worship of lord Ganesh, the destroyer of all obstacles. The priest guides the groom and bride's parents in offering flowers, sweets and prayer to lord Ganesh.
- Arrival of the Bride (Kanya *Aagaman*): The bride enters the hall and is escorted to the mandap by her maternal uncle and aunt, signifying that the bride's maternal side approves of the union. In other parts of India, the bride is escorted by her sisters, cousins and close female friends.
- Exchange of Garlands (*Jai Mala*) – Var Mala Ceremony: Once the bride approaches the mandap, the bride and groom exchange floral garlands, signifying their acceptance of one another.
- After this, they are taken to the mandap where the Kanyadaan ritual is performed. At this point, the

bride's father pours sacred water in his daughter's hand and places her hand in the groom's hand, officially giving away his most precious gift to the groom. The groom's sister or cousin then ties the end of the groom's scarf to the bride's saree or scarf (*dupatta*) with betelnuts, copper coins and rice, symbolizing unity, prosperity and happiness. The knot represents the eternal bond of marriage.
- Lighting of the Sacred Fire (*Vivah Hawan*): The priest then lights the sacred fire or Agni. Fire symbolizes the divine presence as a witness of the ceremony. Commitments made in the presence of fire are made in the presence of god.
- Circling the Sacred Fire (*Mangal Phere*): The bride and groom walk around the sacred fire seven times keeping in mind the four aspirations in life: duty to each other, family and god (*dharma*), prosperity (artha), energy and passion (karma) and salvation (moksha). The bride, representing divine energy, leads the groom in the first three rounds, while the groom leads in the last four rounds, signifying balance and completeness. In some cultures, the bride and groom walk around the fire four times, with the bride leading in the first three rounds, and the groom leading in the final round. The bride's brother usually places rice grains in her hands after she completes each round to signify his pledge to always support and protect her in times of need. Once the couple has completed the four rounds, there's a race to see who will sit down first. It is said that whoever sits down first will rule the house!
- The Seven Sacred Steps (Saptapadi): The couple takes seven steps together, taking a sacred vow with each step:

1. Together they will live with respect for one another.
2. Together they will develop mental, physical and spiritual balance.
3. Together they will prosper, acquire wealth and share our accomplishments.
4. Together they will acquire happiness, harmony and knowledge through mutual love.
5. Together they will raise strong, virtuous children.
6. Together they will be faithful to one another and exercise self-restraint and longevity.
7. Together they will remain lifelong partners and achieve salvation.

- When they return to their seats, the bride will move to sit on the groom's left side, taking the closest possible position to the groom's heart. The groom then offers the bride lifelong protection by placing a mangalsutra, or sacred necklace made of black and gold beads, around her neck and applying sindoor (red vermillion powder) on the crown of her forehead. These two offerings signify the bride's status as a married woman and the groom's devotion to the bride. The bride and groom also exchange rings at this time and feed each other sweets.
- The association of human fertility cult with the coconut is prominently manifested during wedding rituals across India. The fruit is often placed in a pot which is a metaphor for the womb, while the nut itself, a symbol or life, confers fertility on the bridal couple. In Gujarat it is customary for the bride to present the coconut to the groom at the time of the marriage. The coconut is then

preserved as a precious memento by the husband throughout his life. The coconut is covered in embellished fabric and container which the bride carries with her into her new home.
- Blessings for the Married Couple (aashirvaad): Women from both families whisper blessings into the bride's ear. The couple then bow down to the priest, their parents and elder relatives and touch their feet to receive their final blessings. The guests shower the newlywed couple with flowers and rice to wish them a long and happy marriage.

6.3 Post-Wedding Rituals

Going away of the Bride to the Groom's house (Bidaai/Vidaai):

The indian wedding is a cherished moment, which is more of a dream come true. However, after the dream realizes, it's time for the bride to leave her house. This emerges out as the most painful moment of all. This is what the Indian wedding Vidai ceremony is all about. The bride says her final goodbye to her family and the father gives his prized possession to the Groom's father. The procession ends joyfully, yet is often bittersweet for those closest to the Bride and Groom. It takes place after the wedding rituals are completed. During the vidaai ceremony the bride is accompanied by her parents and associates, which lead her outside the doorstep of the house. Before crossing the doorstep, she throws back three handfuls of rice and coins over her head, into the house. This symbolizes that the bride is repaying her parents for all that they have given her so far. Thereafter the bride's father takes her to the groom's vehicle and they leave to the grooms house.

When the bride arrives at her new home, her mother-in-law welcomes her with the traditional prayer. At the entrance, the bride places her right foot onto a tray of vermilion powder mixed in water or milk, symbolizing the arrival of good fortune and purity. With both her feet now covered in the red powder paste, she kicks over a vessel filled with rice and coins to denote the arrival of fertility and wealth in her marital home. The elders present bless the couple. Ornaments and saris are presented to the bride. She and her groom sit on a wooden plank and the Bou Bhat ceremony begins. Women blow conch shells, ring bells, and take up wailing. The bride does not eat any food in her in-laws house. That night, the bride wears a new sari. The bedroom is tastefully decorated with flowers. The flowers and clothes come from the bride's house along with the sweets. She then enters her new home and begins her new life with her husband and carry on the traditions and rituals of her new family home. A few days after the wedding day, the newlywed couple return to the bride's home. The thread which was tied on the bride's wrist by the priest is cut.

Marriage is a sacred vow between a man and woman and the Bible offers many verses that offer guidance for married couples, husbands, wives, newlyweds and engagement. God created man and woman and woman for man. What God has put together, no one can put asunder. Marriage was designed by God for companionship and intimacy. The bible also says that husbands and wives are equal partners, man shall leave his father and mother and cleave to his wife.

²² And the rib, which the Lord God had taken from man, made he a woman, and brought her unto the man. ²³ And Adam said, This is now bone of my bones, and flesh of my flesh: she shall be called Woman, because she was taken out of Man. 24 Therefore shall a man leave his father and his mother, and shall cleave unto his wife: and they shall be one flesh.

Genesis 2:22-24

⁶ But from the beginning of the creation God made them male and female. ⁷ For this cause shall a man leave his father and mother, and cleave to his wife; ⁸ And they twain shall be one flesh: so then they are no more twain, but one flesh. ⁹ What therefore God hath joined together, let not man put asunder.

Mark 10:6-9

6.4 Hindu Symbols

- The Swastika:

As much as the swastika was the symbol of the German Nazism and all it stood for, similarly the swastika is a key symbol that is used in hinduism. It is one of the oldest known symbols second to the Cross of Christ. Traditionally, when the swastika is drawn facing right handed or clockwise as below, it is a good luck symbol. It is sometimes claimed that when it is drawn left facing or anti-clockwise, it is a bad omen and it is labelled a "sauwastika", however there is little evidence of this distinction in Hindu and Buddhist history from which it is supposed to derive. Hindus all over India still use the symbol in both representations for the sake of balance, although the standard form is the left-facing swastika.
Swastika the word has its root in the world Suwasti meaning 'all is well'. If you look closely then you would find a cross with extended arms in the Swastika

symbol. This is true symbol of the entire cosmos to hindus.

- Aum/Om/Ohm:

This is the most important Hindu symbol and is found in every prayer and temple and represents Brahma (is the Hindu god *deva* of creation). It is also a sound used to focus the mind on godly energy, considered a sacred sound.

- Saffron:

Saffron is not only worn by hindus, but also by Buddhists and Muslims, but symbolises different things. For hindus it shows the rejection of material things while Muslims see it as a military colour. It also represents fire and Brahma.

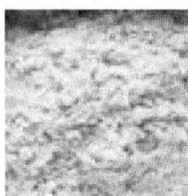

- Trisula:

Also spelled "Trishula," this trident is an important symbol in hinduism. The trihsula (also spelled trishul or trisula, Sanskrit for "three spear") is a trident spear that is the emblem of the god Shiva. The weapon symbolizes empire and the irresistible force of transcendental reality. The three prongs of the trishula represent Shiva's three aspects of creator, preserver, destroyer.

- Yantra:

A yantra is a geometrical diagram representing the universe. It is used in hindu worship and meditation, especially in tantrism (movement within Buddhism combining elements of Hinduism and paganism). A yantra is quite similar to a it can be a three-dimensional object of worship as well as a two-dimensional diagram.

6.5 Red String (mauli/kalava)

It is customary for hindus to tie a red thread - commonly called a mauli or kalava - on the wrist at the beginning of a religious ceremony. The thread is tied on the right wrist of men and the left wrist of women. The literal meaning of mauli is 'above all'. Here the reference is to the head that stands high. With the moon perched on top of Shiva's head he is referred to as candramauli. In most cases, wearing the string simply symbolizes an allegiance to the hindu faith. However, the meaning of this iconic red thread -- which plays a part in many hindu rituals and is commonly worn in day-to-day life, goes well beyond its status as a simple symbol of commonality. The colour red is extremely significant in the hindu faith, symbolizing both purity and, as the colour of the deity, Shakti, prowess. Other Hindu deities that wear red often represent bravery, generosity or security. Oftentimes, the mostly red string features white or yellow braids or accents.

6.6 Sathya Sai Baba

Sri Sathya Sai Baba was an Indian guru. He claimed to be the reincarnation of Sai Baba of Shirdi, who was also considered by his followers to be an avatar, spiritual saint and miracle worker, and who died in 1918.
The reputed materialisations of holy ash and other small objects such as rings, necklaces, and watches by Sathya Sai Baba along with reports of miraculous healings, resurrections, clairvoyance, bilocation, and alleged omnipotence and omniscience were a source of both fame and controversy; devotees considered

them signs of divinity, while sceptics viewed them as simple conjuring tricks. He further faced accusations over the years of sexual abuse and fraud—charges he denied as smear campaigns. The Sathya Sai Organisation, founded by Sathya Sai Baba enables its members to undertake service activities as a means to spiritual advancement and has over 1,200 Sathya Sai Centres (branches) in 126 countries. Through this organisation, Sathya Sai Baba established a network of free hospitals, clinics, drinking water projects and schools. He died on 28 March 2011 from respiratory failure, at age 84. He predicted that he would die at age 96 and would remain healthy until then. After he died, some devotees suggested that he might have been referring to lunar years, rather than solar years, and using the Indian way of accounting for age, which counts the year to come as part of the person's life. Other devotees have spoken of his anticipated resurrection, reincarnation or awakening. He was and is still worshipped by many with many children being named after him by using the "Sai" in his name.

6.7 Dasavatara: Ten Avatars of Vishnu

The ten most famous descents of Vishnu are collectively known as the "Dasavatara" ("dasa" in Sanskrit means ten). The first four are said to have appeared in the Satya Yuga (the first of the four Yugas or ages in the time cycle described within hinduism). The next three avatars appeared in the Treta Yuga, the eighth descent in the Dwapara Yuga and the ninth in the Kali Yuga. The tenth is predicted to appear at the end of the Kali Yuga in some 400,000 years' time. 10 Avatars:

- Matsya, the fish
- Kurma, the tortoise
- Varaha, the boar
- Narasimha
- Vamana, the dwarf
- Parashurama, Rama with the axe
- Rama, Ramachandra, the prince and king of Ayodhya
- Krishna (meaning "dark coloured" or "all attractive") appeared in the Dwapara Yuga along with his brother Balarama.
- Gautama Buddha (meaning "the enlightened one") appeared in the Kali Yuga (specifically as Siddhartha Gautama)
- Kalki ("Eternity", or "time", or "The Destroyer of foulness"), who is expected to appear at the end of Kali Yuga, the time period in which we currently exist.

6.8 Ashrams

Traditionally, an ashram is a spiritual hermitage or a monastery. Additionally, today the term ashram often denotes a locus of Indian cultural activity such as yoga, music study or religious instruction, the moral equivalent of a studio. An ashram is also a place of spiritual retreat. Usually there are permanent residents as well as visitors who come for retreats. Ashrams usually have practical rules to make sure the atmosphere stays spiritual and meditative. For the permanent residents these rules have become a way of life. For visitors they are voluntarily taken on, usually for spiritual cleansing purposes.

6.9 Yoga & Meditation

Meditation is a practice in which an individual trains the mind or induces a mode of consciousness, either to realize some benefit or as an end in itself. Meditation may also involve repeating a mantra and closing the eyes. The mantra is chosen based on its suitability to the individual meditator. Meditation claims to have a calming effect and directs awareness inward until pure awareness is achieved, described as "being awake inside without being aware of anything except awareness itself." In brief, there are dozens of specific styles of meditation practice, and many different types of activity commonly referred to as meditative practices. Outside of Hindu culture, the word "yoga" is usually understood to refer to the practice of meditative movement or Hatha Yoga.

- Hatha Yoga is only one part of the Hindu traditions of Yoga and Tantra. It is one of the paths leading to the ultimate goal of Raja Yoga, or contemplation of the One Reality.
- Kundalini yoga is a tantric form of yoga focused on awakening the kundalini, the latent psychic energy that lies at the base of the spine, and making it rise through the seven chakras to the top of the spine.
- Jnana yoga is for people who are reflective and seek knowledge find their divinity through rationality and spirituality.
- Bhakti yoga is the path to god through love and devoted service. It insists on god's otherness and teaches love of god through adoration.
- Karma yoga is the path to god through work. Be productive and strive to work towards high rewards and work unselfishly.

- Raja yoga is known as the path to reintegration, a way to god through psychophysical experiments. Self-searching could be one way of describing Raja Yoga. Looking inward to discern the humanness from the godlikeness and bringing them together. It involves meditation and self-discipline.

The bible clearly warns against meditation and the practice of yoga given that it is directly linked to hinduism. Yoga is bound up in Eastern religious metaphysics and is not an innocent form of relaxing the body and the mind. The goal of yoga is the same as that of hinduism, which is realizing that one is brahman, the underlying impersonal God of the Universe in Hinduism.

Now the Spirit speaketh expressly, that in the latter times some shall depart from the faith, giving heed to seducing spirits, and doctrines of devils;

1 Timothy 4:1

Know ye not that ye are the temple of God, and that the Spirit of God dwelleth in you?

1 Corinthians 3:16

6.10 Hindu Superstitions

Most Indians are highly superstitious. Many aspects of their life are linked to some superstitious belief and some of these are even mentioned in religious literature. Most superstitions were born with an aim to protect and were based on sound reasoning. With time, however, much of the reasoning has been forgotten and the beliefs appear unsubstantiated. But there are also many beliefs that have no reason behind them and are just simply bizarre.

- The most auspicious omen is to see an elephant when one is on a journey, for it represents Ganesha, the god of good luck and the remover of obstacles.
- If a crow is heard cawing at one's house or if someone drops a kitchen utensil means that they should expect guests to come to their home.
- If any person that is part of a group that are conversing or near the group conversing happens to sneeze, this means that the story they were discussing is true/validated.
- One should neither clip one's nails at night nor use scissors for fear of angering evil spirits.
- One should not clip their nails inside the house as this spells bad fortune for the home.
- A persistent belief is that one must not sweep the floors after the sun sets; else the god Lakshmi would also be swept away from the home.
- If a person hiccups, it is believed that someone is talking about him or remembering him.
- Breaking a mirror is extremely inauspicious as it means 7 years of bad fortune for the person who broke it.
- Women with long hair are not allowed must have their hair tied up and covered whilst walking or travelling at night, it is said that evil spirits can attach themselves to women through their long hair.
- When a family arrives home late at night, the head of the household (usually male) must light a match in front of the door, blow it out and then throw it over their shoulder, this chases away evil spirits

that may have travelled back with them during the journey home.
- When the right hand itches it means good fortune and the reverse applies to the left hand. Some believe that if the palm of the right hand itches, that money is coming their way.
- Twitching of the right eye is considered inauspicious and of that of the left eye, auspicious.
- If a person sees a hearse they must touch strands of their hair to prevent any evil from the hearse getting to them.
- If one gives chillies as a plant or spice to another, the person receiving the chilli must in turn give the person money of any value, if not evil shall befall both people.
- It is bad when a cat crosses your path or road, especially black cats. If that happens, people mostly return to their homes or pray to god and proceed on their path.
- When a coconut is broken in the temple, it should part in to two regular and equal halves and not break in an angle into the eyes of the coconut. A decayed or rotten coconut foreshadows serious mishap to the devotee.
- When the first tooth of a child falls out the fallen tooth is carefully placed in a lump of cow dung, and thrown over roof in the belief that such action will hasten the re-growth of the child's tooth.
- It is a bad for a person to stand with hands placed behind the head when trying to relax, since it can cause the death of parents.
- One should never touch or try to chase a praying mantis that is in the home, as it is seen that god is physically present in their home.

- One should not chase or kill a cream/white lizard from their home, as it is considered good fortune is upon them.
- It is so common to find a string of lemons and chillies hanging on the doorway of shops, offices and homes. Doing this is supposed to ward off the evil eye and bring in good luck.
- Pregnant women must stay indoors during an eclipse in order to ensure that their babies are not born with any deformities. They are also not allowed to sew or cut vegetables during an eclipse.

7. **Hindu Deities**

7.1 **Brahma**

Seen as the creator of the world whose four heads and four arms represent the four points of the compass, it is thought that Brahma would have a dominant role within hinduism. Though he represents one of the three main forms of Brahman, he is very much subordinated to Vishnu, who represents the sustaining aspect of Brahman and Shiva who represents the destructive aspect. In fact, one story tells of Brahma's fifth head being burnt up by Shiva's third eye. He may be shown holding a vase of water, symbolizing the water from which the universe evolved, a rosary for counting the passage of time, a sacrificial spoon linking him with the Brahmin priests and their traditional role in the offering of sacrifices and the four Vedas, ancient sacred books of the Hindus. He is also at times shown with a disc and an alms bowl. He may be depicted on a lotus throne. He is often bearded, and may wear a black or white garment.

7.2 Durga

The name 'Durga' means 'Inaccessible' and this may reflect something of the mystery at the heart of this deity. Though loving and kind to those who worship her, as the consort (wife/partner) of Shiva in her warrior form, she symbolizes the violent and destructive qualities of the Mother Goddess (Shakti). These qualities are explained by a story from the Hindu tradition according to which she was born fully grown from flames which issued from the mouths of Brahma, Vishnu, Shiva and other lesser deities who created her for the purpose of destroying the buffalo demon, symbol of death. The weapons which she holds which may include Shiva's trident, Vishnu's discus, a bow and arrow, a sword and shield, and a javelin are for the destruction of evil and the protection of good. The eight arms with which she is at times shown have been interpreted as representing health, education, wealth, organization, unity, fame, courage and truth. Other images show Durga with ten arms. Her vehicle is a lion or tiger which further emphasizes her violent and aggressive qualities.

7.3 Ganesha

The image of Ganesha is one of the most distinctive ones within Hinduism. The image has an elephant's head and a large human body usually colored pink or yellow. The elephant's head symbolizes the gaining of knowledge through listening (ears) and reflection (large head). The two tusks, one whole and the other broken, reflect the existence of perfection and imperfection in the physical world. There is a wealth of symbolism associated with the 'pot belly'. It has been interpreted as reflecting an ability to digest whatever experiences life brings. Or, to draw on another motif to be found in hinduism, that in some sense the whole universe is contained inside him. It may also be seen as a sign of well-being and of his role as a provider of earthly riches. Usually shown with one leg on the ground and the other one folded as if he were meditating. This reflects a balance between the practical and spiritual life, a theme which is repeated in the symbolism of some of the objects associated with him. In his hands he holds such objects as a rope or noose, to trap the things which attract the mind to the world, and a goad or iron hook, to represent the need to control desires. But he is also typically shown with a bowl of sweetmeats representing earthly prosperity and well-being. He may also be shown with an axe or trident, both of which link him with Shiva. Other symbolic objects which may be associated with Ganesha are a shell, water lily, mace and discus.
He is pictured with four arms symbolizing such aspects of hinduism as the four Vedas (ancient sacred books), the four aims of hinduism and the four stages of life. His vehicle is a rat or a mouse as these creatures are known for their ability to gnaw through barriers. The combination of the elephant and the rat or mouse ensures that all obstacles, of whatever size,

are removed. The fact that a rat/mouse and food are often shown around or under his feet has also been interpreted as reflecting the idea that desires and wealth are both under his control. Ganesha is worshipped as the deity who removes barriers and bestows wisdom and good fortune. Many hindus have an image of Ganesha on their shrines and pray to him before they begin their worship of other deities. He is also worshipped at the beginning of any new venture such as a wedding or the building of a new house. Ganesha is often shown with an open hand, palms upturned, sometimes holding a gift to show him granting favors to his devotees.

7.4 Hanuman

Hanuman, whose image is in the form of a monkey, is particularly associated with the Ramayana, the story of Rama and Sita. In the story, Sita, Rama's wife, is kidnapped by the evil, ten-headed demon Ravana who carries her off to his fortress in the island of Lanka. At great risk to his own safety, Hanuman finds Sita and then returns to help Rama build a bridge over to the island to rescue Sita. During the ensuing battle, Rama's brother Lakshmana was fatally wounded. Hanuman was sent to fetch healing herbs which grew on a particular mountain. Unable to identify the herbs, he uprooted the whole mountain and brought it back to the site of the battle thus saving Lakshmana's life. Images of Hanuman often show him holding the mountain in his hand. As a model for human devotion to God, he is often depicted with paws clasped together in reverence. He is a symbol of strength and loyalty and represents the concept that animals are also a creation of God. Hanuman is also regarded as a god in his own right and as the son of the wind god he is able to fly and change shape at will. He is one of the few gods without a consort. The worship of Hanuman, therefore, symbolizes the worship of the Supreme Lord, for acquiring knowledge, physical and mental strength, truthfulness, sincerity, selflessness, humility, loyalty, and profound devotion to the Lord.

7.5 Kali

Kali, which means black, represents the terrifying aspect of the Mother Goddess, whose kindly or benign aspect is reflected in the goddess Lakshmi. She is usually depicted naked or wearing a tiger skin, with dishevelled hair and

eyes rolling with intoxication. She has fang-like teeth, and her lolling tongue dripping with blood hangs from her mouth. Around her neck is a necklace of skulls. She is usually shown with four arms, two of which hold severed heads while the other two hold a dagger and a sword. A strangling noose also features in some of the images. She dances on the body of her partner Shiva. Though her hands are blood stained, one is often raised in a gesture of protection or assurance in the midst of destruction. Kali reflects the Indian tradition of bringing together seemingly contradictory aspects of life and some see a link with the ancient worship of the Great Goddess as an Earth Mother whose power was shown both in the fertility of the earth and in the receiving of the bodies of dead. Kali represents the realities of life and death. Kali, the devourer of time (kala) stands for the frightening, painful side of life which all who desire to progress spiritually must face and overcome.

7.6 Krishna

Krishna, 'one who attracts or draws' people or 'one who drains away' sins is the eighth and most important avatar of Vishnu, embodying joy, freedom and love. He also often appears as a god in his own right. In the Bhagavad Gita he is the divine instructor of Arjuna and the supreme Deity. In later tradition he is Krishna the cowherd, who, from being a wonderful and mischievous child, grows into a youth loved by the gopis, the cowherd girls. His involvement with the gopis in amorous dance becomes the model of passionate union with God. Some images show him in dance mode, playing his irresistible flute to summon the gopis. He is also shown in images of power, e.g. destroying the evil snake, Kaliya, who has poisoned the life-giving waters of one of India's sacred rivers. He is typically depicted with blue-black skin, wearing a yellow loin cloth and a crown of peacock feather. Krishna as a baby: A model of the baby Krishna features in the Hindu festival of Janamastami which celebrates the birth of Krishna. The baby Krishna is ceremoniously swung in his cradle/hammock at midnight in the midst of feasting and singing. Janamastami is celebrated during August/September.

7.7 Lakshmana

(shown at left, behind throne.)

Lakshmana was a half-brother to Rama whose story is told in the Ramayana, one of the most popular stories in the Hindu tradition. Lakshmana accompanied Rama and Sita in their exile and shared their struggles. In the great battle with ten-headed demon Ravana, Lakshmana was fatally wounded but was restored to health when Hanuman, the god-king of the monkeys, brought to the battle field the mountain on which grew special healing herbs. Lakshmana symbolizes the ideal of sacrifice. He leaves his young wife behind in the palace and chooses to accompany his brother (Rama) in exile. He sacrifices the amenities of his personal life to serve his elder brother.

7.8 Lakshmana

Lakshmi, one of the forms of the Mother Goddess, is the goddess of fortune and wealth and the partner of Vishnu. She is commonly called "Shri" a title given to many gods and saints but especially to Lakshmi. She is associated with the festival of Diwali as the bringer of blessings for the New Year. As goddess of good fortune she is depicted with four arms. Two of her hands hold lotus flowers and a third pours out wealth in the form of gold coins. Her fourth hand is held out in the gesture of blessing. But she is also the goddess of beauty and as such is shown as a young and beautiful goddess decorated with jewels and with only two arms. She is often depicted seated on a lotus being showered by two elephants who are pouring pots of water over her head. The lotus is a symbol of fertility and purity as it grows with both power and beauty form the mud. In India with its lack of a constant dependable supply of water, water is a symbol of plenty. Lakshmi's vehicle is a white owl.

7.9 Parvati

(here with Shiva and their son, Ganesha)

Parvati, daughter of the Himalayas, represents the gentler qualities of the Mother Goddess. Her docile obedience to her husband, Shiva, is seen as a model of the worshipper's relationship to God. It should be noted, however, that behind Parvati lies the power of the Mother Goddess which is seen by many Hindus to be greater than that of the deities themselves.

7.10 Rama

Rama which means 'one who permeates and who is present in everything and everyone' is the seventh avatar of Vishnu. The Ramayana, which is one of the most popular stories in the Hindu tradition, tells of

Rama's exploits. As a young prince he performs heroic acts and in due course wins the beautiful Sita as his wife after succeeding in bending a great war bow. Cheated of his rightful role as successor to his father the king, he goes off into exile. Sita and his brother Lakshmana insist in going with him.  One day Sita is kidnapped by the ten-headed demon Ravana and carried off to his stronghold in the island of Lanka. Helped by Hanuman, the god-king of the monkeys, Rama eventually defeats Ravana and his army in battle and rescues Sita. They then return to their kingdom where Rama is given his rightful place as king. Rama is the model of reason, right action and commendable virtues. He is often depicted with a tall conical cap which symbolizes his royal status. Rama represents an ideal man, as conceived by the Hindu mind. In the story of Ramayana, Rama's personality depicts him as the perfect son, devoted brother, true husband, trusted friend, ideal king, and a noble adversary. Sita and Rama are the model wife and husband in the Hindu tradition.

7.11   Ravana

Ravana is the ten-headed demon who features in the Ramayana, one of the most popular stories in the Hindu tradition.

Ravana kidnaps the beautiful Sita, wife of Rama, and carries her off to his stronghold in the island of Lanka. Helped by Hanuman, the god-king of the monkeys, Rama eventually defeats Ravana and his army in battle and rescues Sita.

7.12 Sarasvati

Sarasvati is the partner of Brahma and is the goddess of wisdom and the arts and as such is widely revered. She particularly attracts the worship of students. She is usually depicted as very fair-skinned, beautiful and elegant and dressed in a white garment. Objects associated with Sarasvati are the vina (an Indian stringed musical instrument), a flute, a manuscript and a book. Sanskrit, the ancient sacred language of Hinduism, is said to have been created by her. Her vehicle is usually shown as a peacock but she may also be seen with a swan or a goose, the vehicles associated with her consort, Brahma. Sarasvati is the Goddess of learning, knowledge, and wisdom. She is worshipped by all persons interested in knowledge, especially students, teachers, scholars, and scientists.

7.13 Shiva

Shiva is one of the three main forms of Brahman, the Supreme Spirit or Power of the universe. In this role Shiva represents the power of destruction. But as the old has to be destroyed to give rise to the new, he is also seen by his followers as the lord of creation. Perhaps the greatest of the Hindu deities, he is given a range of titles which include Maha-deva (great god), Maha-yogi (great ascetic), Nata-raja (lord of the Dance). Shiva has over 100 names, including Shankar and Shambhu. He is also known as the 'Blue-throated'. This title arises from a story in the Hindu scriptures which recounts how he drank the poison which would otherwise have destroyed the world. His name means 'auspicious' or 'kindly' and this should be kept in mind in any interpretation of the symbols associated with him. Shiva is the destroyer of our illusion and ignorance that stands in the way of our perfect union and enlightenment. Shiva's consort (wife or partner) may take several forms and these reflect the different aspects of his character and  qualities. Parvati reflects the gentle aspects whereas Durga and, even more so, the mysterious goddess Kali, reflect the fiercer elements. Ganesha, the god depicted with an elephant's head and a human body, is one of Shiva and Parvati's sons. His most characteristic weapon is the trident, a reminder of his role in the whole process of creation, preservation and destruction. It may also reflect the three qualities of goodness, passion and darkness which are in all things in different proportions. His most characteristic weapon is the trident, a reminder of his role in the whole process of creation, preservation and destruction. It may also reflect the three qualities of goodness, passion and darkness which are in all things in different proportions.

Another typical feature of images of Shiva is his third eye which represents both spiritual insight and the ability to burn up anything which may hinder such insight.

The three horizontal lines on his forehead have been interpreted as representing the three sources of light - fire, sun and moon; or his ability to see the past, present and future. The three lines may also, as with the trident, represent the three qualities of goodness, passion and darkness. Shiva is also typically depicted with snakes around his neck or across his body. The snake may represent the evolutionary power within the human body, the spiritual power which may be developed through yoga and also Shiva's power to deal with death. Rosaries show his mastery of the spiritual sciences. He is frequently depicted sitting on a tiger skin, the symbol of the cruel forces of nature, over which he is lord. Shiva's vehicle is Nandin a white bull which represents strength and fertility. As the bull is ridden by Shiva, it shows the god's control over these powers. In this image he sits in meditative pose reflecting peace and perfect inner harmony. Lord Shiva is the Lord of mercy and compassion. He protects devotees from evil forces such as lust, greed, and anger. Lord Shiva annihilates evil, grants boons, bestows grace, destroys ignorance, and awakens wisdom in His devotees.

7.14 Vishnu

Vishnu is one of the three main forms or manifestations of Brahman, the Supreme Spirit or Power of the universe, and represents the sustaining power of Brahman. It is thought that the name Vishnu means either to 'pervade' or 'to take different forms'. These two ideas are brought together in the doctrine of avatars associated with Vishnu. An avatar is a 'descent' or 'incarnation' of a deity. It is believed that Vishnu pervades the universe by descending to earth in different forms when the forces of evil threaten to overcome the forces of good. The most important avatars are Krishna and Rama. Vishnu's consort (partner or wife) is Lakshmi. Lakshmi, one of the forms of the Mother Goddess, is the goddess of fortune and wealth.

Vishnu may be depicted with two or four arms. When shown with four arms, these represent his power over both the four points of the compass and the four stages of life through which the 'twice born' Hindu man was thought to travel. Images of Vishnu combine compassion and strength. The four symbols most commonly associated with Vishnu are the conch shell which represents water and the first sound of creation, the lotus which symbolizes the unfolding universe, the mace which is interpreted as the power of knowledge conquering time and finally the discus which is associated with the conquering of evil and ignorance. Vishnu may be recognized by the U shaped symbol on his forehead. His vehicle is Garuda, depicted either as a crowned eagle or as a bird with a man's head. He is a powerful opponent of evil. The hood of snakes' heads which shelter him represents the endless cycles of creation and reflects one of the central stories of creation in the Hindu tradition. Three hands hold three of the standard symbols, conch shell, discus and lotus and the fourth is held in the traditional hand gesture symbolizing protection.

When a sincere devotee of the Lord controls his desires, the Lord fulfills the devotee's genuine desires and helps him on his path.

Chapter 3: Witchcraft

Written By: Tanja Davey

"A) the occupation of the devil's agents exercising his dark powers for the carrying out of his will. B) An institution of satanic priests and priestesses of darkness. C) Female lust, and the practise of spiritism and necromancy. Spiritually, the practice of abusing creation for one's own purposes by the imposition of demonic desires upon the will and lives of others using magic, sorcery and other occultic means."- The prophet's dictionary Paula A. Price.

The Devil uses every means which is available to him to trap humans in his web. One of these tools used to trap is witchcraft and other practises linked to it.

When it started

It is safe to say that witchcraft has been around for a very long time. Traditional / Heritage witchcraft represents the most ancient form of Witchcraft. Since the very first dealings God has had with man, He has made His opinion regarding the practise of witchcraft very clear and has clearly indicated that He was not the power behind it. This gives us a good indication of how long witchcraft practise has been around. Although practised in secret at times and in many different ways, according to local beliefs and traditions, it has definitely made its comeback in recent years.

[18] Thou shalt not suffer a witch to live.

Exodus 22:18 (KJV)

Witchcraft has, through the course of history, been able to adapt, change and grow. Just like an undercurrent, it has had a presence in all societies and cultures across the world. Today, as never before, witchcraft can be practised openly under the protection of religious tolerance.

Witches actually state and believe that witchcraft emerged as a revolutionary and radical response to the cruelty of Christianity and other Abrahamic religions.

Tradition

The word witchcraft or witch is a controversial subject; one with a complicated history, which is even more complicated today. Its definition is just as elusive and varied as the people who practise it today. Witches are possessed by the spirit of witchcraft, making them the personification of total human wickedness. This spirit of witchcraft is one of the most feared of all wicked spirits. It drives witches to do evil. Witches, through witchcraft, have an extremely real and evil impact on people.

As we try to tackle the beast (that is witchcraft), you as the reader will come to see that even witches themselves cannot be clear or stand in agreement on what they may or may not believe. The fact of the matter is that every witch is a deceived individual that does not serve the one true God. Not only are they deceived about the essential falseness of their often sincerely held beliefs, but they are also in some cases deceived about the source of their misguided belief system.

In a poll taken on the Debate.org website the question were asked if Witchcraft was indeed a religion. The result was that 57% of people said yes and 43% said no.

By this we can see that there are people that see witchcraft only as a worldwide magical practice, or a skill, that is utilised as a magic tool.

What my intention with this chapter is, is to cut through the mumbo jumbo in the effort of clarifying what witchcraft as a religion entails. To people who consider witchcraft as a religion or spiritual tradition, say it envelopes their entire lives.

It is a way of life that shapes their personalities, their morals and their behaviour. To them it is not just casting spells or a "fly by night", "quick study" religion that can be mastered in one or two years. It is seen as a persistent process of learning, study and devotion. They believe that having witchcraft as their chosen religion is a choice to do, see and react to the world in a certain way. It is not just chosen religion but a way of life.

A lot of people are under the misconception that witchcraft is the same as modern day Wicca, which is incorrect. Witches have started to use the term "traditional Witchcraft" in the attempt to remove and distinguish themselves from Wicca. Traditional Witchcraft refers to the beliefs and practices of Crafter families, individuals, and underground organizations that base their practices on the chants, spells, superstitions, collections of oral lore, documented witchcraft practices and rituals.

Witchcraft consists of many individual traditions that may differ greatly from one another at times.

A "Tradition" is the organisation or variety of Witchcraft which witches follow and practise, very much like a denomination. A Tradition can come from a common ethnic or historic background. Sometimes a tradition will have a specific name, which usually is in the language of the relevant culture. More commonly, the name of the tradition is simply from the culture from which that organisation's beliefs are derived from.

Each continent, country, culture, family, village, and area has their own tradition, inventory of rituals and magical practises and items and sometimes traditions may even merge.

Traditional Witchcraft is an umbrella term for:-

- **Specific tradition :-**
  Clan of Tubal Cain
  Cultus Sabbati

- **Cultural-based witchcraft :-**
  Brujeria: Mexican Witchcraft;
  Stregheria: Italian Witchcraft;
  Seidr, Spae-crafte, Teutonic: Nordic Tradition
  British Tradition
  Celtic Tradition
  Welsh Tradition

    Cornish Tradition
    Asian Traditions
    Pictish Tradition
    Pow-wow Tradition
    Caledonii (Hecatine) Tradition

- **Practice-based traditions :-**
  Dianic
  Arcadian
  Hedge witchery
  Green witchery
  Kitchen witchery

- **Personal tradition: Unique to an individual :-**
  Ceremonial Witch
  Solitary Witch
  Augury Witch

Please note the traditions mentioned above are only some of the traditions and there are many more.

Although there are differences between traditions, there are also the fundamental basics elements which most traditions will follow. Traditional Witchcraft observes practices such as Sabbaths and full moon in the way their ancestors did. They do not abide by the Wicca Rede or Threefold Law but have their own structure of dealing with ethics of the "do's and don'ts" of witchcraft. Because of their notoriety for working with "darker magic's", secrecy is an important factor in witchcraft. There will always be things that will never be written in books or known to the general public.

Generally speaking, Traditionalists do not believe in or have any singular deity(s) or any other gods /

goddesses. They believe in the "powerful force" known as nature. Although some Traditional Witches may accept deities and / or a god and goddess, they tend to use them differently than a Wiccan would. They don't see them reigning over the Universe; Traditionalists tend to focus on using spirits.
Then there are those traditional witches who's "path" involves no gods, no formal rituals and no worship. They can then be classified as being atheists by the truest definition of the term

A student from "Heritage Academy", "Flowing River", says the following about being a witch: "A witch has nothing to do with gods, goddesses, harm none, or thou shalt and thou shalt not. Rather than strict moral codes, the witch would rather seek what is best for them in a given situation. A witch does not whine and grovel before some altar for some god / goddess to answer their problems or get permission; instead a witch takes responsibility for themselves and fixes the problem. Witches use spoken charms to accomplish what they desire." - Topic of discussion-"what witchcraft do or do not believe in: - study hall witchcraft 101 "Lucifer in witchcraft"

These witches feel that witchcraft has liberated them from the "bonds" of cultural and spiritual conformity so that they are free from having to "bow", "whine" and "grovel" before some god / goddess. Instead of being bound to some "strict moral code" they are free to the take responsibility for themselves and can do what is right for them. Correcting and manipulating problems through the use of magic / spoken charms brings about the outcomes that they desire.

Each witch has the freedom to practice and decide for themselves their own chosen religious beliefs and paths. "Awake the witch" website declares witchcraft as the "most democratic" religion on earth. Witchcraft has a tailor made package to suite everyone's needs. Like Buddhism and Taoism they take the middle road; witchcraft is something that says "life is never "black or white."

But the word of God only speaks of two roads and not three. It is as Timothy says, witches are looking for a path that will sooth there itching ears. The Bible states unmistakeably and very clearly that there is only one God.

³ "For the time will come when they will not endure sound doctrine, but according to their own desires, because they have itching ears, they will heap up for themselves teachers; ⁴ and they will turn their ears away from the truth, and be turned aside to fables."

2 Timothy 4:3-4

⁵ "I am the Lord, and there is no other; there is no God besides Me. I will gird you, though you have not know."

Isaiah 45:5

"The difference between believing in God and in many gods is not one of arithmetic. [For] 'gods' is not really the plural of God; God has no plural. But herein is revealed the depravity of polytheism. For they prefer to worship a god they make, rather than the God who made them."- C.S.Lewis

⁶"And the person who turns to mediums and familiar spirits, to prostitute himself with them, I will set My face against that person and cut him off from his people.

Leviticus 20:6

One puzzle piece of Witchcraft is Spiritualism, or "SPIRITISM". Spiritism has existed for thousands of years and it is the attempt to contact the "spirits" of the dead with demons impersonating the dead human beings.

Witches also call these familiar spirits Imps. Familiar spirits is found within 17 verses of the Old Testament and it refers to these spirits as guides of sorcerers and necromancers. Familiar Spirits possess humans, so any words of revelations that come from a person that is possessed by a familiar spirit, can never come from the living God. These demons are under the control of Satan to tempt, harass, and try to control people. Demons are filled with hatred with no exception. They despise even those on earth who serve them.

In ancient times the term was derived from the generational spirit that was supplied or assigned to a family line or to a family by Satan. This familiar Spirit is what gave a family its supernatural knowledge, worldly possessions, success and spiritual wisdom

[27] "A man or a woman who is a medium, or who has familiar spirits, shall surely be put to death; they shall stone them with stones. Their blood shall be upon them."

Leviticus 20:27

These demons / familiar spirits serve and help witches as a primary source of power, in the effort of harming others supernaturally, through sorcery, spell, hexes, charms and astral travel. This sprit will make itself useful whenever the witch is practicing the ways of the

Craft. Familiar spirits also reinforce curses; they fuel harassment against others and carry out spells and bewitchments.

Witches describe the relationship that they have with the familiar spirits as a very special kind of working relationship. They see this bond as being "forged through mutual love and trust." This bond is formalized through the creation of a blood link. This blood link is done by feeding the creature or Imp a bit of the witch's own blood. These demon spirits are what give a witch's workings "special power". However, these familiar spirits are also deceiving spirits; they pretend to serve humans but actually seek to possess and manipulate humans so that they can dominate mankind and do as they please to further the kingdom of the devil.

Many of the demons that are described in "the Lesser Key of Solomon", (Valfor, Paimon, Buer, Purson, Gaap, Malphas, Shax, Alloces, Amy, Amdusias, and Belial) manifest and act as familiar spirits. These demons can be described as being more powerful demons or higher ranking demons.

Let us look at some of these 72 demons that can be found in "The Lesser Key of Solomon"

King Baal (Bael): According to le Grand Grimoire, Bael is the head of the infernal powers and the first king of Hell. He is also listed as the first demon in Wierus "Hierarchy of Demons". He has three heads; a toad, a man, and a cat. He speaks in a boisterous, but well-formed voice, and commands 66 [10]legions of

---

[10] Jesus lived in roman times. So we know that when spoken of a legion

demons. Bael teaches the art of invisibility, and may be the equivalent of Baal, one of the seven princes of Hell.

Duke Agares: He rules the eastern zone of Hell, and is served by 31 legions of demons. He makes runaways come back, and those who stand still to run. He can also cause earthquakes, teaches languages and finds pleasure in teaching immoral expressions. He also has the power to destroy dignities, both temporal and supernatural." He is depicted as a pale old man riding a crocodile.

Vassago: The Third demon on the list is a Mighty Prince that declares things past and future, and helps to discover all things hidden or lost. He has 26 Legions of demon spirits under his control.

"The Lesser Key of Solomon is a grimoire or spell book focused on demonology. "Ars Goetia", is the first section of the book and contains descriptions of the seventy-two demons as well as the appropriate hours and rituals to conjure them. This book was famously edited by Aleister Crowley in 1904 as The Book of the Goetia of Solomon the King.

"Give no regard to mediums and familiar spirits; do not seek after them, to be defiled by them: I am the LORD your God."
Leviticus 19:31

He and the authors of the Scriptures would have made the comparison using the Roman army. And in the Roman army a legion was a unit of 3,000–6,000.

"And the person who turns to mediums and familiar spirits, to prostitute himself with them, I will set My face against that person and cut him off from his people."

Leviticus 20:16

Animism is another important pillar to witch's beliefs. Animism is a primitive religion that believes everything, including animals, plants, rocks, mountains, rivers, and stars have a spirit. People practising Animism have idolized animals, stars, and idols of any kind for thousands of years. They believe each spirit is powerful and can either help or hurt them. These spirits are worshipped, feared and attended to in some way or another. Animism has believers practicing spiritism, witchcraft, divination and astrology. They use magic, spells, enchantments, superstitions, amulets, talismans, charms, or anything that they believe will help to protect them from the evil spirits.

As with any and all false religions, animism is simply just another calculated scheme of Satan to open a door into people's lives for demons to enter. The Bible cannot be clearer about its disapproval towards those who practice spiritism. It is an abomination to God and despite Gods clear instructions, many throughout the world are still continuously being deceived by the devil who continues destroying, killing and devouring people through the practice of Animism. This is one of the reasons [11]hell has to continuously enlarge itself. (Deuteronomy 18; Leviticus 20; Isaiah 47).

---

[11] Mary K Baxter A Divine Revelation of Hell, Jesus showed her that every time that there is an earthquake, hell is enlarging.

¹⁴ Therefore hell hath enlarged herself, and opened her mouth without measure: and their glory, and their multitude, and their pomp, and he that rejoiceth, shall descend into it.
¹⁵ And the mean man shall be brought down, and the mighty man shall be humbled, and the eyes of the lofty shall be humbled:

Isaiah 5:14-15 (KJV)

⁴⁴ "You are of your father the devil, and the desires of your father you want to do. He was a murderer from the beginning, and does not stand in the truth, because there is no truth in him. When he speaks a lie, he speaks from his own resources, for he is a liar and the father of it."

John 8:44

Ancestral worship, also a form of animism, plays a huge roll in false religions and is also an important element of traditional Witchcraft, nowhere more so than in Africa. Ancestors are not seen as gods but more as "respected" or "honoured" ones. They are consulted for advice, help and protection. Hereditary witches believe it is a very unique experience to be able to, unlike non-traditional witchcraft Lineage witches, call their ancestors by their secret names to "Watch and Ward" in special rites. Witches, who come from a generational line of being in the Craft, carry a power and magic which has an intense "life-force" (demonic force) and will of its own. The demonic world sees these witches as thoroughbreds because of the demonic strongholds such bloodlines carry. Worshipers believe it is to their advantage if an old person dies who likes them. This person will then be willing to help them from the spirit world.

Traditional witches believe that long before the first "gods" were ever considered; deceased ancestors were prayed and appealed to grant knowledge, power and favours. Witches believe that the living inherits the qualities of their ancestors and that when they then die they join their ancestors and add, in turn, their own unique achievements and personal power to that legacy.

Witches try to communicate with their "ancestors" in different ways such as meditation, talking, singing or just being quiet, waiting on the ancestors to speak first. Others try more direct methods by using objects or tools such as candles, pins in bottles and Ouija boards. Yet another path of communication with ancestral spirits or the "Otherworld", is by making use of large amounts of alcohol and drugs; even more specifically the use of entheogens. In his book "The Satanic Witch" Anton LeVay tells a witch that no one should deter her from using drugs. - "Entheogens: a chemical substance, typically of plant origin, that is ingested to produce a non-ordinary state of consciousness for religious or spiritual purposes"- google.

For Zulu's it is of the utmost importance to use 'holy' smoke called "impepho" or "impehepo". "Impepho" is a herb that is used during tribal and private rituals, sacrifices, and in order to communicate with ancestral spirits. This type of 'holy' smoke ritual, under various façades, is a common practice in witchcraft around the world, and is also seen in American Indian and Aboriginal ancestral worship. Witches of all types inhale the smoke, which has a sedative and / or hallucinative effect, to induce trances, visions, and dreams.

This is an advert on the iThonga website selling "Impepho" products.

"Impepho Bunch"
"Impepho is a plant used in rituals and ceremonies to create a link between humans and the Spirit world. It is generally burnt as an offering, but it can also be ingested or bathed in. Impepho has proven anti-microbial, pain relief and anti-inflammatory properties."

Witches have ancestral shrines in memory of their loved ones who have passed away. These shrines can be inside or outdoors. These shrines can be full of photos and memorabilia or it can be as simple as a just a photo and candle. It may even just take the form of a skull, a rose and a candle upon a rough stone. To witches it is much more important to physically have a shrine than what appears on it. Personal offerings to ancestors are made on lunar, daily or weekly cycles.

The worshipping of ancestral spirits breeds hate, suspicion and fear; there is nothing noble about it. The bible tells us that when a person dies they either go to heaven or hell. They do not continue to be present on earth, after death, to influence the lives of others.

[27] "And as it is appointed for men to die once, but after this the judgment"
                                                                 Hebrews 9:27

The truth of the matter is that the dead are not conscious of what is going on, on earth so attempts to communicate with them are of no use.

"For the living know that they will die; But the dead know nothing, And they have no more reward, For the memory of them is forgotten."

Ecclesiastes 9:5

Any messages that seem to come from a dead loved one actually originate from demons. Jehovah forbade the Israelites to attempt to talk to the dead or to participate in any other form of spiritism; this still counts to this day. Believers are always in fear of infuriating the ancestors which makes them slaves to these demonic spirits.

[10] "There shall not be found among you anyone who makes his son or his daughter pass through the fire, or one who practices witchcraft, or a soothsayer, or one who interprets omens, or a sorcerer, [11] or one who conjures spells, or a medium, or a spiritist, or one who calls up the dead. [12] For all who do these things are an abomination to the Lord, and because of these abominations the Lord your God drives them out from before you."

Deuteronomy 18:10-12

The Bible is adamant in its disapproval of ancestral worship and all the ceremonies that go along with it. Witches and people who get guidance and help from conferring with ancestral spirits are deceived. They do not know the truth concerning the dead and that they are no longer around. Anyone who engages in this practice of contacting the dead is God's enemy.

³ "For in the eighth year of his reign, while he was still youn6g, he began to seek the God of his father David; and in the twelfth year he began to purge Judah and Jerusalem of the high places, the wooden images, the carved images, and the molded images.
⁴ They broke down the altars of the Baals in his presence, and the incense altars which were above them he cut down; and the wooden images, the carved images, and the molded images he broke in pieces, and made dust of them and scattered it on the graves of those who had sacrificed to them. 5 He also burned the bones of the priests on their altars, and cleansed Judah and Jerusalem."

2 Chronicles: 34:3-6

What needs to be remembered about all these "familiar", "spirit guides" and "ancestral spirits" is that when the devil rebelled against God and God cast him out of heaven, a third of the angels chose to go with him. All of these spirits mentioned above are nothing more than those renegade angel / demon spirits who rebelled against God and joined forces with Satan; and now masquerade as these helping hand spirits. These demons provide the "dynamic" in false religions worship. Any other "god" worship other than God the Father, God the Son and God the Holy Spirit is nothing more than worship of demons. These spirits are actively deceiving humans and that is the reason God instructs us in his word to test the spirits.

¹⁸ "And He [Jesus] said to them, "I saw Satan fall like lightning from heaven."

Luke 10:18

⁴ "Beloved, do not believe every spirit, but test the spirits, whether they are of God; because many false prophets have gone out into the world. ² By this you know the Spirit of God:

Every spirit that confesses that Jesus Christ has come in the flesh is of God, ³ and every spirit that does not confess that Jesus Christ has come in the flesh is not of God. And this is the spirit of the Antichrist, which you have heard was coming, and is now already in the world."

1 John 4:1-6

The exhilaration and feeling of having the power to create, destroy, control, and impress at will, makes witches live in the delusion that they are powerful and invincible. This power comes at a price.

Witches sell their souls to Satan in return for strong and powerful demons to be at their beck and call and for the power to call up and send forth guiding, familiar, and other demonic spirits to "do the witch's bidding" for them. These demons will 'help' the witch achieve desired goals.

Witches might believe and say that they have full control over these demons or (as they would call them) 'angels,' 'spirit guides,' 'familiar spirits,' 'fairies,' 'orbs,' 'spirit helpers', but unfortunately just the opposite is true; Instead they become demon-harassed or demon-possessed.

It is not the witch but the demons that are in charge of what is happening to them. In reality, witches are constantly in danger of demonic torture, destruction, and death. Witches will try to gain control over these demonic spirits but their efforts will not prevail.

These powerful demons may promise witches love, beauty and help but instead they will cause suffering and a lot of pain to the witch. Powerful demons can even knock a person unconscious and be in complete control over a person's body and the demons will enjoy giving many of witches' even worse problems.

The happiness they used to have is gone. They have anxiety attacks and more fears. Although they may have brief periods of excitement at times, they no longer have peace of heart.

Any person or witch who thinks they are in control of Satan and his demons will soon find out that that force has control over them. The devil and his demons will dictate to witches and people what they could and couldn't do.

When Satan has this form of possession over a person, there is no limit on their spirit, soul, body, loved ones, and life. The witch has, in effect, written out a blank cheque to the greatest villain in the world. The only way out of a pact with the devil is through Jesus's blood and power.

The power remains with the spirits and it is a power to control the minds and bodies of men and women! Instead of gaining hoped-for power, those who delve into witchcraft and allied evil arts are themselves overpowered! They are captured and become depressed, mean, and hateful just like the demons now in possession of them.

Another aspect that goes hand in hand with this is when people deceive others by claiming to be Christian and then in the same breath mentioning that they have received a "gift" from a mother or grandmother. They are people that are disobedient to the Lord and whose gifts are directly from one source,

Satan. Do not be a victim of this deceit. As Christians, we need to stay close to Jesus's feet, the word of God warns us to be sober and vigilant.

[8] "Be sober, be vigilant; because your adversary the devil walks about like a roaring lion, seeking whom he may devour."
1 Peter 5:8

[14] "And no wonder! For Satan himself transforms himself into an angel of light."
2 Corinthians 11:14

"European psychiatrist L. Szondi has shown a high correlation between involvement in spiritualism and occultism, on one hand, and schizophrenia on the other. The tragedy of most sorcery, invocation of demons, and related practices is that those who carry on these activities refuse to face the fact that they always turn out for the worst. What is received through the Faustian past never satisfies, and one pays with one's soul in the end."- J.W. Montgomery, Principalities and Powers: the World of the Occult, p. 149.

"Dr. Carl A. Wickland, M.D., a physician, accomplished spiritist, and researcher in psychology became an acknowledged authority in the area of spiritism and the occult Wickland's life was similar to that of the great Emanuel Swedenborg, the famous spiritist of the eighteenth century. Though both Swedenborg and Wickland practiced spiritism extensively, both issued stern warnings about its dangers. He said 'a great number of unaccountable suicides are due to the possessing influence of spirits. Some of these spirits are actuated by a desire to torment their victims' (Wickland, Thirty Years Among the Dead, p. 132).They have no worry or problem tormenting their own followers!

A very diverse subject in witchcraft is the belief in the devil. The very first thing witches will say, especially those who claim to believe in gods or goddesses, is that they do not, and nor will they ever, believe in the devil or his existence. Even when one talks about a Satanic Witch, they would say that it is a contradictory statement as they do not believe witches believe in Satan. They are of the opinion that he, the devil, is merely a Christian concept and refer to him as the "dark" side of Christianity. But true to false religions, there will always be contradictions to their belief basis, because it is all built on lies.

There are however, witches that believe that "authentic witchcraft" (meaning real and true witches, unlike those who have shunned the belief in "The Devil") understand what their ancestors believed about him and why. To them the devil represents "intellectual, sexual and moral freedom." They believe he is not evil, and to them he is a symbol and figurehead of an undiscriminating force of nature, in a silent war against religious conformity. He is a reminder to them that actions have consequences and that they should live for today because there is no such place as heaven. They are also in strong agreement with the Luciferian philosophy that God is an invention of the ruling priesthood who wants to create a new-world order to rob people from free thought and basic human rights. God is the devils enemy and the bad guy.

"He [Lucifer] recognizes that life is suffering and that the price of living is death. Witchcraft is his gift to the World; the light that allows us to reduce suffering and live life to its fullest pleasure." – Study hall "witchcraft 101"- "Lucifer in witchcraft"

Although many witches deny knowing or serving the devil, it has been said that during the Middle Ages Witchcraft flourished; the supernatural was very popular. The initiation process of becoming a witch had only two requirements:

- The newcomer must join of his / her own free will; and
- The newcomer must be willing to worship the Devil.

"Witches: Practitioners of witchcraft. According to tradition witches are skilled in sorcery and magic. Witches can be male or female. Most have been feared and abhorred because they are believed to be vindictive, cast evil SPELLS upon others and consort with evil spirits." – Encyclopaedia of Witches, Witchcraft and Wicca; Rosemary Guiley.

"A Witch is one who has power over her own life. One who makes her own rules, one who refuses to submit to self-denial, who recognizes no authority with a greater esteem than her own and who is more loyal to herself than to any abstraction. One who is untamed, one who says "I am a witch" aloud three times. One who transforms energy, one who can be passionate about her ideal / values as they are changing, one who is explosive, whose intensity is like volcanoes, floods, wind, fire. One who is disorderly, chaotic, one who is ecstatic one who alters reality." - found in the "Daughters of the Moon" tarot deck.

Each witch has their own individual "gifts" and "powers". When witches get challenged by one another, this challenge may lead to the death of the weaker witch; the victorious witch taking or receiving all the demonic "power" from the deceased witch. Worldwide, witches have always been associated with evilness and death and they are among the most frequent causes of premature death. Witches are not burdened by any pre-defined moral or ethical code such as Wiccans threefold law or Rede. Human mythology explains that the first witches were people who made a deal with the god of death, and hence this is the reason they gain power from the deceased. The question is, is Satan not said to be the administrator of death? Let's look at the following scripture in the bible:

[14] "Inasmuch then as the children have partaken of flesh and blood, He Himself likewise shared in the same, that through death He might destroy him who had the power of death, that is, the devil, [15] and release those who through fear of death were all their lifetime subject to bondage."

Hebrews 2:14-15

Notice what verse 14 says: "him who had the power of death". After Satan was cast out of heaven he became the administrator of death; as a result all witches made a deal with the devil.

Some witches are also supporters of the tradition of The Golden Dawn, which gave birth to the entire New

Age movement and grew out of the work of the Rosicrucians.

Rosicrucianism is a secret "society" which contains strong occultic teachings such as ESP, clairvoyance, and spiritism. Rosicrucianism borrows ideas and beliefs from various different religions in an attempt to unify them under a central theme.

Rosicrucianism rejects the divine authorship of the Bible and does not hold and value in the scriptures. They believe Jesus Christ was born of Gentile parents. That also believe the He did not die on the cross, neither did He ascend to heaven and furthermore isn't the only Savior. They believe in Self-effort with their motto being "Try". Rosicrucianism was also influential to Freemasonry.

The purpose of a witch is to wreak havoc, destruction and bloodshed and through the help of demonic power, they can even heal people from a distance. Some witches may even lean towards more secretive and darker forms of magical practices like satanic witchcraft (as it was practiced by Anton LaVey and the Church of Satan, for example the satanic witch), Luciferians or Gnostics witchcraft. The highest form of witchcraft is Luceferian witchcraft. Some witches may even practice Santeria, Hoodoo or any other number of traditional magical practices emanating from countries and cultures around the world.

Some witches are healers who have a vast knowledge of herbs, and minerals, and are better known as shamans, traditional healers or medicine men; they may also be known as a "Green Witch". A saying exists between witches or in witchcraft that states that the definition of a witch is "a walker between the worlds." This phrase includes shamans. It alludes to the fact that witches have one foot in the physical or natural world and one foot in the spiritual world, but both feet firmly rooted. They believe they, as witches, act as gates between the natural and spiritual world. They see themselves as a crossroad in aiding both sides, a partnership between humans and spirits for "the good of all.

Let's take a closer look at some beliefs of witches from different part of the world.

Navajo Skin walkers / Shape Shifters / Witches; this is the dark side of Native Americans and is known as "bad medicine".

The Navajo nation lives in a large area in New Mexico, Arizona and Utah which consists mostly of desert and mountains. The word for a "skin walker" in Navajo is "yee nadlooshii". This means walk / travel like an animal. Skin walkers and shape shifters practice a form of black witchcraft that is unique to the Navajo and has no resemblance to black magic practised by their European counterparts. The Navajo practises are kept very secret from outside observers and they will never show any outward signs of their "powers" until they allow a person to see or when a person physically becomes the subject of the craft.

The initiation into becoming a Navajo skin walker calls for the most evil of deeds, such as murdering a close relative, normally a sibling. They are also known to be involved with necrophilia, eating of corpses, grave-robbing, incest and holding of nocturnal sabbats.

They are humans who have acquired immense supernatural / demonic power which gives them the ability to transform into animals, and, even into other people. Although they have the ability to turn into any animal they choose, they are generally seen in the forms of a coyote, owl, fox, wolf or crow.

"Shape-shifting simply gives the occultist or witch the power to obtain abilities and strengths [think of the various super-hero movies, comics, and TV shows so popular today] in a new form, allowing them to do things which they could not do in the natural."

Becoming a witch is even seen as desirable for the purpose of protection. They see it as a form of counteracting spells that can come against them, and use it for their greedy desire to accumulate wealth in the form of material goods. It is well known that witches will cause someone to die, just so that they can rob the deceased's grave of all their possessions.

Africa is notoriously known as a home for witchcraft. The belief in witchcraft and witches using supernatural powers to harm others forms part of common cultural knowledge and is part of everyday life in Africa. African Witchcraft activities are best described as a form of 'sorcery'. It inflicts emotional, physical and spiritual harm on its victims.

Amongst African people it is well-known that witchcraft is the cause of a variety of sicknesses such as; misfortunes, cause of barrenness, impotence, accidents, death, stomach-ache, unemployment and even the prevention of people finding someone to marry.

Most African cultures have traditional "healers or shaman" and they use Shamanic Witchcraft. Shamanism is the name used to categorise the ways of the Shaman. Other Names that are also used are Medicine Man, Witch Doctor (Inyanga) and Sangoma.

In Southern Africa there are three classifications of people who use Shamanic Witchcraft, more commonly known as traditional "healers". With this type of witchcraft they use trance techniques such as drumming, dancing and the use of plant matter to induce an altered state of consciousness.

These shaman or traditional healers contact demon spirits whom they believe are their ancestors to assist with advice or healing power. Furthermore, they believe that they are working with the spirits of animals and plants, both in the physical and non-physical worlds. (Animism).

Let's look at the three most notorious traditional healers in Southern Africa:

The thakathi/a, translated as "witch"; they are commonly female and are seen as a spiteful and evil people who operate in secret to deliberately harm others.

The inyanga, translated as "witch doctor"; they are almost always male and are referred to as healers, particularly in third world regions. In these primitive societies, traditional healing is more often used to cure sicknesses than modern medicine. They are not just used for healing; Africans also seek help with love and financial problems. They are also known for their ability to break curses, place curses on rivals, assisting in protecting individuals from evil spirits and to treat ailments believed to be caused by witchcraft. Here we find a couple of contradictions, firstly using Satan to combat Satan and secondly placing a curse on your enemy?

[9] Therefore God also has highly exalted Him and given Him the name which is above every name, [10] that at the name of Jesus every knee should bow, of those in heaven, and of those on earth, and of those under the earth, [11] and that every tongue should confess that Jesus Christ is Lord, to the glory of God the Father.

Philippians 2:9-11

[17] Then the seventy[a] returned with joy, saying, "Lord, even the demons are subject to us in Your name."[18] And He said to them, "I saw Satan fall like lightning from heaven. [19] Behold, I give you the authority to trample on serpents and scorpions, and over all the power of the enemy, and nothing shall by any means hurt you.

Luke 10:17-19

[27] "But I say to you who hear: Love your enemies, do good to those who hate you, [28] bless those who curse you, and pray for those who spitefully use you."

Luke 6:27-28

The word of God says there is ONLY one name and that is Jesus. Everything shall bow its knee to Him and demons will be cast out. He has a Name that is above all Names and His is the only name to whom demons are subject to.

[17] "Then the seventy[a] returned with joy, saying, "Lord, even the demons are subject to us in Your name."[18] And He said to them, "I saw Satan fall like lightning from heaven. [19] Behold, I give you the authority to trample on serpents and scorpions, and over all the power of the enemy, and nothing shall by any means hurt you. [20] Nevertheless do not rejoice in this, that the spirits are subject to you, but rather[b] rejoice because your names are written in heaven."

Luke 20:17-20

A common practice in Africa, a means by which to obtain protection from evil, is by a witch doctor making an incision in a person's flesh. This practice is in complete contradiction to the word of God, let's take a look:

[28] "You shall not make any cuttings in your flesh for the dead, nor tattoo any marks on you: I am the Lord."

Leviticus 19:28

We also see in 1 Kings 18:27-29 how the prophets of Baal also made incisions in their flesh. This is also seen as a blood ritual made to Satan and his demons.

[27] "And so it was, at noon, that Elijah mocked them and said, Cry aloud, for he is a god; either he is meditating, or he is busy, or he is on a journey, or perhaps he is sleeping and must be awakened." [28] So they cried aloud, and cut themselves, as was their custom, with knives and lances, until the blood gushed out on them. And when midday was past, they prophesied until the time of the offering of the evening sacrifice. But there was no voice; no one answered, no one paid attention."

1 Kings 18:27-29

Betty Miller explains in her book "Exposing Satan's Devices Workbook" that the commandments received by Moses from God (Leviticus 19:28) spoke directly against a witchcraft practise or ritual that was done in those days to mourn and memorialise the dead. She goes on to say that even tattooing (also spoken against in the commandments) has its origins in witchcraft.

Witch doctors and healers are notoriously known for the practise of "Muti" Magic. The word "muti" means "medicine" in Zulu. This is not meant in the sense of modern medicine but this is medicine manufactured by using "traditional" means. Human body parts (especially those of children), are ground up and combined with items such as roots, herbs, seawater and animal body parts to prepare potions and spells for clients. These medicines can be rubbed onto the skin, into open wounds or even be consumed. In the instance where body parts are harvested from a live victim, the victims are first identified and 'purchased' in a transaction, often for a minimal amount of money. If the body parts are taken from a live victim, so much the better The begging for mercy and agonizing screams from the victim just before he succumbs to shock, calls many powerful demons to the witchdoctor and 'client,' who then proffer these horrendous sacrifices in exchange for a so-called 'blessing' from Satan. It is believed that the more torturous and brutal the murder and the more the victim suffers, the stronger the "muti".

Witchdoctors use sexual parts to 'strengthen' libido or to buy fertility and a human heart is used to enhance bravery.

When body parts from a deceased are needed, they are often obtained illegally from hospitals or stolen by grave robbers from freshly buried corpses. Traditional healers or witch doctors often roast and pulverise the body parts into an ash, or even grind body parts up, before combining them into their potions and spells. Even the water used to wash corpses in the hospital mortuary is being sold to traditional healers.

And the cost of these body parts?

A human brain costs about R1000 and other parts, from internal organs to body fat, fetch from R400 to R1000.

One hospital accused of the trade of body parts for "muti" is the second-largest hospital in the Southern African country of Swaziland. The organ trade at Raleigh Fitkin Memorial Hospital in the city of Manzini has been described as "an open secret" by critics such as Rev. Grace Masilela.

In March 2010 in Pietermaritzburg, South Africa, a Zululand man was jailed for 20 years by the Pietermaritzburg High Court for helping to murder a friend's sister to obtain her body parts to be used in Voodoo type rituals. Mathenjwa Mangomezulu, 45, father of five, earlier confessed to the murder. He said he and his friend Mcwecwe Mngomezulu killed Mcwecwe's 75-year-old sister Nongoziba by twisting her neck. They then cut out her tongue, oesophagus and eyes. They threw her body over a cliff, where it was found a few days later. Mcwecwe intended selling his sister's body parts to a witchdoctor (or "Shaman" to be politically correct) for R5000.

Mathenjwa, who had never been to school, said he was paid R600 for his role in the murder, committed in December last year. Judge Kate Pillay found substantial and compelling circumstances in his favour, so that she did not have to impose the prescribed life sentence, so (as so often happen in South Africa) he will probably be out in a few years' time and will be able to sell some other victim's body parts. Yes, wouldn't all societies be better off they embraced Paganism and Shamanism? (IOL News for South Africa)

Towards the end of 2012 reports of mass exhumations took place in the dead of night in Benin. Over 100 corpses were dug up from a cemetery near Porto Novo and these corpses were mutilated for the purpose of obtaining body parts that could be sold on the black market.

The witchdoctor enslaves their clients / patients, and people that visit and consult with the witchdoctor's lives may even be shortened.

Sangomas / Shamans: These can be seen in modern terms as a diviner or fortune teller and they are usually female. Sangomas believe it is a "spiritual calling", not a chosen profession. They believe training could only take place once the 'Ubizo' has been identified. Ubizo is the 'calling' which comes from the ancestors to become a Sangoma. The Ubizo is identified during consulations / readings with other Sangomas. Without the Ubizo / calling, no Sangoma will be initiated as student into the lineage.

Sangomas can predict a person's future, identify guilty parties in crimes and can (to some degree), practise medicine. Sangomas believe they have a contact with three types of ancestors. Firstly, blood ancestors down the Father's line, secondly, blood ancestors down the Mother's line and thirdly 'adopted' ancestors whom they have an affinity for from other cultures, (e.g. Tibetan Buddhists, North American Indians etc.) When someone wishes to contact the ancestors for help in the making of an important decision, a sangoma is consulted as a medium. In order to make contact with the ancestors, the sangoma goes into a trance-like state. They are then able to connect with the spirit world or experience various sensations such as smells, feelings, voices or visions. Some may have this experience of ancestral 'contact' through dreams. In the case of a healing ceremony the Sangoma will usually 'throw the bones' to make a diagnosis. It is generally believed that it is the "ancestors" who position the layout of the bones after they are thrown. There is a problematic, deep-rooted belief in witchcraft amongst Africans. Even some people who go to church will still make use of a sangoma or witch doctor for financial help and healing.

Living out in Africa it is often spoken about as to how some of the most influential people in churches are the biggest into witchcraft.

There is also a belief amongst Africans that witches can curse someone just by thinking of the person or victim. They use hair and body faeces to bewitch or cure victims, they practice cannibalism and shape shifting; turning into animals like hyenas and eating the flesh of someone who has died.

In Africa the belief is that becoming a witch happens through inheritance or through marring into a "witch-family". They can also be initiated with a ritual done by other witches, or by naming a child after a deceased witch. The "spirit" (this is not the witches' real spirit but a demon) will then possess the child or baby. One can also become a witch by cultivating evil in their heart; this would mean that everybody is potentially at risk of becoming a witch.

What Africans believe about witches is generally the same as the rest of the world, but their "opinion" about witches differs among the various tribes of Africa. In Africa, witches are feared more than the God. With Africa being such a big continent with so many different nations, the cultural terms may differ amongst the tribes. The Mandari witches are believed to dance on their victims graves. Lugbara witches from Uganda dance naked and the Ganda and Nyoro, also from Ghana, believe witches eat corpses. The Kagura tribe of Tanzania believes that witches act in strange manners such as walking on their hands, cannibalism, incest and are know not to recognise, follow and obey the general norms and constraints of society.

In Eastern Africa, more specifically Tanzania, a major evil has become big business in witchcraft. Similar to the myth of the precious Rhino horn having healing properties, Albinos are often not just the subject of fear, hatred, and ridicule, but are also the victims of witchcraft through muti magic or practice. In a continent of dark-skinned Africans, albinos (people with a rare genetic disorder that leaves the skin, hair and eyes without pigments – giving the victims the label of "ghosts" or "zeroes") are being attacked and brutally murdered. Their body parts such as arms, fingers, genitals, and ears are being hacked off with machetes and knifes. Even their blood is used. They are a highly prized commodity on the black market, believed to contain magical powers. No matter what the age, even children are amongst the victims. According to Red Cross statistics at least 50 albinos were murdered for their body parts in 2009 alone.

An IRIN report guesstimates that a "complete set of albino body parts", including all four limbs, genitals, ears, nose and tongue, can sell for about $75,000 in Tanzania. www.thinkafricapress.com/society/african-witchcraft

Fishermen on Lake Victoria are believed to weave albino hair into their nets to improve their catch. Miners in the Mbeya coal-fields have been known to splash albino blood on the ground, wear albino muti charms (often body parts or albino flesh ground up into paste) and bury albino bones, all to "attract" gems and gold to the surface. - Article posted 11 October 2013 on website www.altereddimensions.net

In the Congo, a witch known as 'Ndoki' is believed to have the power to bring poverty to a whole community. In regions like Kenya witches are believed to be associated with shape shifting, turning into animals from the region such as snakes, lizards and various birds. The Luhyia of Kenya believes that witchcraft is used by people who are jealous and are seeking revenge.

Africans believe in witchcraft at the most extreme levels and are deeply rooted in the tradition, something which has been passed on from generation to generation. Many people brush off claims of cannibalism, sacrifices, killings and the hacking and harvesting of body parts for muti and shape shifting. They either think it is too frightening or too silly to consider, but brutal killings and sacrifices are a fundamental part in the progression through the ranks for a witchdoctor. Witchcraft is alive and well.

"You cannot conquer what you don't confront and you cannot confront what you don't identify." - Paula White

Rituals

Witchcraft is seen as the practise of "Low magic", folk magic or thaumaturgy. High Magic, also known as theurgy, is known to be used in more of a ceremonial witchcraft setting.

There are many types of rituals; from simple magical rites for different daily needs, up to festive and worshipping coven rites. The aim of formal rituals and spells at all levels are to manipulate and to cause a positive change, effect or outcome for the person who casts or carries out the ritual. They are trying to bring about healing, peace, reconciliation or whatever is in the spell casters will. But the main purpose is to raise their own level of awareness, even though it may be for a few moments, so they can feel connected to a higher power, even feeling like the source of divinity - David Colon

The practice of magic in Traditional Witchcraft is central to their religion and the belief amongst witches is that every ritual, action or spell performed connects them to everyone who has ever performed the same ritual before.

In general, tools used in rituals by traditional witches do not bear a resemblance to the "working tools" of wiccans. Traditional witches tend to use things like Stangs / staff, bells, besoms, Cencer / Thurbile, cauldrons, cords, candles, skulls, (of people or animals), hammers, mirrors, various stones, Chalice (cup or horn) horns, wands and some traditions may even use daggers as well. This sets them apart from the new-age symbolism. On the other hand some Traditions may not use any tools at all!

Magic is also seen as a tool and can be used by anyone regardless of their beliefs. It is understood to be an inactive and hidden power that can be activated if a person or witch knows the proper chants and rituals to tap into this "power". When this power is mastered, they will have unusual powers and control to achieve supernatural things. Magic uses supernatural powers over natural powers.

"Magic is a part of occult study, along with systems of divination and alchemy. In general, magic is the activity of trying to cause change toward a desired end through symbolic means. The objectives of Magic and the elements of its practice vary from one system or culture to another".

We see in Exodus 8:3 what an important role magic played in the rituals of the Egyptian high priests. It was through the deception of magic that the Egyptians thought that their gods were real and had power. We see that magic was used in an effort to mock God by imitating the miracles God performed through Moses. The type of plagues that God pronounced upon Egypt corresponded with an Egyptian god or goddess.

Let's look at the second Egyptian Plague of the Frogs coming from the Nile River.

The second plague, as we all know, was that of the frogs sent to infest the Egyptian homes. The frogs came up from the river and were found everywhere, in their houses, in their food, in their clothing, in every place imaginable. From the greatest to the least, no one in Egypt escaped the plague of frogs. Pharaoh's magicians were also able to make frogs appear in their attempt to imitate the power of God, but only Moses was able to make the frogs go away. This was an attack on a famous Egyptian goddess, Heket. A frog symbolised good luck, but yet with the plague they were everywhere and were dying and polluting everything. Their "new life representations was being racked up in dead piles".

Mozambique experienced terrible flooding in February and March 2000. Approximately 800 people were killed, 1,400 km² of arable land was affected and 20,000 head of cattle were lost. Many people lost everything they had. Many of the people in Mozambique, who very little in the first place, lost even the little bit they had. Who can forget the story of Rosita Mabuiango's being born in a tree?

My parents, who lived in Mozambique at the time of the floods and who still live there today, lost all their crops too. No one could understand why God would allow something so dreadful to happen to a country that was just starting to recover from a civil war that began in 1977 and lasted for 15 years.

But true is the word of God to His prophet Isaiah when God said:

[8] "For My thoughts are not your thoughts, Nor are your ways My ways," says the Lord. [9]"For as the heavens are higher than the earth, So are My ways higher than your ways, And My thoughts than your thoughts."

Isaiah 55:8-9

Years later we met a Pastor who told us that before the flood sangomas would tell the people of Mozambique that, if they would pay them an amount of money, they would be protected from flood waters. The people who believed did what they were told, sincerely believing that if they did so, that these sangomas would have the power to protect them.

[7] "Do not be deceived, God is not mocked; for whatever a man sows, that he will also reap

Galatians 6:7

[7] "Jesus said unto him, It is written again, Thou shalt not tempt the Lord thy God

Matthew 4:7

Then God decided to show up and exposed the wicked lies in a big way. There had not been such a flood in 50 years. We should realise that God is not just a little "wimpy" God. He is mighty and powerful.

[18] "For the wrath of God is revealed from heaven against all ungodliness and unrighteousness of men, who suppress the truth in unrighteousness, [19] because what may be known of God is manifest in them, for God has shown it to them. [20] For since the creation of the world His invisible attributes are clearly seen, being understood by the things that are made, even His eternal power and Godhead, so that they are without excuse, [21] because, although they knew God, they did not glorify Him as God, nor were thankful, but became futile in their thoughts, and their foolish hearts were darkened. [22] Professing to be wise, they became fools, [23] and changed the glory of the incorruptible God into an image made like corruptible man—and birds and four-footed animals and creeping things

Romans 1:18-32

[5] "The mountains melt like wax at the presence of the Lord, At the presence of the Lord of the whole earth."

Psalm 97:5

[5] "The mountains melt like wax at the presence of the Lord, At the presence of the Lord of the whole earth. 6 The heavens declare His righteousness, And all the peoples see His glory."

Psalm 97:5-6

Magic comes in two forms; white magic and black magic.

White magic: This is described as the use of supernatural powers / magic for the use of "good". Witches who practice white magic say it is used for selfless purposes and that it is a compassionate, kind and caring magic. They believe its origin is not evil but that it is borne out of love, wisdom and positive energy. They believe that at its worst, it is one human being caring and a lending a helping hand in the growth of another's spirit. They also believe they are operating under a strict threefold return law or Rede.

Black Magic: The principal target of black magic is meant to hurt someone and / or something. Witches who are seen as practitioners of Black magic are feared and are not taken lightly by others. Not only is black Magic believed to harm people, but it is also believed that it draws upon evil beings for powers. They are known to conduct negative acts in order to inflict danger, eliminate and punish enemies and perform acts which are spiteful in nature for their own selfish gain.

Black magic or White Magic, all Magic is magic. In truth there is no such thing as "white magic," something that is safe to do, or magic for a good purpose. There is no such thing as "nice spirits." All of Satan's demons are evil and cruel like their master. Black and white magic are one and the same, regardless of the label you put on them. In order for the devil to trick ignorant people, magic has been separated into two categories. When this is boiled down however, any form of magic that is performed makes use of assistance from demonic forces. Every time a person accesses the demonic, a link is established between the person using the magic and a demon, forming an ungodly and evil soul tie. This allows the witch or person to be used for the purposes of the kingdom of darkness, whether they do so willingly or not. Demons do not need to ask permission, they will take whatever they can. They want human souls and are waiting in line to move into the body of the unsaved or vulnerable person; even more so if that person is willingly involving themselves with occultic practices, seeking power from the kingdom of darkness. White magic is often the antechamber that leads to black magic.

The opinion or belief that, as long as intent differs, a witch is either good or bad, is another false doctrine of the devil. But is it ever possible for Satan to do or be good? Even though it may seem that he performs good deeds such as healing, this is only done to trick people so that they can become entangled in his web, and ultimately fall under his control.

In God's eyes, magic is colourless and the power behind the magic is the same dark force, no matter in what form the world tries to package it. Magic is magic and God hates all magic.

The bible does not make light nor any exception for the use of, what is in a man's opinion, good or bad magic. There is no exception to the rule when it comes to magic. The Bible affirms the ugly reality and not the fantasy of magic. The Bible cannot make itself any more clear on its condemning and forbidden the use of magic. It comes down to the source behind the magic that matters. We can see in 2 Timothy 3:8, Jannes and Jambres who were the magicians in Pharaoh's court, use supernatural power (from Satan) to resist Moses. (2 Corinthians 11:13-15)

[8] "Now as Jannes and Jambres resisted Moses, so do these also resist the truth: men of corrupt minds, disapproved concerning the faith;"

2 Timothy 3:8

[13] "For such are false apostles, deceitful workers, transforming themselves into apostles of Christ. [14] And no wonder! For Satan himself transforms himself into an angel of light. [15] Therefore it is no great thing if his ministers also transform themselves into ministers of righteousness, whose end will be according to their works."

2 Corinthians 11:13-15

It should never be forgotten that at the heart of witchcraft is the desire to control people, circumstances and situations for gain. Unspeakable acts of evil take place in witchcraft, there is no such thing as a good witch or good witchcraft.
Not only do rituals vary from tradition to tradition, but they also vary from group to group within the same tradition. Some groups work in robes while others work in the nude (it is said that not many traditional witches work in the nude as they see this as being disrespectful). Some rituals are performed outdoors and others may be carried out indoors.

A key factor to rituals is the spoken word during the spells. Spells are often oral texts that are passed down (without change) from generation to generation. Because of the manner in which spells are passed down, spells will often contain ancient words and even might be in a foreign language.

In the performing of rituals, there is once again a dispute on how the rituals should be performed.

Witches, like those who live in the Trobriand Islands believe the smallest deviation from the ritual can render the spell useless, whereas amongst the Azande tribe from Sudan it is believed that magical rituals are flexible and that spells are unformulated.

There are also other occult practises that witches use in rituals which fall under the "umbrella term" of Magic.

Sorcery: is a broad term for the influence of a person or event through witchcraft. "Sorcerer" (male) and "Sorceress" (female) are the titles given to particularly skilled witches. Sorcery can be utilised by an individual or be performed in groups. This is done for the advancement of the purposes of the witchcraft and is also a way and means in which to gain power. The power can be executed through various means such as mixing of potions and poisons or even in the using of magic spells, charms, rituals, incantations and cursing. They will also wear amulets in an effort to protect themselves from others or use divination to predict the future. Furthermore, they may call on the deities or ancestral and familiar spirits, use sorcery in the domination of the opposite gender and even use this for the elimination of their enemies

Divination: This is the pagan answer to true prophecy or prophesying. This can be seen as a humans attempt to know and to be able to control the future. Divination is the attempt or the practise of using omens, dreams, astrology, necromancy and other magic powers to uncover hidden information, foretell the future and in an attempt to obtain knowledge. It is also used to know the thoughts of others so that they can be manipulated and controlled.

There are several methods of divination that can be practiced and it can be split in to two generalised groups or sections.

The first of the methods which seeks to obtain direct knowledge from the unseen realm / demonic spirits, are Ouija boards, automatic writing, crystal balls, or clairvoyance.

Secondly, there are those methods which attempt to interpret certain signs, omens, or events such as tarot cards, horoscopes, handwriting analysis, palm reading, use of animal entrails, the flight of birds and many more.

The Babylonians were famous for [12]hepatoscopy. This practice is mentioned in the Book of Ezekiel 21:21:

[21] "For the king of Babylon stands at the parting of the road, at the fork of the two roads, to use divination: he shakes the arrows, he consults the images, he looks at the liver."

Ezekiel 21:21

The liver was considered the source of a person's blood and hence the basis of life itself. Many times you will find witches and Satanist eating the liver. From this belief, the Babylonians thought they could discover the will of the gods by examining the livers of carefully selected sheep. A priest known as a "bārû" was specially trained to interpret the "signs" of the

---

[12] The Latin terms haruspex, haruspicina are from an archaic word haru "entrails, intestines" (cognate with hernia "protruding viscera", and hira "empty gut"; PIE *ǵher-) and from the root spec- "to watch, observe". The Greek hēpatoskōpia is from hēpar "liver" and skop- "to examine".

liver, and Babylonian scholars assembled a monumental compendium of omens called the Bārûtu.

The liver was divided into sections, with each section representing a particular deity.

In Africa the liver and entrails of a crocodile are said to be the most powerful to be used for charms, and whoever can get a hold of them is said to be able to cause the death of any person he / she pleases. Witchdoctors also perform a rain-making ritual that is said to be done with charms made from an ox's blood and gall.

What we know of the devil is that he cannot create anything. He is not our creator, God. He is still a creation of God almighty and will and can never be an authentic creator of anything. What he is, is a thief and a copycat. He can only mimic things. Since he rebelled against God and was cast out of heaven, his main focus has been his WAR against Father God. He will steal, kill and destroy whatever or whomever to achieve what he wants. This is what he attempts to do, hijack and steal the spiritual gifts of the Holy Spirit.

Gifts of the Holy Spirit	Counterfeit Gifts
Gift of revelation	
Word of wisdom Word of knowledge Discernment of spirits	Clairvoyance, ESP, Clairaudience, Foreknowledge, premonitions Telepathy, direct experience of another's thoughts
Power Gifts	
Gift of faith Gift of healing Gift of working miracles	Faith through concentration of the mind And will; superstition.

	Psychic and mediums healings. Supernatural manifestations.
Gift of encouragement.	
Gift of prophesy Gift tongues Gift of interpretation of tongues	Fortune-telling Demonic utterances Fortune-telling

Witchcraft activities are very luring because of the fascination people has with the unknown. People are intrigued by it mysterious nature. For generations and even today there is a vacuum in the religious world. Many Christians denies the supernatural as well as the working of the Holy Spirit and this is where the occult is filling in the vacuum.

People are curious to know more and it is this curiosity that catches them. Through the occult people have discovered the reality of another dimension and the possibility that they might be able to obtain some of that power for themselves. The curiosity seekers is looking for a spiritual source that will able to help them to control or hurt others and give guidance on the future. When someone is not using God's Holy Spirit they are using the Devil.

All forms of horoscopes, Tarot cards, psychics, palm readings, fortune telling, crystal balls, Ouija boards, astrology, worshipping or contacting the dead, and sorcery are of the devil.

[1] "Now the serpent was more cunning than any beast of the field which the Lord God had made. And he said to the woman, "Has God indeed said, 'You shall not eat of every tree of the garden'?"[2] And the woman said to the serpent, "We may eat the fruit of the trees of the garden; [3] but of the fruit of the tree

which is in the midst of the garden, God has said, 'You shall not eat it, nor shall you touch it, lest you die.[4] Then the serpent said to the woman, "You will not surely die. [5] For God knows that in the day you eat of it your eyes will be opened, and you will be like God, knowing good and evil."

Genesis 3:1-5

Genesis 3:1-5 provides us with a very good example of how spiritual deception can happen in a person's life. The root and basic philosophy of all occult teaching is found in this passage. The occult interpretation of this text is as follows:

"You will not die": subtle introduction of reincarnation. "You will know all things": this quest for knowledge is central to the occult world. They thrive on the power that knowledge brings them in the search for "truth". "You will be as or like God." In principle you are God. The goal of life is to rediscover your true self through self-realization.

Those who move in the psychic realm and circles hold these same ideals at the core of their belief system. They might try to use different terms or different entry points to establish their teaching, but they all ground their primary religious teaching on the roots of the principles of Genesis 3. Psychic Communication and the Dead: Russ Wise.

Many people advertise themselves as fortune-tellers etc., and say that theirs is a "gift from God" or that they received it from their mother or grandmother. The University of Chicago's National Opinion Research Centre reports that "roughly one in three Americans believe that they have personally communicated with the dead."

The one problem is that this is never a free gift, there is always a price to pay and there are always strings attached. This "free gift" comes at a fee! Even the slightest dabbling for the shortest period of time can cause serious trouble and it becomes very difficult to leave that world.

There are even Christians who find nothing wrong with reading their weekly horoscopes in newspapers and magazines. Do not think for one moment that there is no harm in reading horoscopes. The reading of horoscopes supports the act of faith in something other than God, and it is a form of divination. We cannot determine God's will for our lives through horoscopes.

People also ask the question but what about the "good" Psychics that help the police in solve crimes? When you're loved one is missing or murdered would God not understand. The police should rather turn to Prophets and Apostles that walks with God as the Holy Spirit will direct them.

Let take a look at a case that appeared on CNN LARRY KING LIVE that aired on April 29, 2004. Carol Pate, a psychic helped to find a kidnapped, Arkansas teenager who never showed up home after work. His family was mystified, and one of the biggest manhunts in Arkansas history took off. As a last resort, police brought in a psychic and this is what she described she did.

"I hold the photograph in my hand, and I tune into the energy of the individual. The individual has a signature energy, and I'm kind of like a radio. I tune into their station, and once I get that signal, I then know if they're alive or dead, what they're thinking, what's happened to them." Carol Pate.

"I saw that he was alive. I saw that he was with these men, one man in particular. I began to describe basically what had happened, that he had been kidnapped from the parking lot of the store, and that he had been put, I think it was in a truck, and that I then saw where they were taking him. And then I saw the house and what it looked like, and I described the house. And I noted a belt buckle that the man had on, it was very distinctive and described him" Carol Pate.

"I use what's known as **psychometry**. I work as a radio station. I fine tune my frequency to the frequency that I'm touching, and I can get any type of information that I basically need."

What exactly is psychometry?

"**Psychometry** is a psychic ability in which a person can sense or "read" the history of an object by touching it. Such a person can receive impressions from an object by holding it in his/her hands or, perhaps, touching it to the forehead. Such impressions can be perceived as images, sounds, smells, tastes - even emotions.

Psychometry is a form of scrying - a psychic way of "seeing" something that is not ordinarily seeable.

Some people can scry using a crystal ball, black glass or even the surface of water. With psychometry, this extraordinary vision is available through touch" What

You Need To Know About... Psychometry By Stephen Wagner.

"And he made his son pass through the fire, and observed times, and used enchantments, and dealt with familiar spirits and wizards: he wrought much wickedness in the sight of the LORD, to provoke him to anger."

2nd Kings 21:6

Even if it seems that the information is accurate it is still evil and satanic. It is never right to do wrong in order to get a chance to do right! It's wrong for local police authorities to consult with psychics in an attempt to locate missing persons. Satan's program is always very much like the real thing. However, the glory ultimately goes to himself rather than to Father God, his creator.

But some might say, "wouldn't you not want to try every means possible to find a loved one if they were missing?" God will never give the go ahead to use that which He forbids. You are consulting with demons and the devil. God answers prayer and He wants us to come to Him. This is not a godly practise, and Christians should stay way!

Demons are ordered with the distinct goal of presenting a counterfeit spirituality to mankind, in the attempt to meet the growing needs of human's curiosity. Although it may be possible for the enemy to mimic a gift of the Spirit, he cannot mimic the Fruit of the Spirit! We know that God, through His Holy Spirit, gives as free gifts. Occultic powers focus on the mind, but the truth comes through the Spirit and is a ministry of the Holy Spirit. All the devil need is a small opening in the door to get his foot in the door. If given even the slightest of space, he will take the door off of the hinges! The word of God says:

²⁷ "nor give place to the devil."

Ephesians 4:27

And that we should have nothing to do with evil practises.

¹⁴ "Do not be unequally yoked together with unbelievers. For what fellowship has righteousness with lawlessness? And what communion has light with darkness? ¹⁵ And what accord has Christ with Belial? Or what part has a believer with an unbeliever?"

2 Corinthians 6:14-15

From Numbers 23:21-23 and Leviticus 20:6, 27 we can see that the wrath of God, for "dabbling" in these abomination will not only be upon you, but also your descendants. The wrath of God will prevail whether this is done in ignorance, or blatant disobedience to the Word of God. It is one and the same thing to God, but He also tells us that His pleasure, goodwill and blessing will be upon each and every one who walks "clean" from these practices.

Astral Travel

Astral projection is the term used when a temporary separation takes place between the spirit and the physical body. The astral body, that appears in the form of a mist and yet looks like the person's physical body, is literally projected into the astral dimension or occultic world with the help of a demon, and can travel to physical locations and even be sent on missions. In the astral dimension, things are very different from the real world. Time is distorted and extended; an hour in the astral dimension can be like a few minutes in the physical dimension.

Astral projection can happen as part of the sleeping process, by shutting out your mind or can be attained when you are in a deep meditative state. In her book "Out on a Limb" Shirley Maclaine explains how she "blanked" out her mind to open a doorway for demons to enter. By doing this she forged the link between her conscious mind and spirit, enabling her to experience and control her spirit body. Shirley Macleaine "Out on A Limb" Bantam Books.

One of the goals in Witchcraft is to be fully aware of the astral projection. This is called conscious astral projection. Through conscious astral projection a person can actually recall events that have taken place during the astral journey. The astral body is employed by the conscious mind to explore not only various places on earth but different realms within the dimensions. Within the Astral plain there are seven dimensions of existence in occult philosophy.

The astral body may exit out of the Solar plexus, Third eye, Crown or Heart chakras or people will simply find themselves suddenly looking down at their physical bodies.

Witches, born into a family of witches and witchcraft, are taught from infancy to "Astral Travel". "Astral travel" is actually a product of dissociation. Part of the mind and spirit of a person (or witch in this instance) dissociates and leaves the body behind in order to survive. Once this ability has been developed, an adult mind and spirit (also in a dissociate state) will take or guide the infants mind and spirit through the "astral pathways" The Astral body is always attached to the physical body by a long Silver Chord.

It is very seldom that an astral projection is actually witnessed by someone that has never been involved or is not part of the occult world.

The vast majority of traditional witches do not believe in casting circles. It is believed that every place is sacred. They call on spirits and ancestors to guard the sacred places.

Often rituals may only be performed at specific places and times such as "Hallowed" grounds. Hallowed grounds are literally a geographical area that is claimed by a witchcraft group / tradition or denomination as their grounds. This area can vary from being as small as a few meters or as large as several provinces. When a witch tries to leave the witchcraft cult it is most often necessary for them to be physically and completely removed from this hallowed ground / area. Witches see themselves as being physically and spiritually bound to this hallowed ground and to every living plant and animal that lives and grows on it.

"Sacred" ground is a primary site or temple where corporate worship is performed. These sites are generally found on raised areas such as hills, and are mostly found on private properties. These temples or sacred grounds can be places such as basements, abandoned houses, warehouses, bridges or deserted areas. Sacred ground is just as it suggests, sacred! They will try to keep these grounds away from the general public's view, so that they will not be easily seen. Witches will protect and keep these places secret and protected at all cost, even if it costs them their lives.

A witch's house can also be dedicated and made to be "hallowed" or "sacred". Human blood is used to anoint furniture, silverware and even the dishes to create a safe sanctuary for the witch. After the witch has done this blood anointing, private rituals can be done. Witches also gather together on a regular basis to combine their powers in order to accomplish what they cannot do on their own and worship the witchcraft deities.

Wiccans and Eclectic Witches have what is referred to as a Book of Shadows. Although Traditional Witches do not follow any specific religious book, they do make use of something similar, a Grimoire. Grimoire is a book of rituals and teachings which is usually handwritten by individuals. The name Grimoire is used as a general term, because of the secrecy that reigns supreme; the actual name of this book is kept a secret in most traditions. Even when the name for this book is discussed, it sometimes varies between the traditions. In most traditions, the Grimoire is composed by an individual, and the rituals in the book are often written in symbols, signs or pictures so that it cannot be easily understood by an outsider. The rituals in the Grimoire have rituals based on the traditions of the particular denomination, passages of individual add-ons and on occasions, contents that might have been copied from a "master" book.

Witches are also known to use blood magic. They believe power is obtained through blood and blood sacrifices. Another reason blood is used is because it is thought that blood personalizes the spells. God's word says:

"The life of the flesh is in the blood."
Leviticus 17:11

This verse is true about both the spiritual and the physical realms, and because of this, there is always a blood sacrifice with every ritual. Blood from animals, humans, menstruation, placenta and even blood from self-mutilation is used. We talked about this with the Prophets of Baal, cutting themselves, and even witch doctors making incisions in the flesh. The fertility cult deities that some witches serve are soothed through "blood". Cutting to draw blood symbolizes life sacrifice and offering of their lives to evil spirits.

We read in Mark 5:1-20 about a man that lived among the tombs of the Gaderenes. This man also cut himself because of demonic possession. Jesus delivered this man and sent the legions of demons into a herd of pigs. Satan hates all of humanity, including those who foolishly become his slaves.

[1] "Then they came to the other side of the sea, to the country of the Gadarenes. [2] And when He had come out of the boat, immediately there met Him out of the tombs a man with an unclean spirit, [3] who had his dwelling among the tombs; and no one could bind him, not even with chains, [4] because he had often been bound with shackles and chains. And the chains had

been pulled apart by him, and the shackles broken in pieces; neither could anyone tame him. [5] And always, night and day, he was in the mountains and in the tombs, crying out and cutting himself with stones."

Mark 5:5

In Africa, scarring is used in tribal initiation as a sign of bravery. This is made with razor blades. This very painful process starts at puberty and continues into manhood. Each tribe has its own distinctive tattoo designs. It is usually done on the face and include black ink. These are seen as magic symbols to assist in keep away evil spirits.

The concept of "blood sacrifice" as part of religious rituals goes back to the dawn of mankind. Since blood represents life, it is believed in many religions that by offering up blood or using blood in rituals, this has the power of passing on this source of life, giving power to protect, heal and create.

Charles Walton, a 74-year old agricultural worker and a witch himself, was found murdered on the night of 14 February 1945. The native of Lower Quinton, Warwickshire England, was killed as a blood sacrifice on a day that is notoriously known for blood sacrifices. It was a particularly gruesome murder. They found him lying face up, with his own pitchfork driven through his throat. This was done with such brutal force that it nearly severed his head. Slashed into his chest was a large cross-shaped wound, made with the billhook that was left stuck in his ribs. The famous witch, Margret Murray, spent a week in the area conducting her own investigation and later publicly stated that she believed Walton might have been a human sacrifice in a

Candlemass ritual performed by "traditionalist" witches who were still using the Julian calendar. The old Julian was a calendar in use until the middle ages. On this calendar, February 14th actually fell on February 2nd. And February 2nd is the festival day of Imbloc / Candlemass. This is one of the witches Great Sabbats and propitiatory sacrifices are made on Great Sabbats.

Menstrual blood is seen as "water that gives life". Witches believe that their "power" as a female witch is active during the years when a woman experiences her menstrual cycle. Witches will actually coordinate their menstrual cycles to sync with the phases of the moon. By doing this the witch makes sure that she is in her cycle on the night of full moon. All the witches will then gather at the sacred ground, chanting and dancing around a stone altar in order to anoint mother earth.

The placenta is another very important item in the witch's life. The placenta is considered to be an aphrodisiac and is used in the treatment of infertility if eaten.

In some parts of the world, the placenta of a child is preserved from birth until such time as the child reaches a certain age; at this point a ritual is then performed. The placenta is roasted in a barbecue fashion for the whole family to eat together. This practise has serious consequences for the family. An evil soul tie forms between each of the family members. To spouses who marry into a family that partakes in such practices, and where soulties like these are in place, it has disastrous effects. These soul ties have the tendency to lead marriages straight towards divorce.

Another well-known ritual in Africa is where parents bury their children's placenta next to the family witch doctor or Sangomas house / hut.

"Ye shall not eat anything with the blood: neither shall ye use enchantment, nor observe times . . . Regard not them that have familiar spirits, neither seek after wizards, to be defiled by them: I am the LORD your God."

Leviticus 19:26, 31

In some instances believers have no idea that their families have partaken or participated in such rituals.

These rituals cause a person's spirit, not only to be placed in a spiritual prison, but they may even experience recurring dreams where they hear drums beating and have ancestral spirits calling them back to their homeland in order to service the family altar. Their placenta acts as a spiritual magnet, drawing them back to their past. It is known that these dreams may occur every time a believer intends to move forward in his relationship with God.

The Ancestral involvement in occult and demonic activities does have an effect on our own lives and is one of the leading causes of demonization. Christians should never participate in traditional practices and / or rituals involving the slaughter of animals to appease their ancestors.

Demons and demonic bondages are inherited, so if your family has been involved in any of these practises the Christian needs to make sure that these doors to the spiritual realm have been closed through prayer, confession and the blood of Jesus in order to ensure that the demons are removed from their life and their future. We need to know that we are no longer under the "Old Law" and as a result any sin that is not brought / confessed under the blood of Christ gives Satan legal right to our lives.

The moon

The moon plays a very important role in the lives of witches and has significance for their magical rites. Traditional witches place more emphasis on full moons than they do on the sabbats. To them, the moon not only controls the tides, but it regulates fertility and breeding habits of many species, including humans. Full moons are the strongest time for "dark" power and more magic is performed on Full Moons than at any other time.

There are thirteen Full Moons in every year and Witches believe that by adjusting their lives to the lunar phases they live in harmony with the dominant forces of nature, thereby increasing their effectiveness and success with their spell-work and Magic.

The way in which witches celebrate the lunar moons can differ from witch to witch. The celebrations can be something elaborate or as simple as meditating in front of a candle. Witches are very legalistic about magic and the lunar moon. They believe only certain forms of magic are appropriate for each specific moon, and believe this is the only magic that should be practiced in this specific period.

New Moon: This marks the beginning of the lunar cycle. During this period there is no visible moon in the sky. To witches it is a time of renewal and transformation. This is a very active time for magic and spell casting, especially for the Southern Hemisphere. Spell casting and magic can be carried out from the day of the new moon to three-and-a-half days thereafter. They believe that their magic will be most effective if the process is started within three days of the new moon. Long-term magic, that will occupy the entire waxing cycle, should begin on or as soon after the new moon as possible.

Waxing Moon: This is the period of time between the new moon and the full moon. Waxing moon takes place from seven to fourteen days after the new moon. It is perceived that the power of female witches are growing and gaining power during this phase, just as the moon grows fuller every night. Witches tend to practise magic involving any kind of growth during this time. Rituals for increase, empowerment, the enhancement or conjuring up of things desired are performed during this phase of the moon. Magical workings should include things such as recovery from illness, increasing willpower, courage, motivation, improving relationships, inspiration and luck. This is also seen as a time in which blessings should take place.

Full Moon Magic: The Full moon period is from fourteen to seventeen-and-a-half days after the new moon. These are the nights when the entire moon is completely visible in the sky and it rises at sunset and sets at sunrise. The Moon appears full in the sky for two or three nights.

"The Ways of magic are aligned with the full moon" and witches see the Full Moon representing the full abundance of nature's power which is available to the witch. This is the time that the power is flowing at its peak.

The full moon is an excellent time for most magical works. Witches can often accomplish, in one night, what they might have taken weeks to accomplish. Witches believe that the full moon is a time for "empowering" or "positive" magic.

This is a time for rituals of prophecy, protection, and divination. The power of the Full Moon is also used for banishing unwanted influences in their life. Full moons are also known to enhance shamanic shape-shifting work. It is known that werewolves famously shape-shift during the full moon. The werewolf cult has actual known ties to the ancient witch-cult. Although, on the nights immediately preceding and following the full moon, the moon may appear to be completely full, there is only one full moon per month and only one night when the moon is truly a "Full Moon". The full moon is also traditionally a night of festivity and the infamous witch's sabbath.

This is where, yet again, there are differences in some of the witch's beliefs. There are some traditional witches who believe that magic should not be performed during a Full Moon, other witches consider the Full Moon as a time where magic is at its strongest and yet others who see this time as a time of rest. Just like the tides, the moon appears neither to be coming nor going and simply seems as if it were standing still in the sky.

Waning Moon: This is the period from three-and-a-half to ten-and-a-half days after the full moon. During the waning moon, the moon is fading or shrinking from Full moon to New Moon. Witches believe that the female power is weakening as the moon is waning / fading. This is seen as the appropriate phase for "destructive" or "negative" magic; for instance cursing, also known as 'owl blinking' in the West. They are able to remove or separate themselves from unwanted things or issues such as illness, bad habits, negative behavioural patterns and emotional garbage. Gemma Garry.

The Dark Moon "dark of the moon": This includes the last three days of the lunar cycle and three days prior to the New Moon. This is when the moon appears to be absent from the night sky and generally no magic is performed during this time. This is a time for Vision quests and deep meditation and divination (fortune-telling). During this time witches may feel there is less energy available for physical activities, seeing this period as the polar opposite of the energetic and festive atmosphere of full moon. The best magic for this period, they believe, is no magic at all. The dark moon is a time for ridding oneself of bad habits a time for new projects, self-improvement and binding spells. "Vision Quest is an attempt to achieve a vision of a future guardian spirit, traditionally undertaken at puberty by boys of the Plains Indian people, typically through fasting or self-torture. It often involves the "quester" spending time alone in nature in search of a personal vision that becomes a vision to support the entire community". Huffington Post; Article by Maddisen K. Krown

Blue Moon or 13th Moon
The lunar cycle is slightly shorter than a calendar month, resulting in some months having two full moons in the same calendar month. The second full moon is called a blue moon. It is not physically blue in colour and does not carry any special attributes as it is just a regular, cyclical full moon. A Blue Moon occurs infrequently, hence the saying: "Once in a blue moon". A Blue Moon can occur at any time during the year. Black Moon, is the second New Moon in a month. Black Moons are considered to be stronger than regular New Moons. as is the case with a Blue Moon, this is also an infrequent occurrence.

GOD FORBIDS THE WORSHIP OF THE SUN, MOON AND STARS

[14] "Then God said, "Let there be lights in the firmament of the heavens to divide the day from the night; and let them be for signs and seasons, and for days and years; [15] and let them be for lights in the firmament of the heavens to give light on the earth"; and it was so. [16] Then God made two great lights: the greater light to rule the day, and the lesser light to rule the night. He made the stars also. [17] God set them in the firmament of the heavens to give light on the earth, [18] and to rule over the day and over the night, and to divide the light from the darkness. And God saw that it was good. [19] So the evening and the morning were the fourth day."

Genesis 1:14-19

Although this scripture does not tell us how God made the sun, moon, and stars, it does tell us is that God is the one who made them and why He made them. He placed them in the sky to fulfil specific functions:

- ➢ To divide day from night
- ➢ For signs
- ➢ For seasons
- ➢ For days
- ➢ For years
- ➢ To give light upon the earth
- ➢ To rule over day (the sun) and night (the moon)
- ➢ The sun and moon were made to praise the Lord

[3] "Praise Him, sun and moon; Praise Him, all you stars of light"
Psalm 148:3

We can see that God created the sun, moon and stars. He has assigned them to; exercise dominions, to determine important matters on earth (such as dividing day from night), to indicate seasons, to give light upon the earth and to rule over day and night.

[14] "Then God said, "Let there be lights in the firmament of the heavens to divide the day from the night; and let them be for signs and seasons, and for days and years; [15] and let them be for lights in the firmament of the heavens to give light on the earth"; and it was so. [16] Then God made two great lights: the greater light to rule the day, and the lesser light to rule the night. He made the stars also. [17] God set them in the firmament of the heavens to give light on the earth, [18] and to rule over the day and over the night, and to divide the light from the darkness. And God saw that it was good."
Genesis 1:14-18

God Himself is the God of heaven and earth. We need to remember that planetary movements and alignments are ordained by the Lord according to His sovereignty and His divinely ordained laws of the heavens. The problems associated with the un-godly worship of the sun, moon and stars developed when the enemy hijacked these alignments through sorcery and witchcraft to use these alignments against God's Kingdom.

It is no secret that the moon has been an object of worship for centuries. However, what is generally unknown to people is that at least three-fifths of the world is still steeped in the worshiping of the moon in one form or another, to a more or lesser degree.

[19] "And take heed, lest you lift your eyes to heaven, and when you see the sun, the moon, and the stars, all the host of heaven, you feel driven to worship them and serve them, which the Lord your God has given to all the peoples under the whole heaven as a heritage."

Deuteronomy 4:19

We, as the body of Christ and the Church are the only spiritual "police force". As born again believers we are equipped and empowered in the Name of Jesus to stop this illegality which has gone on unchecked for ages. We need to apply the Blood of the Lamb on the alignments and pray that every single un-godly plant our Heavenly Father has not planted shall be up-rooted. We also need to ask God to lay an axe to every un-godly tree, root and plant in the heavens and our lives.

[13] "But He answered and said, "Every plant which My heavenly Father has not planted will be uprooted."

Through sorcery and witchcraft, the enemy has used these alignments against God's Kingdom and His children by getting humans to worship the sun, moon and the stars. In some cultures babies are being dedicated, in one way or another, to the heavenlies. Through these sort of un-godly practises sorcerers can manipulate these alignments to affect these children. Swazi fetish priests decide the day of festivals by examining the moon. In Swaziland, major decisions are made in relation to vital aspects of the highly demonic Inkwala festival, also known as the "Festival of the First Fruits." During the months of November to February the highly demonic Inkwala festival is held. This is known, in the Swazi culture, as the national prayer. The evil activities that take place during this Inkwala festival are declared "holy" by the Swazi King who himself is steeped in witchcraft practises.

Many of the Swazi people blindly support this Incwala ceremony, not understanding or knowing about the evil rituals that take place behind the scenes. For example the Swazi King interacts with a serpent spirit called LaMlambo. Bestiality also takes place and the King ejaculates into bull horn so that it can be used during the ceremony. It is even sometimes mixed into food used for the celebrations. The monarch then publicly has sexual intercourse with two of his wives. "They are known as "Tesulelamsiti", which means this is where the king cleanses himself and removes all his dirt. Inside the two women is where Mswati leaves his demonic evils so that they carry it whilst he remains clean." It is said that these two wives serve only this purpose in the royal family. - **Sithembiso Simelane**

For a more in-depth look please do a web search of... **"What happens at the annual Incwala ceremony, an account is given by a former Inyatsi regiment, Sithembiso Simelane"**. He is attempting to shine a light on what really happens behind the scenes at the first fruit festival, better known the Incwala ceremony. This is what he has to say: "The above account is my own. It is meant to open Swazi people's eyes and minds so that they see beyond the government's propaganda that Incwala is holy. I must state that Pastor Justice and other pastors were correct when they said Incwala is un-Godly. Indeed, nothing can be Godly with a man having sexual intercourse with a bull every year, having sexual intercourse with two of his wives in full view of other men, yearly causing at least one young boy with a bright future to go insane with the use of muti, and forcing many men to abandon their own fields so that they can go and weed his own fields." **By Sithembiso Simelane**.

Another scary truth is during full moon phases there are more rapes, violent crimes and manic tendencies. The Daily Mail published an article where the Sussex police force have done a study claiming that with each full moon the number of violent disturbances recorded increased significantly. Inspector Parr, who led the study, compared the number of violent crimes reported with the dates of each full moon and discovered a distinct connection.

Michal Zimecki of the Polish Academy of Sciences did an analysed study which took into account human and animal behaviour during lunar activity. He claimed that the full moon could affect criminal activity and health, leading to an increase of crime and hospital admissions. He said that the effects were so marked that it "may be helpful in police surveillance and medical practice".

"Incidence of crimes reported to three police stations in different towns in the period of 1978–1982 was also studied. The incidence of crimes committed on full-moon days was much higher than on all other days, i.e. new moon days and seven days after the full moon and new moon."- Zimecki M. – The lunar cycle: effects on human and animal behaviour and physiology pg 3

"The number of accidents occurring during the full-moon day was lowest, the highest occurring two days before the full moon. Accidents were more frequent during the waxing than during the waning phase, but no signify differences were noted when the lunar month was divided into the four intervals of the lunar cycle."- Zimecki M. – The lunar cycle: effects on human and animal behaviour and physiology pg 3

Let's look at another two independent studies; one done by [13]German scientists in 2000 showing that during the full moon there were a significant rise in binge drinking, and the second a psychological study published in 1998 showing that there was a rise in violent incidents in the maximum security wing at Armley jail, Leeds, England, where 1,200 inmates were held.

Jodi Tasso and Elizabeth Miller published an article in the Journal of Psychology called "The effects of the

---

[13] Read more: http://www.dailymail.co.uk/news/article-460050/Theres-violence-moons-say-police.html#ixzz2xS4aiYna

full Moon on Human behaviour." Here is the summary of that article.

"Summary"

"Data was gathered in a large metropolitan area over a period of one year as to nine categories of 34,318 criminal offenses committed during the phases of the full moon and non-full moon. It was found that the eight categories of rape, robbery and assault, burglary, larceny and theft, auto theft, offenses against family and children, drunkenness, and disorderly conduct occurred significantly more frequently during the full moon phase than at other times of the year. Only the category of homicide did not occur more frequently during the full moon phase. The results support further exploration and research related to cosmic influences on man's behaviour."- www.tandfonline.com/doi/abs/10.1080/00223980.1976.9921376

Sangomas believe in protecting their ancient sacred sites. One such a site is Howick waterfall in Kwa-Zulu Natal. The sangomas hold a ceremony to honour their ancestors, the spirit of the waterfall and the earth as the "mother ancestor". At the bottom of the waterfall they will talk to the earth spirit that lives there and is known in the Zulu tradition as a "Makhosi-Inkanyamba". This is a type of serpent spirit that is both a guardian and ancestral protector of the land and sacred places.

Witchcraft has had dire consequences for the continent of Africa. Being such a dominant belief in African culture, it continuously poses problems and plays a huge factor in Africa's dysfunctional political, religious, social and economic balance.

Many African politicians are linked to or with traditional healers such as sangomas and witchdoctors. It was reported on July 24, 2013 on the news website praag.org, that a group of Gauteng traditional healers or Witchdoctors had performed a ritual for the former, and now deceased, President Nelson Mandela. This ritual took place outside the Pretoria hospital where Mandela had been treated for a recurring lung infection. During the ritual, the traditional healer's burnt incense in a pot, knelt on the ground, sprinkled tobacco, sang and summoned Mr Mandela's ancestors to heal him. Khubane Mashele, the chairwoman of the traditional healers' interim council of Gauteng, said they asked the ancestors of Mandela, the great kings and soldiers of those who had passed away during the struggle, to heal the former President. Nelson Mandela has since passed away at the age of 95.
Sapa: See more at:
http://praag.org/?p=7716#sthash.UDjDMZKg.dpuf

A lot of controversy has also surrounded the current South African President Mr Jacob Zuma. It has been reported on numerous occasions and through more than one newspaper, locally and internationally, regarding the president's participation in witchcraft ceremonies. In January 2014, the "The Daily Sun" reported that Mr Zuma had told supporters in KwaNyamazane, Mpumalanga, South Africa, that whilst in exile during the apartheid era, he would infiltrate South Africa and bewitch the authorities.

Although the presidency stated that the media report of President Jacob Zuma practising witchcraft during apartheid was "ridiculous and misleading", this has not been the only report about the Presidents involvement with witchcraft.

In yet another article, this time in "The Star" newspaper of November 2012, reporter Bongani Hans wrote an article on Mr Zuma allegedly having participated in a witchcraft ceremony in which 12 cows were slaughtered. It was said that Mr Zuma turned to his ancestor for help for the upcoming election, as it was alleged that people wanted him removed as the current leader of the ANC. As this ritual, which took place at his homestead in Kwa-Zulu Natal, not only were 12 cows slaughtered, but incense was also burned and Zulu warriors danced and sang songs. Mr Zuma went on to win that election in Mangaung.

Another prominent politician which has also made headlines relating to her involvement in witchcraft practises of ancestral worship, is DA leader and Western Cape Premier Helen Zille. An article was published by "Die Burger" saying Ms Zille had visited a sangoma and sacrificed a sheep in honour of her ancestors. It was stated that Ms Zille visited the traditional healer in the Cape Town township of Khayelitsha where the ceremony was performed. Allegedly other DA branches in the townships had also been told to slaughter sheep and goats in her honour. Ms Zille has never denied these claims.

It is the love of power and money and its importance in their lives that has resulted in people looking towards other gods for help. But it is not just the "high and mighty" that resort to these means. Witchcraft is deeply rooted in the DNA of the African continent and its people.

Within Africa, where poverty is the norm, it isn't strange to hear all the stories of people seeking the help of their local witch doctors to obtain personal, political, and financial gain. In Malawi, where 53% of the population lives below the national poverty line and 90.4 % live on less than $2 per day, money and even basic foods stuffs are hard to come by. - FINICA.org

Many Malawians seek help from witch-doctors or the Sing'anga. Some of the stories that are told sound surreal or made up, but to these people it is very real. Out in Africa you walk face to face with evil.

Among some of the Malawians, especially in the more remote parts of the country, it is well known that people obtain riches through the help of witchcraft or a Sing'anga. The Sing'anga has many ways of carrying out these "get rich" rituals.

Firstly, there will always be some agreement made between the witch doctor and the "client" regarding price. The price will always be high and at times the payment may even be someone's life or the persons own sanity. It is also well known when an agreement is made and should the person renege on their word, the punishment could involve them losing their minds through being cursed by the witch doctor's wrath.

People selling goods at the market will go to the witch doctor and buy a "charm" from the witch doctor. They will then be instructed to place the charm in their pocket and, when selling their goods at the local market, they are to rub or touch the charm. It is alleged that in this way more people will come and buy goods from their stall.

Some Malawians tell of "medicine" that the witch doctors provide and they are generally instructed to wash their face with the "potion" in order to obtain riches or a better harvest from their crops.

Others talk of witch doctors sending people to graveyards at night in order to steal dead bodies, so that the body parts can be sold for money.

There are those that believe in order to obtain riches that you are required to kill your children or even sleep with one of your parents.

Others mention that if a person requires someone to be killed, they would obtain medicine from the witch doctor and while they mix the medicine together, the person is to call out the name of the victim they want murdered.

There are many stories that are told and as you listen you hear the desperation in some of their voices. You can see the strongholds of generation after generation of demonic strongholds and curses and how deeply rooted witchcraft is and how strong it flows in their veins. It can only be broken by Jesus who made a mockery of the devil and his demons at the cross!

[15] "Having disarmed principalities and powers, He made a public spectacle of them, triumphing over them in it."

The truth to the practitioner of spells: demons are not under the command of humans; they are under the power of Satan. They will do whatever they themselves, or Satan desires. It might appear to the practitioners of false religions whom use demons in incantation, that these demons are subject to them, but this is just a lie. Demons deceive humans in the effort of luring the human into the kingdom of darkness. Once the human is adequately wrapped up in demon worship, the demon may decide to take control over the human, resulting in the human being a slave to the demon.

Holidays

Throughout the ages, traditional witchcraft holidays / festivals and sabbats celebrations can differ considerably because of the various regions, traditions, cultures and people. Each witch chooses for themselves which of the festivals to observe or not. Traditional Witches may not celebrate all eight sabbats, placing their focus more on the times of the year and the extent to which the daylight lengthens or shortens. Again, it needs to be emphasised that it all depends on the individual witch.

For the witches that don't believe in gods and goddesses, it is the seasonal changes themselves that are honoured, not the lives of any gods or goddesses. Traditional Witchcraft is an agriculture-based tradition that follows the tides of planting and harvesting. Some traditions celebrate harvest festivals, while another traditions may celebrate solar tides. As the holidays are based on the tides and changes of nature, they differ depending on where you go. For example nations that live in tropical climates usually recognise only two seasons, the wet and dry or the changing "skin colour" of the earth; from green to brown or vice versa. Many of these people feel that by honouring, thanking and appeasing the gods of the earth, or the "Nature force" depending on the belief, the more abundant their harvest or a hunt may be.

The Greater Sabbats (also known as the cross quarter days) are known as the "Fire Festivals" and they mark the transitions of the seasons. These Greater Sabbats are the mid-points or peaks of the Lesser Sabbats. They are called the Greater Sabbats because witches believe that they are at their highest energy level at the peak or mid-point of such events. On the Greater Sabbats, propitiatory sacrifices are made in an effort to gain divine favour and to avoid retribution or reckoning from their deities or the "forces of nature". The Lesser Sabbats mark the quarters of the year and links back to the agriculture-based tradition that witchcraft is. The solstice and equinox marks the transitions of the sun. The solstice marks either the longest day or the longest night, and the equinox marks the points where day and night are equal. Let's take another look at what C.S Lewis said in this following passage "Failure to Submit to the Ultimate God". "Furthermore, if the pagan realized that Nature and God were distinct; The One had made the other; the One ruled and the other obeyed, then he or she would not worship the gods but rather the God."
C.S Lewis-article written by Scott Robert Presbyterian /church Southside, Texas www.inplainsite.org

[25] "Who changed the truth of God into a lie, and worshipped and served the creature more than the Creator, who is blessed for ever. Amen."

Romans 1:25

We should worship the one who created all things and not the creation. Witches prefer to worship things and the gods they make instead of the God who made everything.

[15] "And saying, Sirs, why do ye these things? We also are men of like passions with you, and preach unto you that ye should turn from these vanities unto the living God, which made heaven, and earth, and the sea, and all things that are therein

Acts14:15

Winter solstice/ Yule
Northern Hemisphere: December 21 / Southern Hemisphere: June 21,

This is a Lesser Sabbat. This festival, the winter Solstice, celebrates the rebirth of the Sun God into infancy.

Unbeknownst to some believers, what we were brought up to believe about Christmas actually has its roots in paganism and witchcraft.

The tree with lights, Yule log, holly and red candles are all ancient pagan and witchcraft symbols. The Christian practice of putting up a Christmas tree is derived from the ancient Pagan tradition of bringing a Yule tree in to the home in order to welcome nature spirits into the festivities.

³ "For the customs of the peoples are futile; For one cuts a tree from the forest, The work of the hands of the workman, with the axe. ⁴ They decorate it with silver and gold; They fasten it with nails and hammers. So that it will not topple."

Jeremiah 10:3-4

Witches sacrifice a child at midnight Christmas Eve and leech emotional energy from the Christians' "holiday spirit."

Laa'l Breeshey / Candlemas / Imbolog / Imbolc (pronounced iv-ole) also known as Feast of the Light, Groundhog Day or St Bridget's day.

Nothern Hemisphere: February 2 / Southern Hemisphere: August 2

Imbolc, is one of the Great Sabbats and is celebrated at the peak of winter. It is one of the four main Fire Festivals. It is native to Celtic culture and love magic is practised on this day.

"Love magic is the attempt to bind the passions of another, or to capture them as a sex object through magical means rather than through direct activity. It can be implemented in a variety of ways, such as written spells, dolls, charms, amulets, potions, or different rituals":- From Wikipedia, the free encyclopaedia

Among the Greeks this day is called "Antihestria", the Festival of Flowers and the Romans call it the feast of Juno Februata, the Virgin Mother of Mars. Pope Sergius and Church leaders tried to "Christianise" this day by declaring it a celebration of the Purification of the Virgin Mary, calling it "Candlemas".

In Scotland and Ireland this feast is celebrated on the 2nd February as the Feast of St. Bride and in the Highlands it is celebrated on 13th February.

The festival is sacred to the Celtic solar and fire Goddess Brigid. Brigid's primary symbol is the sun wheel or fire wheel and it is a version of the ancient swastika that represents the cosmic life force.

In the United States, February 2nd is celebrated and known as "Groundhog Day." It is foretold that if a groundhog or hedgehog comes out from his winter sleep and sees his shadow as a result of it being a sunny day, he will run back into his hole and winter would continue for another six more weeks. If this does not occur, as a result of it being overcast or a cloudy day, he would then remain outside and winter would be over. The groundhog / hedgehog custom relates to the worship of serpents.

Flower crowns, lighting of candles, rituals of new beginnings and Groundhog Day are all customs rooted in "The Old Ways". White or pale blue candles may be lit during the ritual and can be taken home to burn later, when a magical new beginning is needed. In the Greek festival of Antihestria, flowers crowns were placed on any child who had reached the age of three during the past year. - The Old Ways by Doug and Sandy Kopf. It is a time of birth, purification and initiation. It is seen as spring cleaning on both a physical and spiritual level. This is so the spirit of the Old Year can be driven out.

Ostara /the Vernal /Lady Day / Spring Equinox
Nothern Hemisphere: March 21 /Southern Hemisphere: Sep 21

This is a lesser Sabbat and is regarded as the first day of spring in the Northern Hemisphere. For the Southern Hemisphere, Spring Equinox more closely resembles the beginning of autumn, in physical terms. This is a celebration of the "Revitalization of the Earth". This is a very powerful time for the practise of magic and this is a festival focused on fertility.

The Easter symbolism of rabbits, eggs and lambs is derived from the Spring Equinox. A sacramental bonfire is lit and witches leap over the glowing coals to encourage human and crop fertility. The decorating of eggs have always been symbols of fertility and in 17th century France, gifts of decorated eggs were given to new brides, in hopes they would bear many children.

In many cultures the egg is not just seen as a symbol of life or home of the soul, but many cultures also believe creation "hatched" from the Cosmic Egg laid by either a goose or a fairy-tale or legendary bird. In Russia the egg is the symbol of all good fortune and decorated eggs are given as gifts to loved ones and buried in graves to ensure rebirth.

A seemingly Christian custom, the Hot Cross Bun, actually has its origins in Old witchcraft Ways. At a spring festival, dedicated to the goddess of moon and hunting "Diana", the Early Anglo-Saxons ate wheat cakes which were decorated with crosses. In Hertfordshire, England, ruins of an altar to Diana of the Crossways has been found and the area is famous for its Hot Cross Buns! It was also believed that preserved pieces of hot-cross bun can be used as a protective charm against fire or for healing purposes.

The poor little bunny, another fertility symbol, for obvious reasons has been assigned to the role of 'egg-delivery boy' in modern times. The Moon-Hare was sacred to goddesses all over the world.

Beltane/ Beltaen or May Day
Nothern Hemisphere: May 1/ Southern Hemisphere: 31 October

This one of the great Sabbat days and is a Celtic festival of fertility, renewal, purification and another of the Fire festivals. In ancient times, Fire Festivals were seen as a time of sacrifice and purification. As a result, at all fire festivals, human and animal sacrifices took place. The spilling of blood is to nourish the earth or soil.

In Beltane they built fires on hilltops across Britain as acts of magic, trying to charm the sun back to its summer glory. According to Irish mythology great bonfires were bearers of the news of summertime, in the hopes of good harvest, prosperity and wellbeing to all.

The Druids would create a need-fire / wild-fire on top of a hill, believing that bonfires brought good luck in the form of prosperity and health to livestock. They would then rush the village's cattle through the fires to purify them. Sky-clad / nude witches would jump between two flames to guarantee protection and in an effort to secure husbands and safe pregnancies; girls would jump over the coals or ashes.

May Day and Beltane day, although they are linked and share commonalities, are actually unconnected. May Day and Beltane both celebrate new growth and fertility, but Beltane is a Celtic Festival and May Day originated from a Germanic festival. The holiday was also known as "Roodmass" in England and "Walpurgisnacht" in Germany. May Day is associated with dancing around the May Pole, an ancient fertility symbol which once was one of England's most important festivals and oldest surviving religious rites. May Poles were raised and young people would dance and sing around them. Phallic symbols, meant to impregnate the earth, were enjoyed and were then followed by nightlong feasting and sex.

On "Walpurgisnacht" or May Eve, European witches were said to attend the Grand Sabbat of the year at the Brocken Mountain in Germany. It was generally believed that wild orgies, supervised by the Devil, were held here.

Summer Solstice / Midsummer /Litha
Nothern Hemisphere: June 21/ Southern Hemisphere: December 21

This is a lesser Sabbat and is one of the three "spirit nights" where interaction with the spirit world or ancestor spirits takes place. It is a time of divination and the gathering of magical herbs (like St. John's Wort) to hang above the door in order to ward off thunderstorms and evil influences. As this falls approximately in the middle of the growing season throughout much of Europe, this day is also known as being the longest day of the year. Abundance, warmth, and fertility are celebrated.

Lammas/ Llughnassad
Nothern Hemisphere: August 2 /Southern Hemishere: February 2

Lammas is a Great Sabbat. It marks the end of summer, the beginning of fall and that relates to the beginning of the harvest cycle. In Irish Gaelic, the feast was referred to as 'Lugnasadh', a feast to honour the funeral of the Irish sun-god Lugh.

One of the traditional witchcraft traditions on Lammas Eve was the lighting of a huge cart wheel which had been smeared with tar. It was then rolled down a hillside and it's smooth passage (or not) was a sign for the harvest that was about to come. This ritual inspired the popular firework called the "Catherine Wheel", while the "Midsummer Fire Wheel" depicted the motion of the sun in the sky. This fiery wheel of Lughnasadh symbolises the sun descending from the height of the sky into the "underworld".

The blood sacrifice of animals and humans was seen as an act of life and not death, especially in the case of a human victim, whose soul was believed to go straight to heaven or to the realm of the Gods. In some cultures to be selected as the victim for sacrifice was regarded as a great honour as it bestowed divinity.

Autumn Equinox
Northern Hemisphere: Sept 21 / Southern Hemisphere: March 21

The festival of Harvest End or Harvest Home coincided with the Autumn Equinox in September when the days and nights were equal. In Scotland two corn dollies were made from the last bundle of corn, which were considered to contain the spirit of the grain / corn goddess, and they were dressed in handmade clothes. These dolls were known as the Corn Maiden or Corn Mother, the Kern Baby, the Mare, the Old Wife, the Old Hag or the Old Witch and they represented the harvest of the past year and the year to come. They were placed above the fireplace to bring fertility and prosperity to the household. When the early ploughing began In January, these corn dollies were buried in the first furrow to bring a good harvest. Although Wiccans and American neo-pagans have been calling Autumn Equinox "Mabon", it is not the name generally used in the Traditional Craft.

Samhain (pronounced sow-ain) / All Hallows Eve/ Halloween
Northern Hemisphere: Oct 31/ Southern Hemisphere: May 1

Shamhain, Halloween or All Hallow's Eve is seen as the most powerful Sabbat of the year. It is also known as the Feast of the dead. It is in exact opposite to Beltane on the wheel of the year; Halloween is Beltane's dark twin. As with many things in witchcraft, the pronunciation depends on where you live in the

world; 'Sow-in' in Ireland, 'Sow-een' in Wales, 'Sav-en' in Scotland or 'Sam-hane' in the U.S.
This is a festival dedicated to the dead. Halloween is one of the three 'spirit nights', a night of power with a great deal of interaction with ancestral and dead spirits. Not only is this the festival or celebration most associated with witchcraft, but this is an important day for divination, séances, scrying with mirrors, mediumship, telepathic conversation and tarot card readings.

Although this might be the Celtic New Year, many other ancient cultures like the Mexicans celebrate this day. "Los Dias de los Muertos" or Mexican day of the dead shares some origins with Halloween.

In some traditions two circles are cast at Halloween, one for the living and one for the dead. Using a circle or the "act of circling" to make contact with or enter the spirit world has always been a prominent feature of ritual and folk magic. It is a ritual act associated with nocturnal visits (usually at midnight or during the full moon) to prehistoric burial grounds, crossroads, ancient standing stones or churchyards built on pagan sites. At these places a ritual can be done to prompt visions of the future or a manifestation of the Horned God, 'a Lady on a white horse', spirits who are guardians of the treasure, faeries or long dead pagan priests who will reveal secret knowledge. "Once there, if you were brave, you could dance or walk three, seven or nine times widdershins, backwards or forwards or deosil around the hallowed ground."

Moving deosil means to cast a circle or to invoke demons and moving widdershins is to banish demons.

The act of circling or casting the circle is a ritual metaphor for gaining access to the "Otherworld"/demonic realm, crossing the boundaries between the worlds and making contact with demons spirits. We might know that these are demonic spirits but witches believe that this is a very special time and that they are actually making contact with witches that has died and is returning to act as spirit guides.

The sangomas believe that the year is split into seven celestial turns, each occurring when one of the seven constellations waxes in power. They also believe that the time at which an individual is conceived and comes into the world is an indication of their place in the "weave". Sangomas often call it the colour of their thread - although these are not colours that can be seen by the eye, but rather the colour of purpose. Thus, when the time comes again for the waxing of an individual's sign, this is a time for celebration, for this is when he is most active in fulfilling his cause; when his colour is on top of the "weave". There is no particular order in which signs take precedence in the sky, but they all "have their moment" at some point in a given year. On the night that the constellation is at its brightest in the sky, the immediate day following this event is the day that the sangoma who was born under that sign must make the pilgrimage back to their home. They are then to pray and fast and contemplate the skies until another sign waxes brightest in the heavens, calling a different sangoma home.

Marriage

In Witchcraft "Handfasting" was the word used in the once Celtic / Anglo-Saxon lands of Scotland and Northern England to refer to a traditional marriage ceremony. During the Handfasting, ritual couples were literally tied together, hence the saying "tying the knot".

With this ritual the bride and groom's hands are tied together with a red cord or ribbon. The cord that was used during the ceremony was then kept by the couple as a reminder of their vows. In some traditions each wedding guest ties a ribbon around the couple's hands, showing the community's support and recognition of the couples bond.

The Hand-fasting can take place in one of three forms.

- Hand-fasting for a year and a day: The temporary agreement of being married for a year and a day is actually known as hand-fasted. They will then live together as a married couple for a year and a day. After this time has lapsed each person may choose either to part ways and find another mate or to make it official, if both spouses agree.
- Hand-fasting for life: When the couple has decided to make it official for life this is then called hand-fasting. The witches' couple would then again have a similar ceremony as previously carried out at their union, but this time the wraps and knots will be fastened tightly. These ceremonies were generally held in Beltane because Beltane was chosen because of it emulating, the sacred union of the God and Goddess. Beltane is all about sex and fertility.
- Hand-fasting for life and all others

Hand-parting / Divorce: The cord is tied at the beginning of the ceremony and is then cut at the end. This was however, not the common practices of hand-fasting.

Other

Witches in the church

The absolute hatred for Christianity makes churches a big target for witches. It is notoriously known that witches will infiltrate a church and perform many rituals and spells against, not only the congregation, but specifically target the church leadership.

They are sent in to churches as "plants" and will try to become part of the church and be seen to fit in. One of the first places a witch will infiltrate is the prayer groups and intercessors. With prayer being the power base of a church they will do everything to interfere with prayer, the powerbase of every spirit filled church.

They will use manipulation and lust or anything in their power to kill, steal and destroy. They love destroying peoples prayer life, so be aware if you are being attacked in your prayer life. We need to ask God for discernment if this happens as this may be witchcraft coming against your powerbase, which is your prayer life.

Another destructive weapon used by witches is performing rituals that place demons onto their body parts so that they can seduce and flirt with men and woman. They will sit in church dressed very provocatively in the attempt to flirt with the married men and woman. The demons, which are placed on their body parts during these rituals, will cause men's eyes to be drawn to the witch's body part in question. Witches know the power of seduction and lust, and more specifically they know where men can be weak and they will concentrate on this and take advantage.

One of a witch's strongest weapons is sex Magic. Sex Magic: "[14]The use of sex (e.g. intercourse - actual or symbolic) within a ritual or spell-casting session to facilitate or augment the efficacy of a given magical rite. That is, sexual activities are used to accomplish the desired goal of the occultist".

Another very powerful ritual that they perform in church is caging. They will form, in the spirit, a circle around the pulpit and they will "cage in" the pastor or person delivering Gods word, in an attempt to prevent the message from getting out. As was the case in Matthew 18:19, where believers can come into agreement about a particular situation, so to can the enemy come into agreement. They stand in agreement stopping the word of God going out and reaching the hearts of the congregation. The agreement needs to be broken between these witches, it needs to be separated. These agreements are very powerful. We would need to isolate, separate and break this "spell" all in the Name of Jesus, after which we would need to start uprooting the bars that they have planted (in the spirit) around the pulpit to cage the message in.

---

[14]www.inplainsite.org/html/modern_world_of_witchcraft.html#sthash.z3aAVkor.dpuf

We need discernment. We also need to know, as a born again believer, the authority we have in the Name of Jesus.

> ¹⁷ Then the seventy returned with joy, saying, "Lord, even the demons are subject to us in Your name."
>
> **Luke 10:17**

> ⁴ You are of God, little children, and have overcome them, because He who is in you is greater than he who is in the world.
>
> **1 John 4:4**

David star hexagram

> ²⁶ "You also carried Sikkuth[a] your king[b] And Chiun,[c] your idols, The star of your gods, Which you made for yourselves. ²⁷ Therefore I will send you into captivity beyond Damascus," Says the Lord, whose name is the God of hosts."
>
> **Amos 5:26-27**

a. Amos 5:26 A pagan deity
b. Amos 5:26 Septuagint and Vulgate read tabernacle of Moloch.
c. Amos 5:26 A pagan deity

> ⁴² Then God turned and gave them up to worship the host of heaven, as it is written in the book of the Prophets: 'Did you offer Me slaughtered animals and sacrifices during forty years in the wilderness, O house of Israel? ⁴³ You also took up the tabernacle of Moloch, And the star of your god Remphan, Images which you made to worship; And I will carry you away beyond Babylon.'
>
> **Acts 7:42-43**

The so-called "Star of David" is essentially a "hexagram," and has nothing to do with King David or God's people.

Like the obelisk, the six-pointed star was an Egyptian idol used in idol worship in 922 B.C. when King Solomon married the daughter of Pharoah, turned to pagan gods and the occult and became involved in idolatry, magic and witchcraft. Solomon built an altar to Ashtoreth and Moloch as well as developed the six-pointed star, causing God to become very angry with him.

The hexagram is used in magic, witchcraft, sorcery and occultism as well as being used in the casting of zodiacal horoscopes by astrologers. "It was considered to possess mysterious powers." - A Concise Encyclopaedia of Freemasonry.

Sorcerers believed it represented the footprint of a special kind of demon called a 'trud'. The hexagram is used to conjure up demons which do the bidding of the witch, and to keep the witch safe from the demons (while standing in the hexagram).

[15]The hexagram is also a symbol of the sex act, reproduction or sexual union. The triangle pointed downward is a female symbol and the triangle pointed upward is the male symbol. When the triangles are interlaced it represents sexual union of the active and passive forces in nature.

---

[15] Albert G. Mackey provides us with the occult explanation in his book, The Symbolism of Freemasonry, [p. 195, 1869 A.D.]

[16]Speaking of the sexual connotation of the hexagram, another witch revealed: "When the male triangle penetrates the female triangle, it produces the six pointed crest of Solomon or hexagram, the wicked symbol in witchcraft."

Harry Potter

Harry Potter phenomenon is a series of seven fantasy novels written by the British author J. K. Rowling. "The Harry Potter is unprecedented in children's literature."- Diane Roback, children's book editor, Publisher's Weekly, quoted in USA Today, December 2, 1999.

"It's mind-boggling. It would be easy to attribute Harry Potter's success to some form of magical intervention." Jean Feiwel, Scholastic representative, quoted in Los Angels Times, October 22, 1999.

Since the release of the first novel, Harry Potter and the Philosopher's Stone, on 30 June 1997, the book series had sold between 400 and 450 million copies (as of July 2013) making it one of the best-selling book series in history. It has been translated into 73 languages and the last four books repeatedly set records as the fastest-selling books in history, with the final instalment selling approximately 11 million copies in the United States within the first twenty-four hours of its release.

Harry Potter is a training manual of all sorts of witchcraft, it is real and very dangerous. Children might not be able to take one of the books and

---

[16] Freemasonry and Esoterica

actually cast a spell but these books encourages children to seek out real spell books and furthermore encourages play-act or role play in being wizards and witches. Children are even being confused into thinking that the characters and "world" such as the Hogwarts School of Witchcraft and Wizardry are real.

Rowling, herself, said this: [17]"I get letters from children addressed to Professor Dumbledore, and it's not a joke, begging to be let into "Hogwarts", and some of them are really sad. Because they want it to be true so badly they've convinced themselves its true."

Although she has tried to deny it, Rowling has since childhood, has tried to learn everything she could about witchcraft.

[18]"I truly am bemused that anyone who has read the books could think that I am a proponent of the occult in any serious way. I don't believe in witchcraft, in the sense that they're talking about, at all. . I don't believe in magic in the way I describe it in my books."

But according to a childhood friend, Ian Potter whose last name she used in her book titles, Rowling used to dress-up as a witch all the time. Ian's younger sister, Vikki, also remembers those childhood days of growing up together.

[19]"Our favourite thing was to dress-up as witches. We used to dress-up and play witch all the time. My

---

[17] Rowling, Newsweek, July 1, 2000.
[18] "Success Stuns Harry Potter Author," Associated Press, July 6, 2000.
[19] Ian Potter and Vikki Potter, quoted in Danielle Demetriou, "Harry Potter and the Source of Inspiration," Electronic Telegraph, July 1, 2000.

brother would dress-up as a wizard. Joanne was always reading witchcraft stories to us. We would make secret potions for her. She would always send us off to get twigs for the potions."

Besides the obvious astronomical book sales the marketing machine behind the Harry Potter craze exacerbates the effect of the madness. You can currently find anything from Harry Potter dress-up setts (including a cape and wand), Harry Potter Chess sets, Lego or a Harry Potter Levitating Challenge Game and many more.

What is more worrying is the double standard morels of the characters in the book. The seemly "good guys" kill, lie and steel.

[8] But the cowardly, unbelieving, abominable, murderers, sexually immoral, sorcerers, idolaters, and all liars shall have their part in the lake which burns with fire and brimstone, which is the second death."

Revelation 21:8

In the book "A Divine Revelation of Hell" the Lord appeared to Mary K. Baxter in a human form, in dreams, in visions and revelation each night for forty nights. During those visits He showed her the depths, degrees and levels of torment that lost souls undergo in hell. On one of the forty nights they reached the cells in Hell and Jesus said: "This cell block is seventeen miles high, starting from the bottom of hell. Here in these cells are many souls that were in witchcraft or the occult. Some were sorcerers, mediums, drug peddlers, idol worshipers or evil people with familiar spirits. These are the souls that worked the greatest abominations against God. The Lord took her to the third cell. His bright light illumined the inside of the cell. In the cell was an old woman sitting in a rocking chair, rocking back and forth, crying as though her heart was breaking? From the agonizing expression on her face she (Mary) could see the lady was suffering from some unseen torment, and although ashen in colour it appeared as if she had a body (which was unusual in hell). Suddenly right before Mary's eyes the woman began to change forms, first to an old, old man, then to a young woman and then to a middle-aged woman then back to the old lady. The changing seemed to take place only every couple of minutes. Jesus said that when this lady lived on earth she was a witch and a worshiper of Satan. She not only practised witchcraft but she also taught witchcraft to others. From the times as a child, her family practised the black arts and they loved the darkness rather than the Light. God called her to repentance but she only mocked the Lord and said that she enjoyed serving Satan. Mary K. Baxter A divine revelation of Hell

This will unfortunately be the fate of all witches if they do not repent and turn away for their witching ways and except Jesus as their Lord and saviour, as reminded to us below.

[6] "Jesus said to him, "I am the way, the truth, and the life. No one comes to the Father except through Me.

John 14:6

We should rise up against the witchcraft that has been practised in our families for generations. Witchcraft pollutes our land and it leads to violence, crises and dictatorship in governments.

God says that all witchcraft is bad. This includes all kinds of magic, any charms for protection or destruction; all of it. Do not be deceived. Christians do not need protection from Satan. God is the only protection that you will ever need. Satan is a defeated creation and not an all-powerful God. God's angel guards those who honour the Lord and rescues them from danger.

[7] "The angel of the Lord encamps all around those who fear Him, And delivers them."

Psalms 34:7

According to the word of God, Christians should never get involved with witchcraft of any kind, even if they believe it is for a good purposes or cause.

Chapter 4: Kabbalah

Written By: Nyasha Muzvidzwa

Kabbalah is a tradition of knowledge concerning God, the Universe and humanity. The word means "to receive" and we, who are created in the image of God, can receive this wisdom and knowledge which was given at the beginning of time (Kurt Browne).

In Berg's teachings, Kabbalah is a "spiritual technology" that "promises nothing less than a world wholly free of chaos, destruction, and death." The wisdom of Kabbalah, he says, is meant for all creeds - "Christians, Muslims, Hindus, Jews, and all humanity. After all, everyone is entitled to happiness and a fulfilling and productive life free of chaos." Many Jewish leaders have deplored Berg's version of Kabbalah as watered down Judaism, "snake oil for the soul." Others see it as a sinister cult. (Berg, What's a Kabbalah wedding).

According to the bible, God is the one who knows what our lives entail and offers a life of happiness, but does not promise a life free of chaos, destruction and death. The following verses will support this.

"For I know the plans I have for you, declares the Lord, plans to prosper you and not to harm you, plans to give you hope and a future".

Jeremiah 29:11

"Brothers, as an example of patience in the face of suffering, take the prophets who spoke in the name of the Lord. 11 As you know, we consider blessed those who have persevered. You have heard of Job's perseverance and have seen what the Lord finally brought about. The Lord is full of compassion and mercy".

James 5: 10-11

It had obvious theological applications, but much interest also focused on discovering the timeless underpinnings of all world religions and on healing the breach among Christians, Jews and Muslims (Nash, 2008).

Classical Judaic Kabbalah

The Kabbalah (Hebrew: hlbq, "received" or "tradition") has its roots in an oral tradition of Jewish mysticism, extending back to biblical times, perhaps even to Moses or Abraham. That tradition was viewed as divine revelation, interpreted and commented upon by generations of mystics and scholars. However, the Judaic tradition eventually became overlaid by Pythagorean, Platonic and Neoplatonic metaphysics (Nash, 2008).

Belief

Kabbalah teaches that the Torah is the revealed word of God; the universe itself, it says, was created out of Hebrew letters (Whats a Kabbalah wedding)
The English word mysticism has its origins in the word mystery. Jewish mysticism may be understood similarly as a process of opening oneself up to the mystery of the Torah. It is a means to cultivate a sense of the wondrous powers of Torah, thereby initiating one into the presence of God: "Open my eyes that I may see wonders out of your Torah" (Psalms

119:18). Nah?manides uses this verse to explain that the Torah is greater than is apparent from an ordinary empiricist perspective; it transcends the natural realm to reveal the divine powers (Alan Brill).

"Open my eyes that I may see wonderful things in your law".
Psalms 119:18

The verse above comes directly from the King James version and the last word "law" was replaced by "Torah" according to the belief of Kabbalists.

Not that the Kabbalists weren't iconoclastic. Recognizing how perilously close to heresy some of their ideas skirted, as well as the psychological risks attendant upon the intense religiosity they cultivated, until recently its teachers flatly refused to accept students who weren't married, male, deeply versed in Torah and Talmud, and committed to obeying Jewish law . "Even after one has achieved the spirituality of an angel, one must still abide by the commandments like a simple Jew," declared the Baal Shem Tov, the mystical 18th-century rabbi who founded modern Hasidism (Whats a Kabbalah wedding).

If Kabbalah is so Jewish, how did the Catholic-raised Madonna and the Baptist-raised Britney Spears, along with Demi and Ashton, find their way to it? As early as the 1400s, there were Christian adaptations of Kabbalah. Kabbalistic texts and teachings have also had a significant influence on alchemy, Rosicrucianism, and other occult movements, and, through them, on a vast array of contemporary beliefs that fall under the rubric "New Age." But that is not why Kabbalah has been cropping up on the gossip pages. The Kabbalah of Madonna, Demi, Barbra Streisand, Britney, Posh Spice and so many other celebrities is very much the creation of one man, Philip Berg (Whats a Kabbalah wedding).

The Kabbalah also provided a guide to spiritual development, inviting seekers to explore the nature of Divinity and its creation as well as the higher reaches of the human psyche. The original sefiroth, numbered 1-10, were known by the following archetypal names: Kether (rtk, "Crown"), Chokmah (hmkx, Wisdom"), Binah (hnyb, "Understanding"), Chesed (dsx, "Mercy"), Geburah (hrwbg, "Judgment"), Tifareth (tr)pt, "Beauty" or "Harmony"), Netzach (xcn, "Victory" or "Eternity"), Hod (dwh, "Splendor"), Yesod (dwsy, "Foundation"), and Malkuth (twklm, "Kingdom"). Gedulah (hlwdg, "Greatness") was used as an alternative name for Chesed, and Din (Nyd, "Severity") as an alternative to Geburah. Tabun (Nwbt, "Intelligence") was an alternative to Binah (Nash, 2008). The Sefer Yetzirah discussed 32 paths, or netivoth (singular: nativ, bytn), to God. Ten of those "paths" corresponded to the sefiroth, while the remaining 22, each identified by a letter in the Hebrew alphabet, became identified with the relationships among them. The netivoth offered seekers distinctive spiritual challenges and opportunities (Nash, 2008).

When it started

The birth of that major feature of the western esoteric tradition was made possible by the confluence of traditions in the High Middle Ages and Renaissance when Jewish mystical texts and insights became available to Christian scholars. The Christian

Kabbalah first appeared in Florence in the early 15th century and spread to Germany and the rest of Europe. (Nash, 2008).

The Christian Kabbalah was part of a more general investigation of occult traditions which included Hermeticism—a combination of astrology, alchemy and magic. Unfortunately, from the standpoint of the tradition's purity, Hermeticism steered the Christian Kabbalah away from its intellectual and mystical roots toward a preoccupation with magic. Not surprisingly, ecclesiastical authorities became increasingly suspicious, although hostility was also motivated by prevailing anti-Semitism. In any event, the Christian Kabbalah—like its Judaic antecedent—never became a mass movement; it remained the pursuit of a small elite of scholars, aristocrats and churchmen (Nash, 2008).

The modern Judaic Kabbalah owes a great deal to the work of a community of 16th-century Jewish scholars who settled in Safed (Tzafed), Galilee, traditional burial site of the second century rabbi Shimon bar Yochai, mentioned in the Zohar. (Nash, 2008). Preeminent among the Safed scholars were Moses ben Jacob Cordovero (1522–1570) and Isaac ben Solomon Luria (1534–1572). The former was a Spanish émigré, one of tens of thousands of Jews expelled from Spain in 1492, while the latter was born in Palestine of German parents. Cordovero and Luria proposed alternative versions of the Tree of Life, providing a new understanding of geometric relationships among the sefiroth. Their work drew attention to the rich symbolism of polarities which is so much a feature of modern Kabbalistic study(Nash, 2008).

The Safed school also promoted belief in a primeval cosmic catastrophe in which the sefiroth were shattered by influx of the divine force. That catastrophe is referred to as the "breaking of the vessels."11 God had to repair the sefiroth in order for the universe to come into permanent manifestation; but the damage had longer-lasting implications. "Shards" of the broken vessels, each of which contained a divine spark, were scattered throughout the world, and devout Jews are responsible for gathering the shards to re-establish divine order (Nash, 2008).

Bridge to Christian Europe

The Kabbalah came to the attention of western Christian scholars through several channels. Important Kabbalistic schools had been established in Moorish Spain and in Provence in the south of France. The Provençal scholar and mystic Isaac the Blind (c.1160–1235) compiled and edited the Bahir and the Sefer Yetzirah. Moses de Leon (1250–1305), who lived in Castile, compiled the Zohar and added extensive commentary. The newly available books, written in Hebrew or Aramaic, 13 soon became available to Christian scholars (Nash, 2008).

Traditions

The Spiritual Tradition of Africa goes back to that time of creation. It recognises one God. Itongo for the Zulus, Olodumare for the Yoruba, Nyame for the Akan of Ghana and many other names. This being brought forth existence and there are many creation stories which talk of a time when life was pleasant and good, but the bad choices of humans brought suffering and toil (Kurt Browne).

Then Jesus said to his disciples, "If anyone would come after me, he must deny himself and take up his cross and follow me".
Matthew 16:24

This verse clearly states that there is only one God and in order to follow him, you have to die to self and follow him wholeheartedly. There is no other God to follow unlike the many mentioned gods according to the spiritual tradition of Africa.

An example to support this was the mentioned Bini story from Nigeria which tells of the sky being close to the earth in the beginning and nourishing all beings, but because of human greed and selfishness the sky rose up high above the earth beyond the reach of mankind (Kurt, Browne).

"In the beginning God created the heavens and earth".
Genesis 1:1

God created heavens and earth, but it does not talk about the sky being close to earth or the sky rising above the earth beyond the reach of mankind according to the writer Kurt Browne.

The Kabbalistic tradition tells us that when Adam and Eve were expelled from the Garden of Eden, the Holy One sent the Archangel Razile to give them a Book of Secrets to enable them to regain Paradise. This is the

Book that is ever present and in it are the answers to the ancient questions, "Who am I?", "Why am I here?" and "What is life about?" (Kurt Browne). They believe that the constant yearning to know all these answers is what enable people to find meaning and purpose in life through experiences on earth (Kurt Browne).

"So the Lord God banished him from the Garden of Eden to work the ground from which he had been taken. [24] After he drove the man out, he placed on the east side of the Garden of Eden cherubim and a flaming sword flashing back and forth to guard the way to the tree of life".

Genesis 3:23-24

Nothing is mentioned in the verses following their departure from the garden about an Archangel Razile giving Adam and Eve a book of secrets in order for them to regain paradise.

Kabbalah is believed to have at its core, the university and the Oneness of God, which is able to be adopted into any spiritual tradition in which God is one. It is one of many mystical traditions that give us a key to understanding out root and heritage. It teaches about Universal Laws and Principles and shows that all humanity is from the One source (Kurt Browne).
It is believed that we can use the Kabbalistic model to reconnect with our ancestral root to give us realisation that in the wisdom of our past lies the hope for our future. For in our past is Truth, the highest ideal. The key is to take responsibility for ourselves and destiny (Kurt Browne).

Rituals

Principle of Kabbalistic teaching

Below, I am going to examine four componets of African Spiritual Traditions using Kabbalistic insights and knowledge.

The Tree of life is a map of the Universe and in it are all the laws and principles within existence. It starts with God and ends with God. I AM THAT I AM. The Mende call this Supreme Being Ngewo-Ngewo, the Yoruba: Oludumare, the Creator and Sustainer, and the Nuer of Sudan call him Kwoth. The Akan of Ghana know God as Nana Nyame, the Only Great One, who is sometimes regarded as a female and sometimes as a male (Kurt Browne).

In the world of Spirit there are parts of God which deal with the governing of the universe in general, and the affairs of humanity on earth, in particular. There are forces that build up, others that break down, and those in equilibrium. In African Traditions these forces are called Orishas, Divinities, Deities or Spirits (Kurt Browne).

To the Kabbalistic they are Archangels whose job is to work in the world of Creation or Heaven, under the will and direction of the Holy One. Their work is transpersonal and cosmic (Kurt Browne).

In order to understand a cosmic principle, consider the principle of healing throughout all of creation, both seen and unseen, from the healing of a star, planet or solar system to the healing of a cell. Mother Earth needs healing and so do nations and communities. A cut finger heals, as does a wound on an animal or tree. That is the cosmic principle that comes through the powerful rituals of the Dagara people of Ghana, the cote D'Ivoir and Burkina Faso, indeed, all African Spiritual Traditions (Kurt Browne).

It is believed that God is the only one that has the power to heal anyone no matter what they are going through.

News about him spread all over Syria, and people brought to him all who were ill with various diseases, those suffering severe pain, the demon-possessed, those having seizures, and the paralyzed, and he healed them.

Matthew 4: 24

The souls of humans live on after death and can reincarnate back into humanity. The world of formation is where most of us live for much of the time. It is the realm of psychology (psyche – soul in Greek), where our thoughts, feelings and deep emotions shape our lives. In our souls we have free will and through our choices we reap what we sow. At his level, we develop a personality based on out past incarnation, our upbringing, tribe and culture. Our thoughts, feelings and actions are coloured by our parents, tribal customs and society. As we become adults "the choices we make dictate the life we lead" so our responsibility in the first instance is to ourselves, and then to the family and society as we grow and refine the soul through experiences, crisis and pleasures of everyday life (Kurt Browne).

The psychological world is the realm of the newly dead and those waiting to be reborn. It is the place of the Ancestors, those who look after us and know and share the human experience. The more evolved Ancestors become the companions of the light and they are there to guide the destiny of a people or nation. It is our interaction with them that brings about harmonious living for a family, people or nation (Kurt Browne).

In the physical world there are songs, dances and rituals concerning life experiences of birth, circumcision, initiation, marriage and death. These ceremonies of initiation mark the cycles and rhythms of life. They demonstrate the human condition on earth as we evolve and grow in consciousness. (Kurt Browne).

Each time we are born our souls are clothed with a physical body as a vehicle in which to live and fully experience this world. In our bodies we can see, feel, touch, taste, smell and hear the world around us. Those who are awake recognise the uniques positions of human beings who are able to be conscious of being conscious. This, with the gift of free will, enables us to ascend to the highest heaven or descend to the lowest hell. Here in physical existence, the four worlds are present in the NOW. It is the place where God can hold God in the mirror of existence (Kurt Browne).

"And if the spirit of him who raised Jesus from the dead is living in you, he who raised Christ from the dead will also give life to your mortal bodies through his Spirit, who lives in you".
Romans 8:11

Holidays

Of all the holidays, Hanukah and Purim are considered special. There are a number of reasons for this. First, they are not written in the Torah. Second, it is said that when all corrections have been made, all the holidays will be cancelled except those two. Third, the two holidays are directly connected to the rebuilding of the temple.

Purim

The Sages of Kabbalah teach that during the holiday of Purim you can come closer to real joy by overcoming a very powerful form of negativity - doubt. On Purim, a unique spiritual energy is available, an energy that has the specific ability to eliminate the seed of doubt from your consciousness. You can tap into this energy through the tools of Kabbalah, masquerade, and getting out of your normal thought patterns.

How do you get out of your normal thought patterns? Believe it or not, through celebrating, enjoying cocktails and dancing. The spirit of revelry is used as a spiritual tool on this one night of the year to help you break through the rational thinking which limits you.

The masks worn on Purim remove the psychological masks you normally wear, taking you to the level where you can see how your fears and doubts stop you from fully realizing how amazing you really are. Purim is regarded as a magnificent night of revelry (K holidays, 2014).

Pesach

According to Kabbalah, a tremendously powerful technology is encoded and concealed inside the celebration of Pesach. Unlocking the code unlocks your limited thoughts and opens your mind to the infinite possibilities life serves you each day.

In there intensive 4 week course you will discover the specifics of the Pesach methodology, tools and technology. You will uncover the ancient roots and learn how it can give you the courage to dream big. Whether you are thinking of attending your first Pesach with The Kabbalah Centre or you have been coming for years, you will gain an incredible amount of insight into the tools and technology behind Pesach by attending this course (K holidays, 2014).

Lag Ba'Omer

Although the Omer is a time of diminished Light, there is one day during this period that is supremely powerful. The thirty-third day of the Omer is one of the most powerful and important days of the year, yet it remains the least known of all the connections made available to us annually.

The thirty-third day of the Omer is the day when Kabbalist Rav Shimon Bar Yochai left this physical reality. Rav Shimon Bar Yochai, one of the greatest souls to ever walk this earth, is the author of the Zohar. Kabbalah teaches that the day of his death is important because when people leave this world, on that day all the spiritual energy and Light that they revealed throughout the course of their lives is released into the comos (K holidays, 2014).

Shavuot

Raising the immortality rate. Stay up with us as we soar through the night, ascending to the highest of peaks - immortality. Through our joy and unity – and the power of our kabbalistic connections – we will transmit this Light out into the world at large, raising the immortality rate for all humanity (K holidays, 2014).

Tu B'Av

Tu B'Av, referred to as the Day of Love by the kabbalists, begins one of the highest levels of connection of any time of the year.

What's so great about a holiday most of the world has never celebrated?

Kabbalah gives an all access pass to the secrets of the universal time-table, a cosmic Cliff-Notes informing them of the best time to do, or not to do, certain actions. On Tu B'Av, all masculine and feminine forces in the universe, from the celestial bodies to the tiniest of insects, unite in harmony.

Every creation in the world experiences total completeness. The earth and the cosmos are in perfect balance. Soul mates have the opportunity to reunite, reconnect and reinforce their relationships. And for this reason, it is a day of love.

Happy hearts. Open lines of communication. Being understood. Surrounded by people who bring out the best – and help the members with our worst. Isn't this what we're all after? (K holidays, 2014).

The 9th of Av

Approximately 2500 years ago, the Babylonians destroyed the Holy Temple in Jerusalem. The date of the destruction was the ninth day of the Hebrew month Av.

Two thousand years ago, the Romans destroyed the second Temple in Jerusalem. The entire city was sacked, the slaughter reportedly so widespread that the cobblestone streets were knee-deep in blood. The date of the destruction and massacre was the 9th of Av. The Kabbalists tells us that the 9th of Av is the one day of the year when the force called Satan (our Adversary) rules for the entire twenty-four-hour period.

Remember that according to this religion the force called Satan is not a demon or a devil but a negative force of consciousness whose sole nature is receiving, chaos, selfishness and space. This adversarial entity, the source of human ego, was created to test and challenge humankind so that our transformation from selfish to selfless would be difficult and challenging, thus ensuring that we truly earn our place in paradise . (K holidays, 2014).

Rosh Hashanah

Kabbalists teach that Rosh Hashanah is the time during which your life for the following year is determined. This means that instead of living life according to the fickle finger of fate, you can control how your life unfolds.
The Zohar explains that every year on Rosh Hashanah, your actions of the past year are

examined, and the effects of your actions from the previous year come back to you.
If during the entire year your deeds were positive, the effects will be positive. But if you're like the rest of us, you have committed (even inadvertently) unfavorable actions, and it is possible that you will experience some degree of chaos (K holidays, 2014).

Only a kabbalistic Rosh Hashanah can free you from this potential darkness and wipe your slate clean. This means you can begin the New Year refreshed and lighter and better equipped to face your new challenges head on, without being bogged down by last year's residue (K holidays, 2014).

Yom Kippur

Yom Kippur is not a day of fasting, mourning or atoning. Rather, it is a day of feasting. We feast on five gigantic meals during this powerful day of connection. However, the meals that we consume are of a spiritual nature. We receive our nourishment from the highest levels of the spiritual atmosphere, the realm of Binah. This nourishment gives us the sustenance we need for the manifestation of our fulfilment, health, wealth, and family for the next twelve months (K holidays, 2014).

Sukkot

This seven-day holiday follows Yom Kippur. Each of the seven days connects to one of the seven dimensions (Sefirot) that directly influence our reality. During the connection of Sukkot, we receive what Kabbalists call surrounding Light and Inner Light for the entire year to come. Surrounding Light helps us from the outside to expand our spiritual potential for the coming year. Inner Light protects our innate Light from inside, while also pushing us to expand our vessel so that we can hold more surrounding Light (K holidays, 2014).

Hashanna Rabba

All night shadow checking
They check their shadows under the moon to make sure our New Year will be a good one. Strange? Kabbalah teaches the blueprint of our entire year can be read in our shadow cast by the moon on this special night. After weeks of preparing our new vessel, we've got this last chance to check for any problems that might arise.

We can still fix it, but only on this night. The seal for the New Year is made here (K holidays, 2014).

Chanukah

Kabbalah clearly offers connections and consciousness that can help you create miracles. But there's only way to tap this energy - DESIRE. When you have a heightened sense of awareness of the world around you, you can get a glimpse of what's really going on. Chanukah is a cosmic event that brings the cycles of your life into harmony. It's an awesome power that rekindles your passion for life, making your connection to self and others so much stronger.

The flame of a single candle seems insignificant in daylight. But in a dark room it can illuminate the entire cosmos (K holidays, 2014).

Wedding

The Cosmic Roots of Marriage

When a man and woman unite in marriage, their personal union draws its power from the cosmic marriage that underlies the whole of existence -- the bonding of the divine masculine and feminine energies emerging from the Creator's Infinite Light to generate existence, a world, and life (Kabbalah of marriage).

Indeed, the entire Seder Hishtalshelut--the kabbalistic blueprint of the spiritual infrastructure of creation--is modeled on a male-female dynamic: masculine "lights" (orot) unite with feminine "vessels" (keilim), masculine "wisdom" (chochmah) unites with feminine "understanding" (binah), male "holiness" (kedushah) unites with female "immanence" (shechinah), and so on. On each level, masculine and feminine energies unite to "give birth" to the next link in the chain of spiritual "worlds" that channel the flow of divine vitality into our world (Kabbalah of marriage).

The Kabbalists tell us it is in the union of a man and a woman in body and in spirit. When that union is made under the conditions it deserves, with the right preparations and mindful focus, its waves ripple outward through substance of reality. No facet of the cosmos is left untouched, unaltered. Every voice of the Creation resonates in unison as an orchestra plays back the soloist's melody. And so the lives of that man and woman, their children and their children's children are filled with the music of the heavens down on earth (Kabbalah of marriage).

Nothing is more sacred than this union, the very fount of life itself. And nothing is more crucial to our mission in this world. All of life, all of being, depends on the harmony of male and female, a harmony placed in our hands and hearts. That it is why, for most of us, it presents the greatest challenges we ever face (Kabbalah of marriage).

So if you want to know what a Kabbalah wedding would look like, you need search no further than the Kabbalah Centre, whose invention it is. Their website explains the sort of wedding Demi and Ashton were planning: "While many of the customs seem to be Jewish," it reads , "The kabbalistic wedding ceremony is full of understanding, wisdom, and connections that essentially sew the two soul-halves together, creating one new whole soul. There are seven blessings recited in this process, reading from the Zohar, from Psalms, and other key factors." (What's a Kabbalah wedding).

In other words, it would look pretty much like a traditional Jewish wedding, with some additional readings from the Zohar, the central, 13th century Kabbalistic text, and some mystical interpretations. The seven blessings mentioned on the website are direct from a traditional Jewish wedding (they're called the sheva brachot and are for wine, Creation, the Creation of humanity, human reproduction, the future of Zion, the happiness of the bride and groom, and the reign of love and peace in a restored Jerusalem) (What's a Kabbalah wedding).

Presumably, as she'd do in a traditional Jewish wedding ceremony, Demi will walk in a circle around Ashton (foiling any demons who might wish to spoil their union); perhaps a ketubah (a Jewish wedding contract) would be read, answering the question of whether the two stars signed pre-nups. Ashton would stamp on a wine glass (Daniel Matt, The Essential Kabbalah).

Ceremonies

If there is no such thing as a traditional Kabbalah wedding, Kabbalah is downright lusty on the subject of marital relations. Indeed, the Zohar and other major Kabbalistic texts are filled with blush-inducing erotic metaphors. At the very heart of the Kabbalah are the Sefirot, the ten divine emanations by which God enters the world. As sacred as they are, the Sefirot are described in the most carnal of terms. Binah, or divine understanding, is the womb; she receives seed from Hokhmah, divine wisdom, and gives birth to the seven lower Sefirot. The Shekhinah, the immanent spirit of God, is feminine in the Kabbalah's depictions; she is the bride of Tif'eret, the glory of God, "the Holy One, blessed be He."(Daniel Matt, The Essential Kabbalah). When human beings perform mitzvot (fulfill divine commandments), the Shekhinah is aroused with desire; she is penetrated by Yesod, the phallus or conduit through which the forces of divine creation are released into the physical world. Human lovemaking mirrors this divine union, uniting the corporeal and the spiritual realms. "When sexual union is for the sake of heaven, there is nothing as holy or pure," declares the Iggeret ha-Qodesh, an anonymous 13th century manuscript. "The union of man and woman, when it is right, is the secret of civilization." (Daniel Matt, The Essential Kabbalah).

Chapter 5: Zion Christian Church (ZCC)

Written By: Matthew Dean

Before You Start Reading: *This bears **no** reference to a church in America of the same name (http://www.zionchristian.org).*

South Africa is known to be a predominantly Christian country; about 70% of the population is classified as Christian. But, as with many countries, the term is used broadly. This Chapter is about one of the largest denominations in South Africa; we will show you the problems with it.

What is the ZCC?

This is about the Zion Christian Church in Southern Africa (hereafter referred to as ZCC as they are known). It was started in 1910 by Engenas Lekganyane. He was a former member of the Free Church of Scotland, Apostolic Faith Mission and Zion Apostolic Church. He allegedly had a vision from God in 1910 and founded the ZCC. It was initially based in Thabakgone in the Limpopo Province and was officially registered as a church in 1942. Today its headquarters are at Zion City in Moria, Limpopo Province.

Every Easter, ZCC members flock in their thousands to Moria on a pilgrimage. Its current leaders are Barnabas Lekganyane and Saint Engenas Lekganyane, the grandsons of its founder.

The ZCC has flourished on the idea of celebrating

traditional African culture and was affected by the exclusion of Black people from the main churches during Apartheid. You see, back in those days there was a lot of racial segregation and some mainstream churches would actually have churches for White people and churches for Black people (one notable rebel was Beyers Naudé, a Dutch Reformed minister who left the Broederbond and ministered in Soweto).

Although its members do not express any hatred towards White people, its breakaway from the mainstream was mainly because they wanted to escape colonialism, slavery and the idea of "White Christianity". But also, Engenas Lekganyane clashed with "White" Christian church leaders over his actions.

He practiced and welcomed polygamy, which means that a man can have many wives. The ZCC also uses external symbols, especially staffs in worship and wearing robes.

But the core foundations come from a Pentecostal church in America; the *Christian Catholic Church* (now called [20]*Christ Community Church*) founded by John Alexander Dowie, which is based in Zion, Illinois. Not a very "kosher" church! Also it was influenced by the Pentecostal missionary John G Lake, who started working in Johannesburg in 1908. Worth noting is that many Western Pentecostal branches do not include the ZCC as being Pentecostal.

---

[20] http://www.ccczion.org

John Alexander Dowie.

Who is in the ZCC?

In Southern Africa, it's not hard to identify a ZCC member Followers proudly wear a broche on their chests; a green ribbon with a metal star, with ZCC inscribed on it. Male members will also wear a "captain" style hat with the ZCC star on it. I don't think it is compulsory – I know ZCC members who don't wear them – but it is *very* common to do so. And virtually always, the followers are Black Africans (it has nothing to do with race, but that's just what one observes. I have been told of members from other groups, though I've never observed one).

A ZCC star. Either on a "captain's hat" or on a broche (seen her).

So what's wrong with a star?

Now, personally I don't see the need for symbols – even the crucifix. No Christian should engage in using images. But the use of the star is a concern. You see, the five-pointed star has almost always been associated with evil. Today, the star is used in the flag of *every* Communist country's flag as a [21]symbol for Communism. In case you didn't know, Communism was founded by a Satanist, Karl Marx, and was devised by him to *deliberately* be anti-Christian.

Separately, the star is also used as a symbol in Freemasonry, Satanism, Paganism and Witchcraft.

A Christian brother at [22] Christ Movement has done a video to show you that the ZCC star comes from Satanism; as the Pentagram of Baphomet is an upside-down star. But you should also know that the "not upside-down" star is *also* a

---

[21] http://en.wikipedia.org/wiki/Red_star#Symbol_of_communism
[22] http://www.youtube.com/user/Christmovement1303

holy symbol in Paganism and witchcraft! See the similarities.

ZCC star - Pagan Pentagram - Satanic Pentagram. See the similarities?

Why do people join the ZCC?

The main reason for the ZCC having many followers is that it combines Christianity with traditional beliefs. This is clearly a bad thing! One of the core traditional practices is the prayer to and worship of ancestors.

²⁷ Then he said, I pray thee therefore, father, that thou wouldest send him to my father's house:
²⁸ For I have five brethren; that he may testify unto them, lest they also come into this place of torment.
²⁹ Abraham saith unto him, They have Moses and the prophets; let them hear them.
³⁰ And he said, Nay, father Abraham: but if one went unto them from the dead, they will repent.
³¹ And he said unto him, If they hear not Moses and the prophets, neither will they be persuaded, though one rose from the dead.

Luke 16:27-31

²⁷ And as it is appointed unto men once to die, but after this the judgment:

Hebrews 9:27

In other words, when you die, you will either be in Heaven or Hell; so then how can there be a spirit floating around on earth?

I have heard it said by someone who combines Christianity with ancestral beliefs; that to pray to God, they must go through Jesus – and to pray to Jesus, they must go through the ancestors. Besides the painfully obvious:

⁶ Jesus saith unto him, I am the way, the truth, and the life: no man cometh unto the Father, but by me.
⁷ If ye had known me, ye should have known my Father also: and from henceforth ye know him, and have seen him.

John 14:6-7

Throughout the Old Testament, sorcerers often claimed to make contact with the dead and this is

sorcery! Sorcery is another factor in traditional beliefs; they believe in witchcraft and the ZCC offers them protection from evil, sorcery, superstitions and sickness.

What does the Bible say about sorcery, or about people trying to communicate with dead people?

[10] There shall not be found among you any one that maketh his son or his daughter to pass through the fire, or that useth divination, or an observer of times, or an enchanter, or a witch. [11] Or a charmer, or a consulter with familiar spirits, or a wizard, or a necromancer.
[12] For all that do these things are an abomination unto the LORD: and because of these abominations the LORD thy God doth drive them out from before thee.
Deuteronomy 18:10-12

[31] Regard not them that have familiar spirits, neither seek after wizards, to be defiled by them: I am the LORD your God.
Leviticus 19:31

I have often had ZCC members write to me, angry for writing this article. Most will simply say I'm bad, but some will seek to defend the ZCC. The one thing that they always fail to do is read the above Scriptures. One member even told me that they are proud to engage in witchcraft as it makes them feel proudly African! I don't care at all about national pride, tribal pride, or indeed any pride. One can debate from now till the end of time. But there is witchcraft in the ZCC and the Word of God calls that an abomination. Period!

ZCC Baptism

Baptism is very important in the ZCC; but members may *only* be baptised in a river; not just any water. Baptisms are also conducted in the name of Lekganyane! (this was part of an ex-ZCC testimony, but I have heard it said that baptisms are done in the name of the Father, Son and Holy Ghost - well I sure hope so!).

[19] Go ye therefore, and teach all nations, baptizing them in the name of the Father, and of the Son, and of the Holy Ghost:

Matthew 28:19

(In other words, do not baptise in the name of Lekganyane! Can it be any more clear?)

ZCC Calls Their Bishop Christ!

The ZCC believes their leader, Lekganyane, is Jesus Christ!

[24] For there shall arise false Christs, and false prophets, and shall shew great signs and wonders; insomuch that, if it were possible, they shall deceive the very elect.

Matthew 24:24

If you watch this [23]video, you will see a ZCC congregation sing in mantra that "Jealous Down Ramarumo" (that is, Bishop Ramarumo Lekganyane) is Christ.

[24]This is an excerpt from the website of the South African Tourism board, writing to promote the ZCC.

---

[23] http://www.youtube.com/watch?v=q-1GroRtm4g
[24] http://www.golimpopo.com/fact-details_zion-city-moria_8.html

Remember, this is a government organisation writing this! (Their words are in *italic*)

The belief that the religious and administrative leader of the church (or bishop) **is a mediator between the congregation and God; that, like Christ, he can perform supernatural acts.** *The use of different mechanisms for faith-healing.*

These include the laying-on of hands; the use of holy water; drinking of blessed tea and coffee; bloodletting with needles (now obsolete); the wearing of blessed cords or cloth and the burning of blessed papers called mogau and faith-healing.

I can only answer this claim with Scripture:

[5] For there is one God, and one mediator between God and men, the man Christ Jesus;

1 Timothy 2:5

[6] Jesus saith unto him, I am the way, the truth, and the life: no man cometh unto the Father, but by me.

John 14:6

And if this is not clear enough, it is believed that Lekganyane sees every believer – only God has that power! A former member of the ZCC said that Lekganyane would show him people whom he should go and interact with by means of dreams and visions; he would get confirmation from him that he was sent by other prophets of Lekganyane. Members are also told that Lekganyane can control their minds! There are even sacrifices offered to him! I have been advised by former members that the element of mind control is very high and real in the ZCC.

Lekganyane. NOT CHRIST. Pictured left of Jewish Rabbi Moshe.

Faith Healing

Pentecostal churches are big into faith healing. The Pastor will put his hand over you and either pray for healing, or cast out a demon. The ZCC has taken this and turned it into a seriously Pagan practice; "healing" by means of intercession with ancestral spirits (sorcery!) and "sacred tools" such as "holy sticks" (now they are heading for idolatry!). They also believe that they can heal both humans and the environment, even simultaneously.

What are their "sacred tools"?

ZCC Bishops and "Prophets" each have a staff. They are used to provide protection from evil, because they have been prayed over. They use them with faith healing. They also use flags which have been prayed over, again for protection against evil spirits; but also as a symbol of the Holy Spirit (symbol? Idolatry!) and to be placed at the houses of new members as motivation.

Just in case you need reminding that idolatry is seriously anti-Christian – just a few of the many Bible verses condemning it:

[17] And ye have seen their abominations, and their idols, wood and stone, silver and gold, which were among them:
Deuteronomy 29:17

[12] For they served idols, whereof the LORD had said unto them, Ye shall not do this thing.
2 Kings 17:12

[4] Thou shalt not make unto thee any graven image, or any likeness of any thing that is in heaven above, or that is in the earth beneath, or that is in the water under the earth.
Exodus 20:4

Holy Water?

Yes, they have so-called Holy Water. They call it "Blessed Water". This is just plain sick - literally. As a part of faith healing, members are asked to drink this water. And then they must force themselves to vomit it out! They consider this to be a way of expelling their sickness from their bodies, be it physical or spiritual sickness. The water is seen to be purification from evil, sin, sickness and ritual pollution; this stems from traditional beliefs.

Holy Tea? Holy Products?

Apparently the ZCC even has holy tea. The name varies by language; in seSotho it is "Tea ya bophelo" (tea of life). In Zulu it is "Ndhayela". It is known as "tea without sugar". Again, it gets drunk and, by some, vomited out. Actually, the ZCC has an entire range of products; labelled with a picture of Lekganyane. Tea, coffee, body lotion, perfume, and nobody know where or how they are made. Nor are ZCC members allowed to ask. Just shut up and buy them! I have received two sources of information, from clergy that was formerly in the ZCC, that they are made from - among other things - flesh from dead bodies! (note: this is a claim)

Holy Ash?

The ZCC considers ash to be clean and pure, and after it is prayed over, becomes an agent for healing and protecting against evil spirits. Ash is mixed with water, then it will be drunk, used in a bath or put on door posts and window frames. It is also put in the "Holy Tea". Other substances used for healing are lime, blue stone, Epsom salts, milk and blue soap.

Symbolism

There are many symbols that are important within the ZCC. They have a Holy Mountain, where one feels closer to heaven. Another symbol is water, a symbol of cleansing and purification. They also have trees, stones, and candles. They also have a 'Holy City' (an earthly Zion) which would be Moria.

ZCC clergy often wear robes that are white (purity), blue (water), or green (vegetation); all of these symbolise group identity and the wilderness of human life. Other robe colours are khaki (dust) and red (blood of the Lamb). Star and moon-shaped ribbons or patches can sometimes be found on the back of the robes. Crosses are often worn or carried by members. ZCC members sometimes carry a bunch of sticks tied together by wool. Many men (but not all) do not shave their facial hair, so that they look more like Biblical prophets.

Gospel of What?

There are mixed ideas about what the Bible tells us in the ZCC. They do hold it in very high regard. But a ZCC member, for example, said that the Bible was God's message and a map of our lives. Everything about us was revealed in the Bible. The purpose of the Bible was to teach about God and what God was saying today. Another ZCC member said that the Bible was a book that gave us 'God's words'. Yet another commented that the Bible was a guide of how to live. One member stated that the Bible strengthened and helped a person encountering problems. Another Zionist said that the purpose of the Bible was to teach people the word of God, and to reveal the good and the bad things in life so that people could choose for themselves how to live – boy does this sound familiar:

[5] For God doth know that in the day ye eat thereof, then your eyes shall be opened, and ye shall be as gods, knowing good and evil.

Genesis 3:5

ZCC members are taught how to give to the church. This comes down to forced tithing. The golden rule of thumb is: if a church pressurizes or forces you to give them money, run away!

Ruled By Fear

ZCC members are bound by fear. They are led to believe that if they leave the ZCC, they will become mentally disturbed. They are told that Lekganyane has the power to control their minds because they are baptised in his name. Or, if they do something, they are told that if they tell other people, their legs will be cut off. So when a ZCC member claims to know nothing, oh they do; but they are bound by fear to keep quiet!

Below is some stunning testimonies. I also received messages from other followers and ex-followers alike. The pattern is the same - fear of physical intimidation or curses if and when they leave the church. To those I say:

[2] As the bird by wandering, as the swallow by flying, so the curse causeless shall not come.

Proverbs 26:2

Secrets and Ranks

Almost like the Freemasons, there are different levels within the ZCC. One new member was murdered because he got exposed to the secrets of the ZCC by accident!

The "captain" rank is the one where you get exposed to human flesh sacrifices to Lekganyane, which are given in his sanctuary at Mount Moria. It is claimed that those who are in the know will use secret codes.

When referring to "seeds" they are referring to human body part sacrifices. This new ZCC member, who was accidentally in the presence of captains, didn't know this, so collected real seeds as "crops". He entered the private room with a group of captains and they opened their bags of "seeds" to offer sacrifices to Legkanyane. The new member's bag had normal seeds in it. When they made him open his bag, they immediately knew he wasn't a captain, and could possibly expose their secrets because he didn't follow the procedure to reach their level; so they killed him!

The sacrifice of human flesh may seem like hogwash. But it does happen in worldwide. In Aprica it is referred to as "muti". Obviously it is illegal, and people of traditional beliefs are supposed to use herbs instead; at worst animal body parts. But those who truly believe in it want "the real thing" which is *human* body parts. For example, for someone to have a high-powered job and lots of money, they will bury a hand under their house's entrance "for good luck". They would say in their defense that the bodies were already dead; but often people have been murdered for their body parts. It is a real problem in Africa!

In Closing

Here we have yet another example of why you cannot just assume that an organisation which claims Christianity is automatically Christian. While the ZCC claims Christianity, it is anything but! Its founder and leader is worshipped as a god and mediator, sometimes with dire consequences. Its members are subjected to sick rituals and "medicines" in a bid to "heal" them. It has levels of knowledge within the ZCC which are similar to the Freemasons. It is rife with idolatry, sorcery and witchcraft. It claims to worship God and His only begotten Son, Jesus Christ, and to use the Bible – yet its level of paganism, in the form of "traditional beliefs" would even make regular pagans look decent.

Testimony of Mercy

This is the written testimony of a woman, whom I shall call Mercy (she wishes for her full name and details to be concealed), which I received on 24 June 2012.

I am so very tired, having spent almost the whole day and night on the ZCC issue. I remembered of many other events that took place while I was still a ZCC member last night but have since forgotten. I will however write them down and send them to you at a later stage. I also could not edit, please do so. Please remove my surname on the testimony but my name: Mercy.

I challenge the ZCC bishops to stop teaching every member of their church to be prophets. Who do they prophesy to if they are all prophets? When I asked my father after leaving ZCC what I can do to be a prophet, he said the spirit will come to me - I do not have to be taught. To prove this right, I searched for how some of the biblical great got their power, Moses - Exodus 3:1, Jesus – (?) 2:39-40, 46-52, David – 1 Samuel 16:13, Elisha - 2 Kings 2:9, Solomon - 1 Kings 3: 5 and Samson (?). They were not taught like the ZCC members.

Since we are not all ZCC members, they must forbid their prophets to keep watching us and interceding our spirits. When I pray, they often interrupt me spiritually telling to say something about Lekganyane.

The star bishop apparently tells his congregation that all SA citizens will become ZCC members. This to me will be the end of the world.

I agree 100% with the message in this article. Although my father is a pastor in another church, I had a vision that appeared so strongly that it shook me. In the vision I saw someone say 'you have to be a ZCC member'. You have no choice.' I have never been so scared in my life even though I had a million visions before, though not about ZCC.

I eventually joined the church from 2005 to 2008. I will regret this for the rest of my life. I was taught to become a prophet, which they do for all their 3mllion plus members. They could not succeed making a prophet. They started accusing me a sinner and cursing me. They prophesised my parents, siblings, friends, colleagues etc. are bewitching me. I was eventually left alone and avoided my family members, not taking their calls and wanting them in my car because I was told they want to kill me. One prophet was at the Alex branch who said my mother was bewitching me. They have a policy that a women should not touch a men's khaki uniform. However, they prophesised in the Moria Star church that I must dress my then 5 year old son with this khaki uniform. This is despite me asking why they give me such a message when it's against their policy. The answer was that 'the ZCC ancestors and mine have agreed I should do so'. I once received a message from one of their prophet which I decided not to execute and I was punished for that and labelled "high headed, stubborn, think I know better cause I'm educated", and all that. Knowing this, I decided to buy the khaki the same weekend. What happened there after was sad - I had a vision that a ZCC spirit is now with all my father's family. Within 3 months I lost an Audi A4 and I still owed R140 000. I left my job for 2 weeks because one of the prophets was a student in 2007 at the university where I work, she sent a strong message while I was still at work. Since I didn't have any work left for the day, I left for home and never came back for 2 weeks, just hating my work that I loved so much. My students supported me since I had never missed my lecturers with them, but my colleagues were made to hate me so much that I had to leave the university for another one. My brother lost his car and him, and his wife, my parents and a small child almost died when I had a vision when the ZCC bishop said he will fight for me against my family who want to kill me. They almost died even though they lost a car that insurance refused to pay for. As we speak they interfere with my spirit such that anyone of their so called prophets can talk to me spiritually with no other person physically present hearing. They stress me out since they have evil spirit in me. At the university where I work, I have some ZCC students in my class. When I'm teaching, they distract me with their evil spirit saying m bad lecturer, don't know what m saying etc. It happened such that I had to keep on asking other students to pray for me and themselves against the spirit since it affected them too. Their prophets are forever following me and saying things spiritually that hurt and disturbs me. They make me forget what I want to say and also follow me every time I go to the bank. A closer person had witnessed this. While at the former university, they turned all my colleagues against me that they signed a petition for me to be fired although they failed. Earlier on when I joined the church, the star one, during the daily eve prayer service, there was an announcement for somebody to drive the pastor home. I thought to myself, I can't do it since it's late and m only with my 4 year old child. There were men with cars but they singled me out since I was the only women driving on the day. I heard pastors say " we will show her who we are". They could have mentioned that I'm the one who must drive the male pastor home. I suffered since then and they won't leave me alone. I'm only living though the grace of God. I went back to my father's church and Rhema church who all prayed for me and still do so. I have since then experienced God's power, loving mercy, grace, forgiveness ... I pray and would like the people of SA and the world to pray against the ZCC church that steals - my money and Car, and also destroy. They must stop teaching everybody to be a prophet. The Bible says, some will be pastors, others prophets, counsellors etc. yet everybody for them are a prophet. Who do they prophesize. I hear in some of their branches some members take their guns along to so they won't be prophesized. ZCC people know your every move - day and night they have one of them watching you. If I go to Mpumalanga, North West where nobody knows me, I find them waiting and interfering in my spirit. Every new member at ZCC receives this verse - Jeremiah 1:5.

Jeremiah 1:5: *Before I formed thee in the belly I knew* *thee; and before thou camest forth out of the womb I sanctified thee, and I ordained thee a prophet unto the nations.*

Yet more than 2 years as a member, the bishop appeared to me saying I shouldn't be in this church but my father's church. Yet I wonder why he still sends his prophets to me long after I have left the church. This is one reason why some church pastors warn people against churches like the ZCC because they do nothing other than to 'finish you off'. If you want to see that they are false prophets - look what is happening to Shilowa, a long time member of the church. Why didn't they prophesize his future direction as a politician? The bishop told the congregation that he will be in parliament through his people - he's only causing chaos since he wants one of his there.

While at ZCC I registered for my PHD and was also granted as scholarship - I received a message in a vision that I joined ZCC so I can be successful. Since they prayed for me to register for the PHD and the scholarship, they will take it away which eventually happened. I have resumed my studies with another institution though they are still sending evil spirits there for my progress to be delayed. One day I was at the Moria Star when they asked for people to assist with some cleaning. I volunteered with others members there. One of the pastors looked at me and said "Some people joined this church for their god to answer them - for blessings". He even sand song called 'nkarabe' which means "God answer me" - for what I ask you for.–

While worrying about the ZCC prophets, that they

keep track of all the plans I have, what I'm doing, where, when I had a vision of God giving me the two scriptures. Please read them. Jeremiah 29:8-9 and Jeremiah 23:1-4; 11-12.

Jeremiah 29:8-9: *For thus saith the LORD of hosts, the God of Israel; Let not your prophets and your diviners, that be in the midst of you, deceive you, neither hearken to your dreams which ye cause to be dreamed. For they prophesy falsely unto you in my name: I have not sent them, saith the LORD.*

Jeremiah 23:1-4: *Woe be unto the pastors that destroy and scatter the sheep of my pasture! saith the LORD. Therefore thus saith the LORD God of Israel against the pastors that feed my people; Ye have scattered my flock, and driven them away, and have not visited them: behold, I will visit upon you the evil of your doings, saith the LORD. And I will gather the remnant of my flock out of all countries whither I have driven them, and will bring them again to their folds; and they shall be fruitful and increase. And I will set up shepherds over them which shall feed them: and they shall fear no more, nor be dismayed, neither shall they be lacking, saith the LORD.*

Jeremiah 23:11-12: *For both prophet and priest are profane; yea, in my house have I found their wickedness, saith the LORD. Wherefore their way shall be unto them as slippery ways in the darkness: they shall be driven on, and fall therein: for I will bring evil upon them, even the year of their visitation, saith the LORD.*

They watched my bank account and made sure I'm

left with nothing at the end of the day. In 2008, they said I know too much and that they have taken 4 things from me - car, an investment house I had bought, my job, another job I had for additional income plus the fact that I had to cede my studies; I must be killed.

They prophesied that I will not leave until the end of 2010 since I am not becoming their prophets. This despite the fact that I followed the commands and drank their so called Tea of Life - the one you referred to as the holy tea. One of the pastors told me that I would lose everything if I don't practice prophetic, I think that's before I lost my assets.

They also prophesied that my elder son wants to kill me where I ended up cancelling my life assurance to punish my son so that when I die he won't get a cent. I also saw the bishop in the vision telling me that my siblings were also planning to kill me for my life assurance.

I hope to hear more testimonies from other people who suffered like myself. Together we can stop these hypocrites who are destroying our beloved country and its beautiful people.

The challenge we have now is convincing people that this is really a true testimony. I destroyed all my uniforms after leaving the church and anything that reminds me of them. There a story last year of a ZCC woman who burnt her 2 or 3 children to death and I thought they might have been showed to do so in the vision. Another story is four people who died at one of their branches after drinking the tea prepared for them at the church; the only explanation was that the person who did so was not a pastor. No one ever took them to task, nor were there any police investigations. The stories were broadcast on television.

Testimony - Mokgadi

This is a testimony, information I received on 18 September 2012 – from Mokgadi.

I greet you beloved in the name of our Lord Jesus Christ. I grew up in ZCC church, where my Dad was a priest. My problem was that we never prayed in the name of Jesus. We prayed in the name of Egenas, Edward and Barnabas Lekganyane. Though the congregation does not see it, they deny God the Father. They call themselves 'dichewana', meaning 'orphans'. Remember, the Bible teaches us that we have a Father in Heaven. Even the songs that they sing they also deny the Lord Jesus Christ.

"*Mong-wa rena oa re lwela, empa rona ga re mmone. re tla dula le Ramarumo, re tshepe ena fela*" meaning: "Our master is fighting for us though we do not see him. We will stay with Ramarumo and trust him only"...

Every activity that takes place there is evil, not Biblical. They drink teas and water from rivers. This water is prayed for by unrighteous men who have denied the gift of righteousness from Christ. Yes, they carry Bibles, but they only believe in what the prophets say. When the ZCC prophet calls a member or anyone to give them a message, the first they kneel down. The victim is facing the prophet. Then the prophet will say "*Go bolela Ramarumo Lekganyane*" meaning

'Ramarumo Lekganyane is speaking". The member has to respond with amen, meaning "I agree". In this scenario the prophet will reveal the problems or what might come to pass and the solution (which is the instruction of what the ancestors and Ramarumo wants the victim to do).

Most times members are instructed "*Go phulwa*". I don't have an English word for this, but in details, the member has to go to a priest, who will use a needle in the nostrils, hands and feet. Blood will start coming out. They say sickness is also coming out from there. This is also denying the power of the Blood of Jesus, trampling it underfoot.

And also for protection in their homes, they use 'holy water' from the river, stones from the mountain on four corners of the house, (scatter) salt all over in the house, and they burn coffee (Trekker or FG) that will smell for more than two weeks in the house and on your clothes.

Another thing is that a uniform sends a message e.g. policemen. Now these people have their uniforms which are also for protection (or so they believe). But this uniform sends a message that "I belong to a church". Paul once asked: "Why do u say I am of Paul, I am of so and so'... it shows they do not belong to Christ because all nations shall come together and worship one God.

Jesus is the way, the truth, and the life. We can get to the Father only through Him!

Testimony - Margaret

This is a testimony, which I received on 17 December 2012 - she wishes to remain anonymous, other than giving the name Margaret.

Where do I begin?

You know, I've been dating my boyfriend since early 2009, to date. He was never one of those guys who attended church, but last year a friend told him that he should go with him to the ZCC church. He then told me that they are just trying to help him. You know, the saddest part of this whole thing is that I really think that he is being brainwashed by this so-called church.

It has affected our relationship so much; at times I couldn't understand what kind of a church is trying to help someone by giving them tea, some so-called holy water and all sorts of things.

I recently went to the church without telling my boyfriend. I was called out and this guy was giving me a prophecy. He said that my future is bright, a tokoloshe is living in me and that I should do exactly what is expected of me. They even told me that I will become a prophet, which is funny because they told my boyfriend the same thing.

I went with this gentleman at work to the church. I told my boyfriend about me being there and he said that his friend told him that I will go to the church.

What's so scary about the ZCC church is that they brainwash the people only to gain more followers.

Recently I received an SMS from the guy I work with, saying if I don't act now the [25]tokoloshe will kill me.

My response to him was that my GOD is powerful and nothing will beat the power of a prayer. His response: "Enjoy your festive season".

To be honest, I regret why I even went to this church. I really don't ever see myself at the ZCC church. As for my boyfriend, I really pray for him every day.

Please don't use my name, rather use Margaret or anonymous.

---

[25] This is a demon that brings fear to especially African people. We find this demon especially in the rural areas. He is small in height. Some African's believe if their beds are high this demon cannot climb on the bed.

Chapter 6: William Marrion Branahm

Written By: Daniel Phaladi

In my 34 years of life I have never encountered such fierce resistance from the enemy and an extreme spiritual warfare that took place while compiling this chapter. Satan tried everything in his book to stop me from writing and completing this.

I thank my friends, brothers and sisters who were praying and fasting for me through the time of writing and completion of this. I cannot name you here, for obvious reasons, but Thank you and may God bless you.

I was born in a Message home. It was later on in my life when I was 16 years old in 1994 when I first had an encounter and experience with the Lord Jesus Christ. A more detailed account of my life is tabled under Annexure A of this book, for those who may wish to grow through it to understand the a particular way in which God chose to reveal Himself to me.

Events giving Rise to the article.

In the year 2009, I was led by the Holy Spirit to undertake a study on Mystery Babylon, which appears in Revelations. 17 and 18. As I went through this study, I went through many scriptures, the Holy Spirit made me to realize by the Bible, that the Mystery Babylon of Revelations 17 and 18, CANNOT in anyway or form be Rome. I combed through scripture starting in the Old Testament, to make sure scripture lines up with Scripture, and I came to the same conclusion. The Mystery Babylon, cannot be Rome!

The Mystery Babylon of the end-time could only be a military and economic super power that controls Trade and Stock Exchanges, and has its military presence is upon the entire continent, therefore could only be America.

I then then also undertook a study on the beast of Rev 13, and although I will not get into much details now about, I realized by scripture, It could not be the Roman Catholic Pope. The study I undertook about the beast was far more extensive and far reaching than anything the Holy Spirit ever revealed to me. What gave me peace, was that it agreed and with rest of the scriptures which relates to the beast, i.e. Book of Daniel, Revelations and the words of the Lord Jesus Christ.

At this time, I started to wonder, if the Bible is so plain about Revelations 18, as well as the beast, how come are these "revelation" different from WMB's revelations about the same topic. In the Church ages, WMB states in church ages "Each individual of that group is one who has the ability to hear what the Spirit is saying by way of the messenger. Those who hear are not getting their own private revelation, nor is a group getting their collective revelation, BUT EACH PERSON IS HEARING AND RECEIVING WHAT THE MESSENGER HAS ALREADY RECEIVED FROM GOD"

So in other words, with this above statement, no individual or group can receive revelation from God, that is Different from what the messenger has. It really does not matter how much scripture one could produce to prove that Rome CANNOT be Babylon of Revelations 17, The Messenger said it was Rome, and further that the Beast was the Pope. And one day they will elect a Pope from the United States, who will through the confederation of churches form an image unto the beast.

Acts Of The Holy Spirit (54-1219E) I believe, one of these glorious days, when this united confederation of church goes together, and the new pope is brought out of the United States and put over there according to prophecy, then they'll form an image like unto the beast.

So, being afraid of being labeled as someone that wants to introduce "new revelations" to The Message, I simply showed my Parents, and a friend of mine from church I trusted with my "findings" before I shelved them, not to look at them again.

On 9 May 2013, as I was in a study room preparing a sermon, the Holy Spirit spoke to me and said something that left me puzzled. Again, to understand the manner by which He speaks to me, you can read through my personal testimony on Annexure B. He said that "Dispensationalising' His Church in Revelations is absolutely wrong and he hates it, because it is His complete Church. Now, to some that may not be familiar with this word, dispensationalism of the Church, is when you take the 7 churches that appear in the book of Revelations Chapter 2 and 3, and you "compartmentalize them" into dates. For example, the church of Ephesus, becomes not a church, but a church age, and its time starts from 53AD to 170AD.

He expounded to me that, the 7 churches in the book of revelations, represents the entire God's church, till the end. Its obstacles, its challenges, and what it will need to do, to overcome. So He is addressing those spirits that will be present in his Church till the consummation. Because I have never been able to prove "the voice" wrong regarding the Bible, I undertook a study more on this topic of dispensationalism more especially regarding the "Church Ages".

These things which the Lord was revealing to me, bothered me to a very large degree because they were totally different and in my cases seemed to be directly opposed to the revelations of the Messenger -WMB who received these revelations directly from the angel.

My dilemma began to get severe because the further I continued to check all these "revelations" I received from the Holy Spirit with the Bible, the more I could not prove them wrong by the Bible. I then started to ask myself, why would God indeed reveal anything to me, because all I need to do is to listen to the Tapes of the Prophet, who is the only one who has the ability to receive revelation from the Lord.

It was at this time, that I decided to do something about this predicament I found myself in. I had vigorously studied and researched many books of other denominations in order to be able to testify with knowledge when I am testifying to someone of a certain sect. For example If someone is Catholic, I needed to state exactly what their doctrine said which was not in line with Bible in order to "win" them to the Lord. I had however, **never** in my life, studied and researched my own church's doctrines and beliefs. As long as the prophet said it, I believed it, and that settled it. So, because I had so far received "2" revelations from the Lord that were different to what WMB says, I decided to initiate something I never did before.

I was going to try and establish scripturally where WMB got the doctrines he preached and taught, specifically the Church Age doctrine and the Mystery Babylon. I had no problem fully believing that the 7 Angels revealed to him that Revelations 17, mystery Babylon is Rome and Pope is the beast of Rev 13, but I wanted to learn from which Biblical point of view the Angels were saying it from. After all, we don't just believe things because they came from Angels of heaven, we need to see if they are Biblical. Paul said in…

But though we, or **an angel from heaven**, preach any other gospel unto you than that which we have preached unto you, let him be accursed.

Galatians 1:8

Where does VICARISU FILII DEI (666) originate from?

The next study I undertook was where WMB states as the quotes below that 666 in Rev 13 is Vicarivs Filii Dei, which after converting the Roman Numerals added up to 666.

WMB states: (54-0515 QUESTION AND ANSWERS) "**it's over the throne of the pope** where he sets on his throne. It's wrote up there, VICARIVS FILII DEI (57-1006 QUESTIONS AND ANSWERS ON HEBREWS) **The pope wearing a triple crown, Vicarivs Filii Dei**, all those things which I've heard and so forth, it's absolutely the truth. A religious group that governs every nation under the heavens, and it does. There it is; it's those... (58-0927 WHY ARE WE NOT A DENOMINATION)
I stood that close to the triple crown of the pope in a glass: Jurisdiction of hell, heaven, and purgatory. See? So, those things, I've just come from there, just come from Rome and know it's the truth. Now, we know it's pictured out. 62-1111E WHY I'M AGAINST ORGANIZED RELIGION In the Roman numeral **over the Vatican, or over the Pope's throne**, is written, Vicarivs Filii Dei 63-0319 THE SECOND SEAL JEFFERSONVILLE IN TUESDAY In other words, **up over the Vatican** (Now, I've been right there.) it's wrote Vicarivs Filii Dei

From the above quotes, I could not really establish if the letters Vicarivs Filii Dei are "over the throne", "on the triple crown" or "over the Vatican". So I decided to do some independent research to find more about Vicarivs filii dei, and its origins, if there are pictures of the throne/Triple Crown that one could spot those words.

My research led me to a man by the name of Andreas Helwig who in the year 1612 took 15 titles from "the donation of Constantine" and did some trial and error, by converting them into roman numerals and trying to find out which of the 15 titles when converted them in Roman numerals would add up to 666. He found this title Vicarius filii Dei added up to 666, but he first had to convert the **U** into a **V** and preferred it, and said it was a title of the Pope therefore used it to say the Pope's title is 666. (Do simple research on Andreas Helwig 1612) Encyclopedia states In 1866, Uriah Smith was the first to propose the interpretation to the Seventh-day Adventist Church.[12] See Review and Herald 28:196, November 20, 1866. In The United States in the Light of Prophecy he wrote

The pope wears upon his pontifical crown in jeweled letters, this title: "Vicarius Filii Dei," "Viceregent of the Son of God;" the numerical value of which title is just six hundred and sixty-six The most plausible supposition we have ever seen on this point is that here we find the number in question. It is the number of the beast, the papacy; it is the number of his name, for he adopts it as his distinctive title; it is the number of a man, for he who bears it is the "man of sin."

Uriah Smith passed this statement on to the Seventh Day Adventist as fact, and no more a trial and error by Andreas Helwig. I then tried to verify if Vicarius Filii Dei is in fact a title of any pope, and I discovered that one of the titles of the Pope was "Vicarius Christus" (Vicar of Christ). The Seventh Day Adventist's realizing that Vicarius Filii Dei is not the title of any pope states that -"Because the Catholic Church says it would not have bothered them to have that title Vicarius Filii Dei as a title of a Pope, it means it IS the title of the pope. It's the same as saying to your friend, "because you won't mind owning a gold mine, it means you a have gold mine"

I went to independently found out that Vicarius filii Dei is not a title of any pope, (Kindly do own research on this topic in order to verify) but also found this in most urban legends dictionaries, that the Pope's triple crown is written Vicarius filii Dei.

The extract below was written on one urban legend dictionary: (An urban legend is a myth that has been told over time, sometimes taken as fact when it is actually a myth. An example of an urban legend is that, [26]Camel stores water in its hump in the back)

*One classic urban legend claims the pope's crown or **Papal Tiara** contains the words* Vicarius Filii Dei *which when numerised adds up to 666, the number of the **antichrist** mentioned in the **Bible**. Though the story has no basis in fact (all papal crowns dating from the sixteenth century onwards are on public show and none contain the words), 'belief' in the 'myth' has continued,* Seventh Day Adventist elders in the 1941's went over to the Vatican because they could not believe that Ellen G White their prophet was wrong about this, they were given access to all crowns, all

---

[26] From an Urban legend dictionary

rooms, inspected everything, until they were satisfied that indeed, there was nothing that had an inscription of Vicarius Filii Dei, and since then, most of them have stopped that claim, but still insist the Roman Catholic Church is Rev 17, and the Pope is the beast of Rev 13.

The only problem I had with this at this time is that The Prophet was at the Vatican and he saw it, (58-0927 WHY ARE WE NOT A DENOMINATION) **I stood that close to the triple crown of the pope in a glass**.

So I decided to park this Vicarius Filii Dei, and not to come to any conclusions yet, and went on to rather to research the Church-ages,

"Church Age" Doctrine

Why does the Holy Spirit tell me that God's church is not dispensationalised in "ages", when in fact, it was of the major doctrines of WMB and this revelation was brought by the Angel? The main reason that WMB sets as a basis for the church age doctrine is that God will never have two major prophets on earth at the same time.

51-0929 OUR HOPE IS IN GOD: There never was in the age, any two major prophets on the earth at one time.

61-0428 GETTING IN THE SPIRIT: And it's strange, but through the Bible, He never had two prophets, major prophets in at the same time

63-0116 THE EVENING MESSENGER: Never did He

have two major prophets on the earth at one time.

63-0319 THE SECOND SEAL

And never two major prophets on the earth at the same time.

It is at this point I searched the scriptures and history to find the truth of the above statements. Please do your own research, do not purely rely on my findings. I only realized after many years that it was imperative to search things with the scripture to see if it they were true. I always believed investigating and doing any research amounted to "questioning" therefore "doubting" the Prophet.

But it is written in:

[10] And the brethren immediately sent away Paul and Silas by night unto Berea: who coming thither went into the synagogue of the Jews.
[11] These were more noble than those in Thessalonica, in that they received the word with all readiness of mind, and searched the scriptures daily, whether those things were so.
Acts 17:10-11

I found that Ezekiel and Daniel both prophesied between 593 and 570 BC. Hosea, Amos, and Jonah all prophesied between 755 and 750 BC. Haggai and Zechariah prophesied to the people of Judah at the same time (see Ezra 5:1). In the New Testament, God will send "My two witnesses" to prophesy at the same time (Rev. 11:1-14).

After establishing through history that indeed there

has been major prophets prophesying at the same time, then I needed to know, where does the theory of the "Church Age" originate from then. Upon the study of writings by different writers, I came across the writings of a man by the name of **Clarence Larkin** a Baptist minister. Clarence Larkin published a book in 1919 called the Book of Revelation illustrated. I have with me a complete copy of the Book of Clarence Larkin, and I will give to anyone who would like to read the copy. The book of Revelations by Clarence Larkin has broken down Churches in Rev 2, into Seven Church **Ages**.

Upon further reading and inspection of the book, I found some things that at first I refused to believe. This could not happen for real. I discovered that WMB's Church-age doctrine and the revelation of the seven "Seals" were a perfect copy of Clarence Larkin's book. I read the book over and compared it with our Church ages/Seals. I was shaking, in complete denial and disbelief and said to myself, "no I am actually dreaming." This can't be true. Only the Messenger had this revelation "Directly" from God. Downloaded straight from heaven. I remembered very well, how after WMB preached the Church Ages, how "the Pillar of fire" went and drew the church-ages as they had been preached on the board, in order to confirm and vindicate that the church ages and their messengers were correct. Kindly look at the chart below for just one example of the similarities between Church Ages by Larkin and WMB.

WMB did not attempt to alter the dates from Larkin, except as can be seen above, the 1st and the last Church "Age". I was in complete denial. I actually thought that probably Larkin "Stole" WMB as his own,

However, I realize the book was published in 1919.

I have included as annexure to this book, a little portions from Clarence Larkin's book and the exposition to the seven church ages by WMB in order to make own comparisons.

	Clarence Larkin (From *The Book of Revelation*, 1919)	William Branham (From Church Ages sermons and books, 1960 onwards)
Ephesus	70 A.D. to 170 A.D.[2]	53 A.D. to 170 A.D.[3]
Smyrna	170 A.D. to 312 A.D.[4]	170 A.D. to 312 A.D.[3]
Pergamos	312 A.D. to 606 A.D.[5]	312 A.D. to 606 A.D.[3]
Thyatira	606 A.D. to 1520 A.D.[6]	606 A.D. to 1520 A.D.[3]
Sardis	1520 A.D. to 1750 A.D.[7]	1520 A.D. to 1750 A.D.[3]
Philadelphia	1750 A.D. to 1900 A.D.[8]	1750 A.D. to 1906 A.D.[3]
Laodicea	1900 onwards[9]	1906 onwards[3]

At this point I started to wonder, who is this Angel, that will allow someone to copy someone's work, and repackage it as his own as the messenger whom only him has the ability to hear from God, and then confirm this "Truth" on the Board? Who is this Angel? This will be investigated further in this chapter. However, while trying to pierce pieces together about this angel I found the following Quote:

WMB's Three High Words

Experiences #3 , December 21, 1947 (tape #47-1221) Have you noticed, always, after I ask or rebuke over a spirit, I'm always perfectly silent for a few moments? Who's noticed that in the meetings, let's see your hands. Have you noticed that? Now, here's what it is. There's three words that I have to repeat at that time. See? And it's the **three high words of the Bible. No mortal on earth know it.** *See? And when I ask that, and then I feel that drop, then it comes shakes back to a place in return of that spirit. Then the...?... healed. That's the reason you hear me say that. See? That's what takes place. Now, I did that so you wouldn't be questioning me about it coming through the line. So that is true. Now, I know that you noticed a lot of times when I ask to rebuke, I stand still just for a few minutes* **and repeat these three words that the Angel of the Lord told me to repeat.** *Then if I feel it come back, then I know it's done.*

In case you are like me and thought the "three high words of the Bible" as Lord Jesus Christ, you are wrong, he says "no mortal on earth know it". Many mortals know the Lord Jesus Christ. The angel told

WMB words to repeat these "three high words" to "rebuke" a spirit.

The Bible says in **Colossians 3:17** *And whatsoever ye do in word or deed,* **do all in the name of the Lord Jesus***, giving thanks to God and the Father by him.*

Did the Angel tell WMB to do something which was against what the Bible said? Made him to repeat "High Words only Him Alone no mortal on earth knew? The angel gave him words to rebuke spirits other than the name of the Lord Jesus. We will come back too this very important point later, when it becomes apparent why the angel would want to break God's Church in to Church Ages.

Not only did WMB take Larkin's work, he also took scripture references, even examples and phrases as can be se en in Annexure D. And the angel was only too happy to finish the Job on the Board.

It was at this point that I started to have serious Mental Psychological and Spiritual Battle. I went into complete denial, at one point even angry at myself for having read Clarence Larkin's book. The message is all I know and been taught. There is phrase I used to say like a mantra, "Thee prophet said it, I believe it, that settles it", because after all, what the Prophet says is in the Bible.

Now, I know the Seals came from the seven angels, but here I was reading the seven seals by Clarence Larkin, and realizing WMB seals, including scripture references, even examples were given by Clarence

Larkin in his book.

I wondered, then what was the purpose off the 7 angels? Did they come to tell him to photocopy Larkin's work? Surely not. When did the Angels come down again — 28 February 1963, at this time, I started to do my own investigation and study into "Thee Cloud", which is also Jesus Christ.

The SECOND CLOUD???

I have in my home a Picture of The Cloud in my living room. It says Christ on **Mount Sunset.**

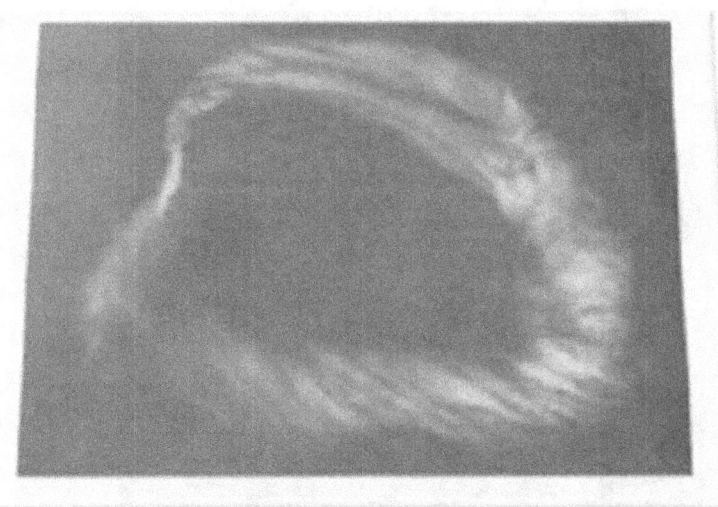

There were articles published about "The Cloud" in Life and Science magazine. The article in Science magazine was written by James E McDonald. I have copied the entire article which was in the science magazine, as well as later publications by James E McDonald.

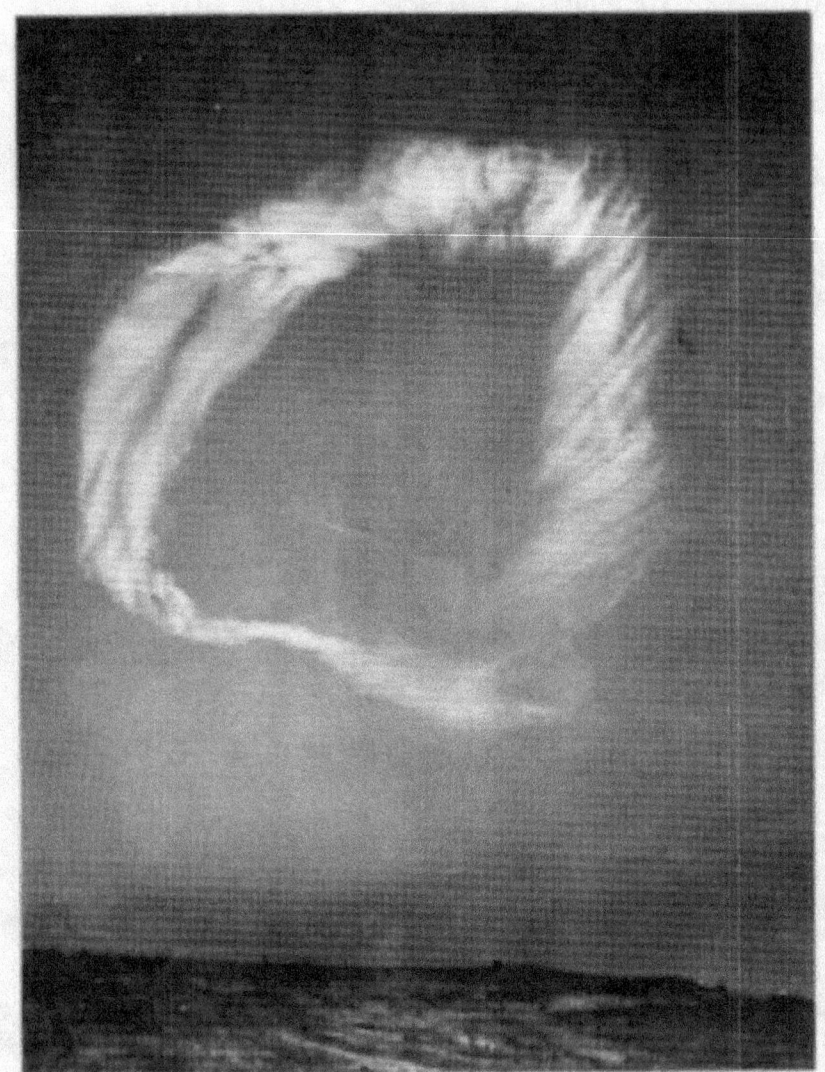

If you research about the man James E McDonald, you will discover that he was a physicist who was interested in UFO's. His whole fascination with "the cloud" was for those reasons that he was hoping that he would come to the conclusion that this "Cloud" was the result of UFO. The first article he wrote on 119 April 1963.

He did not publish only one article about the 28 February 1963 Stratospheric cloud, he kept on studying and writing more facts as he became aware of them, until his final conclusion. Ass you can see from the Newspaper article, the Cloud was Photographed over flagstaff in the evening.

WMB calls the place the Place where the angels met him Sunset Mountain hence many believers refer to this cloud as the Mt. Sunset cloud. The name off the peak WMB was referring to is actually known as Sunset Peak.

When I s started to read the article, the first thing that caught my attention which was even more puzzling to me than anything I encountered so far is that, the article (please see arrow) reported that there was another cloud, **a second cloud**, which was similar in shape, yet smaller size. I had never heard before or been told that there were **2 almost Identical Clouds.** If one was Jesus, I started to wonder who was the other one An Extract from the News article.

The Newspaper article below is clear that the Cloud was taken over **Flagstaff**. WMB states that cloud was above Sunset peak

Many observers reported a second cloud off to the northwest of the main cloud, with shape very much like that of the main cloud, but only about a quarter as large. Correctness of these reports has been established from some of the first photographs that have come in from northern Arizona. The cloud was evidently moving generally southeastward, though visual reports are in some conflict on this point; this point can only be resolved from further studies by triangulation.

Now, science took the picture of It, you seen it, went on Associated Press. They didn't know what it was. There's a Cloud hanging, twenty-six miles high. That's fifteen miles, or twenty, above even where vapour's at. They don't know what it's all going about, and they're trying to investigate it. **And there, right under It, I was standing.** *And those seven Angels roaring out their voices, of those Seven Seals, standing there. And the witness, three of us, as a witness of the things that was prophesied on the tape, "Sirs, What Time Is It?" And there now they're trying to find out. It's a mystery to them. (LORD JUST ONCE MORE HOT SPRINGS AR V-20 N-10 FRIDAY 63-0628A, par 42)*

*And He said, "He is wigged." Watch in the book, before it ever happened, I said that. And that day when that happened, it went up. And then you turn that picture sideways, if you've got "Look" magazine or "Life" magazine. Turn it sideways. There He is, just perfectly Hofmann's Head of Christ, **looking right down where I was standing**; there it is in the*

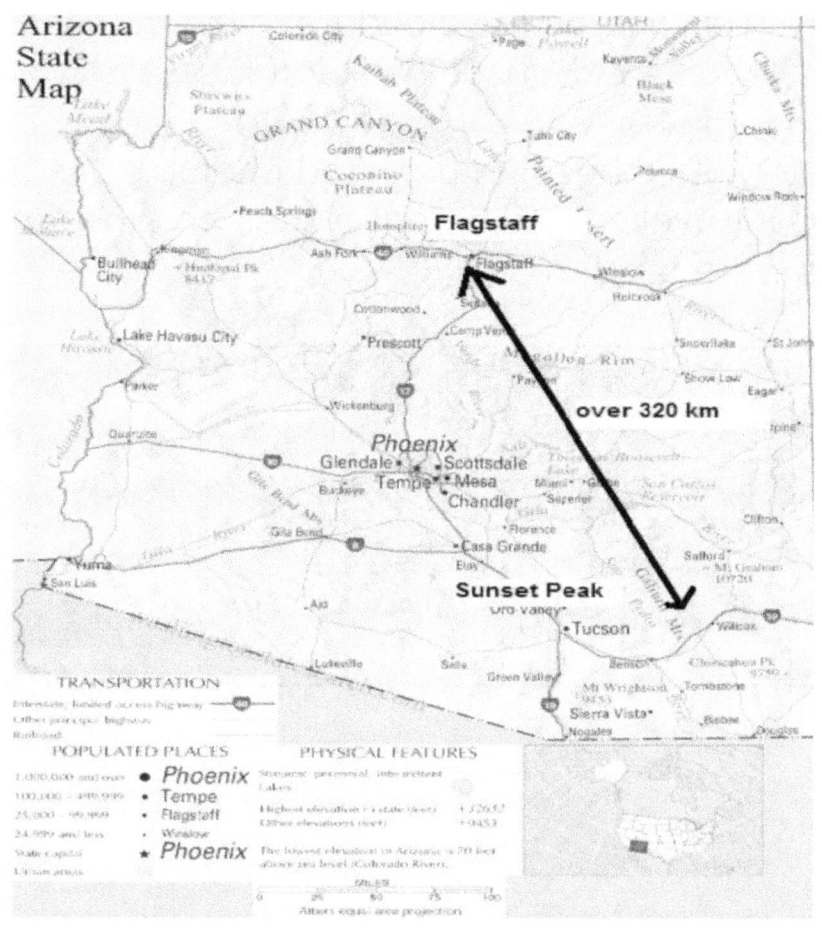

magazine. How many people have seen it? 'Course, you've all seen. There, looking right back, proved exactly the revelation was correct. (WORKS IS FAITH EXPRESSED SHREVEPORT LA V-7N1 FRIDAY 65-1126, par 255)

Let's see the hands. And now, the "Life" Magazine picked it up. And I have the article here this morning in the "Life" Magazine there, of the show... Now, here it is, **the same time I was there.** See the pyramid or the Cloud? (emphasis added) (STANDING IN THE GAP JEFF IN V-6N-7 SUNDAY 63-0623M, par 82)

As you can see, the that Flagstaff is over 320 kilometres from Sunset Peak (Mt Sunset), How was it possible that WMB was standing right under it. Some may say, well, maybe the cloud travelled from where he was standing at Sunset Peak to Flagstaff.

Fortunately life magazine provided photographs of this cloud as it travelled to different places and the time the pictures were taken.

6:10 P.M., N.E. OF PRESCOTT

6:15 P.M., N. OF PHOENIX

6:30 P.M., W.N.W. OF WINSLOW

These are different locations and different time 6:10 Pm N.E of Prescott, 6:15 P M N of Phoenix, and 6:30 PM N.W of Winslow.

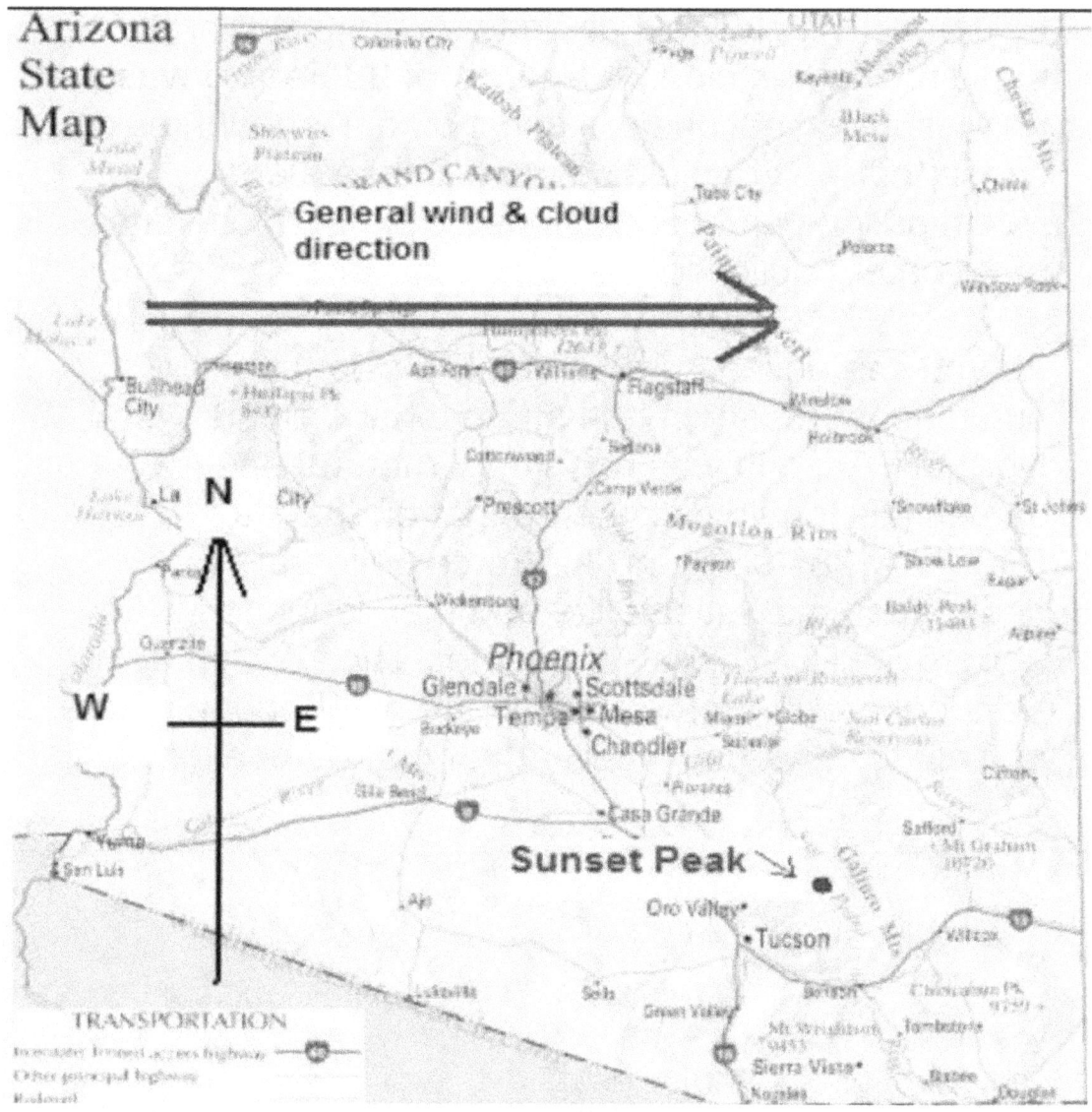

Therefore based on the above account we can see that the cloud was moving in this direction:

Why would the Angels of God/Jesus get carried away by the wind? It then became clear (and extremely scary) that the Cloud did not come near Sunset Peak (Mt. Sunset) at all. Since we had only the first article by James E McDonald given to us that he cannot explain what the cloud formation of 28 Feb 63 was, and his investigations are continuing, it should make sense that we should also have Subsequent investigations and conclusions by him. Which states all his later publications and conclusions.

As you can notice from James E McDonald subsequent research, the stratospheric cloud over Northern Arizona was not a supernatural one. Dr James McDonald discovered that on that day (February 28 1963), the Air Force deliberately destroyed a secret satellite and they launched it aboard a TAT (Thrust Augmented Thor) rocket at Vandenberg Air Force Base in the neighbouring state of California was an aftermath of that detonation.

The Air Force

Vandenberg AFB Launch History Extract

Date	Launch Time PST/PDT	Vehicle	Pad/Silo	Comments
1963 FEB 13	Unknown	Atlas D	576 A-1	SAC launch. Flag Race
1963 FEB 16	Unknown	Titan II	395-C	AFSC launch. Awful Tired
1963 FEB 19	Unknown	Scout	PALC-D	AFSC launch. Blue Scout V
1963 FEB 28	Unknown	Atlas D	576 A-3	SAC launch. Pitch Pine
1963 FEB 28	Unknown	TAT/Agena D	75-3-5	AFSC launch. Farm Country
1963 MAR 9	Unknown	Atlas D	576 B-3	SAC launch. Tall Tree 3
1963 MAR 11	Unknown	Atlas D	576 B-2	SAC launch. Tall Tree 2
1963 MAR 13	Unknown	Scout Junior	PALC-A	AFSC launch
1963 MAR 15	Unknown	Atlas D	576 B-1	SAC launch. Tall Tree 1

ce has since declassified the launch history of Van den berg Air Force Base and it is freely available on this websites.

(http://www.spacearchive.innfo/vafblog.hhtm) By examining the report it's clear that indeed there was launch activity on that day:

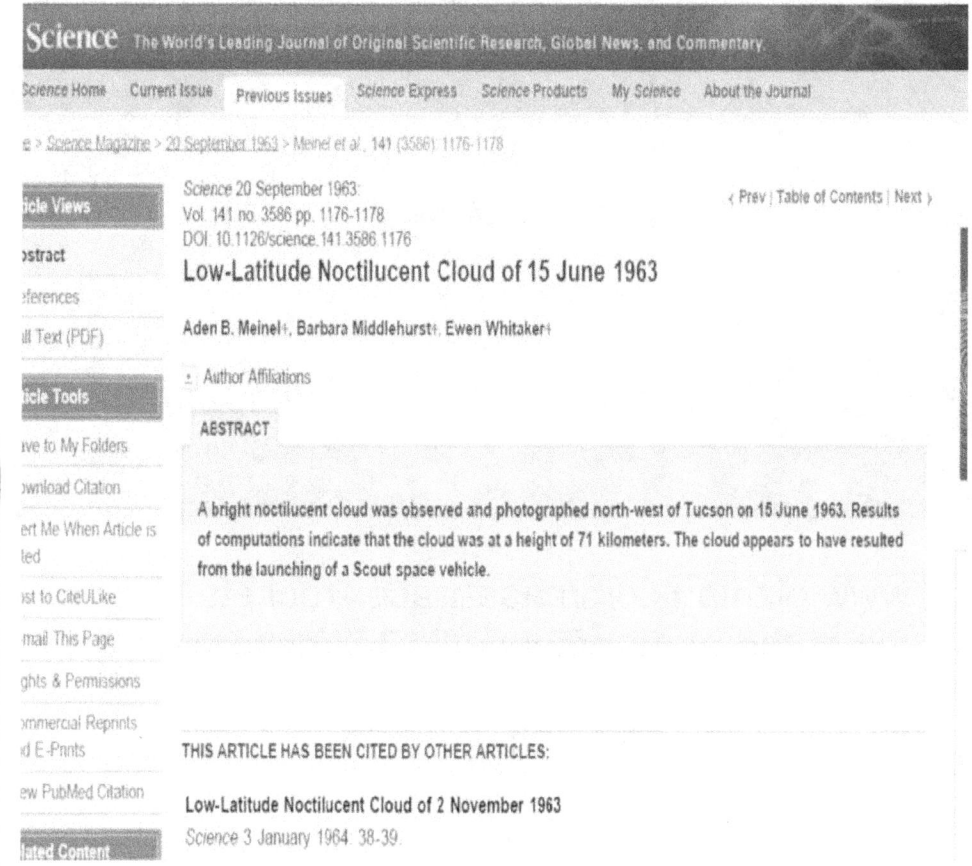

There were more sightings of stratospheric clouds, in June 19963 as well as November 1963.

The above article is found in
http://www.scienncemag.org/content/1411/3586/11766.abstract

Similar clouds have been formed by Nasa Rockets.

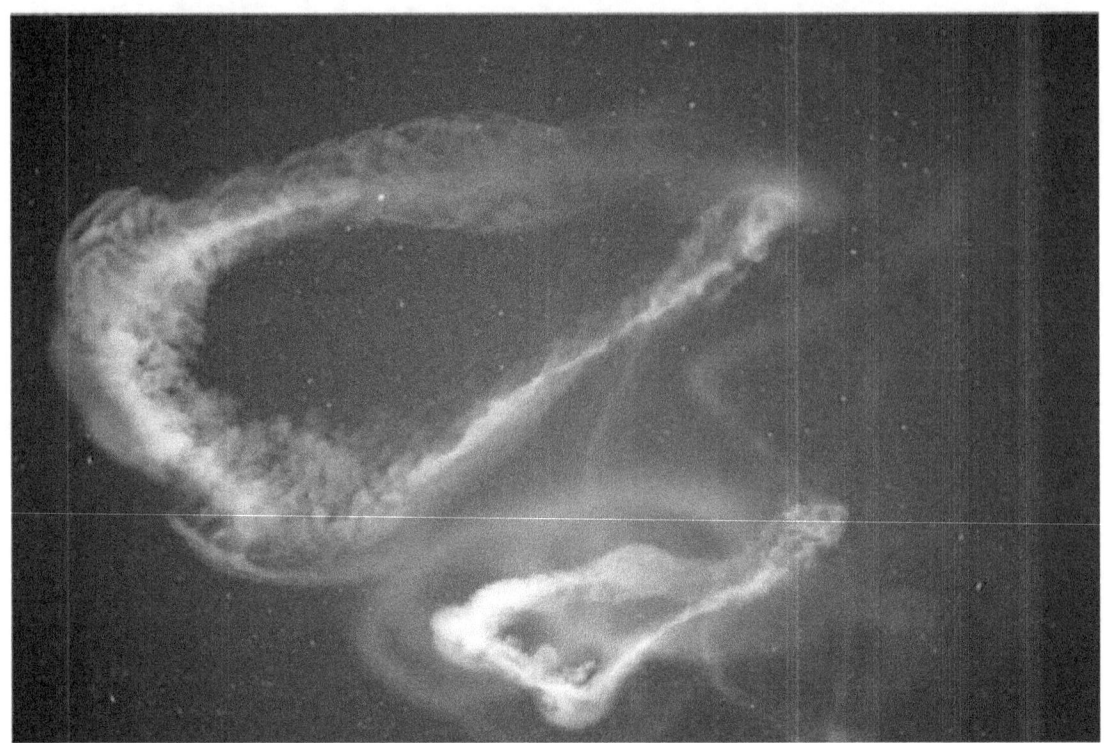

http://www.gizmag.com/nasa-tracer-rockets-form-ringed-clouds-at-the-edge-ofspace/21972/pictures#12

Below is an excerpt from one website.

"Dr. McDonald concluded that the Cloud was the result of a test missile which was launched from Vandenberg AFB and detonated nearly directly overhead earlier in the day of February 28, 1963. The steady, high speed stratospheric wind carried the Cloud to where it was later discovered over Flagstaff, Arizona after sunset."

Now, the most shocking fact, which I refused to believe, in fact, which was one of the most compelling discoveries that made me write this letter, was the revelation that there was no way WMB could have been hunting Javelina Hogs on 28 February 1963 because of the regulations for hunting season. I understood from different accounts that WMB only went Javalina Hog hunting on the 6th of March to the 9th March.

I promised myself to disbelief this fact, until I had actual copies of the Hunting Regulations of Javelina Hogs of 1963. When I did receive the Hunting Regulation itself (Please see below),

```
T-12, JAVELINA HUNT REGULATIONS      ARIZONA GAME & FISH DEPARTMENT

SEASON: March 1 - March 10, 1963, inclusive
LEGAL ANIMAL: One javelina, any age, either sex.
BAG & POSSESSION LIMIT: One javelina, See Commission Order P-36
OPEN AREA: Statewide, EXCEPT Three Bar, Santa Rita, Tucson Mountain, Robbins
           Butte, and Arlington Wildlife Areas, and Game Management Unit 20,
           and posted portions of the Cibola and Topock Wildlife Areas.
    A valid Class F or G licnese and valid javelina tag must be in possession of any
person hunting javelina.
FORT HUACHUCA MILITARY RESERVATION SPECIAL JAVELINA HUNT:
SEASON: March 1 - March 10, 1963, inclusive.
NUMBER OF PERMITS: 125
DESCRIPTION OF AREA:
    The Fort Huachuca Military Reservation lying within Game Management Unit 35.
    The Fort Huachuca Military Reservation shall be open only to hunting by properly
licensed civilian and military personnel attached to Fort Huachuca.
    Hunters will be selected by drawing with the numbers of civilian and military
hunters to be determined on the basis of the ratio of civilian to military applications.
Application blanks will be available beginning January 28, 1963, at Fort Huachuca.
Applications will be received at Fort Huachuca on or after January 28, 1963, and
before noon on February 15, 1963, and quota for the hunt will be filled by public
drawing at Fort Hucahuca in the presence of Arizona Game and Fish Department per-
sonnel on February 15, 1963. Permits will not be valid until countersigned by the
Commanding General, or his representative, at the time and place designated by him.
    All hunters must personally check into and out of the area through a checking
station as designated by the Commanding General.
```

The copy of the Regulation above states depicts that the hunting season started on 1 March 1963 and ended 10 March 1963. - WMB said he was "Standing right under the cloud", which happened to be 320 kms from Mt Sunset, and appeared a day before the hunting season started. "Time Travel" is given a brand new meaning. I said surely, this cannot be happening to me. I am dreaming. I have listened to the "vindicated" voice since I was a baby. I needed someone to wake me up, because I was dreaming. This became too much for me too bear. For a couple of days I went into a state of total denial. Then minor depression. I rebuked myself for having found out all these things, which are FUNDAMENTAL to our doctrine. This is what sets us apart from the denominations and Pentecostals, who are Pentecostal babies and can't understand spiritual things.

I have attached a high resolution picture of the cloud of "Life Magazine" below. That's the clearest picture one can get of the cloud. Please take a very long and good look at it and let me know if you see any face of Jesus. Please look very hard. You can enlarge the Picture to a lot of pixels, if you think maybe "Jesus" may be hiding.

To think that the beginning of this year in 2013, I was speaking about the Jubilee of "the Cloud". 50 years since the cloud appeared on Mt. Sunset, I was rejoicing.

At this point I said; Surely WMB cannot start stories so people can believe him. No, there is something I must be missing. In trying to find if WMB was prone to "making up" stories, I came across this article about the man from Windsor. This article it proved to me, that yes, WMB could change stories with no problem at all without any problems. Please make sure you are strong enough to handle what you are about to see, before continuing. I know the emotional turmoil it threw me in. Just make sure that you are ready to uncover the reality and the truth of what this Message truly is, there is an expression that people normally make "This is not for Sissies". Please do not hate yourself that you did not see this all the time, there is a time appointed by God for everything.

The Man from Windsor

WMB often tells a story of from Windsor, who wrote Cancer on a prayer card, but he was lying, he wanted to deceive WMB. The first time WMB tells this story is below:

__Moses' Commission (50-0110)__ Then a few nights after that, I was over at Windsor, Ontario. Had fourteen thousand at that meeting there. There was a man in the meeting who thought that this was just a bunch of make-up. He went and got a prayer card in one of the lines, pretending that he was sick and in need. And he went and wrote on the prayer card he had all kinds of diseases and so forth like that. And he come around and give it into the man, the prayer line manager. I never see the cards. They take the cards down there. He thought, "I'll just see what this is all *about." Then when he come in and put that on a prayer card down, he come walking up. I said, "Good evening, sir." He said, "Howdy do." And I took a hold of his hand. There was no vibrations. I looked at him; I seen him and two men, standing in a room across a table making up about... I said, "Why would you purpose in your heart to try to deceive somebody?" I said, "God is apt to strike you dead right now."*

E-42 And he fell down on the floor and begin to screaming to the top of his voice. He said, "God, have mercy on me." I said, "Why would you do that, friend?" He said, "Brother Branham, I--I thought it was just make-up. I--I--I honestly, is there forgiveness for me?"

There was

When this man that tried to deceive WMB asked for forgiveness, WMB said "There Was". The man was indeed forgiven. That is what every Christian should do, forgive. And WMB states that there was forgiveness for him.

But the next time he tells the same story, it has changed. The story has gone from the one of love and forgiveness, to the one of showing the power of WMB and his God of wrath.

(1) South Africa testimony (54-0902)

And I looked around. And after a while, then it broke to a vision. And I seen him setting at a table with another man. And they were sitting. And a woman was standing there with a dotted dress on. And there was a green thing hanging over the table, like this. And they had made up together that it was mental telepathy, and they was going to prove it from the platform. And that was revealed and told him who he was and what church he belonged to.

E-15 Brother, I said, "Now, the things that you put on the plat--on your prayer card, is on you. You have it now." That was right. He fell down, grabbed a hold of my pants leg. I said, "Sir, that's between you and God, not me." I said, "That's between you and God." **Far as I know, the man's in eternity today, dead.** *See? Now, you can't play church.*

The first instance, this man was forgiven, however, WMB's God has changed from a forgiving God to a God of punishment. So this man was no longer forgiven. In 1954 he was in eternity dead. However the story keeps changing over time.

(2) Blind Bartimaeus (56-0407)

And the man grabbed me by the pants leg, he said, "Pray for me, Brother Branham." I said, "That's between you and God now. It's out of my hands. He's done spoke it. That's you now."

And the man's laying bedfast to this day.

The man that was dead in 1954 is now bedfast in 1956. Is this man a Zombie? Believe it not, the story keeps changing!!

(3) Jehovah-Jireh (56-1209E) *And I said, "I have nothing to do with that. You cursed yourself. So you have what you put on the prayer card." And screaming, he run from the building. There it was.* **I don't know what ever happened.** *See?*

(4) Blind Bartimaeus (57-0127E) *I said, "Now, the...?... And grabbed...?... on the platform by my pants and I said, "The thing that you put on your prayer card, TB and so forth, is on you now."* **The man died about a year later.**

(5) Thirsting for Life (57-0630) *And I said, "The things that you put on your card, you have. Both cancer and TB." And he fell down on the platform. But the last time I heard him, I never heard no more, just a letter from some of the people, that* **he was in a serious condition.** *So we're not playing church.*

(6) The Queen of Sheba (58-0208) *I said, "Now, what was on your prayer card you have."* **He died about six months later with a cancer.** *Uh-huh, uh-huh.*

(7) Christ outside the door (58-0330E)

How many was at the Windsor meeting to see that critic, that preacher? **They packed him out paralyzed, and he's still paralyzed.**

(8) Have not I sent thee? (62-0124) *I said, "The things that you got on your card is upon you."* **He died about six weeks after that.** *Don't you never do that.*

How could one man that wrote cancer on the prayer card, the cancer he did not have, have so many endings to him?? He was forgiven, then he is dead, later he is bedfast, he is paralyzed, he died after 6 weeks, he died after 6 months. I don't think we will ever know the truth about this man's ending, that is if this story even happened at all. WMB said the "I am God's voice to you". If he is indeed God's voice to us, I think I expect a little bit of more honesty from "God".

These statements below also made me realize that WMB had the capability to fabricate and paint completely different picture from reality, in order to invoke "sympathy". You will soon realize for WMB to say things without any basis or truth in them was basically no problem at all, as long as it "vindicated" him. Below is an example of where WMB is explaining to someone why he does not have good English grammar. WMB states:

*And he said--he said, "You use some of the awfullest words." Said, "You really tear up the--the--the...?... English." And I said, "Yes, sir." I said, "I'm aware of that." He said, "Why, the people that you speak before," said, "you ought to be ashamed of that grammar." I said, "I am, but it doesn't do me any good. I just don't know no better." And he said... "Well," he said... I said, "**When I was a boy, my father died**. I had ten children to take care of, and I had to work and support my mother and the children. Then since the Lord has sent me out, why, I have--haven't had a chance."*

So far, this story sounds like a perfect reason why WMB did not have good English. His father died when he was still a boy, and he had to take care of 10 children. Now lets look at the facts.

51-0501 EXHORTATION.OF.DIVINE.HEALING

My father died early fifty-two, with a heart attack.

Life story (51-0415A)

Daddy was eighteen years old; mama was fifteen when I was born,

Now, if WMB's dad was 18 years old when he was born, and he died when was 52, that means when he died, WMB was 52 – 18 = 34 years. So the "Story" that his father died when he was still a boy is not true. Purely fabricated. Why?

I then sadly found myself, looking into every bit of story that we tell people when we are testifying to them, its validity.

1933 Ohio Baptism (As John the Baptist….)

We tell people about the 1933 Baptismal Service as Narrated by WMB, how a light appeared when he baptized the 17th person and spoke "As John the Baptist was sent to forerun…ect". This happened when he was baptizing 500 people, and there were thousands on the banks to witness this event.

According to different Quotes, this is what WMB said happened on that day. Please find all the quotes attached as Annexure D

As you read through the quotes, look for the following key points that Brother Branham makes throughout his various accounts of this event:

- The event occurred in 1933 when Brother Branham was baptizing converts in the Ohio river at the foot of Spring Street.
- Different dates are given for the event, but he most consistently states this occurred sometime in June, 1933.
- The event occurred before Brother Branham and Hope were married in June, 1934.
- This was his first revival, or first group
- Roy Davis was still his pastor when this revival was held. He had just recently been ordained as a Baptist minister.
- There were a lot of people in attendance; between several hundred to thousands. Brother Branham baptized around 500 people.
- As he was baptizing, he heard a voice tell him to "look up".
- A light appeared and a voice spoke something to the effect of "As John the Baptist was sent forth to forerun the first coming of Christ, you have the Message that'll now forerun the second Coming of Christ."
- All the local papers packed the article of it. The Louisville Herald, or Herald Post ran a front page story with a headline similar to "A mystery Light hangs over a local Baptist minister while baptizing at the foot of Spring Street in Jeffersonville, Indiana."

> The associated press picked up the story and it was carried in papers around the US and Canada.

Remember, in particular, that WMB was baptizing his first converts as he stated while preaching

The Pillar Of Fire in Jonesboro, Arkansas on May 9, 1953:

*And He… When I was–I was a young Baptist preacher **baptizing my first converts, five hundred of them down on the river, my first revival…** I had about three thousand attend at the revival. And my education was so poor, till **my girlfriend** read the Bible while I preached.*

Upcoming Tent Revival

On May 6, 1933 Roy Davis began to advertise an upcoming tent revival in the Jeffersonville Evening News:

See newspaper advert below:

...URDAY, MAY 6, 1933

...vice at County Farm.
  6:30 Christian Endeavor
  7:30 Worship, "The Saint Among Sinners."

FIRST PENTECOSTAL BAPTIST
DR. ROY E. DAVIS, Pastor

Saturday Night

The usual interesting meetings will be held Saturday night. These Saturday night meetings are getting more and more interesting.

The pastor will be in charge.

Sunday Morning

Sunday School 10 a. m.
C. E. Myers, Supt.

Sunday evening 6:30 o'clock P. B. Y. P. U.

7:00 o'clock Senior P. B. Y. P. U. meets with Halbert Davis leading.

Sunday Night

Beginning promptly at 7:30 o'clock a very special musical program will be featured.

8:15 o'clock the pastor will deliver his ninth sermon of a series of the subject of Pentecost.

The public is invited to attend these meetings.

A tent revival will begin soon under the direction of a noted evangelist. Announcements of this meeting will be made later.

"The Pappers Packed The Article Of It"

FIRST PENTECOSTAL BAPTIST
DR ROY E DAVIS, Pastor

Saturday Night

The interesting study of the Psalms will be resumed Saturday night. These studies are creating considerable interest among Bible students

Sunday Morning

Sunday School 10 a m

C. E Myers, Supt. This Bible school is now well over the 100% mark in every department and on all points.

Sunday Evening

Junior Young Peoples' meeting 6:30

Senior Young Peoples' meeting, 7:30;

Sunday Night

The evangelistic meeting will be in charge of sister Florence Myers, who will preach Sunday

The pastor was called to Detroit, Michigan Saturday, where he is arranging to bring back several minis

Just a few days later, the June 2nd edition of the Jeff News packed this article Fersonville Evening News on the front page:

ool large enough to ac
en hundred persons
bid at its next meet.
be Friday, June 9 at

was appointed by Dr.
tigate the cost of con-
imming pools in this
also determine as far
type of pool best suit-
of the community. Del
was named as chair-
mittee.

ecorator Is
alls City Store

Garn, expert interior
he Dupont Duco Com-
uct a Duco demonstra-
Saturday, June 2 and
of the Falls City Elec-
dware Company on

ter, business manager
ly Company, advises
o consult Miss Garn
g problems and to see
e the famous Duco pro
vice is free, and the
ally invited to avail
arn's assistance.

fersonville zone, is wearing that
told you so" expression since his return from the big race at Indianapolis
where five Studebakers finished the
full grind of the Memorial Day classic, while three of them were among
the first ten "in the money."

Mr. and Mrs. Vorgang, who motor-
ed to the capital city for the annual
event, returned enthusiastic over the
performance of the Studebaker stock
cars and the impression made on the
100,000 visitors that thronged the
speedway.

"It goes to show you that 'class will
tell' whether it be a contest among
human beings, a horse race, or the
gruelling 500-mile test of automobile
engines," said Mr. Vorgang in his enthusiastic resume of the event.

Goldblume Beer to Wash Indiana Throats June 10

Evansville, Ind., June 2—Cook's
Goldblume beer will be on the market
about June 10, according to Adolph
Schmidt, president of the F. W. Cook
Company. He is unable to state as yet
what the average output will be.

our Name In The Supplement?

uto license numbers and serial numbers of one dol-
circulation today which are scattered throughout
ORIAL SALES SUPPLEMENT of the EVENING
d distributed to all non-subscribers in Jeffersonville
iting holders to a set of two volumes of the Popular
dia' are presented herewith to EVENING NEWS
that they may have the opportunity to determine
ey are holding any of the lucky numbers. The names
ses of two residents of Jeffersonville are also printed
everage supplement today. Search the ads. You may

oped that the persons receiving this Pictorial Supple-
realize the advantage of being regular subscribers to
daily paper, and in this way the circulation of The
ews will be increased more than ever.
umbers for this week are as follows:
Licenses—291,999; 290,469.
Bills—N56277431-A; T25393350-A
residents—John Dolan, 426 Watt St., J. B. Murphy,
Market St.

rs of these numbers will be given the encyclopedia
office of the NEWS & JOURNAL upon presentation
with any of the serial numbers or upon presentation
ownership of the auto license numbers.

numbers will be printed in all advertisements in the
Sales Supplement today. If you, Mr. Subscriber,
d any of the above numbers tell your friends, who
scribers to read the advertisements presented in the
t today, for they may hold the license or serial
titling them to this valuable reference encyclopedia.

ordinance regulating the use of its
lands.

That is constructive legislation;
and if other northern counties will fol
low Oneida's example, they will save
themseves a lot of future grief.

Unregulated settlement and land
use have cost upper Wisconsin much
money. Men have gone into the woods
or the cutovers, selected what lands
they pleased, and used them for any
purposes they pleased.

That would have been all right and
in line with America's historic individ-
ualism, if the fate of such men had
been their own affair alone.

But it never was. Always their prob
lems became public problems. Always there came demands, sooner or
later, for a road to give ingress and
egress to an isolated home; or for a
school for isolated children; or for
other services from government.

Being scattered all over the map, it
soon was clear that these independent
settlers were costing the public a lot
of money. To build a road into a community is one thing; to build a separate road into each of many scattered clearings is quite another. To build
schools for a compact community is
no great problem; to build schools for
scattered homesteads may mean to
build a separate school for a single
family, in instances.

So it has been going in many parts
of northern Wisconsin. The unregulated use of lands has meant scatter
ing public functions over wide terri-
tories; and, in instances, giving individuals or families services costing
ten times the amount of taxes the
family would pay in a lifetime.

Wise land use is important from
the public standpoint. Oneida county
realizes that. It now is saying to its
citizens:

"Here are good agricultural areas
and if you want to engage in farming
you must do so in these areas. Here
are recreational areas where you can
build summer cottages or resorts.
Here are forest areas and if you
choose to buy these you must grow or
harvest trees."

By that process there will yet be
sound development in Oneida county
and a gradual decline in the public
load that comes of too little planning
in the use of land.

FOURTEEN CONVERTED

Fourteen conversions are report-
ed in a tent meeting conducted at
Eighth and Pratt streets by the
Rev. William Branham.

SHOT SUCCUMBS IN NEW ALBANY

Was One Of Few to Survive Ride

David Albin alias "Cockeye" Mulli-
gan, said to be a "big shot" of Chicago gangdom and one of the few
gangsters to live through a ride, died
an ungangster-like death with his
shoes off in a New Albany Hospital
Thursday, it was learned here Friday.

Albin was visiting Walter Mattox,
who has built an expensive mansion
on the McCulloch pike a short distance from New Albany. Stricken
with a sudden kidney stone attack Albin was rushed to St. Edward's hospital and died there Thursday.

The George Barker gang took Albin for a ride several years ago, but
he recovered from a chest wound.
Chief of Detectives William Schoen-
maker of Chicago gave Albin a going
over last week, scorning Albin's protest that he was a "respectable busi-
nessman." The chief told Albin he was
a "public enemy, unworthy of consid-
eration." Albin obtained release on a
writ of habeas corpus and came to
visit Mattox.

Mattox is under bond to answer fed
eral liquor charges which grew out of
a raid on his home Derby day.

Judge Kopp Names Board of Review

Judge George C. Kopp appointed
Claude Conner, New Washington dem
ocrat and Harry C. Poindexter former
mayor of Jeffersonville to serve on
the Board of Review at the Court
House Monday. Mr. Conner and Mr.
Poindexter with County Treasurer
Charles V. Babb, County Auditor Ot-
tis B. Fifer and County Assessor Mil-
lard Badger will meet for thirty days
at the Assessor's office to pass upon
the valuation of real estate and to con
sider taxation problems.

The law requires that a democrat
and a republican be appointed upon
the board to serve with the county officials. Both Claude Conner and
Harry C. Poindexter are well quali-
fied for the appointment as the men
have a thorough knowledge of the val
uation of real estate.

Perhaps you nearly missed the article. Here is it below.

There is no mention of a mysterious light or a huge

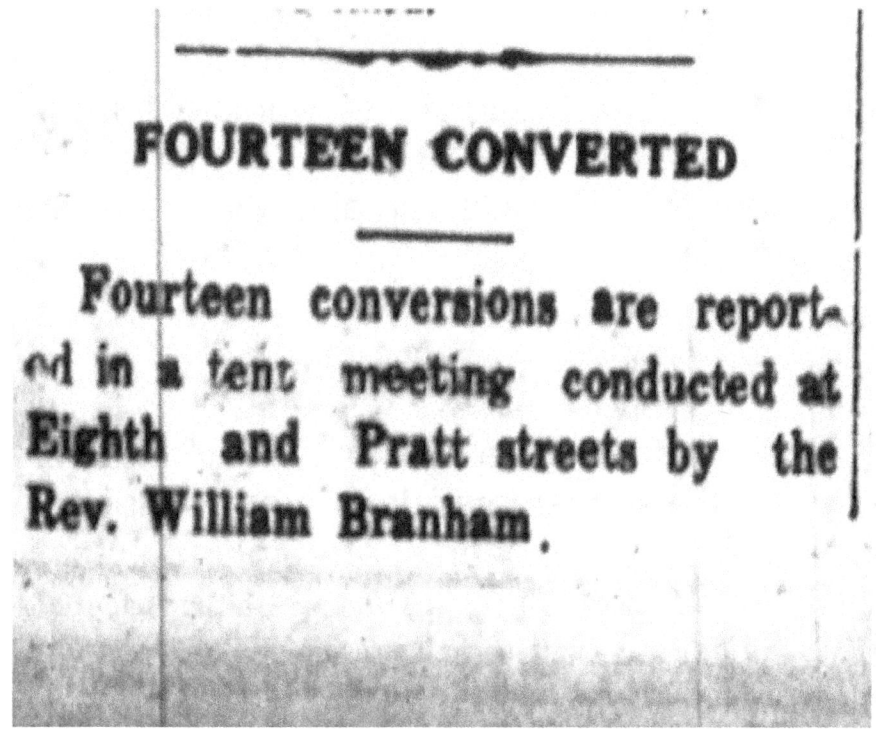

crowd at the river for a baptismal service being held by Brother Brannham. Other people have been searching for this article for years, and to date, such an article has never been produced. In this sleepy river town, this would have been a huge story.

How does 14 people become 500 people?, " Light hanging over Baptist minister", then there is a light, then a voice speaking "A*s John the Baptist was sent forth to forerun the first coming of Christ, you have the Message that'll now forerun the second Coming of Christ*"

Please note that even this message changes over time from **you have the Message** *that'll now forerun* *the second Coming of Christ* it changes overtime to **you will forerun** *thee second Coming of Christ.*

Failed Visions and Prophecies

Please note, in this article, I do not wish to delve into False prophecies, failed visions, i.e. Municipal bridge, Africa Trip, Brown Bear, and 1977 etc. At this point, an objective reader of this article can already see where the wind is blowing.

Fear

I soon discovered the above was just the tip of an Ice Berg, as you will discover later. It is rather strange how People have always been scared to find out for themselves if what was said by WMB is true due to the fear which is induced on the followers. "One word against it, it will never be forgiven", "a woman once said she won't even give this Message to my cow, when she died, she was screaming, definitely going to hell", "a brother was sitting in the meeting resenting WMB, then he fell down dead", who on earth would want to put your life in danger by investigating the things he said.

" You will cross the line and there won't be ever mercy for you". But the Holy Spirit commanded not to fear but to do like the Bereans in Acts 17:10 -11 *And the brethren immediately sent away Paul and Silas by night unto Berea: who coming thither went into the synagogue of the Jews. 11 These were more noble than those in Thessalonica, in that they received the word with all readiness of mind, <u>and searched the scriptures daily, whether those things were so</u>.*

Look at the example we have been told and have told many others about the pillar of fire that appears over WMB.

WMB: "*The mechanical eye of this camera won't take psychology. The light struck the lens.*" *And so, you have the picture now. And one of them's in* **Washington, D.C., in the religious Hall of Art,** *with a note under it, "The only supernatural being that was ever photographed in the history of the world."*

First and foremost, there **NEVER** existed anything called Religious Hall of Art in Washington D.C. then and there still is not such a hall today. This was yet another fabrication by WMB. At this point, I know there are some "Message believers" that are starting to say, no, not everything can be a lie!! I mean, The FBI questioned the photo. Sorry to disappoint you. George Lacy never worked for the FBI at **any point.** George Lacy was a freelance examiner of questioned documents who used to work off Texas, and he only examined the photograph because Gordon Lindsay hired his services.

Turning churches into Church ages

Now, at this point, I would like to return to my initial puzzlement, why the Lord told me that He hates the compartmentalization of His church into dispensations.

[20] The mystery of the seven stars which thou sawest in my right hand, and the seven golden candlesticks. The seven stars are the angels of the seven churches: and the seven candlesticks which thou sawest are the seven churches.

Revelations 1: 20

It is clear from the above scripture that the Lord Jesus is explaining to John the mystery of the golden candlesticks. Why would God, replace a mystery by another mystery of the seven churches, which still needs to be explained? The second explanation being that the seven churches are not really **churches**, they are **church** ages. In other words by coming up with seven church age theory, we are simply saying that the Lord Jesus did not explain the real mystery to John.

Why would Jesus Christ say that in;

[18] For I testify unto every man that heareth the words of the prophecy of this book, If any man shall add unto these things, God shall add unto him the plagues that are written in this book:
Revelations 22:18

Then later on the same Jesus sends angels, to give WMB revelation, that Jesus forgot to add the word "age" to the "seven churches" and even come in a "pillar of fire" and draw these church ages on a board.

Yes the book of Revelation is full of symbols, however in this particular case, The Lord Jesus Christ clearly explains the mystery of the candle sticks to John.

Let us objectively look at the Church age doctrine does by the filter of the Bible. First of all, it divides the church of God into dates. Then it does not stop there, it then finds an "angel" for each age. I will not dwell at this point into the Roman Catholic "Messengers" (angels) that WMB chose as church age messengers. After an angel is allocated his church age, he is then

responsible for that church age. That is why we keep on hearing "Luther and his group", "Wesley and His group".
"Paul and his group". Is this true? Did Paul really have a group that was his? Let's hear what Paul says himself.

[11] For it hath been declared unto me of you, my brethren, by them which are of the house of Chloe, that there are contentions among you. [12] Now this I say, that every one of you saith, I am of Paul; and I of Apollos; and I of Cephas; and I of Christ.

1 Corinthians 1:11-12

It is clear from what Paul is saying, that he did not want any "group" saying they are his and does not want any "group" to be named after him. Why do we then allow someone to give him a group?

WMB said he is preaching what Paul is preaching. But we see what Paul says here dividing the Church of God by "messengers" Paul, Apollos, Cephas." Is wrong. It therefore becomes obvious that God does not want His church divided by Time, Geographical location, this is simply unbiblical.

Why did WMB say he is against denominationalism when his very core doctrine of Church ages does exactly that, "Compartmentalize/Denominationalise" the church of the living God in time. This is like telling a child not to play in the garden because he will damage the flowers, then you come with an 18 wheeler 30 Ton truck and destroy the "Entire" Garden.

Why did he then Compartmentalize/Denominationalise the Church of God into dates? The reason is simple. If he didn't compartmentalize the Church, he couldn't place himself as "**The Leader of the The group**". So this had to be done, so he could be the "Messenger" of Laodicean Church "**Age**".

Every seed shall bring forth of its kind.

Now this is where things start to get interesting.

I grew up in the Message. And growing up, I had the "privilege" of attending different message churches around South Africa. Now as a child of a pastor, you get to witness many things that a lay member does not get to see. You get to witness **the real contentions** and the "utter hatred" amongst "Message Pastors". Now I used to wonder, why is there so much divisions and "blasting of other pastors in this message".

To my friends who know nothing about the message, there is something called "blasting". Now blasting is mostly when a Pastor exposes the errors of another message pastor and "blast" it from behind the pulpit. I would then reply myself by saying: "If only our pastors were as sweet and kind and loving as WMB, there would be no divisions.

I have come to realize, the Bible is true. Every seed will bring forth of its kind. Jesus Christ says in John 13:35 *By this shall all men know that ye are my disciples, if ye have love one to the another.* You've got to love Jesus Christ!! He keeps things straight and simple for us. All men are to know that we are Christ's disciples if we have love for one another. Then you may wonder, why then so many carnal comparisons, pure dislikes and avoidance, clicks and clans, certain pastors "band" together and wont invite other message pastors, for different reasons.

You are about to quickly realize, although It appears on the face of it, that WMB is the "mouth piece" of Jesus, from the tongues that were breaking forth in church, and many of the things WMB said himself like "I am God's voice to you". "Elijah of the End time is the Lord Jesus Christ", but as you will quickly notice, **WMB** and the **real Jesus Christ say** "*opposite things*".

In Acts 10:28 *peter speaking in the house of Cornelius: " And he said unto them, Ye know how that it is an unlawful thing for a man that is a Jew to keep company, or come unto one of another nation;* **but God** *hath shewed me that I* **should not call any man common or unclean**.

WMB says "An immoral woman is the lowest thing *that can be thought of in the earth. Excuse this, young ladies. She's nothing but a* **human garbage can,a"sex exposal**.*" That's all she is. A immoral woman is* **a human sexual garbage can**, *a pollution where filthy, dirty, ornery, lowdown filth is disposed by her. MARRIAGE.AND.DIVORCE_ JEFF.IN V-3N-13 SUNDAY_ 65-0221M, par 168)*

Someone may say, But Jesus himself called a woman a dog one day. So, he called someone common or unclean. Not so fast, hold your horses. In the Same book of Acts 10:15 *and the voice spake unto him again the second time, "What* **God hath cleansed***, that call not thou common"*. After the death, burial and resurrection of our Lord Jesus Christ, we gentiles that were alienated from him, he hath cleansed us by his blood. After the blood of Jesus Christ has cleansed his people, the Bible says we should not call any man common or unclean.

Let's hear more what WMB says. And Satan is really working on her today (in these last days), because he is her designer. I could prove that now, to go right back at the beginning. Who started to work on her, Adam or Satan? God or Satan? See? That's her designer. It's her chief weapon to throw men to her filth… You may question me about Satan being her designer, but that's the truth. **Satan designed her. He still does it.**‖ (MARRIAGE.AND.DIVORCE_ JEFF.IN V-3N-13 SUNDAY_ 650221M, par 125)

In other words, God wanted to create a woman, but he couldn't, or had run out of ideas, but for whatever reason, he gave Satan the job to design her. What does the Bible say?

[21] And the LORD God caused a deep sleep to fall upon Adam, and he slept: and he took one of his ribs, and closed up the flesh instead thereof;
[22] And the rib, which the LORD God had taken from man, made he a woman, and brought her unto the man.
Genesis 2:21-22

At this point it is becoming clear, that you are going to have to either 1) Believe **God of the Bible**, **the Lord**

Jesus Christ, or 2) WMB. You cannot mix the 2, no matter how much you try. I do know for a fact that God is NOT satan. Why then did WMB say these kind of things about women.

WMB: Women perpetrate or particip*ate in 98% of all US cities crimes (65-0221M, par 169).* Yes, women are criminals indeed 98% of all crimes? We have played this "quote" over and over on your tapes. The message of marriage and divorce came directly from Angels. And it goes without say that "The Angel" would have told him that a woman is the lowest of all animals on earth (650221M par 182.

"But I can remember when my father's still up there running, I had to be out there with water and stuff, see young ladies that wasn't over seventeen, eighteen years old, up there with men my age now, drunk. And they'd have to sober them up and give them black coffee to get home to cook their husband's supper. Oh, something like that, I said, "I..." This was my remark then, **"They're not worth a good clean bullet to kill them with it**.*" That's right. And I hated women. That's right. And I just have to watch every move now, to keep from still thinking the same thing.* (LIFE.STORY_ LA.CA FOOTPRINTS.BOOK SUNDAY_ 59-0419A, par 87)

WMB said he hated woman. That's right. So he now has to "watch every move" from still thinking the same.

Why does he struggle with hatred for women. Ask yourself this, Why is Allah of Islam, so very much against women, they can't drive, they shouldn't work, they must "cover" their bodies which were designed by satan. Nkosi Yam'.

Why are women hated in every cult? Why do women suffer the most terrible tortures and honour killings and rapes…, Women, Why?

WMB: *You see a woman with a lot of paint on her face, you know what you can call her? Say, 'Hello,* **Miss dog meat**.*' That's what she is,* **like dog meat.**

What have you done women to deserve so much hatred. Until you are nothing but "Human Garbage Cans and dog meat?

You will find the answer in Genesis 3:14

[14] And the LORD God said unto the serpent, Because thou hast done this, thou art cursed above all cattle, and above every beast of the field; upon thy belly shalt thou go, and dust shalt thou eat all the days of thy life:

Genesis 3:14

the *days of thy life 155:* **_And I will put enmity between thee and the woman,_** *and between thy seed and her seed; it shall bruise thy head, and thou shalt bruise his heel.*

So, then do you still wonder why the Message of the Hour bears thee "fruits" of hatred, whilst its Messenger - WMB is full of love..?

WMB: You see a woman with a lot of paint on her

face, you know what you can call her? Say, 'Hello, Miss dog meat.' That's what she is, like dog meat.

Pyramids, UFO's

The Future Home of the Heavenly Bridegroom and the Earthly Bride, August 2, 1964

The pyramid of Enoch casts no shadow *no time of the day. I've been in Egypt at the pyramids. It's so geographically fixed, and in the dimensions of this great geometrical figure;* **that no matter where the sun is, there's never a shadow around the pyramid.**

So, the above statements that Pyramids give no shadows, which was not said only on one occasion because "he's been to Egypt" WMB taught that UFO's are "investigating Judgement angels" and People will be picked up by UFOOs when going up for the rapture (665-0822M, par 68). My personal encounter with UFO's was enough evidence for me to know that they are demons. I have narrated this on my "personal testimony". Now why is the church being prepared for an "alien" rapture?

When one looks at the drawings and markings made inn ancient Egypt, on pyramids, it is clear that they depict many times "Alien" like creatures in contact with men. In fact, the pyramids have many sculptures of these "gods". The sphinx, Pyramids have always been part of the occult. (Advanced Witchcraft). That is why many people who are in the **occult today**, are obsessed with pyramids structures etc.

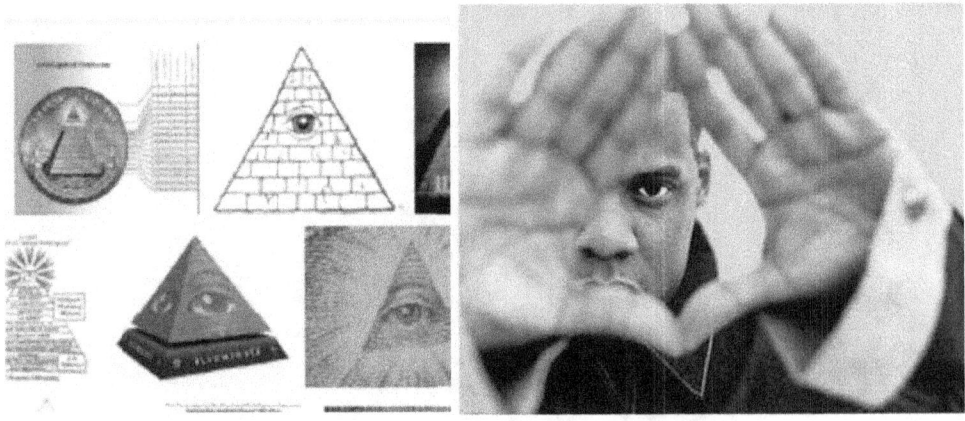

This is what WMB said about pyramids: The 1st Bible was the Zodiac, The 2nd Bible was Pyramids the 3rd is the Holy Bible. Below on the left is the grave of Charles Taze Russell. He is the founder of Jehova's Witness, Compare it with the grave of WMB on the right.

No, you are not dreaming.

W M Branham does not Speak Against Jehovah's Witness

Now, here was another one who said... I'd... I - I appreciate this asking. And Almighty God Who is my Judge, standing here now in this sacred spot... Before I left home, the Spirit of the Lord told me, said this question will be laying on here. And I - I knowed nothing about it, but I knew it would be here. "Is Jehovah Witness a false sect?" See, somebody... And the Holy Spirit, at the place at the. ... Standing in my bathroom before coming down here, God, Who is my solemn Judge, told me, "That will be laying on the platform," and said I wouldn't say nothing about it, just go on. See? So I... You know what I said last night, don't you? All right, that's what it was.

QA, Image of the Beast , May 15, 1954 (tape #54-0515)

It's now going to get a little more interesting:

The Angel

Let us turn to this angel again who gave WMB secret three High Words.

WMB Prays to His Angel and the Angel doesn't mind.

Angel of God, I do not see you. But I know that you are standing near. Please, thou knowest my heart, and know how I love these people. Stand by me tonight. And may not one go through without faith. And I know that your Words have been true. **I've took you at your Word, for you said you were sent from God.** *I believed you. And you've stuck by me. You have confirmed the Word with signs following. Now,* *again tonight, in this March the fifth, this Memorial night, may you stand now and heal every one. Grant it. May every demon be submissive to the Name of Jesus Christ.* **At Thy Word, Lord**, March 5, 1948 (tape #48-0305)

WMB has taught us to say what the Tapes say. That means, he is teaching us also pray this type of prayer that is praying to the Angel.

Why is he worshipping this Angel?

The Bible says

[18] **Let no man beguile you of your reward in a voluntary humility and worshipping of angels**, intruding into those things which he hath not seen, vainly puffed up by his fleshly mind

Colossians 2:18

Kindly note the Angel in the book of revelations told John not to worship him.

According to WMB: This Angel however, has no problems whatsoever with someone praying to him. Holy Spirit "possession"? part 1 But now, on the platform when someone meets me, then…it's not me that's speaking. When you hear my voice speaking when that inspiration is on, I have no more control of that than you know what you're going to say next New Year's day. **I do not have no control of that, it speaks itself.** It's my voice, and I'm listening to myself talk just as you're listening to me now talk. I hear myself, what it says to the people…Sometimes take a hold of their hand, I'll wait there, and after while I'll hear what it speaks, just hear myself speak, talking to the people. **It's a very strange feeling**. And under that anointing, being that my services are so close together, that it's best for me not to be too much under it at a time in one service. *The Angel of the Lord*, May 2, 1951 (tape #51-0502)

You may begin to think you starting to know what is happening, but let me assure you, you don't. The purpose of this chapter, is really going to focus on the last point. Which is my last and final point.

Now you may be thinking, well, everyone makes a mistake once in while, and WMB was just a man full of mistakes, and because he was uneducated, that's why he kept of fabricating things, copying other people's work and so forth. Now you are about to see, this is not just a matter of randomness, just a man, that keeps making errors and fabrications, and hoping no one will find them out, and moving along happy as he goes.

No!! The Agenda of the angel is MUCH bigger than that. If the Holy Spirit hath not shown this to me, I wouldn't have picked this up. This is my Last, and my most important point.

Beyond the Curtain of time

63-0322 THE FIFTH SEAL JEFFERSONVILLE IN FRIDAY

394   And I set there, and then a voice said, "You've been gathered to your people **like Jacob was gathered to his people.**" I said, "All these my people? Are all these Branhams?" He said, "No, they're your converts to Christ." And I looked around, and there was a real pretty woman run up. She looked real... They was all about the same. She threw her arm around me, and she said, "Oh, my precious brother." She looked at me. I thought, "My, she looked like an angel." And she passed by, and that voice said, "Didn't you recognize her?" I said, "No, I didn't recognize..." Said, "You led her to Christ when she was past ninety." Said, "You know why she thinks so much of you?" I said, "That pretty girl was past ninety?" "Yeah," said, "She can never change no more now." Said, "That's the reason she's saying, "precious brother." I thought, "Oh, my, and I was afraid of this. Why, these people are real." They - they wasn't going anywhere. They wasn't tired being there. And I said, **"Well, why can't I see Jesus?"** He said, "Well now, He will - **He will come someday**, and **He will come to you first**, and **then you'll be judged**." Said, "These people are your converts that you've led." And I said, "You mean by being a leader, that I - that - that He will judge me?" He said, "Yes." And I said, "Does every leader have to be judged like that?" Said, "Yes." I said, "What about Paul?" He said, "He will have to be judged with his." "Well," I said, **"if his group goes in, so will mine**, 'cause I've preached exactly the same Word." I said, "Where he batized in Jesus' Name, I did too. I preached..." And the millions screamed out, all at once, said, **"We're resting on that**."

I have heard this testimony being repeated over and

over again. Before the Lord by His grace showed me what is happening, I used to desire and pray to be amongst the "**millions**" screaming "We are resting on that". My eyes fill with water, when I think of His Amazing Grace.

Paul states in the scripture

[6] Therefore **we are** always confident, knowing that, whilst we are at home in the body, we are absent from the Lord
2 Corinthians 5:6

(For we walk by faith, not by sight)

We understand that before the death and resurrection of Jesus Christ, saints of old, which died under the blood of goats and bulls, were kept in a place which some people may refer to as "Paradise" or "Abraham's bosom". The souls of the saints in this place could even be called by witches (Saul and the spirit of Samuel). These souls could not be where Jesus was because they had died under blood of animals. When the perfect lamb of God had shed his blood, he died, buried and was resurrected, we read from the Bible in;

[9] (Now that he ascended, what is it but that he also descended first into the lower parts of the earth?
Ephesians 4:9

[52] And the graves were opened; and many bodies of the saints which slept arose,
Mathew 27:52

Saints that were dead, resurrected. Wow!! Finally, they could be with the Lamb. Prophets of old, that were waiting to be with Christ, could now be with him, their Lamb, their Redeemer, their Savior. The Lord Jesus Christ. What a story!! What an awesome story of Victory.

According to the narration of WMB above, his converts were dead on earth, but where **still waiting** for the coming of the Lord. Just to let you note something, "the Voice" that speaks to him could not have been Jesus because he says "**Well why can't I see Jesus**". So the argument that the voice is Jesus is gone. Now, that is where we start getting interesting preaching's on the "dimensions".

Now, let us forget unbiblical fabrications, let us save us time and stick with the Bible.

The Bibles states, the Saints were resurrected. Abraham resurrected, Daniel resurrected, Jacob Resurrected, Moses resurrected, they went home to be with Jesus Christ. Because Jesus has gone to prepare a place, so that where he is, we may be also.

When I breath my last breath on earth, I will be received by the loving caring arms of the Lord Jesus, he will come and fetch me, for I cannot lead myself home, and he will come for me, and lead me to his side!! Sweetest name in Seraph Song! Sweetest Carol ever Sung! Jesus Blessed Jesus.

But here we find WMB's converts, they are dead!! Yet, they are in a dimension where **Jesus is not there**. In fact, what they say it's scary. They are waiting for WMB to be Judged first! And then depending on which way it goes.., no really, that's what WMB says, he says "**if his group goes in, so will mine**"!! He is basing the entire salvation of his "converts" or should I say "group" on an "if Paul goes with his group". What he doesn't know is that Paul does not believe this "group" doctrine, because Paul does not believe in "dividing" the church of the Lord, as we saw earlier on.

Paul has no group "waiting" for the coming of Lord. If Paul's group was waiting also, then the 2 groups would be together in that "waiting" place. Let's assume the Church Age theory was from God, that would mean Ireneaus is waiting with his group, Columbas with his Group, Martin Luther with his group, John Wesley with his group. In other words according to WMB, there are multiple denominations in heaven with their bosses **waiting** for the coming of the Lord.

This is very important, may the Holy Spirit speak to your heart now. I don't care at this point if you are calling me Serpent Seed, I've crossed all the lines, Son of perdition, the beast" all the wonderful names we call each other in the Message, you can call me anything, I really don't mind, but at this time, will you please ask **the Lord Jesus to reveal to you the real truth**. This is the only point in this letter I'm begging you to pray in your heart as you ponder this.

Just think about this for a while. If there are "Groups" with their leaders, they are dead on earth, but they are not with God, and yet, they are also not together. Why do I say they are not together, WMB did not see Paul there, or Martin Luther, Or John Wesley. He is only seeing his converts. Unless you would like to tell me that, God created different dimensions and heavens for all the "leaders" with their "groups"

"So, in other words God is separating his church in heaven. All true Christians who have had what is called "near death, or death experience, they all describe, the minute their souls left the body, Jesus Christ received them."

Now, look to what they say to him, **He will come to you first!** If you don't see what is happening now, please, let the Holy Spirit open your heart. Where did you see this **ANYWHERE** in the Bible? How could we tell this story over and over again, for so many years without realizing it is talking about a heaven where Jesus is not present!! What do they mean when they say, when Jesus comes, he will come to their leader first? Why then did God send the Holy Spirit, if we are still going to be sent Leaders to be mediators. Please also take note that only He (the leader), is going to be Judged, the entire "group" will not be Judged. "If" he goes in, they go in too.
Is there Purgatory in the Bible? A place where people that are dead go and wait, until people on earth (WMB) comes to be judged rescues them?

This is what Jesus Christ said to the man of the Cross: "*Truly I say to you,* today *you* **shall be with me** in Paradise *(Luke 23:43).* After Jesus Christ is with this man, will Jesus then leave this man alone, and tell him, I'm leaving you in a waiting room with one of the "leaders"?? I will Judge the leader and see if you will make it? What manner of a Gospel is this? What is this thing?? Jesus Christ is a leader of His Church.

Listen to what the "converts" are saying… "we are resting on that". You see, they are not resting on Christ at all. They are resting **on the hope that WMB preached what Paul preached.** Why then was the purpose of him leading them to "Christ" if in the end, their personal relationship with "Christ" does not matter, what matters is that he is their "leader" is Judged. And because he believes he preached what Paul preached, they say they are waiting on that.

Did WMB preach what Paul preached? We have already seen that Paul does not believe in the "group" mentality. Let's investigate the following CRITICAL quotations and compare them with scripture, to see if WMB really preached what Paul Preached.

In a letter to the Galatians, Paul says in **Galatians 5:4** Christ is become of no effect unto you, **whosoever of you are justified by the law; ye are fallen from grace**

³ Are ye so foolish? having begun in the Spirit, are ye now made perfect by the flesh?

Galatians 3:3

WMB says:
The way of a true prophet (63-0119) *Any boy walk around with his britches hanging off his hips, and head hanging back, and his hair hanging down his neck like a Mrs. Kennedy's water-head haircut, and going around like that as a hoodlum. And then call that American?* **You've fallen from grace.**

The choosing of a Bride (65-0429E *Modern church and their theological paint, have their women all with their glory shaved off by their some Ricky added pastor that they got, like a Jezebel if there ever was one: bobbed-hair, shorts, paint, and all fixed up in a theological taste. That's the way the church stands. That's right. But her spiritual character is far from that being the homemaker that Jesus Christ is coming to receive.*

25-4 *If any Christian would marry a woman like that,* ***it shows he's fallen from grace***

Paul teaches that, If you replace the Holy Spirit with laws and regulations you fallen from Grace.

WMB on the other hand stated that your outward appearance showed that you have fallen from Grace. Keeping the law of WMB's angels "Outward holiness" is obedience to the law, it cannot make anyone perfect. Please show me anyone who achieved perfection in **sight of the Lord** because of the hair style, or clothes, or anything that is carnal.

So from the above 2 contradicting CORE teachings for Paul and WMB it is clear, WMB did NOT preach what Paul preached. Now my heart turns to those poor Souls, WMB's converts, that are in a place where there IS NO JESUS, hoping that WMB preached what Paul preached! This brings tears to my eyes.

WMB stated himself that:

53-1112 DEMONOLOGY OWENSBORO KY THURSDAY ^{E-46} Now, **when a believer dies now, he goes straight to the Presence of God**.
It's getting more astonishing.

65-1127B TRYING TO DO GOD A SERVICE WITHOUT IT BEING GOD'S WILL SHREVEPORT LA V-7 N-2 SATURDAY "See? Looking a-pass the curtain of time. There it was just the same as I'm preaching to you all, there they stood. Souls under the altar crying, "How long?"

WMB notices that his converts he saw were not in the presence of Jesus, so then he says they were the fifth seal "Souls under the altar". But this presents a rather **grave doctrinal issue**. During the preaching of the Fifth Seal, which of course came by the revelations of Angels, WMB states that
63-0323 THE SIXTH SEAL JEFFERSONVILLE IN SATURDAY

I always allowed them souls under the altar to be the early Christian martyrs, but we found out last night, **when the Lord God broke that Seal for us**, *it absolutely is impossible. It wasn't them.* **They were gone on to Glory,** *plumb on the other side. And there they was...* **We found out that they were Jews** *that would come up during the time where the -from the calling now of the hundred and forty-four thousand, which we get into tonight and tomorrow and - and between the Sixth and Seventh Seal, the hundred and forty-four thousand is called.*
So, from the above two contradicting statements, it is

quite clear that WMB does not know himself in which dimension his "Converts" end up. All he knows is, where they are, Jesus is NOT THERE!! But you can rest assured. WMB's angel, knows where those people are.

Please do not leave this world without accepting the Lord as your personal Savior by His Grace. You are going to have to choose this day, whether you are going to follow The Lord Jesus Christ or WMB. I can spend the whole year writing just to prove to you that Jesus and WMB say opposite things, and hence the Saints of God are with Him and the "converts" of WMB who is their "Leader" are somewhere else.

Many people may ask me, Why now? Why do you only see this now? Now may I state that, except the Holy Spirit showed this to me by His Love and Grace, I would also today, be a convert of WMB, going to that waiting place where there is no Jesus. I shudder, just thinking about this. It is not him who willeth or runneth, its purely the Grace of God. Not by Power nor by Might, but by my spirit saith the Lord!

Finality and Conclusion

How did it happen then, that so many people find themselves following mighty signs and wonders that are purely against God's word? Had we forgotten that a little leaven leaveneth the whole bread? What you need to form a cult, is to convince yourself that you and your "group" is correct and everyone else is Mark of the beast. In other words, you have to kill the love first for your neighbor. When you don't love your neighbor anymore, then you Jump on to this train, led by Mighty Leaders, with clouds, Angels, Pillars of fire, and Plenty of doctrinal confusion. Since the lord took away the scales in my eyes, I knew that I had to forsake all, I was born in the Message, I have no friends outside the message, I have no other life I know outside the Message church. Now when God is showing me this, and I know the ridicule, that I will be topics in every pulpit, the rejection that I will feel, when people treat me worse than leper, but I said Lord, I would rather suffer now!! I would rather be called The beast, Judas, serpent in the Grass, and all the names that are always in the mouths of Message believers, while they themselves are on the "fast lane" to heaven and the whole world is on a fast lane to hell.

I find it very strange, that we have spoken Many times in the message, how The Pope, will mobilise the World council of Churches and persecute the "little bride". But in reality, Message adherents are the ones doing the persecuting. We are the ones calling people "Dog meats", we are the ones calling denominations the mark of the beast. Of late, I used to feel very righteous and very religious, because I had ticked all the message checklist boxes. No TV, no this and that, and over and above that, I was just beginning to have a ministry where my fame was starting to spread in wider circles. But God called me to his side, he sat down, put his arms around me, and said I love you, I have always loved you. You left me right here, and you went up your Tower of Babel. How does one know that he/she is going up the Tower of Babel?, the higher you go, is the more you look down on people.

If you have a little tiny speck of love in your heart, no matter how drunk you see a woman on the street, you will never call her "Sexual Human Garbage Can". Jesus Christ says, if you love me keep my commandments. The commandments of Jesus Christ are only two. 1)Love the Lord thy God with your heart, 2)and love your neighbour, he says in all these 2 laws hangs ALL the LAW and ALL the prophets. The Kingdom of Jesus Christ is built on Love.

Satan is aware of this that is why he would rather give people a false impression of being "extremely" holiness, while he takes away from their hearts the main ingredient – "Love". He knows, it doesn't matter how Long their skirts are, when they die without love, with that kind of an attitude, When they leave this earth they are heading to a place where there is no Jesus. Their only representation is WMB.

I am prepared for the rejection that is soon to follow. As Daniel, I am even prepared to be thrown in the lion's Den, because I know, My Lord will come and spend the night with me in that Den.

When a Prophet is wrong he is always right

A brother came not long ago to my house. It was at a time I was still waiting for the Javelina Hunt Regulations so I did not want to say anything. He said these words, Brother Dan, do you know when a Prophet is wrong, he is in fact right. He continued to make an example of how Abraham lied, but he was still God's prophet, and How Jonah ran away from God's command to go to Niniveh, but in the end, His disobedience was the main pointer to the Messiah spending 3 days in belly of the earth. This sounds like a credible argument, but you will see now that Satan is horrible and indeed a father of ALL lies.

Why would God then say in

[21] And if thou say in thine heart, How shall we know the word which the LORD hath not spoken?
[22] When a prophet speaketh in the name of the LORD, if the thing follow not, nor come to pass, that is the thing which the LORD hath not spoken, but the prophet hath spoken it presumptuously: thou shalt not be afraid of him.

Deuteronomy 18:21-22

If I apply this brother's reasoning that when a prophet is wrong he is always right, that means ALL prophets are always right, because when they are wrong they are still right. According to him Prophet Lekganyane, and Prophet Mboro and Sangomas "Prophets" are right because no matter how wrong they are **they are** prophets so they are right. Unless he wants to tell me that there are some prophets which are right when they are wrong, and some prophets which are wrong when the wrong? The how do we know which "Wrong Prophet" to exonerate of his wrongness and turn it into right? This is an example of how Satan easily twits the scripture to suit him. But you can search the entire Bible, there is nowhere where God says "When a prophet is wrong is always right". I do not know how many times I've heard this unbiblical statements said behind "Message" Pulpits. Since this argument has been proven false by the Word of God let us put it to rest.

So Now who is the Elijah that is to Come

Many people ask the following questions: *"If Bro. Branham wasn't the fulfilment of* **Malachi 4:5,** *then who is?"*

I used to ask the same question as well, but by the grace of God, this is what the Holy Spirit revealed. As this is an important question and forms the BASIS for having an "End time Elijah" some considerable time is spent on this.

This question that people often asks, *"If Bro. Branham wasn't the fulfilment of* **Malachi** 4:5, *then who is?",* starts by makes very grave assumptions, that God has promised to send an Elijah to the gentiles. Hence why today we have so many "Elijah's", Alexander Dowie, Hebert Armstrong, etc. All their followers believe that their Elijah to be the "real deal". Now Let's pause for a moment to look at the following scriptures:

Is this assumption correct? Do we have to look for a Gentile prophet to fulfil Malachi 4:5?

The spirit of Elijah, and the spirit of Jesus

[13] But the angel said unto him, Fear not, Zacharias: for thy prayer is heard; and thy wife Elisabeth shall bear thee a son, and thou shalt call his name John.
[14] And thou shalt have joy and gladness; and many shall rejoice at his birth.
[15] For he shall be great in the sight of the Lord, and shall drink neither wine nor strong drink; and he shall be filled with the Holy Ghost, even from his mother's womb.

Luke 1:13

[11] Verily I say unto you, Among them that are born of women there hath not risen a greater than John the Baptist: notwithstanding he that is least in the kingdom of heaven is greater than he.

Matthew 11:11

The least in the kingdom of heaven is greater than John the Baptist.

Why?

Because every true Christian has the anointing of the Holy Spirit, which is far greater than the spirit of Elijah.

Why would God send the spirit of Elijah when each believer possesses something greater?

Are we falling short of what God intended for believers by looking for the spirit of Elijah when, in fact, we possess something much greater? Are we really living and attaining to the level of spiritual life that God intends for us?

Read Malachi 4 vs. Malachi 3

WMB stated that John the Baptist fulfilled Malachi 3 but did not fulfill Malachi 4.

However, Jesus told his disciples, referring to John, that **"if you are willing to accept it, he is Elijah, who is to come."** (Matthew 11:14)

The problem is that the there is **only one** reference to Elijah in Malachi, and that is in Malachi 4. So how could William Branham's interpretation that John did not fulfill Malachi 4 be correct **if Jesus specifically referred to John the Baptist as Elijah, a direct reference to Malachi 4?**

Scriptures

And if you are willing to accept it, he is Elijah, who is to come.
Matthew 11:14

Then they asked him, "Why do the experts in the law say that Elijah must come first?" He said to them, "Elijah does indeed come first, and restores all things. And why is it written that the Son of Man must suffer many things and be despised? But I tell you that Elijah has certainly come, and they did to him whatever they wanted, just as it is written about him."
Mark 9:11-13

But the angel said to him, "Do not be afraid, Zechariah, for your prayer has been heard, and your wife Elizabeth will bear you a son; you will name him John. Joy and gladness will come to you, and many will rejoice at his birth, for he will be great in the sight of the Lord. He must never drink wine or strong drink, and he will be filled with the Holy Spirit, even before his birth. He will turn many of the people of Israel to the Lord their God. And he will go as forerunner before the Lord in the spirit and power of Elijah, to turn the hearts of the fathers back to their children and the disobedient to the wisdom of the just, to make ready for the Lord a people prepared for him."
Luke 1:13

Quotes

Audio Letter to Lee Vayle (May 1964, Tucson, AZ)

You think it would be good 7here to let the public know that this wasn't the John of Malachi 4? This is John of Malachi 3, for in Matthew 11, you might quote it like this. See, Matthew 11:9, we put it. But what went ye out for to see? A prophet? yea, I say unto you, and more than a prophet. For this is he, whom it is written, Behold I send My messenger before thy face, which shall prepare thy way before thee. Now, that's Malachi 3, not Malachi 4. The Malachi 4 prophet is to come in this day, when the Lord is going to burn the Gentile world just - or the whole Gentile world up like He did at Sodom. You see? It's going to be Malachi 4 when He did that, not Malachi 3. Malachi 3 was John the Baptist also in the spirit of Elijah. But Malachi 4 here is John-or - or Elijah returning again just before the great and terrible day of the Lord, to turn the hearts of the children. John did it when he come, and this prophet will do the same thing in the - in the Malachi 4. See, there's two different times. And Jesus refers to it here as Malachi 3. "Behold, I send My messenger before My face." Jesus referring to John here... And Matthew 11 refers to it as Malachi 3. "My messenger before My face," not before the great and terrible day of the Lord shall come. I thought you might inject that there and let the public know that Malachi 3 Elijah, and Malachi 4 Elijah, are two different prophets altogether.
QUESTIONS.AND.ANSWERS.4 JEFF.IN 64-0830E

In Malachi 4, this Elijah is to take the hearts of the fathers to the children, and then the hearts of the children to the fathers. Is this the same person? Yes, the same person. All right. **Oh, wait a minute. No. Pardon me; I'm sorry. Just... See the Holy Spirit catch that for me then? No. I thought it said the... See?**

What it was in Malachi 3, there, "I send My messenger before My face," which was Elijah. In Malachi 4 it turns back around and said, "Behold I send Elijah." Malachi 3, He was to take a messenger sent before the face of the Lord Jesus, which was John. How many understands that? Malachi 4, when this Elijah comes, immediately after that - his Message and things, and after the - is the coming of the Lord and the renewing of the earth...
BIRTH.PAINS PHOENIX.AZ 65-0124

Then John, the promised Elijah of Malachi 3, not Malachi 4. Malachi 3, 'cause Jesus said the same thing in - in Matthew the 11th chapter.

...Said, "Then what did you go out to see, a prophet? And I say unto you, more than a prophet. For if you can receive it, this is he who was spoken of by the prophet, saying, 'I'll send My messenger before My face, to prepare the way.'" That's Malachi 3:1. Not Malachi 4, at all. That's a different. Cause, that Elijah come, the world is to be burnt immediately, and the righteous walk out on the ashes of the wicked.

PROVING HIS WORD LA CA 65-0426

not the Elijah of Malachi 4, at all.

Restoration time

Jesus said, *"Elias truly shall first come, and restore all things."* (Matthew 17:11b)

This statement has been interpreted by some to mean that Elijah's spirit is needed again as John the Baptist did not restore all things.

This presents two problems.

First, this ignores Jesus statement, *"that Elias is come already, and they knew him not, but have done unto him whatsoever they listed… Then the disciples understood that he spake unto them of John the Baptist."* **(Matthew 17:12-13)**

In other words, John the Baptist introduced Jesus Christ, who was the only person able to restore man to their intended condition. When John bore witness of the light, he was pointing the way back to the Word of God. *"In the beginning was the Word,"* (John 1:1a) and John the Baptist restored that Word to the people. **Secondly, Jesus said that the Holy Ghost would** *"teach you all things, and bring all things to your remembrance, whatsoever I have said unto you."* **(John 14:26)**

Why would the Lord Jesus Christ send Elijah if we have the Holy Spirit to teach us all things, and if it is the Spirit himself that brings all things to remembrance?

Turning the hearts

An angel prophesied to Zacharias, before the birth of John the Baptist, that he would *"go before [the Lord] in the spirit and power of Elias, to turn the hearts of the fathers to the children, and the disobedient to the wisdom of the just; to make ready a people prepared for the Lord."* (Luke 1:17).

The first, second, and fourth parts of this verse are very clear. The third part says, "the disobedient to the wisdom of the just." Since it is usually children who are disobedient, and usually parents who have wisdom, this part of the verse could be interpreted to read "to turn the hearts of the children to the fathers." If this is the true meaning of the prophecy in Luke 1:17, there is no half-scripture left for Elijah to fulfill.

The Great and Dreadful Day

Malachi 4:5 says that Elijah will come before:

"the coming of the great and dreadful day of the LORD." (KJV) *"the coming of the day of Jehovah, The great and the fearful."* (Young's Literal Translation) *"the great and awesome day of the LORD comes."* (ESV)

The Hebrew word translated as "dreadful" in the KJV includes the meanings "to cause astonishment and awe, be held in awe; or, to inspire reverence or godly fear or awe."
Daniel 9:4

And I prayed unto the LORD my God, and made my confession, and said, O Lord, the great and **dreadful God, keeping the covenant and mercy to them that love him***, and to them that keep his commandments;*

WMB, relies on the "dreadful" interpretation of this Hebrew word when he states in the Church Age Book, See, immediately after the coming of THIS Elijah, the earth will be cleansed by fire and the wicked burned to ashes. Of course, this did NOT happen at the time of John (the Elijah for his day.)

In other words, he subscribes "Destruction" to the meaning of this word. However as can be seen from Daniel 9:4, Daniel says the dreadful God, keeps the covenant of mercy to them that love him. Does dreadful in this scripture mean destructive God? This is where again, Scripture is has been twisted, to the detriment of thousands of "gullible" people to further the WMB "angel's" Agenda.

Jesus' ministry

The following paragraphs are all based on the KJV:

When Jesus was on earth, his ministry was to proclaim *"the acceptable year of the LORD"* (Luke 4:19). Jesus also said that he would send the *"the Comforter, which is the Holy Ghost"* (John 14:26a). Isaiah 61:2 says that the ministry of the Messiah (Christ, the anointed) was to *"proclaim **the acceptable year of the LORD, and the day of vengeance of our God;** to comfort all that mourn"*.

The acceptable year was Jesus' teaching ministry

The comforter (the Holy Spirit) came on the day of Pentecost The day of vengeance of our God would have to be between these two times, as the scripture is ordered this way.

As a result, the "day of vengeance of our God" is not the tribulation, but the day of the crucifixion and burial of Jesus Christ. That was the day that Jesus Christ suffered God's wrath and vengeance for sin on our behalf.

The Law and the Prophets

Jesus said that "all the prophets and the law prophesied until John. And if ye will receive it, this is Elias, which was for to come. He that hath ears to hear, let him hear." Matthew 11:13-15

Paul taught that "Christ is the end of the law for righteousness to everyone that believeth." (Romans 10:4). So, if the law has no dominion over Christians after Jesus' righteousness is imputed to us by faith, then the judgment of the prophets (including Elijah) also have no dominion over us by the same faith.

"Somethings are said to make people to leave, but the bride will stay"

These are some of the things one will hear from a Message church quoting WMB. Now this statement is spoken generally when it speaks about how Jesus said John 6:53 "Except ye eat the flesh of the Son of man, and drink his blood, ye have no life in you." You see, Jesus didn't explain it, he just said it, and many educated people left, because they ddnt understand the "third pull". Now this scripture is quoted when there are impossible things and absolutely pure fabrications which WMB said, (These are way too many to mention, see books "Fall of the legend" and "the rest of Annexure E, by Nathan Rivera), and it is said, it is God, "testing" who the real believer is.

Now this scripture was a commandment by Jesus. The is no way a commandment can be a lie. You are simply telling someone to do something. How can that be a lie. If I say, "please bring a glass of water", this can't be compared with a blatant fabrication and a "un-factual" statement like .. "Man has one less rib than a woman" – WMB; So this argument falls flat on its belly. It is one of the things said to make people even more Fearful of being "trapped" by God by investigating ridiculous fabrications.

Three high Words
I once heard one Message Pastor saying that, the Angel gave WMB three high words because WMB's mouth was constructed with big jaws and he could say things which no man could. You might be laughing now, but the Congregation was applauding in sheer astonishment. Happy that they have a prophet with big Jaws. The pastor then went on to say that the three high words was when WMB was calling the name of God from front to back, like a cassette playing in Reverse. Can we please come back to Christianity, it seems like now we are discussing Voodoo.

Where to from now

Now you may ask me, now who is your "leader". You need a "Leader" no one comes to the wedding feast without a messenger. Everyone comes with their messengers. What an utter misapplication of the Bible. Sometimes I wonder, how did we get to such a place where

we "Butcher" the word of God in broad daylight?
But I know why.

The Angel, we don't know his name, said WMB must make recordings of his sermons, therefore we have more than 1200 books and a few extra, that we must read in order to get "Rapturing faith". We can only get that Rapturing faith not in the Bible, but in the tapes of WMB. You must listen to them "until" you get rapturing faith. So, that is why, people don't even search the scriptures for themselves. It is one WMB tape after the other, no time for the Bible. All the while, having a feeling of righteousness, more than the Jezebels out there in the street. God saw them. "having a form of Godliness, but denying the power thereof".. what is the Power therefore, Love!! Love is the Power of Godliness. Love is everything. The tapes have long choked that love away. One can preach about love everyday, but the fruits will only manifest the seed that was planted.

2 Thessalonians 9 Even him, whose coming is after the working of Satan with all power and signs and lying wonders,

10 And with all deceivableness of unrighteousness in them that perish; because they received not the love of the truth, that they might be saved.
11 And for this cause God shall send them strong delusion, that they should believe a lie: (Believe their outward appearance will earn them a seat in heaven,)
12 That they all might be damned who believed not the truth, but had pleasure in unrighteousness. (Oh Lord, help that none is Damned)

How are the seventh day Adventists made to adhere strictly to the Sabbath and the doctrine of their church? They are told a fairy tale that one day the Pope, through the world council of churches will enforce Sunday as a day of worship. And it is at that time that their "3rd pull" will come, and the ark of the covenant will be found, and some other miracles happen.

How are message believers made to adhere strictly to 1124 tapes and extra books?, they have been told that One day, America will get so broke that they will have to go ask money from Rome. Then Rome will use the world council of churches to "force" us to join a denomination, and take away our Spoken Word books. The sad thing is that, Now in Midyear 2013, Rome is the one who is broke, they have austerity measures, the Eurozone is failing and they are part of it. Rome needs bailout from United States not the other way around. All these tactics are used to make you cling closer to your books believing someone will come fetch them away from you. Sad, Sad.

If anyone knows of a good Christian church I can attend with Sound doctrine, please refer me. (Please, No: Ellen White, Tussel, Moroni, Shembe, Lekganyane, Joseph Smith,Elijahs, Mboro) I just want a simple people who just loves the Lord Jesus Christ and Loves their neighbor. Love is a mystery to Satan. He will NEVER understand love. He can't understand Love. Darkness has never understood light. Light has never ran away from Darkness, but it is Darkness that has always ran away from Love.

God is love. Just break down all the Babylonian Idols, this is Home going time. I am so Thankful to God that he revealed to Daniel in Babylon, that it was time to look up!! Now you see why everyone wants Rome to be the mother harlot, and not America. Because satan will never reveal his true location. While people are still looking for the Pope to take away their "Spoken Word" books and turn their churches into storerooms, the real "fornications" of the great "Harlot" are being fed to the people. Making nations drunk!!

All South African cults, where they have a man as their "leader" have their roots in the USA. No wonder the cult leaders don't want people knowing the real Babylon. Mother of all Occultism and UFO and angel worship.

Don't you find it amazing, that the more hatred Message pulpits spread, calling people "fallen angels", Rickys, Jezebels, and all the names that are always on the message believer's mouth, the church members are clapping their hands and rejoicing. Yes, Lord! Bring Fire! And destroy these atomic Fodders!!

Jesus says in

5 And seeing the multitudes, he went up into a mountain: and when he was set, his disciples came unto him:
² And he opened his mouth, and taught them, saying,
³ Blessed are the poor in spirit: for theirs is the kingdom of heaven.
⁴ Blessed are they that mourn: for they shall be comforted.
⁵ Blessed are the meek: for they shall inherit the earth.

⁶ Blessed are they which do hunger and thirst after righteousness: for they shall be filled.
⁷ Blessed are the merciful: for they shall obtain mercy.
⁸ Blessed are the pure in heart: for they shall see God.
⁹ Blessed are the peacemakers: for they shall be called the children of God.
¹⁰ Blessed are they which are persecuted for righteousness' sake: for theirs is the kingdom of heaven.
¹¹ Blessed are ye, when men shall revile you, and persecute you, and shall say all manner of evil against you falsely, for my sake.
¹² Rejoice, and be exceeding glad: for great is your reward in heaven: for so persecuted they the prophets which were before you.
¹³ Ye are the salt of the earth: but if the salt have lost his savour, wherewith shall it be salted? it is thenceforth good for nothing, but to be cast out, and to be trodden under foot of men.
¹⁴ Ye are the light of the world. A city that is set on an hill cannot be hid.
¹⁵ Neither do men light a candle, and put it under a bushel, but on a candlestick; and it giveth light unto all that are in the house.
¹⁶ Let your light so shine before men, that they may see your good works, and glorify your Father which is in heaven.
¹⁷ Think not that I am come to destroy the law, or the prophets: I am not come to destroy, but to fulfil.
¹⁸ For verily I say unto you, Till heaven and earth pass, one jot or one tittle shall in no wise pass from the law, till all be fulfilled.
¹⁹ Whosoever therefore shall break one of these least commandments, and shall teach men so, he shall be called the least in the kingdom of heaven: but whosoever shall do and teach them, the same shall be called great in the kingdom of heaven.
²⁰ For I say unto you, That except your righteousness shall exceed the righteousness of the scribes and Pharisees, ye shall in no case enter into the kingdom of heaven.

21 Ye have heard that it was said of them of old time, Thou shalt not kill; and whosoever shall kill shall be in danger of the judgment:
22 But I say unto you, That whosoever is angry with his brother without a cause shall be in danger of the judgment: and whosoever shall say to his brother, Raca, shall be in danger of the council: but whosoever shall say, Thou fool, shall be in danger of hell fire.
23 Therefore if thou bring thy gift to the altar, and there rememberest that thy brother hath ought against thee;
24 Leave there thy gift before the altar, and go thy way; first be reconciled to thy brother, and then come and offer thy gift.
25 Agree with thine adversary quickly, whiles thou art in the way with him; lest at any time the adversary deliver thee to the judge, and the judge deliver thee to the officer, and thou be cast into prison.
26 Verily I say unto thee, Thou shalt by no means come out thence, till thou hast paid the uttermost farthing.
27 Ye have heard that it was said by them of old time, Thou shalt not commit adultery:
28 But I say unto you, That whosoever looketh on a woman to lust after her hath committed adultery with her already in his heart.
29 And if thy right eye offend thee, pluck it out, and cast it from thee: for it is profitable for thee that one of thy members should perish, and not that thy whole body should be cast into hell.
30 And if thy right hand offend thee, cut it off, and cast it from thee: for it is profitable for thee that one of thy members should perish, and not that thy whole body should be cast into hell.
31 It hath been said, Whosoever shall put away his wife, let him give her a writing of divorcement:
32 But I say unto you, That whosoever shall put away his wife, saving for the cause of fornication, causeth her to commit adultery: and whosoever shall marry her that is divorced committeth adultery.

³³ Again, ye have heard that it hath been said by them of old time, Thou shalt not forswear thyself, but shalt perform unto the Lord thine oaths:
³⁴ But I say unto you, Swear not at all; neither by heaven; for it is God's throne:
³⁵ Nor by the earth; for it is his footstool: neither by Jerusalem; for it is the city of the great King.
³⁶ Neither shalt thou swear by thy head, because thou canst not make one hair white or black.
³⁷ But let your communication be, Yea, yea; Nay, nay: for whatsoever is more than these cometh of evil.
³⁸ Ye have heard that it hath been said, An eye for an eye, and a tooth for a tooth:
³⁹ But I say unto you, That ye resist not evil: but whosoever shall smite thee on thy right cheek, turn to him the other also.
⁴⁰ And if any man will sue thee at the law, and take away thy coat, let him have thy cloak also.
⁴¹ And whosoever shall compel thee to go a mile, go with him twain.
⁴² Give to him that asketh thee, and from him that would borrow of thee turn not thou away.
⁴³ Ye have heard that it hath been said, Thou shalt love thy neighbour, and hate thine enemy.
⁴⁴ But I say unto you, Love your enemies, bless them that curse you, do good to them that hate you, and pray for them which despitefully use you, and persecute you;
⁴⁵ That ye may be the children of your Father which is in heaven: for he maketh his sun to rise on the evil and on the good, and sendeth rain on the just and on the unjust.
⁴⁶ For if ye love them which love you, what reward have ye? do not even the publicans the same?
⁴⁷ And if ye salute your brethren only, what do ye more than others? do not even the publicans so?
⁴⁸ Be ye therefore perfect, even as your Father which is in heaven is perfect.

Matthew 5

Moving Forward

After reading this article, many of you, just like myself, will be more than surprised, in total shock, disbelief and denial after realizing that the main stories told to get the people to believe WMB are all Fabrications.

I know the first thing many are going to go, is to run to your pastors to ask for clarifications. Rather go on yur knees and say the prayer under the born again section in the beginning of this book and ask for forgiveness and invite the Holy Spirit into your heart to guide and convict you.

Chapter 7: Freemasonry

Alice Ann Bailey (1880-1949), a leading spokesperson of the occultic *Theosophical Society* and member of Co-Masonry confirmed the occultic and Luciferian nature of Freemasonry, stated...

"The Masonic Movement is the custodian of the Law, the holder of the Mysteries, and the seat of initiation... a far more occult organization than can be realized... intended to be the training school for coming advanced occultists."

SOURCE: "President Clinton Will Continue The New World Order"; Dennis L. Cuddy, RESEARCH MANUAL: AMERICA 2000/GOALS 2000, MOVING THE NATION EDUCATIONALLY TO A "NEW WORLD ORDER" Editor: James R. Patrick Citizens for Academic Excellence, 1994, 28-48.

It is tragic that many professed "Christians" fail to recognize the occult nature of Freemasonry; while the occultists themselves, who blaspheme the name of Jesus Christ, openly admit the diabolical nature of Freemasonry.

Alice Bailey states the evil agenda of Freemasonry...

"There is no question therefore that the work to be done in familiarizing the general public with the nature of the Mysteries is of paramount importance at this time. **These mysteries will be restored to outer expression through the medium of the Church** [false church] and the Masonic Fraternity... When the

Great One [Antichrist] comes with his disciples and initiates we shall have the restoration of the Mysteries and their exoteric presentation as a consequence of the first initiation."

SOURCE: "President Clinton Will Continue The New World Order"; Dennis L. Cuddy, RESEARCH MANUAL: AMERICA 2000/GOALS 2000, MOVING THE NATION EDUCATIONALLY TO A "NEW WORLD ORDER" Editor: James R. Patrick Citizens for Academic Excellence, 1994, 28-48.

Alice Bailey plainly stated that Satan would **infiltrate the church** with Freemasonry, which is the training school for coming advanced occultists who will play their part in the establishment of the New World Order of the antichrist. In lieu of such damning evidence, it's hard to imagine that **37% of the U.S. Freemasonry membership are Southern Baptists**.

Albert Pike and other Masonic leaders acknowledge their debt to Kaballah and to the Babylonian Mystery Schools. In his book, *Morals and Dogma*, Pike states: "Every lodge is a temple of religion, and its teaching instruction in religion... Masonry is the successor to the Mysteries."

The Jewish Kaballah, their more occult teachings, is said by many to have been influenced by the Babylonian Mystery religion, and it originated as oral teachings during the Babylonian Captivity of the Jews. Albert Pike (1809 to 1891), a highly influential 33rd Degree Freemason of the nineteenth century, acknowledged that the Masons derived many of their ideas from the Jewish Kaballah. In his 1871 book,

Morals and Dogma of the Ancient and Accepted Scottish Rite of Freemasonry, Pike, says of the Jewish Pharisee tradition...

"The primary tradition... has been preserved under the name of the Kaballah by the priesthood of Israel." Freemasonry is a religion of Jewish mysticism and occultism, which are rooted in pagan Egyptian and Babylonian religions. Here are some more quotes concerning the demonic nature of Freemasonry...

"Freemasonry is not Christianity, nor a substitute for it. It does not meddle with sectarian creeds or doctrines, but **teaches fundamental religious truth.**" (Albert G. Mackey, "Encyclopedia of Freemasonry," page 162)

"**Masonry, like all the Religions**, all the **Mysteries**, Hermeticism and Alchemy, conceals its secrets from all except the Adepts and Sages, or the Elect, and **uses false explanations and misinterpretations of its symbols to mislead** those who deserve only to be misled; to conceal the Truth, which it calls Light, from them, and to draw them away from it." (Albert Pike, "Morals and Dogma," page 104)

"Drop the theological barnacles [timeless Biblical truths] from the religion of Jesus, as taught by Him, and by the **Essenes** and **Gnostics** of the first centuries, and it becomes Masonry, Masonry in its purity, derived as it is from the old Hebrew Kaballa as a part of **the great universal religion** of the remotest antiquity." (J. D. Buck, "Mystic Masonry," page 119)
It is also a known historical fact that **"skulls"** are an object of worship in pagan cultures, the skulls of human sacrifices are be used in occult rituals.

"...a skull and cross thigh bones are still used in the Masonic living resurrection ceremony. A quick calculation leads us to believe that Freemasonry around the world probably possesses a total of some fifty thousand skulls!"

SOURCE: Knight, Christopher and Robert Lomas. THE SECOND MESSIAH: TEMPLARS, THE TURIN SHROUD AND THE GREAT SECRET OF FREEMASONRY, Element, 1997.

Is that bizarre of what? This helps explain the emblem of the *Skull and Bones*, which is the official symbol of the occult group, *The Order of Death* (unofficially known as *Skull and Bones*), to which U.S. Presidents George W. Bush and his father are members. John Kerry is also a member of this evil power-wielding group. Satan is the god of this world (2 Corinthians 4:4), and he operates through occult organizations to hide his true evil agenda.

-By David J. Stewart

Freemasonry is of the Devil

FREEMASONRY AND CULTS!

Joseph Smith founded the **Mormon** church, which is also called the Church of Jesus Christ of Latter-Day Saints. Smith and his followers were Masons. Mormon priests go through the rituals of the first three degrees of Masonry. Mormon sources claim that Masons murdered Joseph Smith. As a result, Mormons aren't allowed to join Masonic lodges, even though their origin is Masonic. ("Scarlet and the Beast," Vol. 1, pages 41-42)

Masons founded the **Jehovah's Witnesses** and the Church of Scientology. Mary Baker Eddie, the founder of Christian Science, was strongly influenced by Freemasonry. Madame Blavatsky, the founder of Theosophy, was a Mason. (Some European lodges have admitted women.) Theosophy is foundational to much of the New Age movement. ("Scarlet and the Beast," Vol. 1, pages 42 and 649-650).
Ron Hubbard, founder of <u>**Scientology**</u>, was also a high-degree Freemason and personal good friend of Satanist, <u>Aleister Crowley</u>.

In 1951, a Mason named Gerald B. Gardner introduced Wicca to mainstream society. Gardner was the first fully public witch of modern times. He made witchcraft more socially acceptable by changing its name to **Wicca** and calling it an ancient religion. There is evidence that Gardner's witchcraft texts were his personal creation rather than being documents handed down from ancient tradition. This would make Wicca a modern Masonic invention rather than the resurrection of an ancient pagan religion. (For a discussion of this, see "Goddess Unmasked" by Philip G. Davis, pages 327-343.)
Ellen G. White, founder of the *Seventh-day Adventists*, has a <u>large Freemasonry Obelisk marking her grave</u>. On the surface, Freemasonry looks wholesome. There is fellowship, loyalty, and the support of good causes such as burn units in hospitals. The Masonic motto is "Making good men better."

Few men understand what they are getting into when they become Masons. Most Masons join because they trust friends, family members, or church members who invite them. Others join for business connections or political votes. Some men join because of Masonic charities. Most men who join have no idea that, during their initiation, they will be required to make solemn blood oaths.

American Freemasonry includes local Lodges, Scottish Rite Temples, York Rite, and the Shriners. Prince Hall is a Masonic order for black men.

The Eastern Star is an auxiliary organization for wives and adult daughters of Masons. There are also Masonic organizations for children -- DeMolay (for boys), Job's Daughters, and Rainbow Girls. These are known as "adoptive" masonry, which means that wives, sisters, daughters and sons of Masons are spiritually adopted into the Masonic order. As a result, they are under the spiritual authority of Freemasonry. (William Schnoebelen, Masonry: Beyond the Light, page 104)

MASONS ARE DECEIVED

For the vast majority of Masons, Freemasonry is a lifelong succession of deceptions. Most Lodge leaders do not realize that they are deceiving their members. For the most part, they are simply reciting the same things they have heard and said, over and over, assuming that they are right and good. However, the Princes and Adepts of Freemasonry deliberately deceive the Masons under them. (See Tom C. McKenney, "Please Tell Me...Questions People Ask About Freemasonry -- and the Answers," pages 123-133.)

Masons take blood oaths, but are told that they are

only symbolic. They participate in rituals that they don't understand, assuming that they must be alright because their Masonic friends have done it.

This paper contains quotations which would shock most Masons because they have never read what the highest Masons say about Freemasonry. Masonry is a system that confuses, deceives and controls men, getting them to do things that they would not do if they understood them.

The highest-level Masons (Princes and Adepts) deliberately deceive the Masons under them. For example, Albert Pike was one of the highest authorities in American Masonry. He was Grand Commander of the Southern Jurisdiction of the Scottish Rite of Freemasonry from 1859 to 1891. He was also Grand Commander of the Thirty-Third Degree, as well as a Prince Adept. His book "Morals and Dogma" is given to men when they reach the 32nd degree. The following quotations from Pike's "Morals and Dogma" show that Masons of the highest level deliberately deceive the Masons below them... "Part of **the symbols are displayed there to the initiate, but he is intentionally misled by false interpretations**. It is not intended that he shall understand them; but **it is intended that he shall imagine he understands them**." (Albert Pike, "Morals and Dogma," page 819)

"There must always be a **commonplace interpretation for the mass** of initiates, **of the symbols that are eloquent to the Adepts**." (Albert Pike, "Morals and Dogma," page 819) [The "Adept" are Thirty-Third Degree and above.]

Even a Thirty-Second Degree Mason will have limited understanding unless he studies the Secret Doctrine and the writings of the Princes and Adepts of Masonry. It is difficult for a man to turn away from Freemasonry because of the many blood oaths which he has made in order to obtain his degrees. Furthermore, he has invested a lot of time, effort and money into Masonry, and many of his friendships and business connections are with fellow Masons. Freemasonry is a religion. Masons meet in temples, such as the Scottish Rite Temple. They have an altar and there is a "holy book" on it. They have prayers, deacons, and religious titles for their leaders, such as High Priest and Worshipful Master. They say that they bring men from spiritual darkness to spiritual light. In some Masonic degrees, they even serve communion. Although Freemasonry is a religion, most Masons deny it. They use double talk and say "We are an order of religious men, but not a religion." Most of them are quite sincere about this. (Tom C. McKenney, "Please Tell Me," pages 81-82)

Most Masons sincerely (but wrongly) believe that Freemasonry is not a religion. How can they be so wrong when they are so sincere? Tom McKenney says, "...they were told upon entering the Lodge that, whatever their religion, Masonry would not conflict with or contradict it. They believed this because sincere men told them so. Those sincere men who told them so believed it because an earlier generation of sincere men had told them the very same thing. And so, **this deception, which originated as a lie in Masonry's dark beginnings, is perpetuated** generation after generation." (Tom C. McKenney, "Please Tell Me," page 82)

MASONRY CLAIMS TO BE SUPERIOR TO CHRISTIANITY

Not only is Freemasonry a religion, its highest authorities claim that it is superior to Christianity. Freemasonry is considered to be the highest and purest form of religion:
"Freemasonry is not Christianity, nor a substitute for it. It does not meddle with sectarian creeds or doctrines, but **teaches fundamental religious truth.**" (Albert G. Mackey, "Encyclopedia of Freemasonry," page 162)
Christianity is even considered to be Freemasonry which has become encrusted with inflexible Biblical doctrines or "theological barnacles".
"Drop the theological barnacles from the religion of Jesus, as taught by Him, and by the Essenes and Gnostics of the first centuries, and it becomes Masonry, Masonry in its purity, derived as it is from the old Hebrew Kaballa as a part of the great universal religion of the remotest antiquity." (J. D. Buck, "Mystic Masonry," page 119)
To better understand Mr. Buck's statement, it is necessary to understand what the Kaballa is. (Kaballa can also be spelled Kaballah, Kabala or Cabala.) Webster's dictionary defines it as:
"1. A kind or system of occult theosophy or mystical interpretation of the Scriptures among Jewish rabbis and certain medieval Christians. 2. Secret or esoteric doctrine or science, in general; occultism; mystic art; mystery." ("Webster's Collegiate Dictionary," Fifth Edition, 1947)
The following definitions give clarity to the above definition of the Kaballa:

"Occult. Of, pertaining to, concerned with, or designating alchemy, magic, astrology and other arts and practices involving use of divination, incantation, magical formulae, etc." ("Webster's Collegiate Dictionary," Fifth Edition, 1947)

"Occultism. Occult theory or practice; belief in hidden or mysterious powers and the possibility of human control of them." ("Webster's Collegiate Dictionary, Fifth Edition, 1947)

Albert Pike also stresses the fundamental importance of the Kaballa to Freemasonry:

"All truly dogmatic religions have issued from the Kaballah and return to it; everything scientific and grand in the religious dreams of all the Illuminati, Jacob Boeheme, Swedenborg, Saint Martin, and others, is borrowed from the Kabalah; all Masonic associations owe to it their Secrets and their Symbols." (Albert Pike, "Morals and Dogma," page 744)

MASONRY IS ANTI-CHRISTIAN

Considering Freemasonry's roots in the Kaballa, it is not surprising that it opposes Christianity. The writings of Masonry's highest authorities clearly show that it actually is antagonistic to Christianity, to the point that Masons are not supposed to mention the name of Jesus in the Lodge.

"A Christian Mason is not permitted to introduce his own peculiar opinions with regards to Christ's mediatorial office into the lodge." (Albert G. Mackey, "Lexicon of Freemasonry," page 404)

"Whether you swear or take God's name in vain don't matter so much. Of course the name of the Lord Jesus

Christ, as you know, don't amount to anything, but Mah-hah-bone--O, horror! You must never, on any account, speak that awful name aloud. That would be a most heinous crime--unmasonic--unpardonable." (Edmond Ronayne, "Masonic Handbook," page 184) James Shaw, a former Thirty-Third Degree Mason, was appointed Chaplain in the Scottish Rite. Since at that time he didn't know how to pray, he got a book of John Wesley's prayers and read one, ending "in Christ's name". For that he was sharply rebuked by his Commander and reported to the Secretary of the Scottish Rite, who told him that he was never to end a prayer "in Jesus' name" or "in Christ's name." (Tom McKenney, "Please Tell Me," page 72)

MASONRY CLAIMS TO PROVIDE SALVATION WITHOUT JESUS

The following quotation shows that Freemasonry promises "assurance of a future life" apart from Jesus. Most people familiar with salvation would take this to be a promise of salvation. However, eternity in hell is a form of "future life." Everybody has a future life. The question is, will they spend it in Heaven or in hell? "The symbolism of the Master's Degree, as we have it now, is necessarily restricted to the First Temple and to the present life; although it reaches a climax in the assurance of a future life all without the aid of the Bible, God, Jesus Christ or the church." (John A. Hertel Company, "The Masonic Bible,' pages 10-11)

MASONS WORSHIP PAGAN GODS

When Masons first join a lodge, they worship G.A.O.T.U, which they are told is the god of their own religion. When they have progressed, they are told that G.A.O.T.U. stands for the Grand Architect of the Universe. Then they search for the true name of God, which they are told was lost. In the process, they are taught that the God of the Bible is the same as the old pagan gods:

"The Masonic doctrine of the unity of God teaches that: (1) The names of the different nature gods (Brahma, Baal, Om, On, Dagon, Osiris, Allah, Molech, and Shango), along with Jehovah, all denote the generative (reproductive) principle in nature. (2) All religions are essentially the same in their ideas of the divine. (3) It is for this express purpose that the simple Mason is instructed to look upon every man's religion as his own." (C. F. McQuaig and James D. Shaw, "The Masonic Report," page 8)

In the Royal Arch Degree (13th degree), the Mason is given a three-syllable name for God. Each syllable stands for a different god. The first stands for Jehovah, the God of the Bible. The second stands for Baal. The third stands for a Chaldean (Babylonian) god. This name signifies that the God of the Bible and Baal are one and the same, being different facets of the same god. (See page 97 of Martin L. Wagner's "Interpretation of Freemasonry" and pages 8-9 of "The Masonic Report" by C. F. McQuaig and James D. Shaw).

According to the Bible, pagan gods are really demons. The conflict between Elijah and the prophets of Baal demonstrates that Baal worship and worship of the God of the Bible are incompatible. (See 1 Kings, chapter 18) Christians are warned that they cannot worship both the God of the Bible and pagan gods.

"What am I saying then? That an idol is anything, or what is offered to idols is anything? Rather, that the things which the Gentiles sacrifice they sacrifice to demons and not to God, and I do not want you to have fellowship with demons. You cannot drink the cup of the Lord and the cup of demons; you cannot partake of the Lord's table and of the table of demons." (1st Corinthians 10:19-21)

The Royal Arch Degree shows that Masons are really Baal worshipers. Most Masons do it without realizing it by participating in rituals that they really don't understand. However, a few top-level Masons (those in highest authority) know exactly what they are doing.

In Old Testament times, the Canaanites worshipped Baal by having men have sexual intercourse with temple prostitutes (both male and female, including children), and by burning babies alive. Other pagan gods were worshipped in similar ways. In some countries, this kind of pagan worship continues to this day. For example, according to eye-witness accounts, children in India are still being drowned in the Ganges River as sacrifices to pagan gods. In this century, Amy Carmichael and her coworkers rescued children from temple prostitution in India.

Most Masons don't understand that they are really worshipping demons when they worship pagan gods. They also have little or no knowledge of the atrocities that men have committed in pagan worship.

MASONIC INITIATION

Before being initiated, candidates for membership do not know that any oath will be involved, much less the bloody nature of the oath. They take the oath a few words at a time, repeating the words as the Worshipful Master says them. Before they start saying the oath, they are assured that nothing they are going to say will in any way conflict with their religion.

At the time that he is led in the oath, the candidate is disoriented, blindfolded, half naked, confused, afraid, and humiliated. He has been stripped of all his clothes and his wedding ring, and has put on something similar to pajamas, with one leg rolled up and the shirt half off his torso. He has been blindfolded with a hood, and had a rope put around his neck. He has been led around during the initiation ritual like a blind dog on a leash. He has no idea who is watching him or how many men there are. He has been told that he is in darkness and must depend on Masonry to give him light.

After having been pressured into taking an oath that he never expected to take -- and which he only partly understood because he was disoriented and only heard a few words at a time -- the initiate is given a written copy of the oath. He is required to memorize it word for word. This is similar to being pressured into signing a blank check, and later finding out what it is going to cost you.

All of this is a powerful means of subjugation and mind control. It can bind men to the Lodge and its authority both mentally and spiritually. (See Tom C. McKenney, "Please Tell Me," pages 66-69 and 124).

MASONIC OATHS

The first degree, or Entered Apprentice, swears, with his hand on the sacred book of his religion (the Bible, Koran, etc.). His oath states various obligations, and concludes:

"I do most solemnly and sincerely promise and swear, without the least equivocation, mental reservation, or self evasion of mind in me whatever; binding myself under no less penalty than to have my throat cut across, my tongue torn out by the roots, and my body buried in the rough sands of the sea at low watermark, where the tide ebbs and flows twice in twenty-four hours; so help me God, and keep me steadfast in the due performance of the same." (Captain Morgan, "Freemasonry Exposed," pages 21-22.)

Penalties for violating oaths of the next two degrees include having his heart ripped out, and being cut in two and disemboweled. A Christian Mason makes these vows with his hand on the Bible, asking God to keep him steadfast in performing it.

Once a man becomes a Master Mason, he is eligible to join the Scottish Rite or the York Rite. Scottish Rite Masonry has twenty-nine more degrees and York Rite has ten more degrees. Each of these degrees includes initiation, with a blood oath. A Thirty-Second Degree Mason is a man who reached the Third Degree (Master Mason) in his local Lodge, and then went through twenty-nine more degrees in the Scottish Rite.

Thirty-Second Degree Masons are eligible to join the Shriners (an American order of Freemasonry). Initiation into the Shriners includes a taking blood oath and swearing allegiance to Allah. (Allah is not another name for the God of the Bible. It is the name of another god, a pagan god.) (C. F. McQuaig and James D. Shaw, "The Masonic Report," page 72)

Membership in the Thirty-Third Degree is by invitation only. Initiation includes drinking wine out of a human skull and taking a solemn oath that their primary allegiance is to the Thirty-Third Degree Masons. (Jim Shaw and Tom McKenney, "The Deadly Deception," page 104)

MASONIC SECRETS

Masons spend their lives carefully guarding secrets -- initiation rituals, secret words, "obligations" (oaths), "signs" (special body language), and secret distress signals (the Grand Hailing Sign, and the question: "Is there no help for the widow's son?") They take blood oaths, promising to allow themselves to be killed if they betray any of these secrets. However, most of these secrets have been matters of public record for over a century.

In 1826, Captain William Morgan (a Mason of the Royal Arch Degree) renounced Freemasonry. He then wrote "Freemasonry Exposed", a book revealing Masonic oaths and secrets. He and his publisher were kidnapped by Masons. Captain Morgan was murdered, but his publisher escaped and told people about the murder. As a result of Captain Morgan's Murder, thousands of Masons became disillusioned and renounced Freemasonry. Some of them testified in court, thus revealing more Masonic secrets. These written court records have been available to the public since 1826. (See the section of this paper on "Masonic Morals" for further information regarding Captain

Morgan's murder.)

In 1869, Evangelist Charles Finney (a former Mason) published a book further exposing Freemasonry. In this book (which was published 130 years ago), Rev. Finney discusses eight books which had already been published by former Masons. One of them was a comprehensive book written by a committee of sixteen former Masons, which gives the signs, tokens, grips, sacred words, passwords, oaths, and hieroglyphics of forty-eight degrees of Freemasonry. It also has diagrams of lodges and drawings representing signs and ceremonies. Another book covers sixty-two degrees of Freemasonry. In addition to the Blue Lodge degrees (which go through Master Mason) and the Scottish Rite and York Rite degrees, a number of European degrees are also described in these books. (Charles G. Finney, "The Character, Claims and Practical Workings of Freemasonry," pages 174-176) Since then, other former Masons have written books exposing Freemasonry.

In 1988, Jim Shaw (a former Thirty-Third Degree Mason) wrote about his personal experience in "The Deadly Deception," a book which he co-authored with Tom McKenney. This autobiography shows the human, experiential side of Freemasonry through the Thirty-Third Degree, in addition to giving secrets, oaths, and rituals. It shows love for the men, while exposing the system.

In 1991, William Schnoebelen wrote "Masonry: Beyond the Light," which describes his personal experience in an "esoteric" degree which is even higher than the Thirty-Third Degree. (This degree is so secret that most Masons have never heard of it.)

MASONIC MORALS

Master Masons promise not to cheat, defraud, or do violence to a Master Mason. They promise not to commit adultery with the wife of a Master Mason or seduce his sister, daughter, or other female relative. These promises only apply to fellow Master Masons. They do not protect non-Masons, Entered Apprentices, or Fellow Crafts and their families.

Masons are required to tell lies and even perjure themselves to protect other Masons. They are also required to obey even orders which they know to be immoral:
"You must conceal all the crimes of your brother Masons, except murder and treason, and these only at your own option, and should you be summoned as a witness against a brother Mason be always sure to shield him. Prevaricate [falsify], don't tell the whole truth in his case, keep his secrets, forget the most important points. It may be perjury to do this, it is true, but you're keeping your obligations, and remember if you live up to your obligation strictly, you'll be free from sin." (Edmond Ronayne, "Masonic Handbook," page 183)

"Right or wrong his very existence as a Mason hangs upon obedience to the powers immediately set above him. The one unpardonable crime in a Mason is contumacy [insubordination] or disobedience." (Robert Morris, "Webb's Monitor of Freemasonry," page 169) According to Masonic oaths, Masons are to be killed if they reveal Masonic secrets. In 1826, Captain William

Morgan, a high-degree Mason, made Masonic secrets public in his book "Freemasonry Exposed." According to the "Masonic Handbook," he was murdered for it. "When a brother reveals any of our great secrets; whenever, for instance, he tells anything about Boaz, or Tubalcain, or Jachin, or that awful Mah-hah-bone, or even whenever a minister prays in the name of Christ in any of our assemblies, you must always hold yourself in readiness, if called upon, to cut his throat from ear to ear, pull out his tongue by the roots, and bury his body at the bottom of some lake or pond. Of course, all this must be done in secret, as it was in the case of that notorious man Morgan, for both law and civilization are opposed to such barbarous crimes, but then, you know you must live up to your obligation, and so long as you have sworn to do it, by being very strict and obedient in the matter, you'll be free from sin." (Edmond Ronayne, "Masonic Handbook," page 74)

The murder of Captain Morgan -- and the kidnapping and attempted murder of his publisher, David Miller -- are described in detail (with extensive quotations from original sources) in the Introduction to the 1998 reprint of "The Character, Claims and Practical Workings of Freemasonry" by Charles G. Finney (pages xxi through xxxviii). (This book was first published in 1869. In 1998 it was reprinted with a Foreword by Ed Decker and an Introduction and Epilog by John Daniel). Pages 6-10 give the death-bed confession of one of Captain Morgan's murderers.

Masons still murder people. In the Foreword to "The Character, Claims and Practical Workings of Freemasonry," Ed Decker tells how he survived attempted murder by Masons (pages i to iii).

MASONRY'S RELATIONSHIP TO THE MAFIA AND THE KU KLUX KLAN

Giuseppe Mazzini, a Thirty-Third Degree Mason, founded a group of revolutionaries called Young Italy. Their goal was to free Italy from the control of monarchy and the Pope. They succeeded, and Mazzini is honored as a patriot in Italy. However, in the process, the Mafia was born. The Young Italy revolutionaries needed money, and they:
"...supported themselves by robbing banks, looting or burning businesses if protection money was not paid, and kidnapping for ransom. Throughout Italy the word spread that "Mazzini autorizza furti, incendi e attentati," meaning, 'Mazzini authorizes theft, arson, and kidnapping.' This phrase was shortened to the acronym, M.A.F.I.A. Organized crime was born." (John Daniel, "Scarlet and the Beast," Vol. I., pages 330-331)
Albert Pike was Grand Commander the Thirty-Third Degree, as well as Grand Commander of the Southern Jurisdiction of the Scottish Rite of Freemasonry. He was also a Confederate general. Pike was influenced by Mazzini. Both were military men who were good at fomenting rebellion. (William Schnoebelen, "Masonry," pages 191-192.)

When the Confederacy surrendered to the Union forces, Albert Pike was determined to start another Civil War so that South could win. He founded the Ku Klux Klan, which instigated riots throughout the South in an attempt to disrupt reconstruction and incite a second Civil War. Pike gave Klansman Jesse James the assignment of robbing Northern banks in order to get money to fund this war. It is estimated that Jesse James and other Klansmen buried seven billion dollars in gold all over the western states. ("Scarlet and the Beast," Vol. 3, pages 76-77)

"Pike the old Confederate general, was a wily strategist who knew that if he could leave behind a secret terrorist society in the south to fight against freedom for black people as a rear guard action, the south's defeat might not be in vain." ("Masonry," page 192)

Two books from the turn of the twentieth century document Pike's direct involvement in founding the Klan: "Ku Klux Klan: Its' Origin, Growth and Disbandment" (1905) by J. C. Lester and D. L. Wilson; and "Authentic History: Ku Klux Klan 1865-1877" (1924) by Susan Lawrence Davis." ("Scarlet and the Beast," Vol. 3, page 76)

In considering this, we should remember that Mazzini and Pike probably saw what they did as doing "whatever it takes" to accomplish goals that were important to them. This is a practical application of the philosophy that "the end justifies the means". Mazzini successfully used guerilla warfare and civil disruption to instigate a civil war in Italy, in order to win freedom from control by the monarchy and the papacy. Pike attempted to do a similar kind of thing in the South, in order to win freedom from control by the North, but he failed.

MASONRY'S INFLUENCE ON AMERICA

The majority of Supreme Court justices were Masons from 1941 to 1971. During this time, prayer and Bible reading were prohibited in schools, and pornography was redefined to allow things that had previously been considered indecent.

Sixteen presidents were Masons. Many judges and politicians are Masons. In 1950, one out of every twelve American men was a Mason, but membership has been decreasing since then.

MASONRY'S INFLUENCE ON THE CHRISTIAN CHURCH

According to a tract produced by Concerned Southern Baptists in 1994, twenty-six percent of Southern Baptist men are Masons, and the percentage is even higher among leadership. Masons are also common in other denominations. For example, Dr. C. F. McQuaig, an Assemblies of God pastor, had so many Masons in his congregation that he did extensive research and wrote "The Masonic Report."

PRIMARY LOYALTY

When Jim Shaw became a Thirty-Third Degree Mason, all of the candidates swore that their allegiance to Freemasonry took priority over all other commitments. Among those present at this initiation were some highly influential men.
"We then swore true allegiance to the Supreme Council of the 33rd Degree, above all other allegiances, and swore never to recognize any other brother as being a member of the Scottish Rite of Freemasonry unless he also recognizes the supreme authority of 'this Supreme Council.' . . . There were some extremely prominent men there that day, including a Scandinavian King, two former presidents of the United States, an internationally prominent

evangelist, two other internationally prominent clergymen, and a very high official of the federal government, the one who actually presented me with the certificate of the 33rd Degree." (Jim Shaw and Tom McKenney, "The Deadly Deception," pages 104-105)

The initiation consisted of two parts. The first involved things that were acted out. One of the candidates went through that, representing the entire group. The second part of the ritual was taking the oath. All of the men formally made the oath, which was sealed by drinking wine out of a human skull.

"One of the Conductors then handed the 'candidate' [the man who represented all of the candidates] a human skull, upside down, with wine in it.

"With all of us candidates repeating after him, he sealed the oath, 'May this wine I now drink become a deadly poison to me, as the Hemlock juice drunk by Socrates, should I ever knowingly or willfully violate the same' (the oath).

"He then drank the wine. A skeleton (one of the brothers dressed like one -- he looked very convincing) then stepped out of the shadows and threw his arms around the 'candidate.' Then he (and we) continued the sealing of the obligation by saying, 'And may these cold arms forever encircle me should I ever knowingly or willfully violate the same.'" (Jim Shaw and Tom McKenney, "The Deadly Deception," pages 104-105)

CAN CHRISTIANS BE MASONS?

Because some Christians are Masons, many people

sincerely believe that Freemasonry is compatible with Christianity. Unfortunately, just being sincere does not protect Christian Masons from having their Christian faith and fervor become weakened by Freemasonry. Christians who become Masons are under two opposing spiritual influences -- Jesus Christ and paganism. The Bible calls this being double minded. The Apostle Paul said:

"Do not be yoked together with unbelievers. For what do righteousness and wickedness have in common? Or what fellowship can light have with darkness? What harmony is there between Christ and Belial? What does a believer have in common with an unbeliever? What agreement is there between the temple of God and idols? For we are the temple of the living God." (2 Corinthians 6:14-16)

FREEMASONS CURSE THEMSELVES AND THEIR FAMILIES

Freemasonry is actually a pagan religion, the worship of pagan gods. It is idolatry. In the Commandment dealing with idolatry, God says:

"...you shall not bow down to them nor serve them. For I, the Lord your God, am a jealous God, visiting the iniquity of the fathers upon the children to the third and fourth generations of those who hate Me." (Exodus 20:5)

BOOKS CITED

Books by Masonic authors are available at lodge libraries and Masonic distributors. Most of them are only sold to Masons. However, they can sometimes be found at used book stores and yard sales. Albert

Pike's "Morals and Dogma" is difficult to obtain. All quotations from books by Masonic authors can be found in "The Masonic Report," which is described in the Bibliography.

The books in the Bibliography are all written by Christians. With the exception of Tom McKenney, the authors are former Masons who renounced Freemasonry. The first two books are available at Amazon.com and regular bookstores. Information for ordering the other three books is given in the Bibliography.

BIBLIOGRAPHY

"The Deadly Deception" by Jim Shaw and Tom McKenny (1988, Huntington House, Inc., Lafayette, Louisiana). This book describes Jim Shaw's experience as a Thirty-Third Degree Mason, his discovery of Jesus Christ, and his deliverance from Freemasonry.

"Please Tell Me...Questions People Ask About Freemasonry -- and the Answers," by Tom C. McKenney (1994, Huntington House Publishers, Lafayette, Louisiana). After Deadly Deception was published, Tom McKenney was invited to answer questions on several hundred talk shows. This book answers the most frequently asked questions about Freemasonry. It is compassionately written and avoids gory details. If you are only going to get one book about Freemasonry, this is a good one to get. It is easy to read, covers the questions that people ask in real life, and doesn't go into a lot of gory details.

"The Masonic Report: New Revised Pastor's Edition" by C. F. McQuaig, with James D. Shaw (1976, Answer Books and Tapes, P.O. Box 1316, Norcross, GA 30091-1316) (Shaw was a former Thirty-Third Degree Mason; McQuaig was a former Thirty-Second Degree Mason.) This book includes many quotations from high-ranking Masonic authorities, books that would be difficult for non-Masons to obtain.

"The Character, Claims and Practical Workings of Freemasonry" by Rev. Charles G. Finney. This book was first published in 1869. In 1998 it was reprinted with a Foreword by Ed Decker, an Introduction and Epilog by John Daniel, and an Appendix by four pastors. (Jon Kregel Inc.; JKI Publishing, P.O. Box 131480, Tyler, Texas 75713; Phone: 800-333-5344.)

"Scarlet and the Beast" by John Daniel (2nd edition, 1995) is a comprehensive, three-volume work totaling over 1,400 pages. It is extensively documented. (The first volume contains 84 pages of Notes, a 13-page Bibliography, an Index, and 11 Appendixes.) This trilogy shows the influence of Freemasonry on world history. It also contains the author's perspective on some end-time prophecies. (Whatever you may think of the author's eschatology, his historical research and documentation are impressive.) Volume 1 shows Freemasonry's influence on American and world history. Volume 2 studies the occult history of Freemasonry. Volume 3 further elaborates on some topics which were covered in Volume 1, including Freemasonry's influence on international finance, drugs, the American Civil War, and assassinations. Individual volumes and the three-volume set can be

ordered from JKI Publishing, P.O. Box 131480, Tyler, Texas 75713 (Phone: 800-333-5344).
SOURCE: The Freemasons

"No one will enter the New World Order unless he or she will make a pledge to worship Lucifer. No one will enter the New Age unless he will take a Luciferian Initiation."
David Spangler, Director of Planetary Initiative, United Nations

Chapter 8: United Church of Christ

The following *United Church of Christ* beliefs are found at God is Still Speaking: About the United Church of Christ:

We believe that the persistent search for God produces an authentic relationship with God, engendering love, strengthening faith, dissolving guilt, and giving life purpose and direction.

What a lie straight from satan's mouth! No amount of persistent searching for God will produce a relationship with God. The Word of God clearly warns in John 3:3, "**...Except a man be born again, he cannot see the kingdom of God.**" Friend, you don't need to seek for God, He keeps you breathing (Acts 17:25). If you would like to be saved, which is the ONLY way to have a relationship with God, then you MUST be born again.

We believe that all of the baptized 'belong body and soul to our Lord and Savior Jesus Christ.' No matter who – no matter what – no matter where we are on life's journey – notwithstanding race, gender, sexual orientation, class or creed – we all belong to God and to one worldwide community of faith. All persons baptized – past, present and future – are connected to each other and to God through the sacrament of baptism. We baptize during worship when the community is present because baptism includes the community's promise of 'love, support and care' for the baptized – and we promise that we won't take it back – no matter where your journey leads you.

The United Church of Christ teaches damnable heresies by claiming that water baptism is required for salvation. Martin Luther's Small Catechism is straight from the pits of Hell. Please read our chapter on Lutheran in Chapter 1 of this book.

United Church of Christ is Satan's religion, which is further proven by their acceptance of openly homosexual people into their organization; while never a word is spoken against homosexuality. Take a look at the abominable photo below...

Chapter 9: Church of Christ

Church of God followers do NOT believe in simple FAITH in Jesus Christ to be saved; on the contrary, they most definitely demand that BAPTISM be added for one to be saved. I spoke at length recently with a Church of God minister who earned his degree from the *Dallas Christian College*. Dallas Christian College DOESN'T make it clear at all that they are indeed a *Church of Christ* college. Why are they deceptive about who they really are?
What are they afraid to tell people? Click on their *"Our Mission"* link and see if Church of Christ is mentioned. It is NOT! By all indications, many Christian people would ignorantly think this was a great college to attend, but it certainly is NOT! It looks innocent enough on the surface doesn't it? That's the disguise they want you to see.

I went to visit their website to read their statement of faith; as I suspected, it was vague. But as clever as the person tried to be who devised this statement of faith, it couldn't escape the discernment of a spirit-filled believer, knowledgeable in the Word of God.

The following quote is taken from their statement of faith:

"...the Church of the New Testament ought everywhere to be restored with its divine plan of admission: faith, repentance, and baptism..."

Did you read that? Did you see the heresy? Is baptism necessary for admission into the Church? No! The very moment you trust Jesus Christ as your personal Savior, asking Him to forgive your sins and come into your heart, you have been born-again and are a member of the body of Christ. Any person who tells you that you have to be baptized to become a member of the church is LYING to you! Isn't it something how misguided ministers will force you to get baptized to join THEIR church, but God accepts ANY repentant sinner into heaven.

You do NOT have to be affiliated with any church, religious group or denomination to go to Heaven. You just need Jesus! Jesus Himself proclaimed in John 14:6 that He is the ONLY way to God the Father. John 10:9 clearly declares that Jesus Christ is the DOOR by which men and women enter into Heaven. John 6:40 teaches that the will of God is **to believe** on Christ. Salvation is simple, we are the SINNERS and Jesus is the SAVIOR.

As I spoke with this sincerely misguided minister, he explained the following order to me as being necessary for salvation:
1. HEAR
2. BELIEVE
3. REPENT
4. CONFESS
5. **BAPTISM (uh oh! This is damnable heresy!)**

Water baptism is NOT required for Biblical salvation! "Repentance" is "a change of mind," not a change of lifestyle. You DON'T have to stop committing sins to be saved, you need to acknowledge your sinnership. Who can give up all their sins? No one! If all sins had to be forsaken for salvation, then NO one could be saved because we are all sinners (Romans 3:23). A changed life is the FRUIT of genuine repentance; and not a part of the ROOT of saving faith. A man's faith is COUNTED for righteousness (Genesis 15:6; Romans 3:4-6).

Jesus said in Matthew 7:21-23 that many who "confess" Him as Lord are not saved, because they have never done God's will (which is to believe on Jesus, John 6:40).
To tell people that water baptism is essential to salvation is a lie of the Devil.

"There is a way which seemeth right unto a man, but the end thereof are the ways of death."
Proverb 14:12

Faith in Christ ALONE equals salvation!

Faith in Christ PLUS anything equals hell!

If I said that I believed I could trust you with my money, that would NOT be faith (that would be optimism). If I entrust you with my money and ask someone to follow you (to keep an eye on you), that is NOT faith either. If I entrust you with my money and don't take ANY precautions whatsoever, that is 100% faith. To add baptism to faith is to add a "work" to faith; consequently, it is NO faith at all. You don't need much faith to be saved, you need "just enough" faith. You need JUST ENOUGH faith to obey Romans 10:13 and "call upon the name of the Lord."

If you have faith even as small as a grain of mustard seed (a VERY small seed indeed), that is all the faith you need. The AMOUNT of one's faith is not of importance for salvation, what is important is that you simply HAVE FAITH. Either you have 100% faith or you do not.

The Church of Christ minister I was speaking with told me that he felt much safer by adding that extra step of baptism to his faith and repentance. How woefully ignorant is he of the Word of God.

The Apostle Paul in 1st Corinthians 1:17 declared...

"For Christ sent me not to baptize, but to preach the gospel..."
1 Corinthians 1:17

According to a Church of Christ minister, Paul was sent by Christ to TEACH the gospel, but not to actually do any of the REQUIRED baptism to be saved. He claims this was done to prevent division in the church. True, Paul didn't want to baptize any of them because of their immature quarreling; however, this had absolutely nothing to do with their salvation. Some of the believers in the Corinthian church were actually fighting over who baptized them. They were making an issue of a non-issue. Paul lays the issue to rest by proclaiming that CHRIST did NOT send him to baptize, but to preach the gospel. It is our FAITH in the gospel of Jesus that saves us, NOT baptism.

I could go on and on about why baptism is NOT necessary for salvation. No one in the Old Testament was ever baptized. These people who claim that the Old Testament is invalid are teaching you wrong. Of course, the law which was against us was indeed nailed to the cross. Yes, the Jewish ceremonial laws are gone. However, we are still expected by God to obey the Commandments (NOT to be saved, but because we are saved and love Jesus). People in the Old Testament (old contract) were saved the SAME way people are saved today, BY GRACE THROUGH FAITH IN CHRIST JESUS (Ephesians 2:8-9). There is NO other way to be saved! It's Jesus or hell, turn or burn friend!

Don't let some misguided individual trick you into believing that baptism is essential for salvation. The Church of Christ claims that since the New Testament didn't actually begin until Jesus died, that the thief on the cross didn't have to be baptized. He is trying to say that there are TWO different plans of salvation (one for the Old Testament and one for the New Testament).
He believes that water baptism was NOT required for Old Testament saints, but IS required for all New Testament saints. This is ludicrous and preposterous!!!! There is NO such teaching in the Bible. There has always been ONE and only one plan of salvation, and that is through the precious shed blood of our Dear Lord Jesus Christ! The Bible plainly teaches that Old Testaments saints were saved the same as New Testament saints...

"To him give all the prophets witness, that through his name whosoever believeth in him shall receive remission of sins."
Acts 10:43

Do you want to be saved? Then look upon Jesus!

> "Look unto me, and be ye saved, all the ends of the earth: for I am God, and there is none else."
>
> **Isaiah 45:22**

Baptismal regeneration is of the Devil. Jesus didn't baptize (John 4:2). In the book of Romans, water baptism is only mentioned briefly in chapter six. Paul NEVER makes any direct command to be baptized! Yet, Paul expresses in Romans 10:1 that it is his "HEARTS DESIRE" for the people to be saved. Paul wanted people to be saved, that is why he went publicly from house-to-house in Acts 20:20 to witness to people. We soul-winners call this the "Acts 20/20 vision." In other words, if your consumed about winning souls to Christ, then your seeing 20/20 as a Christian. Most believers are wearing blinders.

No Caught-up/Rapture or Millennium?

The Church of Christ also DO NOT believe in any type of rapture, but that the Lord would simply return and part the righteous from the wicked. We are clearly taught in God's Word that there will be a "departure" of the saints from this world; hence, the word rapture (which is not itself found in the Bible as the Bible talks about being caught up). The words of the Apostle Paul in 1 Thessalonians 4:13-18 are as clear as can be. In the twinkling of an eye, the Lord WILL return. Read it for yourself. Why can't people just take the Bible at face value? Why do they persist to read in-between the lines? Why do they seek for things that God has NOT placed in the Bible? Luke 17:36 is still in the King James Bible people! Matthew 24:41 is still in the Bible! Two shall be, and one shall remain! The Church of Christ also does not believe there would be a Millennial reign of Christ. Revelation 20:1-6 speaks of the 1,000 year millennium.

The purpose of this article is NOT to get into depth of these individual Bible doctrines, but rather to expose the heretical teachings of the Church of Christ. A study of Biblical prophecy is beyond the scope of this article. The Bible is very clear concerning the departure of the saints from this world (the rapture) and of the Millennial reign of Christ from Jerusalem over the earth. Satan will be bound and imprisoned in the bottomless pit for 1,000 years (Revelation 20:3).

No Eternal Security?

The Church of Christ also believes that a saved person COULD lose their salvation if they got away from fellowship with the Lord.

A saved person could NEVER lose their salvation. I mean, Jesus told Nicodemus to be "born again," NOT born again and again and again and again! Revelation 3:20 is an invitation for us to open the door of our heart to allow the Lord Jesus to come in (John 14:23).

Church of Christ followers also have a problem with Christians who are less than perfect. They for instance do not believe that a Christian could commit murder and still be saved.

The Church of Christ has a wrong view of salvation! The truth is that we DO NOTHING to earn salvation! If we can't do any good works to get saved, then why would doing any bad works make us unsaved?

Let me repeat...

If we can't do any good works to get saved, then why would doing any bad works make us unsaved?
I did nothing to get saved of my own merit. All I did was place my faith in the Lord's work of atonement. It is Jesus Christ and what He did to pay for my sins that gets me into heaven, I had nothing to do with that. Salvation is OF GOD, not man! So then why in the world would anyone conclude that a person has to maintain a certain level of fellowship or righteousness with God to keep one's salvation? It is no less than a WORKS religion!

The Church of Christ is ADDING works to simple faith in Christ! They teach that you MUST be baptized to be saved! They teach that you MUST keep coming back to the Lord (to get your salvation back) every time you get away from the Lord. Listen people, there is NOTHING in the Bible which teaches that we can fall from grace as believers. When the Bible speaks of "falling from grace" it is simply talking about unsaved people who have rejected Christ.

Jesus is the ONLY way to heaven! If you reject Jesus, then you have missed your ONLY buss ticket to heaven. This is the only way to fall from God's grace. You CANNOT lose your salvation!!! If someone is not saved now, then they never were to begin with. As a perfect analogy, I cannot change the relationship between myself and my own child. I could disown my child (which I think is a horrible thing for ANY parent to do), but they would still be my child. Even if my child killed someone, the relationship doesn't change one bit -that is still my child and I am still their parent. Such is this case with God! No matter what we do, we are God's children.

No Tears in Heaven?

There will be tears in heaven for those believers who lived for SELF and hurt other people while upon the earth.

The blood of our loved ones will be upon our hands if we have failed to witness to them. We can't force them to accept the truth, but we CAN love them and tell them the good news of Jesus Christ. There will be tears throughout the Millennium, but all tears shall be wiped away at the end, after the Great White Throne of Judgment. All former things will be passed away (Revelation 21:4). Being a Christian DOESN'T give us a license to sin.

Though our sins are under the blood and all is well between us and God as far as our sin debt, we must still make things right with those we have wronged. Salvation balances the scale of justice between us and God, but the scales of justice must also be balanced between us and those we have victimized or hurt in ant way (Romans 12:19). The Judgment Seat of Christ is going to be a JUDGMENT only for believers, it is not going to be a joyous time for most believers. There WILL be many tears.

Heaven is Not a Physical Place?

The Church of Christ does not believe in heaven as a place. They believed that heaven is only a spiritual existence, NOT a literal place.

What then about the streets of gold and the gates of pearl? What about the mansions which Jesus spoke of in John 14:1-2, how can the Church of Christ denies this as being physical homes.

Chapter 10: Buddhism

Written By: Allen Van Zyl

On 20 June I accepted a task of writing on the religion Buddhism which is yet another false religion. I grasped at the opportunity so as to further my knowledge and also having at the back of my mind a knowledge that one of my brothers was looking at converting to this religion.

Whereas I had already forwarded certain limited information to him about this topic and the briefest of brief reasons of why this is a false religion to follow, I had no real concrete knowledge of this other than what I had "studied" some three to four years prior and could only rely on scripture from the bible, the little I know and the Holy Spirits guidance in my attempted persuasion. Then of course there is the new covenant Jesus left us, the promise of writing the truth / laws on our minds and hearts which can also be construed as our conscience which I believed would help him if he was serious about following the one and only TRUE God.

I recall when I was first spiritually awakened, it happened at a Mighty Men Conference (MMC 2010) held in Greytown, Kwazulu Natal, South Africa. I came away from this evangelistic movement with a passion to learn more. With so many different religions I needed to know which was the correct one to follow, which was the ONLY true God each religion proclaimed Him to be.

I was and have become even more conscious that we have a jealous God, although loving.

> ⁴ Thou shalt not make unto thee any graven image, or any likeness of anything that is in heaven above, or that is in the earth beneath, or that is in the water under the earth.
> ⁵ Thou shalt not bow down thyself to them, nor serve them: for I the LORD thy God am a jealous God, visiting the iniquity of the fathers upon the children unto the third and fourth generation of them that hate me;
>
> **Exodus 20:4-5 KJV**

> ¹⁵ (For the LORD thy God is a jealous God among you) lest the anger of the LORD thy God be kindled against thee, and destroy thee from off the face of the earth.
>
> **Deuteronomy 6:15 KJV**

As such I delved into the "major" religions, when I say "major" I mean the older ones, the religions that have been around since year "dot" because quite simply, in my mind and reasoning any religion that is less than 2000 years old is simply just a waste of time and energy even looking into.

Why? Because if Joe Soap who is a teacher / pastor / priest / spiritual leader (whatever you want to call this person) of a religious movement that started AD (Anno Domini) my first question would be, what happened to all the souls / spirits who died before this date? Were their lives non consequential? Did they just merely exist with no souls / spirits? If with souls / spirits where did these then go when they died? So surely then by reason, God who has always been around must have filtered His belief system into a religion that has been around since the beginning of age for man to follow.

To then become even more complex and a topic that will not be covered herein but may need clarity in your own mind is the age of the earth. Why? Because as touched on above, a religion of sorts must have been around since the beginning of man, God must have set some sort of guideline in place for man to follow. As such I would like to refer you to a chap called Dr Kent E. Hovind who is rather outspoken on this topic of the age of the earth / man.

Unfortunately his worldly reputation has been somewhat smeared as since January 2007, [27]Hovind has been serving a ten-year prison sentence after being convicted of 58 federal counts in the USA. I do however still urge you to view his material and decide the validity for yourself in the spiritual sense.

As a side thought, if you believe in God you must believe in an opposite force to Him, as such, this would be a dark opposing force that is directly competing for the souls / spirits of man. Who best to target than those that speak the truth? Find their weakness, set them up, stage an untruth and not only destroy a reputation but destroy all faith placed in that man that stood up for the TRUE GOD. This was merely a thought that transpired as I wrote the above, saying that, are you positive in your own mind that you are incorruptible or that you are unable to be framed? Just a thought!

Back to the topic at hand.

---

[27] Dr Hovind is a born again scientist who had to be sent to prison to "shut" him up as I believe the Government did not like to hear the truth about the creation and rather wanted to teach the children the evolution theory. This footnote added by Apostle Hélèné Fulton

So in conclusion to the above, some form of religion must be older than the age of man or equivalent to the age of man from inception. Agree? Then lets look at that. What religions claim to have been around then? Which are the oldest religions?

History Timeline of World Religions and its Founders
2,085 BC. Judaism-Abraham
1,500 BC. Hinduism- no specific founder
1000 BC Zoroastrianism - Zoroastrianism founded by Zarathushtra (Zoroaster) in Persia
560 BC. Buddhism- Gautama Buddha
550 BC. Taoism - Lao Tzu
599 BC. Jainism, Mahavira
30 AD. Christianity –Jesus Christ
50-100 AD. Gnosticism-
Reference: http://www.letusreason.org/Cult11.htm

A list of all religions, starting from the youngest to the oldest?

Hinduism - 4000 to 2500 BCE

The origins of Hinduism can be traced to the Indus Valley civilization sometime between 4000 and 2500 BCE.

Judaism - 2000 BCE

Judaism, Christianity, Islam and the Baha'i faith all originated with a divine covenant between the God of the ancient Israelites and Abraham around 2000 BCE.

Zoroastrianism - 1000 BCE

Zoroastrianism was founded by Zarathushtra (Zoroaster) in Persia

Buddhism - 560 to 490 BCE

Buddhism developed out of the teachings of Siddhartha Gautama who, in 535 BCE, reached enlightenment and assumed the title Buddha.

Shinto - 500+ BCE

Shinto is an ancient Japanese religion, closely tied to nature, which recognizes the existence of various "Kami", nature deities.

Confucianism - 500 BCE

K'ung Fu Tzu (Confucius) was born in 551 BCE in the state of Lu in China.

Jainism - 420 BCE

The founder of the Jain community was Vardhamana, the last Jina in a series of 24 who lived in East India.

Taoism - 440 CE

Taoism was founded by Lao-Tse

Reference:
https://answers.yahoo.com/question/index?qid=20061203073051AApmXbX

The above are various people's interpretation of when the oldest religions were "founded", I am no expert and have made my choice, should you wish to investigate this and make your own learned opinion please do so.

How accurate is anything / everything we read? Any human author would / could put their own opinion in their communication. Their own life experience or belief would fall part of the content communicated over to us, hence we have to be able to discern for ourselves what is right and what is wrong. However, how do we know our own thinking has not been corrupted as much as we think we are right? How many of us have had arguments or disputes with someone because their ideologies are different to ours, they are just as forceful as what we are because we both think we are right. So again, are we really right?

What has corrupted us? Is it this world that boiled down to our own personal circumstance and experience? Can we then safely say that this world has corrupted us? If so how can we then trust this world and the contents thereof? Surely that is why it is so important to have the new covenant implanted on our hearts? If the new covenant has been implanted in our minds and in our hearts, if we TRULY reflect and contemplate and "soul search" **in humility**, will we then only find the truth?

[10] For this is the covenant that I will make with the house of Israel after those days, saith the Lord; I will put my laws into their mind, and write them in their hearts: and I will be to them a God, and they shall be to me a people:

Hebrews 8:10

³¹ Behold, the days come, saith the LORD, that I will make a new covenant with the house of Israel, and with the house of Judah:
³² Not according to the covenant that I made with their fathers in the day that I took them by the hand to bring them out of the land of Egypt; which my covenant they brake, although I was an husband unto them, saith the LORD:
³³ But this shall be the covenant that I will make with the house of Israel; After those days, saith the LORD, I will put my law in their inward parts, and write it in their hearts; and will be their God, and they shall be my people.
³⁴ And they shall teach no more every man his neighbour, and every man his brother, saying, Know the LORD: for they shall all know me, from the least of them unto the greatest of them, saith the LORD: for I will forgive their iniquity, and I will remember their sin no more.

Jeremiah 31:31-34 KJV

¹⁵ And for this cause he is the mediator of the new testament, that by means of death, for the redemption of the transgressions that were under the first testament, they which are called might receive the promise of eternal inheritance.

Hebrews 9:15 KJV

And how do we deal with this world in the aspect referred to?

² And be not conformed to this world: but be ye transformed by the renewing of your mind, that ye may prove what is that good, and acceptable, and perfect, will of God.

Romans 12:2 KJV

Having touched on the above very briefly lets now look at one of these religions, a religion founded in or around 560 BC (Before Christ) BCE (Before the Common Era), namely Buddhism.

General

Buddhism appears to be the dominant religion in the east and is appearing to becoming more popular in the west as time progresses.

Buddha means "awakened one" or "the enlightened one." He taught that understanding the true nature of the world is a way to eliminate suffering, in so far as this knowledge remains practical.

Speculation on matters such as God, the nature of the universe and after life was rejected.

He urged his followers to focus on four noble truths and the Eightfold Path:

Four noble truths

All life is marked by suffering
Suffering is caused by desire and attachment
Suffering can be eliminated
Suffering can be eliminated by following the noble eightfold path.

Eightfold Path
Right view
Right intention Ethical conduct
Right speech
Right action
Right livelihood
Right effort
Right mindfulness
Right concentration
In short, the purpose of life is to end suffering.

Buddhism is ranked the fourth largest religion in the world and as in all religions have various variations within the faith however allegedly share certain core beliefs.

There are three main branches or subdivisions in Buddhism, namely Theravada, Mahayana and Vajrayana.

The Buddha was an "ordinary" human before he became enlightened. Enlightenment is compared to waking up, because suddenly a complete transformation of body and mind is experienced when woken up. A Buddha is a person who has allegedly developed all positive qualities and eliminated all negative qualities. One could say that a Buddha represents the very peak of evolution, as he/she is omniscient or all-knowing. With his wisdom, a Buddha really understands the truth, whereas ordinary people live like in a dream, an illusion that prevents us from understanding reality properly.

A Buddha is not the creator of the universe, like "God" in the Christian-Judeo-Islamic sense. They believe there is no creator of the universe given in Buddhist philosophy apart from the karma (actions) of sentient beings (beings with a mind like humans and animals). The Buddha is not omnipotent (all-powerful) like the Christian-Judeo-Islamic "God". (The simple reason is that if he were, out of compassion, he would have long released all sentient beings from suffering.)

The state of a Buddha is not impossible to reach (although it may take many lives and extensive effort).

A Buddha is not hindered by ignorance, but is omniscient (knows everything).

A Buddha is not a passive being; he will use his wisdom to help to other living beings when they are open to his advice.

Respect and compassion for all beings are encouraged.

There appears to be no Buddhist story on how the universe was created.

The current most influential Buddhist master is his holiness the 14th Dalai Lama.

Belief

The purpose of life is to escape the cycle of rebirth (reincarnation / transmigration) and attain nirvana. Nirvana is seen as the cessation of suffering by some and as a heavenly paradise by others.

Nirvana is also described as being the state of final liberation from the cycle of death and rebirth. It is also therefore the end of suffering.

Buddhist ethics have been orientated toward maintaining social harmony rather than the concept like the Christian notion of sin. Their approach to morality avoids absolutes and rigid commandments, instead they are encouraged to weigh and analise situations to come to their own decisions of right and wrong.

In terms of homosexuality, sex outside of marriage their teaching is translated as "Do not indulge in sexual misconduct", there is no decisive answer as to what this misconduct actually is.

Issues such as abortion, whereas they consider abortion as taking a human life, they are reluctant in imposing rigid moral absolutes.

Buddhist women have reportedly faced harsher discrimination especially in Asian institutions

Origin

Buddhism was established on or around 520 - 560 BC / BCE. Although various other dates have been recorded they all appear to fall within this range, founded some 2500 years ago.

It was founded in north eastern India by an Indian prince called Siddharta Gautama who taught for roughly four decades and passed on around the age of 80.

Rituals

Sacred texts are called Tripitaka, it is alleged that Buddhas teachings were only reduced to writing many hundred years later after his death. All teachings prior to that were taught verbally by powers of memorisation and repetition.

Place of rituals usually occur in Temples or meditation hall's.

Rituals include bowing, chanting and lots of silent meditation.

All Buddhists take refuge in the "Three Jewells" which comprise:
The Buddha
The Dharma (teachings)
The Sangha (community)

It is said that the Buddha was reluctant to accept images of himself, as he did not like to be venerated as a person. To symbolise the Buddha in the very early art, one used mainly the Eight Spoked Wheel and the Bodhi Tree, but also the Buddha's Footprints, an Empty Throne, a Begging Bowl and a Lion are used to represent him.

The Eight-Spoked Dharma Wheel or 'Dharmachakra' (Sanskrit) symbolises the Buddha's turning the Wheel of Truth or Law (dharma = truth/law, chakra = wheel).

The wheel refers to the story that shortly after the Buddha achieved enlightenment, Brahma came down from heaven and requested the Buddha to teach by offering him a Dharmachakra. The Buddha is known as the Wheel-Turner: he who sets a new cycle of teachings in motion and in consequence changes the course of destiny.

The Dharmachakra has eight spokes, symbolising the Eight-fold Noble Path. The 3 swirling segments in centre represent the Buddha, Dharma (the teachings) and Sangha (the spiritual community).

The wheel can also be divided into three parts, each representing an aspect of Buddhist practice; the hub (discipline), the spokes (wisdom), and the rim (concentration).

Holidays

There are many holidays and festivals celebrated by Buddhists which differ according to country and tradition.

The Buddha's birthday is the most widely observed holiday, it is celebrated on different days with different rituals in different countries.

Below are a few other holidays:

Buddhist new year
Vesak (Buddha day)
Sangha Day
Dhamma Day
Observance Day
Kathina Ceremony
Festival of Floating Bowls
Elephant Festival
The Festival of the Tooth
Ancestor Day

Wedding Ceremonies

In Buddhism, marriage is regarded as entirely a personal, individual concern and not as a religious duty. Marriage is a social convention, an institution created by man for the well-being and happiness of man, to differentiate human society from animal life and to maintain order and harmony in the process of procreation.
Even though the Buddhist texts are silent on the subject of monogamy or polygamy, the Buddhist laity is advised to limit themselves to one wife. The Buddha did not lay rules on married life but gave necessary advice on how to live a happy married life.

There are ample inferences in his sermons that it is wise and advisable to be faithful to one wife and not to be sensual and to run after other women. The Buddha realized that one of the main causes of man's downfall is his involvement with other women.

Men must realize the difficulties, the trials and tribulations that he has to undergo just to maintain a wife and a family. These would be magnified many times when faced with calamities. Knowing the frailties of human nature, the Buddha did, in one of his precepts, advise his followers to refrain from committing adultery or sexual misconduct.

The Buddhist views on marriage are very liberal: in Buddhism, marriage is regarded entirely as personal and individual concern, and not as a religious duty. There are no religious laws in Buddhism compelling a person to be married, to remain as a bachelor or to lead a life of total chastity.

It is not laid down anywhere that Buddhists must produce children or regulates the number of children that they produce. Buddhism allows each individual the freedom to decide for himself all the issues pertaining to marriage.

It might be asked why Buddhist monks do not marry, since there are no laws for or against marriage. The reason is obviously that to be of service to mankind, the monks have chosen a way of life which includes celibacy.

Those who renounce the worldly life keep away from married life voluntarily to avoid various worldly commitments in order to maintain peace of mind and to dedicate their lives solely to serve others in the attainment of spiritual emancipation.

Although Buddhist monks do not solemnize a marriage ceremony, they do perform religious services in order to bless the couples.

Other

Looking at all these teachings, especially Buddhists aspirations of helping others with all their "rules and regulations or teachings", I see them all in Jesus' one simple teaching.

[34] A new commandment I give unto you, That ye love one another; as I have loved you, that ye also love one another.
John 13:34 KJV

Buddhist theology to me merely symbolises absolute and utter confusion! No direction, no guidance, everything but nothing is right or wrong … what you may believe is right may just be wrong. How would a sociopath fit into this? A sociopath would be a brilliant Buddhist!

Forgive me for saying this but I now believe an aspiring Buddha would be someone happily growing and smoking marijuana / dagga / weed and reducing themselves to a state of euphoria.

I have no doubt in my mind that Buddhism is just another religion imposed by Lucifer to confuse the masses.

Whereas I initially embraced the writing of the above I have found that I have become totally exasperated and irritated and can only assume that it has been the "studying" of Buddhism for this document that has reduced me to this feeling.

In concluding my preamble on the first pages of this document, Christianity is firmly embedded in Judaism.

[17] Think not that I am come to destroy the law, or the prophets: I am not come to destroy, but to fulfil.

Matthew 5:17 KJV

Throughout Jesus' life on earth, he partook in Jewish law and custom, Jesus was born to a Jewish family, He was circumcised, He kept the Sabbath, He celebrated the Passover and much more.

Judaism as well as Christianity believe in the creation of the universe, the first man and woman as well as the lineage from Adam to David…, even to Jesus but that is where the similarity ends which is a topic for another day.

1 The book of the generation of Jesus Christ, the son of David, the son of Abraham.
2 Abraham begat Isaac; and Isaac begat Jacob; and Jacob begat Judas and his brethren;
3 And Judas begat Phares and Zara of Thamar; and Phares begat Esrom; and Esrom begat Aram;
4 And Aram begat Aminadab; and Aminadab begat Naasson; and Naasson begat Salmon;
5 And Salmon begat Booz of Rachab; and Booz begat Obed of Ruth; and Obed begat Jesse;
6 And Jesse begat David the king; and David the king begat Solomon of her that had been the wife of Urias;
7 And Solomon begat Roboam; and Roboam begat Abia; and Abia begat Asa;
8 And Asa begat Josaphat; and Josaphat begat Joram; and Joram begat Ozias;
9 And Ozias begat Joatham; and Joatham begat Achaz; and Achaz begat Ezekias;
10 And Ezekias begat Manasses; and Manasses begat Amon; and Amon begat Josias;
11 And Josias begat Jechonias and his brethren, about the time they were carried away to Babylon:
12 And after they were brought to Babylon, Jechonias begat Salathiel; and Salathiel begat Zorobabel;
13 And Zorobabel begat Abiud; and Abiud begat Eliakim; and Eliakim begat Azor;
14 And Azor begat Sadoc; and Sadoc begat Achim; and Achim begat Eliud;
15 And Eliud begat Eleazar; and Eleazar begat Matthan; and Matthan begat Jacob;

¹⁶ And Jacob begat Joseph the husband of Mary, of whom was born Jesus, who is called Christ.
¹⁷ So all the generations from Abraham to David are fourteen generations; and from David until the carrying away into Babylon are fourteen generations; and from the carrying away into Babylon unto Christ are fourteen generations.

Matthew 1:1-17 KJV

Judaism and Christianity are thus the oldest Faiths and as such should be considered seriously before you decide to embark on any other (what I call) false religion.

Please read our article on Judaism today. If you choose Judaism make sure it is a Messianic Jewish Church who recognise Jesus Christ as the Messiah.

Chapter 11: Amish

Written By: Clara Kudya

Beliefs

Amish believe in one God eternally existing as Father, Son, and Holy Spirit (Romans 8:1-17). They believe that Jesus Christ, God's only Son, died on the cross for the sins of the world. They believe that the Holy Spirit convicts of sin, and also empowers believers for service and holy living. They believe that salvation is by grace through faith in Christ, a free gift bestowed by God on those who repent and believe.

The Amish believe in the Bible as trustworthy guide for living but do not quote it excessively. To do so would be considered a sinful showing of pride. They believe in Jesus Christ and strive at all times to live by the blessings that were taught by Christ in

The Beatitudes
5 And seeing the multitudes, He went up on a mountain, and when He was seated His disciples came to Him. ² Then He opened His mouth and taught them, saying:
³ "Blessed *are* the poor in spirit,
 For theirs is the kingdom of heaven.
⁴ Blessed *are* those who mourn,
 For they shall be comforted.
⁵ Blessed *are* the meek,
 For they shall inherit the earth.
⁶ Blessed *are* those who hunger and thirst for righteousness,
 For they shall be filled.

⁷ Blessed *are* the merciful,
   For they shall obtain mercy.
⁸ Blessed *are* the pure in heart,
   For they shall see God.
⁹ Blessed *are* the peacemakers,
   For they shall be called sons of God.
¹⁰ Blessed *are* those who are persecuted for righteousness' sake,
   For theirs is the kingdom of heaven.

¹¹ "Blessed are you when they revile and persecute you, and say all kinds of evil against you falsely for My sake. ¹² Rejoice and be exceedingly glad, for great *is* your reward in heaven, for so they persecuted the prophets who were before you.

Believers Are Salt and Light

¹³ "You are the salt of the earth; but if the salt loses its flavor, how shall it be seasoned? It is then good for nothing but to be thrown out and trampled underfoot by men.

¹⁴ "You are the light of the world. A city that is set on a hill cannot be hidden. ¹⁵ Nor do they light a lamp and put it under a basket, but on a lampstand, and it gives light to all *who are* in the house. ¹⁶ Let your light so shine before men, that they may see your good works and glorify your Father in heaven.

Christ Fulfills the Law

¹⁷ "Do not think that I came to destroy the Law or the Prophets. I did not come to destroy but to fulfill. ¹⁸ For assuredly, I say to you, till heaven and earth pass away, one jot or one tittle will by no means pass from the law till all is fulfilled. ¹⁹ Whoever therefore breaks one of the least of these commandments, and teaches men so, shall be called least in the kingdom of heaven; but whoever does and teaches *them,* he shall be called great in the kingdom of heaven. ²⁰ For I say to you, that unless your righteousness exceeds *the righteousness* of the scribes and Pharisees, you will by no means enter the kingdom of heaven.

Murder Begins in the Heart

²¹ "You have heard that it was said to those of old, 'You shall not murder, and whoever murders will be in danger of the judgment.' ²² But I say to you that whoever is angry with his

brother without a cause shall be in danger of the judgment. And whoever says to his brother, 'Raca!' shall be in danger of the council. But whoever says, 'You fool!' shall be in danger of hell fire. ²³ Therefore if you bring your gift to the altar, and there remember that your brother has something against you, ²⁴ leave your gift there before the altar, and go your way. First be reconciled to your brother, and then come and offer your gift. ²⁵ Agree with your adversary quickly, while you are on the way with him, lest your adversary deliver you to the judge, the judge hand you over to the officer, and you be thrown into prison. ²⁶ Assuredly, I say to you, you will by no means get out of there till you have paid the last penny.

Adultery in the Heart

²⁷ "You have heard that it was said to those of old, 'You shall not commit adultery.' ²⁸ But I say to you that whoever looks at a woman to lust for her has already committed adultery with her in his heart. ²⁹ If your right eye causes you to sin, pluck it out and cast *it* from you; for it is more profitable for you that one of your members perish, than for your whole body to be cast into hell. ³⁰ And if your right hand causes you to sin, cut it off and cast *it* from you; for it is more profitable for you that one of your members perish, than for your whole body to be cast into hell.

Marriage Is Sacred and Binding

³¹ "Furthermore it has been said, 'Whoever divorces his wife, let him give her a certificate of divorce.' ³² But I say to you that whoever divorces his wife for any reason except sexual immorality causes her to commit adultery; and whoever marries a woman who is divorced commits adultery.

Jesus Forbids Oaths

³³ "Again you have heard that it was said to those of old, 'You shall not swear falsely, but shall perform your oaths to the Lord.' ³⁴ But I say to you, do not swear at all: neither by heaven, for it is God's throne; ³⁵ nor by the earth, for it is His footstool; nor by Jerusalem, for it is the city of the great King. ³⁶ Nor shall you swear by your head, because you cannot make one hair white or

black. ³⁷ But let your 'Yes' be 'Yes,' and your 'No,' 'No.' For whatever is more than these is from the evil one.

Go the Second Mile

³⁸ "You have heard that it was said, 'An eye for an eye and a tooth for a tooth.' ³⁹ But I tell you not to resist an evil person. But whoever slaps you on your right cheek, turn the other to him also. ⁴⁰ If anyone wants to sue you and take away your tunic, let him have *your* cloak also. ⁴¹ And whoever compels you to go one mile, go with him two. ⁴² Give to him who asks you, and from him who wants to borrow from you do not turn away.

Love Your Enemies

⁴³ "You have heard that it was said, 'You shall love your neighbor and hate your enemy.' ⁴⁴ But I say to you, love your enemies, bless those who curse you, do good to those who hate you, and pray for those who spitefully use you and persecute you, ⁴⁵ that you may be sons of your Father in heaven; for He makes His sun rise on the evil and on the good, and sends rain on the just and on the unjust. ⁴⁶ For if you love those who love you, what reward have you? Do not even the tax collectors do the same? ⁴⁷ And if you greet your brethren only, what do you do more *than others?* Do not even the tax collectors do so? ⁴⁸ Therefore you shall be perfect, just as your Father in heaven is perfect.

Matthew 5:1-48

One scripture often quoted in Amish worship services is: "And be not conformed to this world: but be ye transformed by the renewing of your mind, that ye may prove what is that good, and acceptable, and perfect, will of God." (Romans 12:2) They are admonished to live a life that is separate from the world.

The Ordnung (order) is the set of rules for each Amish community. It contains both religious and civil rules written and unwritten. Because the Amish believe in a strictly literal interpretation of the Bible these rules are created in order to keep their members in line with the laws therein. Amish communities are not centrally governed so each group comes up with their own version of the rule. There are two types of Ordnung – those determined in the early history of the religion by conferences (these are usually written down rules) and those passed verbally within each group. The rules are mostly derived from the Bible but those which aren't are justified by the fact that they will cause a person to ultimately become worldly and thus breach the Biblical laws.

The Amish believe in living a life separated from the non-Amish. They quote the Bible to justify this belief: "Be ye not unequally yoked together with unbelievers: for what fellowship hath righteousness with unrighteousness? and what communion hath light with darkness?" (2 Corinthians 6:14).

Funerals are held in the home of the dead and coffins are plain – hand made by the community. Graves are dug by hand because the Amish believe that modern technology is a hindrance to family life – as a result they shun electricity and machinery. In some cases, however, electricity is permitted to warm homes. This electricity is supplied by the community itself via simple devices such as windmills. Because of their other religious convictions, the Amish take no government benefits (and most don't have medical insurance) and they do not serve in the military.
Belts, gloves, ties, sneakers: banned! The Amish have a very simplistic dress style – in keeping with their

overall life philosophy. Their clothes are handmade and are usually of a dark fabric. Coats and vests are fastened with hooks. Men's trousers must not have creases or cuffs. Married men must grow their beards whilst mustaches are forbidden. Amish women cannot wear patterned clothing or jewelry and they are not permitted to cut their hair. The length of clothing, like dresses, is strictly governed by the Ordnung of the community.

The term "church members" means those who are baptized as adults and voluntarily commit themselves to a life of obedience to God and the church. Yes, those who break their baptismal vows are shunned by the Old Order Amish. "Belonging" is important and shunning is meant to be redemptive. It is not an attempt to harm or ruin the individual and in most cases it does bring that member back into the fellowship again.

The Biblical basis for shunning is found in these two verses:

[11] But now I have written unto you not to keep company, if any man that is called a brother be a fornicator, or covetous, or an idolator, or a railer, or a drunkard, or an extortioner; with such an one no not to eat.

1 Corinthians 5:11

[17] Now I beseech you, brethren, mark them which cause divisions and offences contrary to the doctrine which ye have learned; and avoid them.

Romans 16:17

The families of a shunned member are expected to also shun them. Families shun the person by not eating at the same table with them.

⁴ Thou shalt not make unto thee any graven image, or any likeness of any thing that is in heaven above, or that is in the earth beneath, or that is in the water under the earth.

Exodus 20:4

They clearly do not read the verses that pre-seed or follows and therefore take everything out of contex.

⁵ Thou shalt not bow down thyself to them, nor serve them: for I the LORD thy God am a jealous God, visiting the iniquity of the fathers upon the children unto the third and fourth generation of them that hate me;

Exodus 20:5

"Early Anabaptists, the ancestors of Amish and Mennonites, were very evangelistic, going everywhere preaching and teaching. This was a sharp contrast to the "Christian" society in which they lived. Persecution followed and many Anabaptists died for their faith and their zeal for evangelism. In the years that followed, missionary zeal decreased. The church succumbed to persecution and discrimination. Gradually Amish and Mennonites became known more for their traditional practices and their quiet, peaceful way of life and less for their active evangelism. This trend continued until it seemed almost wrong to send members out of the close community to evangelize. Old Order Amish, along with some Old Order Mennonites, have retained this position and desire to remain "the quiet in the land." However, missionary zeal experienced a strong rebirth around the beginning of this century in Mennonite circles and more recently among the Church Amish. As a result of this rebirth of evangelism, Mennonites today number more than one million people in over 60 countries around the world and speak 78 different languages."

"I understand your belief in nonresistance and pacifism. Does this principal extend to personal situations where you are confronted with imminent evil – say a known murderer confronting you and your family in your home? Can you use force to preserve your life in this situation? To what extent? What is the Biblical basis for your position?"

"Both Amish and Mennonites are committed to a lifestyle of peace and non-violence. The Amish people do not believe that women should hold positions of power. The Amish educate their children only up to the eighth grade level.

The Amish believe that if one breaches the Ordnung or other "crimes" such as marrying outside the faith, they are excommunicated. Excommunication is called Meidung (shunning). When an individual is shunned they are expelled from the community and all ties are cut. This means that a shunned member cannot have any contact at all with other members of the group including his immediate family or friends. Needless to say this is the most serious punishment available to the Amish. Meidung lasts until death unless one repents one's crime before the community.

How did it start?

The Amish religion was founded in Switzerland Europe by Jacob Amman (1644 – 1720CE). The name of the Amish is derived from their founders name. The Amish denomination was born out of the strict teachings of Jacob Amman who was a Mennonite. The religion was formed as a way of restoring/preserving the early practices of the Mennonites.

Traditions

The Amish are a congregational organization they do not have church buildings, and hold worship services in private homes. The homes were they hold worship services are sometimes called "House Amish." This practice is based on the following scripture:

[24] God that made the world and all things therein, seeing that he is Lord of heaven and earth, dwelleth not in temples made with hands;

Acts 17:24

Each congregation's leadership is made up with one of the members serving as bishop, one as deacon, and one as secretary. Congregation leaders meet with other congregation leaders from time to time and compare needs, problems, and teachings. Women are not allowed to hold positions of power. Worship services are 3 hours long and they only sing traditional solemn hymns

Rumspringa or "the Amish get out of jail free" card is the Amish term for adolescence. It begins at about age 16 when youth socialize with their friends, and it ends with marriage. The vast majorities of teens in Rumspringa do not leave for urban life but live at home. Prime activities include dating, socializing with peers, testing traditional Amish boundaries (for some youth), and deciding if they will join the church or leave the community. Because most youth are not baptized during Rumspringa the church members are lenient with them.

During this time young adults are most likely to be rebellious against their community and consequently they are treated more leniently so as to not push the youths away. At the conclusion of rumspringa the youth is expected to choose whether he wishes to stay with the community or leave it. If he stays he is baptized and then held to a much higher behavioral standard. Adults who do not behave in a manner deemed fitting by the group are shunned. Most youths who undergo this process opt to stay with the Amish.

Holidays

The Amish celebrate the same traditional holidays as Christian holidays. Holidays observed by the Amish are: Thanksgiving, Christmas, Good Friday, Easter, Ascension Day, Pentecost, and White Monday (the day after Pentecost). The reasons for these observances are too fast and meditate on scriptures related to these days. December 25 is a solemn celebration of Christ's birth and second Christmas on December 26 is a time for visiting and family dinners. Communion services, are held twice each year, in autumn and spring, and these frame the Amish religious year.

Rituals

Two important religious rituals in Amish life are baptism and communion.

The Amish place supreme importance on adult baptism. Those who take the baptismal vow commit themselves to following the ways of Jesus and upholding the *Ordnung* for life. Most young people take their baptismal vows between 18 and 22 years of age, during a Sunday morning service that follows several weeks of instruction for the candidates. Baptism is a lifelong promise before God and other members that they will be accountable to the church for the rest of their lives.

At least five or six months before the ceremony, classes are held to teach the candidates, the strict implications of what they are about to profess. The Saturday before baptism, they are given their last chance to withdraw. The difficulty of walking the narrow path is emphasized, and the applicants are instructed it is better not to vow than to make the vow and break it later on. If they renege on vows and stray from the church, they face excommunication and shunning. On the other hand, if they leave the community before baptism, they will not face any formal sanctions because the Amish respect an individual's voluntary decision regarding church membership.

Those who come to be baptized sit with one hand over their face, representing humility and submission to the church. The candidates are asked three questions: Can you *renounce* the devil, the world, and your own flesh and blood?

Can you commit yourself to Christ and His church, and to abide by it and therein to live and to die?

And in all order (Ordnung) of the church, according to the word of the Lord, to be *obedient* and *submissive* to it and to help therein?

A deacon then ladles water from a bucket into the bishop's cupped hands, which drips over the candidate's head. Then the bishop blesses the young men and greets them into the fellowship of the church with a holy kiss. The bishop's wife similarly blesses and greets the young women who have been baptized.

Communion services, are held each autumn and spring, and frame the religious year. These ritual high points emphasize self-examination and spiritual rejuvenation. Sins are confessed and members reaffirm their vow to uphold the *Ordnung* at a council meeting held prior to the communion service.

Communion is held when the congregation is "at peace"; that is, when all members are in harmony. The eight-hour service includes preaching, a light meal during the service, and the commemoration of Christ's death with bread and wine. Pairs of members wash each another's feet as the congregation sings. At the end of the service, members give an alms offering to the deacon. This is the only time that offerings are gathered in Amish services.

Bundling is the rather odd practice of a young courting couple being bound in two separate blankets and laid together on a bed for intimacy that does not involve sexual contact. The practice has died out in most of the world (it was practiced by some non-Amish too) but in the Pennsylvania Amish communities it is still to be found. In some cases in the past (though perhaps not now) the girl was tied into a sack and her potential husband would lie in bed with her. In modern times it is also not uncommon to see a bundling bed – a bed with a board in the middle to prevent touching.

Weddings

Almost all of the members of the Amish are born into the faith and raised. Converts from outside the faith are rare. Marriages outside the faith are not allowed. The Amish groups of people have a very restricted gene pool and hence they are experiencing several inherited disorders.

Family is the core element of the Amish, boys and girls begin their search for a spouse when they turn sixteen. By the time a young woman turns twenty or a young man is in his early twenties, he or she is probably looking forward to the wedding day. But several definite steps must be taken by a couple before they may marry.

Both must join the Amish church which means being baptized into the Amish faith and following the Ordnung. The Ordnung is a written and unwritten set of rules for daily living that prepares the young people for the seriousness of setting up their own home.

The young man asks his girl to marry him, but he does not give her a ring. He may give her china or a clock. The couple keeps their intentions secret until July or August. At this time the young woman tells her family about her plans to marry.

A whirlwind of activity begins after Fast Day on October 11. Fall communion takes place the following church Sunday. After communion, proper certification of membership is requested, and is given by the second Sunday after communion. This is a major day in the life of the church because all the couples who plan to marry are "published." At the end of the service, the deacon announces the names of the girls and who they plan to marry. The fathers then announce the date and time of the wedding and invite the members to attend. The betrothed couple does not attend the church service on the Sunday they are published. Instead, the young woman prepares a meal for her fiance and they enjoy dinner alone at her home. When the girl's family returns from church, the daughter formally introduces her fiancé to her parents.

After being published, the young people have just a few days before the ceremony. They are permitted to go to one last singing with their old group of friends.

The girl also helps her mother prepare for the wedding and feast which takes place in her parents' home. The boy is busy extending personal invitations to members of his church district.

Blue is a typical color chosen for weddings by young Amish women. Navy blue, sky blue and shades of purple are the most popular colors donning Amish brides in any year. An Amish bride's wedding attire is always new. She usually makes her own dress and also those of her attendants, known as newehockers, (Pennsylvania Dutch for sidesitters). The styles of the dresses are a plain cut and are mid-calf length. They are unadorned, there is no fancy trim or lace and there is never a train. Most non-Amish brides wear their bridal dress once, but an Amish bride's practical dress will serve her for more than just her wedding day. Her wedding outfit will become her Sunday church attire after she is married. She will also be buried in the same dress when she dies. The bride and her attendants also wear capes and aprons over their dresses. Instead of a veil, the bride wears a black prayer covering to differentiate from the white cap she wears daily. And, the bride must wear black high-topped shoes. No one in the bridal party carries flowers.

The groom and his newehockers wear black suits. All coats and vests fasten with hooks and eyes, not buttons. Their shirts are white, and shoes and stockings are black. Normally, Amish men do not wear ties, but for the wedding they will don bow ties. The groom also wears high-topped black shoes, and a black hat with a three and a half inch brim.

All of the attendants in the wedding party play a vital role in the events of the day. But there is no best man or maid of honor; all are of equal importance.

Wedding dates for the Amish are limited to November and part of December, when the harvest has been completed and severe winter weather has not yet arrived. A full day is needed to prepare for the wedding. Most are held on Tuesdays and Thursdays. Mondays, Wednesdays and Fridays are used as days to prepare for or to clean-up after. Saturdays are not used as wedding days because it would be sacrilegious to work or clean-up on the following day, Sunday.

A typical Amish wedding day begins at 4 o'clock in the morning. After all, the cows must still be milked and all the other daily farm chores need to be done. There are also many last minute preparations to take care of before the wedding guests arrive. Helpers begin to arrive by 6:30 a.m. to take care of last minute details. By 7:00 a.m., the people in the wedding party have usually eaten breakfast, changed into their wedding clothes, and are waiting in the kitchen to greet the guests. Some 200 to 400 relatives, friends and church members are invited to the ceremony, which is held in the bride's home.

The ushers, (usually four married couples), will make sure each guest has a place on one of the long wooden benches in the meeting or church room of the home. At 8:30 a.m., the three-hour long service begins. The congregation will sing hymns, (without instrumental accompaniment), while the minister counsels the bride and groom in another part of the house. After the minister and the young couple return to the church room, a prayer, Scripture reading and sermon takes place.

After the sermon is concluded, the minister asks the bride and groom to step forward from their seat with the rest of the congregation. Then he questions them about their marriage to be, which is similar to taking wedding vows. The minister then blesses the couple. A final prayer draws the ceremony to a close.

That's when the festivities begin. In a flurry of activity, the women rush to the kitchen to get ready to serve dinner while the men set up tables in a U-shape around the walls of the living room. A corner of the table will be reserved for the bride and groom and the bridal party. This is an honored place called the "Eck," meaning corner.

The bride sits on the groom's left, in the corner, the same way they will sit as man and wife in their buggy. The single women sit on the same side as the bride and the single men on that of the groom. The

immediate family members sit at a long table in the kitchen, with both fathers seated at the head.
After dinner, the afternoon is spent visiting, playing games and matchmaking. Sometimes the bride will match unmarried boys and girls, who are over 16 years old, to sit together at the evening meal. The evening meal starts at 5:00 p.m. and the festivities usually winds to a close around 10:30 p.m.

The couple's first night together is spent at the bride's home because they must get up early the next day to help clean the house. Their honeymoon is spent visiting all their new relatives on the weekends throughout the winter months ahead. This is when they collect the majority of their wedding gifts.

Typically, when the newlyweds go visiting, they will go to one place Friday night and stay overnight for breakfast the following day. They'll visit a second place in the afternoon and stay for the noon meal and go to a third place for supper. Saturday night is spent at a fourth place, where they have Sunday breakfast.

A fifth place is visited for Sunday dinner and a sixth for Sunday supper before they return to the bride's parent's home. The couple lives at the home of the bride's parents until they can set up their own home the following spring.

Other

The Ordnung is best thought of as an ordering of the whole way of life . . . a code of conduct which the church maintains by tradition rather than by systematic or explicit rules. The question is why the Amish would resort to having a different set of conduct than just follow the bible.

The Amish believe in the Bible as trustworthy guide for living but do not quote it excessively. To do so would be considered a sinful showing of pride, but also the bible, and the Holy Spirit are the only guides that we have. The bible says

[6] My people are destroyed for lack of knowledge: because thou hast rejected knowledge, I will also reject thee, that thou shalt be no priest to me: seeing thou hast forgotten the law of thy God, I will also forget thy children.

Hosea 4:6

The Amish have rejected Gods main source of knowledge and relied on human knowledge as a way of life.

The Amish have deliberately made decisions as to what will or will not be allowed among members of the Amish community. The Amish do not pass judgment on outsiders but they do pass judgments against each other.

Chapter 12: Seventh-Day Adventist

Seventh-Day Adventism [SDA] is a challenging false cult to expose for one who is ignorant of the Scriptures and ignorant of SDA's core hidden beliefs. Many Christians find it difficult to expose SDA's because the false religion plainly teaches faith in Jesus Christ. This confuses many people, which is exactly what Satan intended. Satan is a master deceiver and liar (John 8:44), and the highest Satan award goes to the religious group who can appear the most "Christian" while leading their followers into Hell.

SDA teaches that the archangel Michael became Jesus on earth. This is the same demonic doctrine which Jehovah's Witnesses share. SDA's deceitfully claim to believe that Jesus is God, while maintaining that He was also Michael. You can't have it both ways. There is NOTHING in the Word of God that indicates, even remotely, that Jesus was Michael. The teaching clearly denies the deity of Jesus Christ. Interestingly, the most profound figure in SDA, Ellen G. White, openly denied the deity of Jesus Christ, which fact SDA's today attempt to lie about and deny. History can be corrupted, but the truth cannot. Ellen G. White denied Jesus' deity.

> **"The man Christ Jesus was not the Lord God Almighty."**
> —Ellen G. White (1903, ms 150, SDA Commentary V, p. 1129)

SDA teach a series of heresies, such as the unscriptural "Investigative Judgment" and "soul sleep" and that there is no Hell. SDA's instead errantly believe that the wicked will be annihilated. The Bible has much more to say about Hell than Heaven, and repeatedly warns of flaming fire (2 Thessalonians 1:8-9), everlasting fire (Matthew 18:8) and the vengeance of eternal fire (Jude 1:7) for the wicked.

Psalm 9:17 warns that the wicked shall be turned into Hell. Common sense tells us that the wicked and the righteous **do not** go to the same place; for if they did, Psalm 9:17 would make no sense at all. If the wicked go to Hell, then obviously the implication is that the righteous go somewhere much better. God said that the wicked shall be turned into Hell and all they who forget God. Only a fool would deny the existence of a literal Hell, when we see so much suffering in this present world. If God allows tormentuous suffering in this earthly life, do you foolishly think that He will not do so in eternity? Don't kid yourself! Hell is real.

Please don't go to Hell. Just as Jackie Gleason, who didn't think God would send a sinner to Hell, SDA's will find out the hard way and regret their unbelief for all eternity in the flames of Hell.

SDA is a bizarre false religion. When one studies their prophecies of the future, which is highly unbiblical, this becomes more clear. They have many similar teachings to the Jehovah's Witnesses, twisting dates and numbers to indicate years.

Many books exposing false religious cults, such as Walter Martin's *KINGDOM OF THE CULTS*, foolishly identify Seventh-Day Adventism as a Christian cult. May I say, SDA is a demonic cult. There is NOTHING

Christian about the SDA religion. They openly deny the existence of Hell.

Ellen G. White was deeply involved with the occult and SDA was founded by Freemasons as part of the New World Order's attempt to deceive the masses into following the Antichrist. There's an occult obelisk on White's grave, showing her allegiance to the New World Order, just as Charles Russell (who founded the Jehovah's Witnesses false cult) has a giant illuminati pyramid on his grave. Russell showed his blatant support for the New World Order by corrupting the Bible and writing his own. He named it the *New World Translation*. Truth is stranger than fiction.

All mainstream so-called "Christian" religions were started by 33rd degree Freemasons, including Ron Hubbard, Taze Russell, Joseph Smith (founder of the Mormons) and many others. The Christian Scientist false religion and Oral Roberts were also involved with the occult. As shocking as it may be, the Freemasonry demonic occult is largely composed of Southern Baptists, who are also a part of the New World Order and have gone apostate in recent decades. This is why they are 100% supportive of the Ecumenical Movement.

Overview

In 1782 William Miller was born on the east coast of the United States. As a young man he was a farmer and during the war of 1812, he served as a captain in the American armed forces. In 1833 he was licensed to preach by a Baptist church but was never ordained.

After having studied the Bible for two years, in 1818 Miller announced to the world that in 25 years (March 1844) Jesus Christ would return to the earth. At the height of his ministry, Miller had gathered some 50,000 followers, who had also become known as "Adventists." When March 1844 came and went with no sign of Jesus Christ having returned, Miller recalculated the new date to October 22, 1844. When Jesus did not return on October 22, 1844, the entire Millerite movement collapsed as his followers' Christian faith were destroyed. Miller revamped his doctrine to say that Christ had indeed returned, but that Miller had not understood that Christ first had to come to the "Heavenly Sanctuary," which He is now busy cleaning. Once Jesus has cleansed things up in heaven, He would be coming back to the earth.

The remnant that bought into this lie formed the Advent Church and in 1845 William Miller became its first president. The name was later changed to Seventh Day Adventists and after the death of Miller in 1849 a new false prophet came on the scene, this time a woman, Ellen G. White. At the age of 13, Ellen was taken to a meeting where William Miller spoke and was converted to the Adventist faith. During the month of December, 1844, Ellen was holding a prayer meeting in which she had a vision and felt that she was transported to heaven and shown that Christ could not come back to the earth until the Great Commission has been fulfilled. This revelation was later going to be mixed in with the teaching that Christ had come back in 1844, but that He stopped in the heaven sanctuary to first clean that up. Thus, like with so many other false movements, the leaders in the

Advents movement had to cover up for the false prophecy of William Miller.

On August 30, 1846 Ellen married James White, who had been ordained into the Adventist church in 1843. Her ascension as a "prophetess" in the Seventh Day Adventist Church had now begun.

During her years as the "seer" for the SDA church, she prophesied a number of predictions, which did not come true. One of the most blatant false prophecies she made was when she predicted before the American Civil war, that the Union would not be preserved but that the United States would be divided, slavery would not be abolished but England would intervene and declare war on the United States. Any student of history knows differently. But, like so many other false movements, these failed prophecies are swept under the rug and most Seventh Day Adventists today do not even know about them.

Like so many other cults, the doctrine of the SDA church evolved with time. The doctrine of Saturday as the Sabbath was not preached by William Miller, but came in later. Neither did Miller preach and believe in vegetarianism.
With the collapse of Miller's prediction that Christ would return in 1844, the movement needed a cause in order to survive. After the damage control had been completed and the SDA spin doctors had cured the disease, it was time for the SDA leadership to hammer out some kind of "theology" that could be used to attract new converts to their fold.

The teaching of vegetarianism came from the Whites. In1864 Ellen's husband became ill and Ellen nursed him back to health. After his recovery James and Ellen began to think about food and eating habits. Since just a practical experience would not do the job of changing the theology of the SDA church, Ellen had a "convenient" vision from the Lord, and vegetarianism was not introduced tot he church as a "THUS SAYS THE LORD." In 1866 the Western Health Reform Institute was founded at Battle Creek, Michigan. Despite the new vegetarian diet, James White died in1881.

Ellen was always writing for the SDA denominational publications, and wrote a string of books. One well known book and still pushed hard by the SDA members is, "The Great Controversy." It is important to note that Ellen was a proven plagiarist. The explanation of the SDA Church for her plagiarism, that there were no copyright laws back then does not excuse her "borrowing".

SDA's often make every effort to appear "evangelical", joining in with inter-ministry groups and trying to "blend in" with the Christian community. However, make no mistake about it, they believe they are exclusively correct because they recognize and follow Ellen G. White. Among themselves, they mock the Christian's beliefs, calling our concept of salvation, "cheap grace". They privately consider themselves to be spiritually superior to the rest of us.

The SDA Church made this statement in their "Ministry" magazine of October 1981 and has never retracted it:

"We believe the revelation and inspiration of both the Bible and Ellen White's writings to be of equal quality. The superintendence of the Holy Spirit was just as careful and thorough in one case as in the other."

Cult Beliefs

➢ Great emphasis is laid upon the teaching that the Sabbath day is on Saturday, and if a person does not keep Saturday as Sabbath, he cannot be saved. Ultimately, according to SDA theology, your salvation in the last days boils down to the day you worship on. Simply put, there is no salvation outside the SDA church.

The Bible says we are saved by grace through faith and nothing more.

Ephesians 2:8-9

➢ Ellen G. White taught that all other churches except the SDA church were teaching lies from the Devil. Only SDA members are true and obedient believers; prayers spoken in other churches are only answered by the Devil. *This is a man-made doctrine not found in the Bible.*

➢ They believe that in the last days just before Christ returns, only those worshipping on Saturday will be saved. They particularly believe that worshipping on Sunday will be the mark of the beast. They consider themselves to be the only true, remnant church and all others will be condemned in time. *This is a man-made doctrine not found in the Bible. The mark of the beast will be a literal mark, either in your forehead or in your hand. Revelation 14:9*

- They firmly believe that Jesus is Michael the Archangel and this is the name used for him (Jesus) in the Old Testament; yet also believe that Jesus is God. *Jesus is God, he is the Creator; (John 1:1-3; Colossians 1:16-17; Hebrews 1:1-6) whereas, Michael is just an angel, a created being.*

- They believe that the atonement through Jesus is not complete until He comes again, only your past sins are forgiven by grace up to that point. *The Bible says that the atoning work of Jesus is finished, never again to be repeated. John 19:30; Hebrews 9:24-28*

- They believe in the "sanctuary teaching" that Jesus is now cleaning the sanctuary in the heavens before he can return to the earth. *This is a man-made doctrine not found in the Bible.*

- They believe you will have to stand in the presence of the living God for judgment without a mediator. *The Bible says that there is one mediator between God and men, and that is Jesus himself. I Timothy 2:5*

- They believe you can be sinless, also known as "sinless perfection". Meaning that a person can become sinless while they are still living on this earth in their physical body. *The Bible says that all are born with sin. All throughout the New Testament, the various authors write about fleeing and resisting sin, they themselves struggled with sin. This is a man-made doctrine not found in the Bible.*

- They won't tell you that early Adventists expected the literal second coming of Christ in 1843 and 1844 only to be disappointed. They won't tell you that their 1844 "investigative judgment" teaching was born out of an attempt to cover over this false prophecy. Instead of repenting over this false date, they believe that Christ really came, but INVISIBLY in heaven. As an SDA you now enter a period of "investigative judgment" where every deed you do or don't do is recorded for judgment day. You will even be judged for "idle moments" where you could have been more obedient. *When Christ comes, every eye shall see it (Revelation 1:7). At the Judgment Seat of Christ, we will be judged. 1st Corinthians 3:11-15; 2nd Corinthians 5:10*

- They believe the doctrine of soul sleeping, which states that the souls of believers in Christ are not in heaven, but are sleeping in the graves. *The Bible says those who were saved on earth by receiving Jesus Christ as their Saviour and died are now living a full and joyous life in heaven. Revelation 7:9-17*

- They believe in the final and total annihilation of the wicked, where they will simply cease to exist after the final judgment. This doctrine is in harmony with the Jehovah's Witnesses. *The Bible says they will be cast into the Lake of Fire. Revelation 20:12-15*

- They do not believe in the eternal punishment of Satan and his fallen angels. They believe that the penalty for sinning against a Holy God is merely annihilation. Satan is the scapegoat; the sins of the believers are laid upon him, and he and these sins are finally burned up. *The Bible says that Satan and his fallen angels will be cast in the Lake of Fire. Revelation 20:10-15*

➢ They believe in and demand vegetarianism. *There is no place in the Bible where God demands this. There is nothing wrong if a person chooses to be vegetarian for personal or health reasons, but it should never be tied in with our salvation.*

➢ They believe you should revere their founding prophetess, Ellen G. White, viewing her as having the "spirit of prophecy" referred to in the book of Revelation. Ellen G. White's writing are considered as inspired as the Bible and are used as a authoritative source of truth. In spite of revering her, they won't ordain women as ministers. *Ellen was a proven plagiarist and therefore a liar. God's attributes are truth and light (I John 1:5-6), whereas, Satan's attributes are darkness and lying (John 8:44).*

Seventh Day Adventism (SDA) is a very deceitful false religion. SDA's, more than any other false religion, APPEAR as born again Christians; BUT, they are not. They are of the Devil.

Seventh-Day Adventism is a dangerous cult. According to Wikipedia.com, SDA is recognized as a "Christian denomination." This is frightening indeed...

The **Seventh-day Adventist Church** had its roots in the Millerite movement of the 1830s and 1840s, and was officially founded in 1863. Prominent figures in the early church included Hiram Edson, James Springer White and his wife Ellen G. White, Joseph Bates and J. N. Andrews. Over the ensuing decades the church expanded from its original base in New England to become an international organization. Significant developments in the 20th century led to its recognition as a Christian denomination.

As you will see, *Seventh-Day Adventism* is of the Devil, an apple rotten to the core.

Seventh-Day Adventist Minister, Steve Wohlberg, Exposed

Steve Wohlberg is a *Seventh-Day Adventist* minister, and former pastor of the *Templeton Hills Seventh-Day Adventist Church* in California. SDAs are deceitful, and as a general rule hide the fact that they are Adventists. Steve Wohlberg is no exception. I dare you to look at Mr. Wohlberg's ministry's website and show me where he admits to being a *Seventh-Day Adventist*. In typical SDA fashion, he hides his affiliation. The reason why is quite obvious--because of the embarrassing beginnings of *Seventh-Day Adventism*. SDA was started as a damage control measure, due to a failed prophecy by a wayward Baptist preacher named William Miller (1782-1849). Mr. Miller had predicted that Jesus would return in 1843, and again in 1844, but He didn't. Over 10,000 people had sold their homes, given away all earthly possessions, and quit their jobs, expecting the Lord's return. Can you imagine their disappointment when the Lord DIDN'T return? Miller sinned by setting a date. No man knows when the Lord will return. Miller soon afterwards died, but the SDA cult was born to save face. Miller's followers concluded that they misunderstood the Scriptures, and that Jesus had entered into the Holy of Holies INSTEAD of coming to the earth. They termed this unbiblical event, the *Investigative Judgment*.

SDA is a cult, a false religion, which had it beginnings in false doctrine, failed prophecy, and confusion. This is why SDAs today shy away from revealing their true identity, because it enables prospect followers to do a little "investigative judgment" of their own.

Mr. Wohlberg is a wolf is sheep's clothing. The Word of God warns us about these deceivers (Matthew 7:15).
"White Horse Media is directed by author, radio host, and national seminar speaker Steve Wohlberg. Steve Wohlberg is the author of ten books, hosts the national radio show, World News and the Bible, and writes a monthly column for Wisconsin Christian News. He has also been a guest on over 400 radio and TV shows, including CNN Radio, Cable Radio Network, USA Radio, 3ABN Today, Focus 4, and The Harvest Show."
-SOURCE:
http://www.whitehorsemedia.com/about/

Again, I dare you to look at Mr. Wohlberg's ministry's website and show me where he admits to being a *Seventh-Day Adventist*. Mr. Wohlberg attracts a worldwide following of people, who errantly think he's a true Christian; BUT, he is certainly not. BEWARE of this false prophet! Mr. Wohlberg portrays himself as a true Christian, deceitfully failing to reveal his SDA beliefs. I've looked at several SDA websites, and they all deliberately steer clear of mentioning Ellen White's false doctrine of *Investigative Judgment*. SDA is a very deceitful religion.

Steve Wohlberg even teaches that the Sabbath was not Jewish. Now, that is ridiculous, and he really perverts the Scriptures in a feeble attempt to support his false doctrine. The biggest heresy of SDA is their *Investigative Judgment* doctrine, which is clearly based upon works salvation.

Adventists Teach Salvation by Works!
Here is a quote from Dr. John R. Rice's excellent book, *FALSE DOCTRINES* (pg. 183), available from the Sword of the Lord (which I highly recommend)...
"In article 9 (of 'What Seventh-Day Adventists Believe'), it says, 'that those who are truly converted and love God will diligently study, and give heed to, His Word.' And they give eight Scripture references and none of them say anything like that. The simple truth is that people who are converted do not always 'diligently study' the Bible and do not always obey it in many matters. This is a part of the doctrine of salvation by works which they teach, and that one may keep saved by keeping on working."

Thank God for Dr. Rice's wisdom and uncompromising stand for the truth! The Devil can't deceive us if we shine the light of God's Word upon the darkness. As with most false religions, SDAs talk out of both sides of their mouth. They say one thing here, and then another over there. SDAs will swear on their mother's grave that they believe in salvation by grace through faith in Christ; BUT, then the writings of Ellen G. White, whom they ALL recognize as a prophet inspired by God, contradicts their claims. Here again are the words of Dr. John R. Rice, from his book *FALSE DOCTRINES* (Pg. 188)...

"Mrs. White, the 'prophetess' of Seventh-Day Adventists, is quoted in their book, *Answers to Objections*, by Francis D. Nichol (published by the Review and Herald Publishing Association, Washington, D.C.), page 402, as saying: 'Those who accept the Saviour, however sincere their conversion, should never be taught to say or to feel that they are saved. This is misleading. Every one should be taught to cherish hope and faith; but even when we give ourselves to Christ and know that He accepts us, we are not beyond the reach of temptation ... Only he who endures the trial will receive the crown of life.''

"On page 409 (of *Answers to Objections*) Mr. Nichol says, speaking officially for Seventh-Day Adventists:
'Thus we escape on the one hand, the false doctrine of Universalism; and on

the other, the equally false doctrine of claiming full and final salvation for a man before he has endured 'unto the end.' "

Clearly, SDAs teach that a person must "endure" to the end to be guaranteed salvation in Christ. In contrast 1st John 5:13 states, **"These things have I written unto you that believe on the name of the Son of God; that ye may KNOW that ye have eternal life, and that ye may believe on the name of the Son of God**." We read in Romans 4:3, 5 that Abraham simply BELIEVED God, and was saved WITHOUT any works, **"For what saith the scripture? Abraham believed God, and it was counted unto him for righteousness ... But to him that worketh not, but believeth on him that justifieth the ungodly, his faith is counted for righteousness."** There is NO mention of enduring to the end to be saved. "Enduring" would be a work. Eternal life is a "FREE GIFT" (Romans 5:15; 6:23), paid for by the precious blood of Christ (1st Peter 1:18,19). SDAs teach salvation by works when they require a person to "endure unto the end" to be saved for certain.

Francis D. Nichol, in his book, *Answers to Objections*, states on page 243...
"Here is our position: Only those will be saved who, having been redeemed by the grace of Christ, walk in obedience to all the light that God sheds on their way."

This is the official Adventist position! The above doctrine means that all SDA members must comply with ALL of the requirements of the SDA church to be saved. So, according to SDA doctrine, if you don't tithe, you're not saved.. if you don't keep the Sabbath Day, you're not saved, etc. Jesus NEVER asked anyone to FOLLOW Him to be saved; BUT, rather, only to BELIEVE on Him (John 3:16). Jesus never asked anyone to work for salvation, only believe (Acts 16:31).

Baptismal Regeneration

Here's a SDA website, at http://www.adventist.org, that teaches Baptismal Regeneration. The following LIE of Satan is taken from a *Seventh Day Adventist* (SDA) Church website...

"Through baptism we are truly born again in Jesus." -SOURCE (2nd paragraph from bottom)

What a lie of Satan! No where in the Word of God are we ever told that baptism saves. Lutherans and other Bible-corrupters like to manipulate 1st Peter 3:21, **"The like figure whereunto even baptism doth also now save us (not the putting away of the filth of the flesh, but the answer of a good conscience toward God,) by the resurrection of Jesus Christ."** Usually, the heretics will just take a few words out of this Scripture, failing to quote the entire Verse. If a person were only to consider the phrase, "...baptism doth also now save us," then they might get the WRONG impression that baptism is essential to going to Heaven.

If we read the rest of the Verse, then the truth is clearly seen, "...not the putting away of the filth of the flesh, but the answer of a good conscience toward

God." Being baptized cannot forgive our sins. In fact, getting baptized will just get you wet! 1st Peter 3:21 states that baptism is the "like figure." Romans 6:5,6 plainly teaches that baptism is only the "likeness" of the Gospel, not the Gospel itself. Ironically, SDA's state this on the the above webpage, which is extremely CONTRADICTORY. How can baptism be "symbolic" if it also has the POWER to save. Romans 1:16 declares that the Gospel is the "power" of God unto salvation. Baptism is not mentioned.

You can argue with me all you want, but the SDA quote above requiring baptism for salvation speaks for itself. SDA is of the Devil, as was it's most influential leader, Ellen G. White who openly denied Jesus' deity in her writings.

The Devil is Subtle and Deceptive in Seventh-Day Adventism

Seventh Day Adventists [SDA] profess to believe that faith in Jesus Christ is the only way to Heaven. However, what they don't tell you is that they have a very different understanding of what the term "faith" means. To the Adventist, faith encompasses everything that the Christian life includes.

"To have faith means to find and accept the gospel treasure, with all the obligations which it imposes" (*Christ's Object Lessons,* p. 112).

SOURCE: *SALVATION BY FAITH*, Jan Paulsen; http://www.adventistbiblicalresearch.org/documents/Salvation%20by%20Faith.htm

Obligations? What obligations? Eternal life is a free gift, paid for by Jesus' precious blood (Romans 4:5-6; 1 Peter 1:18-19). SDA is a works-based false religion, which mandates OBLIGATIONS that the Bible does NOT! There can be no obligations for something truly to be a gift! If I tell you that I bought you a birthday present, but first you must complete a list of obligations to have it; then it WOULDN'T truly be a gift! It would be a reward that you had earned.

The entire corrupted mindset of the Seventh-Day Adventist is that you had better do your best, while trusting Christ, and hope your best is good enough when Christ's work of Investigative Judgment is complete. This false doctrine is only taught by Adventists. The term **Investigative Judgment** isn't even found in the Bible. SDA's have their own bizarre demonic cult which is deceitful, packed full of lies and smells with the stench of sewage from Hell. Run, run, run while you can, before you get sucked into the deadly black hole of lies and deceit of Seventh-Day Adventism!!!

Thus, faith to an Adventist means that a person must be water baptized, go to church, faithfully live a righteous life, tithe, keep the SDA Sabbath, et cetera, to be saved in their religion. Of course, that is a damnable doctrine not taught in the Word of God. Seventh Day Adventism is a false religion based upon self-righteousness and a corrupt view of the gospel.

Biblical faith is simply resting in Jesus Christ for salvation (Genesis 15:6; Romans 4:3-5; Romans 10:3-4; Ephesians 2:8-9). Biblical faith imposes no obligation upon the sinner in order to be saved. Faith in the Lord is all that is necessary. Eternal life is a free gift (Romans 5:15;6:23), freely offered (Romans 10:13) and freely received (Revelation 22:17). Salvation is receiving, not giving. The sinner who believes on Jesus Christ, the Son of God, apart from all self-righteousness, will be saved and go to Heaven.

Seventh-Day Adventism is a Satanic Deception!

SDAs talk out of both-sides-of-their-mouth. On one hand they say that Jesus died once; YET, they simultaneously claim that there is a "second phase" to redemption, i.e., their devilish heresy of *Investigative Judgment*. Clearly, something is not right with SDA. You'll find it to be true that one lie always requires another lie to prop it up. For example: Catholics sinfully teach that Mary was born without a sin-nature, and that she never sinned one time. They call this the doctrine of the *Immaculate Conception*.

But this new doctrine posed a big problem for Catholics, because if Mary never sinned, then Mary couldn't die... *For the wages of sin is death* (Romans 6:23). So to remedy the problem, Catholics fabricated another lie to support the first lie, and called it the *Assumption of Mary*, i.e., the false doctrine that Mary was bodily assumed into Heaven and never saw death. Do you see how the Devil does things? William Miller fabricated a big lie when he predicted the Lord's return in 1844, and then his followers fabricated an even bigger lie to cover it up, calling the new doctrine, *Investigative Judgment*. SDA is nothing more than a BIG LIE, as a cover-up to a previous lie.

It is tragic that men and women, in their woeful stubbornness and pride, are willing to corrupt the Scriptures in order to justify their foolishness and sin. SDA wouldn't exist today if it were not for the foolishness of William Miller, who errantly predicted the Lord's return in 1843. SDA was born out of a failed prophecy!!! This fact alone proves incontrovertibly that SDA is a scam, a hoax, and a false religion rooted in man's sinful pride and wickedness.

I plead with you to forsake the *Seventh-Day Adventist* false religion if you are a victim. Acts 16:31 is the only invitation which God ever gave for men to be saved ... **"Believe upon the Lord Jesus Christ and thou shalt be saved."**

The Occult Roots of Seventh-day Adventism
New Age Markings on Ellen G. White's Writings

"There be some that trouble you, and would pervert the gospel of Christ. But though we, or an angel from heaven, preach any other gospel unto you than that which we have preached unto you, let him be accursed."

Galatians 1:7,8

Right: Official Seventh-Day Adventist Logo, shaped as a Masonic pyramid

Seventh-day Adventism [SDA] is a false religion, plagued with deception and lies. It is one of the more subtle religions, being easily

mistaken for a genuine New Testament Church; however, it is not. SDA founder, Ellen G. White, was involved with the occult and has a large Freemasonry Obelisk situated above her grave.

The late Ellen G. White (November 26, 1827-July 16, 1915), known to Seventh Day Adventists as "God's Messenger" or "God's Prophet," used New Age/occult terminology and taught New Age doctrine via some of the pages of her voluminous published works.

Below are citations from her complete published works found at http://www.whiteestate.org. [Quotes are used in accordance with the Fair Use Copyright Law]

New Age/Occult terms: Mother earth, Mother Nature
--Cited from The Health Reformer, March 1, 1871 and The Health Reformer, May 1, 1871
Ellen G. White referred to the earth as Mother Earth:
May has come, with all her beauties of the sunshine, clothing nature with a glorious dress. **Mother earth** has laid off her brown mantle, and wears her cheerful robes of green. The trees and shrubs upon the lawn are decorated with their opening buds and flowers of varied tints. The peach and cherry are covered with blossoms of pink and white, and the pure music from a thousand of nature's happy and cheering songsters, unite to awaken joy and thankfulness in our hearts. {HR, "The Beautiful May" May 1, 1871 par. 1} (Emphasis added)
The trees, shrubs, and flowers, will soon be attractive to the eye, inviting all who delight in the beauties of nature to enjoy life out of doors. The flowers and green foliage have not appeared, but **mother earth** has thrown from her bosom her white mantle, and she

even now bears a cheerful aspect in the bright sunshine and shadows. All should now seek employment some hours every day out of doors. {HR, March 1, 1871 par. 3} (Emphasis added)

Ellen G. White chose Beltane (the highest holiday in Druid witchcraft) as the time to cite a lengthy passage by Fanny B. Johnson that contains New Age terminology and teaches New Age doctrine:

Lovely May is here. Enjoy her, all you who can, while she is with us. Read what Fanny B. Johnson, in *Laws of Life*, says under the caption, {HR, "The Beautiful May" May 1, 1871 par. 4}

Mrs. White endorsed Fanny Johnson's highly New Age passage in which she urged Mother Nature's children to "come out of doors, and take part in the grand entertainment which she has gotten up with wondrous skill, taste, and power":

OUT OF DOORS.
IN BEHALF OF OUR GOOD MOTHER NATURE, I HEREBY INVITE AND ENTREAT ALL HER CHILDREN WITHIN SOUND OF MY VOICE OR SIGHT OF MY PENTRACES TO COME OUT OF DOORS, AND TAKE PART IN THE GRAND ENTERTAINMENT WHICH SHE HAS GOTTEN UP WITH WONDROUS SKILL, TASTE, AND POWER. {HR, May 1, 1871 par. 5} (Emphasis added)

Johnson presented Mother Nature (not the Lord Jesus Christ) as the way for poverty-stricken, burden-bearing human beings to escape from their condition:

MOTHER NATURE WILL TAKE YOU IN HER LAP, WILL WOO YOU WITH THE BREATH OF APPLE BLOSSOMS AND CLOVERS, WILL FAN YOUR CHEEK WITH PERFUME-LADEN AIRS, WILL SOOTHE YOU TO SLEEP WITH DROWSY HUM OF BEES, AND MURMUR OF STREAMS, AND RUSTLE

OF MYRIAD FLUTTERING LEAVES, WILL WAKEN YOU WITH JOYOUS VOICES, WILL TAKE AWAY FROM YOUR SPIRITS THE PEEVISHNESS AND LITTLENESS THAT IS SURE TO GATHER IN A NARROW ROUND OF CARE, AND PUT IN THEIR PLACE SOMETHING OF HER SPIRIT OF CHARITY, AND LARGENESS, AND HARMONY, **AND BRING YOU INTO SYMPATHY WITH THE DIVINE. THERE WAS NEVER BETTER CHANCE FOR POVERTY-STRICKEN, BURDEN-BEARING HUMAN BEINGS TO ESCAPE FROM THEIR CONDITION AND INDULGE IN LUXURIES FURNISHED WITHOUT MONEY AND WITHOUT PRICE.** I PROMISE YOU NATURE WILL SHOW NO FAVORS ON ACCOUNT OF WORLDLY DISTINCTIONS. SHE WILL MINISTER NO MORE GRACIOUSLY TO THE QUEEN OF A REALM THAN TO HER HUMBLEST MENIAL, PROVIDED THAT MENIAL BE LOYAL TO HERSELF. BUT TO THOSE WHO LOOK UPON HER WITH "LOVERS' EYES" SHE MUST OF NECESSITY BE PARTIAL. SHE SHOWS THEM WONDROUS THINGS IN HER PAGES, AND REVEALS HERSELF TO THEM AS SHE CANNOT TO OTHERS. {HR, May 1, 1871 par. 6} (Emphasis added)

Ellen G. White did not disclaim any of Fanny Johnson's New Age teachings and warn her readers to refrain from being wooed by the devil in Mother Nature's garb. An ambassador of the Lord Jesus Christ would contradict Fanny Johnson and insist that Jesus Christ's invitation to the weary is the only one that is valid:

"Come unto me, all ye that labour and are heavy laden, and I will give you rest."

Matthew 11:28

The Lord Jesus Christ offers the only legitimate spiritual rest but the devil seeks to ensnare the weary with a counterfeit rest via Ellen G. White's endorsement of Johnson's "Mother Nature," who is known to New Agers as Earth Mother, or Gaia.

New Age/Occult term: Vital Force

Ellen G. White favored the occult term, "vital force." Vital Force is a foundational concept in New Age doctrine. Vital Force is another name for Chi which is commonly known in the West as life force, vital force, universal energy, vital force, subtle energy, etc.
Chi (also ki, qi or ji) - A "life force" pervading the universe that sustains the body and the material world. These terms and concepts come from Eastern beliefs but are most prominently used in the martial arts and in alternative healing. Both *ki* and *chi* can be seen in the following terms: *Aikido, Tai Chi, Reiki* (energy healing). This force may also be known as the life force, **vital force**, the vital energy, bioenergy, universal life force, or universal energy. **The belief in such a force is at the heart of occultism and is also found in New Age beliefs.** (1) [Emphasis added]

New Agers believe that Vital Force (subtle energy) is a nonmaterial force that sustains life:
vital force (bioenergy, cosmic energy, cosmic energy force, cosmic force, cosmic life energy, cosmic life force, elan vital, energy of being, force of life, force vitale, inner vital energy, internal energy, life, life energy, life force, life force energy, life power, life

source energy, nerve energy, nerve force, personal energy, spirit, **subtle energy,** universal energy, universal life energy, universal life energy power, universal life force, universal life force energy, universal life principle, vital cosmic force, vital element, vital energy, vital energy force, vitality, vital life force, vital life force energy, vitalistic principle, vitality energy, vital life spirit, vital magnetism, vital principle, vital spirit): An alleged nonmaterial "force" that sustains life. (2)

Subtle Energy, vital force, universal life force, etc. (demon spirits) can be manipulated and sent on assignment to perform lying wonders (2 Thessalonians 2:9) via various forms of witchcraft that are often disguised as alternative medical treatments-- such as Reiki and acupressure. Man cannot control or manipulate God (or healings from God)--ever.

Man *can* manipulate demons (which disguise themselves under sophisticated and scientific-sounding terms) *if* he submits to the occult methodology necessary for their cooperation but the result of such sin (even if it is engaged in under the guise of New Age alternative medicine) is eternal destruction in the Lake of Fire.

Examples of Ellen G. White's use of the term, "vital force."

[Bold emphasis is added.] Please note that Mrs. White used the term, "vital force" in the same manner New Agers do today:
God has endowed us with a certain amount of **vital force**. He has also formed us with organs suited to

maintain the various functions of life, and He designs that these organs shall work together in harmony. If we carefully preserve the life force, and keep the delicate mechanism of the body in order, the result is health; but if the vital force is too rapidly exhausted, the nervous system borrows power for present use from its resources of strength, and when one organ is injured, all are affected. [The Ministry of Healing, pg. 234] (3) [**Note**: in this passage Ellen G. White teaches that God gives vital force.]

Food should not be eaten very hot or very cold. If food is cold, the **vital force of the stomach** is drawn upon in order to warm it before digestion can take place. [The Ministry of Healing pg. 305] (4)

Sometimes the result of overeating is felt at once. In other cases there is no sensation of pain; but the digestive organs **lose their vital force**, and the foundation of physical strength is undermined. [The Ministry of Healing pg. 306](5)

These unpleasant symptoms are felt because **nature has accomplished her work at an unnecessary outlay of vital force** and is thoroughly exhausted. The stomach is saying, "Give me rest." But with many the faintness is interpreted as a demand for more food; so instead of giving the stomach rest, another burden is placed upon it. As a consequence the digestive organs are often worn out when they should be capable of doing good work. [The Ministry of Healing pg. 307] (6)

[**Note**: in the passage above, Ellen G. White attributed vital force to nature. Mrs. White's practice of citing

God and nature as the source of vital energy is an example of Christian/New Age syncretism.]
Where wrong habits of diet have been indulged, there should be no delay in reform. When dyspepsia has resulted from abuse of the stomach, efforts should be made carefully to preserve the remaining **strength of the vital forces** by removing every overtaxing burden. [The Ministry of Healing pg. 308] (7)

In the following passage, Ellen G. White links Christian growth with vital force:
Let a living faith run like threads of gold through the performance of even the smallest duties. Then all the daily work will promote Christian growth. There will be a continual looking unto Jesus. **Love for Him will give vital force** to everything that is undertaken. [From *Christ's Object Lessons,* pp. 356-360] (8)

Those who think that perhaps she used these terms unknowingly and innocently taught New Age doctrine, please understand that New Age teachings were not widely known in the United States in the 1800s. Ellen G. White learned these doctrines from someone...and that someone was not God.

Ellen G. White's "Christ" bestowed vital force:
He was the originator of all the ancient gems of truth. Through the work of the enemy, these truths had been displaced. . . . **Christ** rescued them from the rubbish of error, **gave them a new, vital force,** and commanded them to shine as jewels, and stand fast forever. [Manuscript 25, 1890.] (9)

[**Note:** The context of this quote has to do with Mrs. White's defense of her practice of claiming authorship

of material she did not write but she did use the occasion to link Christ with vital force. I ask which "Christ" might that be? It is the New Age Christ who afflicts his followers with subtle energy.]
In the next passage Ellen G. White was correct to warn against the dangers of drugs but that does not negate the fact that she was functioning as an early spokeswoman for the New Age Movement by her continual promotion of the idea that vital force keeps the body in good health. We see Christian/New Age syncretism at work again via Ellen G. White's attribution of vital energy to nature in some passages and to God in others:

People need to be taught that drugs do not cure disease. It is true that they sometimes afford present relief, and the patient appears to recover as the result of their use; this is because **nature has sufficient vital force** to expel the poison and to correct the conditions that caused the disease. [The Ministry of Healing, pg. 126] (10)

Here Mrs. White attributed vital force to God:
The Lord will put new, vital force into His work as human agencies obey the command to go forth and proclaim the truth. . . . The truth will be criticized, scorned, and derided; but the closer it is examined and tested, the brighter it will shine. . . . [*Selected Messages,* book 1, p. 201] (11)

God endowed man with so great vital force that he has withstood the accumulation of disease brought upon the race in consequence of perverted habits, and has continued for six thousand years. . . . [From My Life Today, page 126] (12)

According to Mrs. White, vital force is highly desirable and parents should take care not to deny this force to future generations:
If the mother is deprived of the care and comforts she should have, if she is allowed to exhaust her strength through overwork or through anxiety and gloom, her **children will be robbed of the vital force** and of the mental elasticity and cheerful buoyancy they should inherit. [The Ministry of Healing, pg. 375] (13)

Children who are **robbed of that vitality** which they should have inherited from their parents should have the utmost care. [Vital Vigor and Energy 204] (14)

Rather than tell her followers not to overwork lest they become too tired and run down, Ellen G. White presented the New Age concept that overexertion depletes vital force to the hurt of one's health:
Those who make great exertions to accomplish just so much work in a given time, and continue to labor when their judgment tells them they should rest, are never gainers. They are living on borrowed capital. They are **expending the vital force** which they will need at a future time. [From My Life Today - Page 142] (15)

According to Mrs. White, frequent child-bearing depletes women of vital energies. This of course conflicts with God's command to multiply and be fruitful and 1st Timothy 2:15: "...she shall be saved in childbearing..."

Everywhere you may look you will see pale, sickly, care-worn, broken-down, dispirited, discouraged women. They are generally overworked, and **their**

vital energies exhausted by frequent child-bearing. [Vital Vigor and Energy 203] (16)
While it is a fact that frequent child-bearing can be physically exhausting, giving birth has nothing do with losing a nonmaterial "force" that sustains life.

Mrs. White taught that snacking causes the unnatural stimulation and wearing of the vital forces. The context suggests that an imbalance of the vital forces leads to sin:
Children are generally untaught in regard to the importance of when, how, and what they should eat. They are permitted to indulge their tastes freely, to eat at all hours, to help themselves to fruit when it tempts their eyes, and this, with the pie, cake, bread and butter, and sweetmeats eaten almost constantly, makes them gourmands and dyspeptics. The digestive organs, like a mill which is continually kept running, become enfeebled, vital force is called from the brain to aid the stomach in its overwork, and thus the mental powers are weakened. **The unnatural stimulation and wear of the vital forces** make them nervous, impatient of restraint, self-willed, and irritable. . . . It is difficult to arouse them to a sense of the shame and grievous nature of sin. [Selected Messages, book 1, p. 201.] (17)

The God of the Bible is NOT the god of Vital Force

Ellen G. White, regardless of what she may have stated in her other writings, chose to repeatedly use the occult phrase, "vital force" to promote the pagan belief that "an alleged nonmaterial force sustains life."

The Bible clearly states that it is by the Lord Jesus Christ that all things consist:

For by him were all things created, that are in heaven, and that are in earth, visible and invisible, whether they be thrones, or dominions, or principalities, or powers: all things were created by him, and for him:

Colossians 1:16

And he is before all things, and by him all things consist.

Colossians 1:17

It is in Jesus Christ that we live, move and have our being:

For in him we live, and move, and have our being;

Acts 17:28

The Holy Bible refutes the New Age lie of vital force. It is by Jesus Christ himself, not a nonmaterial force, that all things consist. It is in Jesus Christ (not vital force) that Christians live and move and have their being.

It is God, not Vital Force That Sustains Mankind

This passage was cited earlier in the article, but in conclusion, please note that Ellen G. White taught her followers that vital force has enabled man to live on earth for six thousand years without becoming extinct: **God endowed man with so great vital force** that he has withstood the accumulation of disease upon the race in consequence of perverted habits, and has continued for six thousand years. . . . If Adam, at his creation, had not been **endowed with twenty times**

as much vital force as men now have, the race, with their present habits of living in violation of natural law, would have become extinct. [From My Life Today, page 126]

It is God himself, not a nonmaterial "vital force" who has mercifully sustained mankind's existence upon the earth for all these years.

Ellen G. White promoted the "vital force" doctrine of devils long before Eastern religious thought became prevalent in the United States and other parts of the western world.

Notes:
1. http://cana.userworld.com/cana_occultTerms.html
2. http://www.rodsmith.org.uk/alternative-health/Alternative-health-glossaryU-Z.htm
3. www.egwtext.whiteestate.org/mh/mh17.html
4. http://www.egwtext.whiteestate.org/mh/mh23.html
5. http://www.egwtext.whiteestate.org/mh/mh23.html
6. http://www.egwtext.whiteestate.org/mh/mh23.html
7. http://www.egwtext.whiteestate.org/mh/mh23.html
8. http://www.whiteestate.org/message/littlethings.asp
9. http://www.whiteestate.org/issues/whitelie.html
10. http://www.egwtext.whiteestate.org/mh/mh8.html
11. http://www.whiteestate.org/issues/rev-insp.html
12. http://egwlists.whiteestate.org/Lists/devotional/Message/1185.html
13. http://www.egwtext.whiteestate.org/mh/mh31.html
14. http://healthyliving.benabraham.com/html/vital_vigor_and_energy.html
15. http://egwlists.whiteestate.org/Lists/devotional/Message/1201.html
16. http://healthyliving.benabraham.com/html/vital_vigor_and_energy.html
17. http://www.whiteestate.org/issues/rev-insp.html#footnote-28

SOURCE: New Age Markings on Ellen G. White's Writings

Seventh-day Adventists: Yoked with the United Nations

The Seventh-day Adventist Church hierarchy is yoked with the United Nations and their interests are represented there:
Liaison Office to the United Nations is based at the Church's world headquarters in Silver Spring, Maryland, USA. It serves to both communicate and represent the Church at the UN and also to inform the Church of UN activities of importance and interest. (1)

Seventh-day Adventist leaders partner with the United Nations in many UN-sponsored activities:
The Church benefits from such representation and recommendations, and seeks to partner where appropriate in UN-sponsored activities such a literacy development, humanitarian aid, human rights education, anti-narcotic drug programs, and conventions and declarations of mutual interest such as trafficking in people, children's issues, preventive health, AIDS programs, pollution control, combating intolerance etc. (2)

Indeed, the SDA Church and the United Nations globalists have common goals:
Much of the work of the Church is appreciated and endorsed since it parallels the aims and objectives of the UN as outlined in the UN Charter. (3)

The Seventh Day Adventist high-ranking officials believe that much can be accomplished via their association with the United Nations and consider their work with the UN an essential part of their witness to the world:
The UN Liaison work is considered an essential part of the Church's witness to the wider world, and also provides the Church with updated and relevant

information on programs and plans of the international community. (4)

What kind of witness is the SDA Church accomplishing via their yoke with the United Nations? The United Nations was founded for the purpose of implementing the New Age/World Order. **It is revealing that a religious organization that claims to be "the Remnant Church" (and whose co-founder marked herself for the New Age) considers their work with high-level globalists an essential part of their witness to the world.**

Be ye not unequally yoked together with unbelievers: for what fellowship hath righteousness with unrighteousness? and what communion hath light with darkness?

2 Corinthians 6:14

The Seventh-day Adventist Church falsely presents the United Nations as a benign organization when in fact it is a major vehicle for the one world government of the Beast.

Woe unto them that call evil good, and good evil; that put darkness for light, and light for darkness; that put bitter for sweet, and sweet for bitter!

Isaiah 5:20

Notes:
1. http://un.adventist.org
2. http://un.adventist.org/aboutus/index.html
3. http://un.adventist.org/aboutus/index.html
4. http://un.adventist.org/aboutus/index.html

Chapter 13: Roman Catholicism

Written By: Leeanne Panday-Naicker

Belief

The **Catholic Church**, also known as the **Roman Catholic Church** is the oldest institution in the western world. Today there are more than a billion Catholics in the world, spread across all five continents with particular concentrations in southern Europe, the United States, the Philippines and the countries of Central and South America. What binds this diverse group of people together is their faith in Jesus Christ and their obedience to the papacy. Catholics believe that the Pope, based in Rome, is the successor to Saint Peter whom Christ appointed as the first head of His church. He therefore stands in what Catholicism calls the *apostolic succession*, an unbroken line back to Peter and has supreme authority. Popes can speak infallibly on matters of faith and morals but rarely do so in practice.

Catholics share with other Christians a belief in the divinity of Jesus Christ, the son of God who came to earth to redeem humanity's sins through His death and resurrection. They follow His teachings as set out in the New Testament and place their trust in God's promise of eternal life with Him. Catholicism, however, is distinct from other Christian churches in both its organisation and its teaching. The Hebrew Scriptures (usually known to Christians as the Old Testament and the New Testament) lay the basic groundwork for the Catholic understanding of all reality. They show God as the creator of the world and everything in it, including humanity. Catholics understand the two major parts of the Bible to be "testaments" because they testify to the centrality of Christ in God's plan for the world and the humans within it. They believe that even the stories that do not mention Jesus by name are in some way pointing to his existence and his role in bringing humans back into right relationship with God, which makes the story of Jesus the Christ the most important narrative that Catholics hold to be sacred.

The Catholic Church is Trinitarian and defines its mission as spreading the Gospel of Jesus Christ, administering the sacraments and exercising charity. The Church holds the Blessed Virgin Mary, as mother of Jesus Christ, in special regard and has defined four specific Marian dogmatic teachings:

- her Immaculate Conception without original sin,
- her status as the Mother of God,
- her perpetual virginity,
- and her bodily Assumption into Heaven at the end of her earthly life

Distinctive Roman Catholic beliefs and teachings include:

- God's objective existence;
- God's interest in individual human beings, who can enter into relations with God (through prayer);
- the Trinity;
- the divinity of Jesus;
- the immortality of the soul of each human being, each one being accountable at death for his or her actions in life, with the award of heaven or hell;
- the resurrection of the dead;
- the historicity of the Gospels;
- the divine commission of the church
- the special authority of the pope,
- apostolic succession,
- the ability of saints to intercede on behalf of believers,
- the concept of Purgatory as a place of afterlife purification before entering Heaven, and the doctrine of transubstantiation - that is, that the bread used in the Eucharist becomes the true body of Christ when blessed by a priest

To belong to the Roman Catholic Church one must accept as factually true the gospel of Jesus as handed down in tradition and as interpreted by the bishops in union with the pope. The doctrine of apostolic succession is one of the keystones of the Catholic faith; it holds that the pope (the Vicar of Christ) and the bishops have in varying degrees, the spiritual authority Jesus assigned to his apostles. The voice of the pope, either alone or in conjunction with his bishops in council, is regarded as infallible when speaking on matters of faith and morals taught in common with the bishops.

In addition the Roman Catholic Church stresses that since the members, living and dead, share in each other's merits, the Virgin Mary and other saints and the dead in purgatory are never forgotten.

The Roman Catholic Church teaches that the main motive for ethical behaviour is the love of God. Nothing that God has created is evil in itself, but evil use may be made of it.

The doctrine concerning persons not Catholic is that since God affords each human being light sufficient to attain salvation, *all will be saved who persevere in what they believe to be good, regardless of ignorance. Only those will be damned who persist in what they know to be wrong; among these are persons who resist the church when they know it to be the one, true church.*

When it Started – Origins

The Roman Catholic Church traces its history to Jesus Christ and the Apostles. Over the course of centuries it developed a highly sophisticated theology and an elaborate organizational structure headed by the papacy, the oldest continuing absolute monarchy in the world. The Roman Catholic Church contends that its origin is the death, resurrection, and ascension of Jesus Christ in approximately AD 30. The Roman

Catholic Church can trace its roots all the way back to the original Christian church in Rome.

For almost a thousand years, Catholicism and Christianity were as one. The break or schism between the Church of Rome and other Christian faiths began with the split with Orthodox Christians in 1054 over questions of doctrine and the absolute authority and behaviour of the popes. Throughout the Middle Ages, if you were a Christian, you belonged to the Catholic Church. Any Christianity other than the Catholic Church was a heresy, not a denomination.

Today, however, Roman Catholicism is not the only accepted Christian church, although the Roman Church teaches it is the most authentic form of the faith today.

Thus to be a Roman Catholic means to be a certain kind of Christian: one with unique beliefs, practices and traditions that are distinct from those of other Christians. Nevertheless, the Catholic Church continues to maintain that it alone has carried on the true tradition of the apostolic church and has traditionally regarded dissenting groups as heresies, not alternatives. However, the recent Second Vatican Council declared all baptized Christians to be "in a certain, although imperfect, communion with the Catholic Church."

Traditions

There is a great deal of concern about Catholic tradition these days because, since the 1960's, the Church herself has been heavily impacted by a secular culture which scorns tradition. As a result, many traditions have fallen by the wayside and, clearly, the Catholic sense of identity has been weakened. Tradition has a very specific meaning in Catholicism. It does not include all the customs, art, liturgical forms and disciplines which make up the various human traditions associated with the Faith. Therefore, it is well to start with a definition of Tradition.

Tradition is, in fact, a source of Divine Revelation in Catholicism. While various Catholic traditions may be altered or even abandoned without anything essential being lost, the same cannot be said about Tradition properly understood. But Scripture is also a source of Divine Revelation essential to the life of the Church, and so the question arises of the relationship between the two. The most recent explanation of the role of Tradition in transmitting Divine Revelation is found in Vatican II's Dogmatic Constitution on Divine Revelation. Although not essential to the constitution of the Church, human Catholic traditions are important to us because of how human persons receive their identities and imbibe values.

To further explain "Tradition" in Catholicism – it is literally a "handing on," referring to the passing down of God's revealed word. Tradition first means all of divine revelation, from the dawn of human history to the end of the apostolic age, as passed on from one generation of believers to the next, and as preserved under divine guidance by the Church established by Christ. Sacred Tradition more technically also means, within this transmitted revelation, that portion of God's revealed word which is not contained in Sacred Scripture.

Referring specifically to how Christian tradition was handed on, the Second Vatican Council says: "It was done by the apostles who handed on, by the spoken word of their preaching, by the example they gave, by the institutions they established, what they themselves had received--whether from the lips of Christ, from His way of life and His works, or whether they had learned it by the prompting of the Holy Spirit" (Constitution on Divine Revelation, II, 7).

Canon Laws

Canon law is the name for the Catholic Church's order and discipline, structures, rules, and procedures. The Catholic Church has two Codes: one for the Latin Church and one for the Eastern Catholic Churches. What is a code? A code is a single collection of all the laws of a community in one place, promulgated by a legislator. A code is intended to be consistent, systematic, and logical. The universal legislator of the Catholic Church is the Pope; the official language of canon law is Latin. Canon law is a tool to guide the Church as a large human institution from differing cultures and languages. In short, canon law informs the community on how to conduct themselves and protects the rights of the faithful.

At the time of the First Vatican Council, the leaders of the church decided that the law needed to be consolidated into one codified system. Cardinal Gasparri led the project, and the first Code of Canon

Law was endorsed in 1917 and was in force until 1983.

The code is divided into seven books:

- General Norms
- People of God
- Teaching Office
- Sanctifying Office
- Temporal Goods
- Sanctions
- Procedures

The Code of Canons of the Eastern Churches was promulgated by Blessed Pope John Paul II on October 18, 1990 for all 21 Eastern Catholic Churches. The patron saint of canon law is St. Raymond of Peñafort, whose feast day is January 7.

Prayers

Catholics memorize and teach their children to know certain prayers by heart. Catholic prayer begins and ends with the Sign of the Cross *(In the Name of the Father and of the Son and of the Holy Ghost. Amen)*. Ideally, prayer is offered facing East when possible. Prayers range from daily devotional prayers, special occasions that fall during the year, prayers for the pope, prayers for priests and more… This is a list of some of the prayers that are performed.

- The Lord's Prayer (Our Father prayer)
- The Sign of the Cross
- The Apostles' Creed
- The Nicene Creed
- The Glory Be

- Prayer before meals
- Prayer after meals
- I Confess Prayer
- Fatima Prayer
- Prayer to St. Michael
- Prayer to Guardian Angel ("Angel of God")
- Hail Mary Prayer
- Hail, Holy Queen
- Eternal Rest Prayer
- Act of Contrition
- Act of Faith
- Act of Hope
- Act of Charity
- Act of Reparation to the Sacred Heart

Catholic practices make up the daily life of a Catholic individual and a Catholic society. The morning offering, the invocation of Jesus, Mary and Joseph, the sprinkling of holy water on children at bedtime, the incantation to Saint Anthony, the pleas to Saint Jude to prevent a bankruptcy, the novenas for a sick spouse. All of these many practices is said to fill the lives of the faithful, enrich, comfort and orient them. Often it is difficult to trace their origin. Often the ones which seem most intimate and natural to people were never even introduced by ecclesiastical authority. They emerged as natural, faith-filled expressions of love or joy or thanksgiving or grief or desperation.

Posture and gesture

Posture and gesture is very important in prayers. These are some that are practiced:

Bowing of the Head

- When passing by a Church, the head is bowed and the Sign of the Cross is performed to honor the real presence of Christ in the tabernacle.
- Any time they hear the name "Jesus" (note that "Christ" is His title, meaning "Anointed One"; there is no need to bow the head at just the mention of the word "Christ").
- Men should remove their hats and bow their heads when passing a church or when His Name is spoken; this practice is for both inside and outside of Mass.
- Perform the sign of the cross and bow the head when the priest and crucifier walk down the aisle before and after Mass.
- After Mass, as the priest leaves the Altar, it is also customary to pray for him. (Some make a profound bow instead at these times)

Kisses

- Kissing Crucifixes and Icons (2-D or 3-D)
- Kissing rings of hierarchs
- Kissing a priest's hands: the priest's hands may be kissed when greeting or leaving him because they alone are able to confect the Holy Eucharist. They are also kissed on Palm Sunday when receiving a palm (which is also kissed).
- During the Mass, the priest's hands are kissed by the acolytes/altar boys.

Prostration

Prostrations, which signify total humility and penance, are made during the Rite of Ordination, during rites of religious profession (i.e. entry into religious orders), as penance in religious orders, and by anyone during private prayer before a Crucifix or the Blessed Sacrament. It is also occasionally made by adults, at the priest's invitation, before the Profession of Faith in the solemn Rite of Baptism.

Kneeling

- Any time the Blessed Sacrament is exposed, to show adoration and humility
- Many times during the Mass: during the Prayers at the Foot of the Altar, after the Sanctus, after the Agnus Dei, at the altar rail, and at the Last Blessing
- During Confession, inside or, in emergencies, outside of the Confessional
- When receiving a priestly blessing, inside or outside of the Liturgy. If unable for some reason to kneel, then the head is bowed.
- During private prayer

Veiling

For 2,000 years, Catholic women have veiled themselves before entering a church or any time they are in the presence of the Blessed Sacrament (e.g., during sick calls). It was written into the 1917 Code of Canon Law, Canon 1262, that women must cover their heads -- "especially when they approach the holy table" - but during the Second Vatican Council, Bugnini (the same Freemason who designed the Novus Ordo Mass) was asked by journalists if women would still have to cover their heads. His reply, perhaps innocently enough, was that the issue was not being discussed. The journalists took his answer as a "no," and printed their misinformation in newspapers all over the world. 1 Since then, many, if not most, Catholic women have lost the tradition. This one superficially small act is:

- so rich with symbolism: of submission to authority; of surrender to God; of covering their glory for His glory; of modesty; of chastity, of being vessels of life like the Chalice, the Ciborium and, most especially, the Virgin Mary;
- an Apostolic ordinance with roots deep in the Old Testament and, therefore, a matter of intrinsic Tradition;
- the way Catholic women have worshipped for two millennia, it is part of the heritage, a part of Catholic culture;

Traditionally, single women wear white or ivory head coverings, and married or widowed women wear black, but this isn't a hard and fast rule, and is often ignored.

Novenas

Its name deriving from the Latin word "novem," meaning "nine," a novena is nine days' private or public devotion in the Catholic Church to obtain special graces. They've been prayed since the very beginning of the and a nine-day period of supplication was a pagan Roman and Eastern practice, so novenas were easily accepted by the earliest converts in these lands.

The Christian and Jewish meaning of the number "9" entered into Christian thinking on the matter, as "9" was associated with suffering, grief, and imperfection, making it a fitting number for when "man's imperfection turned in prayer to God" (Catholic Encyclopedia).

The Rosary: Mary's Psalter

The 150 Davidic Psalms (the Psalter of David) have always been prayed by Old Testament Israel, post-Temple Jews, and by Christians for personal prayer, communal prayer, lamentations, praise, thanksgiving, and, in the case of Christians, to demonstrate the fulfilment of prophecy. Lay people who didn't have copies of Scripture or the Breviary and those who were illiterate would substitute 150 Pater Nosters (Our Fathers) or Aves (Hail Mary's) in place of the 150 Psalms they could not read.

The prayers were originally counted by transferring pebbles from one bag to another, but soon enough Christians began to tie a rope with knots on which to count. This evolved further into using beads or pieces of wood in place of the knots, and this soon came to be called the "Psalter of the Laity." Around the end of the first millennium, Rosaries contained the present five decades (sets of ten beads), with the Ave beads shaped like white lilies for the purity of the Virgin, and the Pater beads shaped like red roses for the wounds and Passion of Christ.

It is believed that the Virgin Mary also appeared to the children at Fatima and asked that the Rosary be prayed daily, including the "Fatima Prayer," as part of what must be done in order to prevent Russia from spreading its errors throughout the world. The Rosary, thus, has always been a weapon against heresy and trouble; in fact, the 7 October 1571 victory of Christendom over Islamic warriors at the Battle of Lepanto -- the first naval victory against the infidels -- was said to be attributed directly to the Rosaries prayed by the faithful.

The Rosary beads themselves can be made of stone, wood, crystal -- even bakelite or plastic, and they can be of any colour (sometimes the Ave beads will be of one colour and the Pater beads of another). They are often bought according to one's birthstone, but as a general rule, men prefer black or wood rosaries, and women prefer white or coloured ones. Where the two halves of the Rosary come together is a centrepiece, usually a medal with a depiction of the Sacred Heart, Virgin Mary, and/or a Saint. Most Rosaries are bought pre-made from Catholic gift shops, but there are also many Rosary makers who can put together a customized Rosary with a choice of beads and centrepiece. It takes around 20 minutes to recite the prayers using the rosary.

Stations of the Cross

As early as the 4th century, Christian pilgrims to the Holy Land would walk the route that the Lord Jesus Christ walked as He made His way to Golgotha for our salvation. When Muslims captured Jerusalem and it became too dangerous to make this pilgrimage, Christians replicated the sites back in Europe, and there developed the "Stations of the Cross" devotion (also known as "Way of the Cross," "Via Dolorosa," or "Via Crucis").

The devotion consists of meditating on 14 events -- that number being fixed in 1731 by Pope Clement XII -- which took place during Christ's Passion, from His being condemned to His burial. The Way of the Cross can still be made outside but is usually made inside nowadays, especially during the Season of Lent and most especially on Good Friday.

If you enter a Catholic Church and look along the walls of the nave (where the parishioners sit), you should see 14 representations on the walls which depict 14 events of Christ's Passion that have been singled out for contemplation. It is at these blessed artistic representations, these "stations" -- which can be painted, carved, engraved, of wood, metal, paint on canvas, etc., topped with a wooden Cross -- that the Way of the Cross is made during public liturgy. The Way of the Cross can also be made privately, even at home, with or without "visual aids." When the Way of the Cross is made in groups, each person first makes the Sign of the Cross, makes an Act of Contrition (i.e., expresses penitence through prayer) and mentally intends to gain indulgences, for themself or another.

The 14 stations are:
- Jesus is Condemned to Die
- Jesus is Made to Bear His Cross
- Jesus Falls the First Time
- Jesus Meets His Mother
- Simon Helps Jesus Carry His Cross
- Veronica Wipes Jesus' Face
- Jesus Falls the Second Time
- Jesus Meets the Women of Jerusalem
- Jesus Falls the Third Time

- Jesus is Stripped
- Jesus is Nailed to the Cross
- Jesus Dies on the Cross
- Jesus is Taken Down from the Cross
- Jesus is Laid in the Tomb

Fasting and Abstinence

Practitioners of the Old Testament religion fasted or abstained on Mondays and Thursdays, but Christians opted to take Wednesdays (the day the Lord was betrayed) and Fridays (the day the Lord was crucified) as their penitential days.

Wednesdays and Fridays are still days of penance in most Eastern Catholic Churches (and among the Orthodox), but in the Roman Church, only Fridays, as memorials to the day the Lord was crucified, remain as weekly penitential days on which abstinence from meat and other forms of penance are expected as the norm.

If any of the Fasting and/or Abstinence Days falls on a Sunday or a first class Feast outside of Lent, the requirements (except for the Eucharistic Fast) are totally nullified. Some are excused from the obligations of fasting and abstaining for medical reasons (pregnancy, the demands of extraordinarily hard labour, hypoglycemia, etc.) have to obtain dispensation from their priests.

Abstinence

In the Latin Church, abstinence means refraining from eating the meat from mammals or fowl, and soup or gravy made from them. Fish is allowed, hence Fridays are known as "Fish Fridays." Traditionally, the laws of abstinence apply to all aged 7 and over, but the new Code of Canon Law applies it to all who have completed their 14th year.

Partial Abstinence

Meat and soup or gravy made from meat may be eaten once a day at the principle meal.

Fasting

Fasting is the taking of only one full meal (which may include meat) and two smaller, meatless meals that don't equal the large one meal. No eating between meals is allowed, but water, milk tea, cofee, and juices are allowed. Meat is allowed at one meal (assuming abstience isn't also expected on a given day). Traditionally, everyone over 21 years of age and under 59 years of age is bound to observe the law of fast; but the present Code of Canon Law sets the ages of 18 and 59 as the limits.

Votive Offerings

Votive offerings (a.k.a. "votives" and "ex-votos") are actions or material things vowed to God (or promised to a Saint for their intercession with God) in return for a hoped-for miracle, offered in thanksgiving for already-answered prayer, or given in thanksgiving for blessings not asked for. Votives can range from the humble to the resplendent; great artists have made votives by their own volition or at the commission of wealthy patrons of statues, paintings, hymns, stained glass even entire churches or shrines have been given "ex voto."

Usually, paintings and other artworks offered depict the miracles for which the votive is being offered, and many bear the intials "VFGA" which stand for the Latin "Votum Fecit Gratiam Accepit" -- "Vow made, graces received," simply "E.V." for "Ex Voto" ("in fulfillment of a vow"), or a vernacular equivalent.

Present day ex voto offerings most often take the form of the lighting of candles, the placing of flowers or pictures before icons, and leaving thank-you notes, money, or little tokens on or near the altars or statues of Saints in churches, shrines, or family altars.

Mass

Catholics worship God in a variety of ways, but the chief act of corporate or communal worship is the Liturgy of the Eucharist. In the Eastern churches, Catholic and Orthodox, this is known as the Divine Liturgy; in the West, it is known as the Mass, an English word derived from the Latin text of the priest's dismissal of the congregation at the end of the liturgy ("Ite, missa est."). The Mass has always been the central form of Catholic worship.

As far back as the Acts of the Apostles and Saint Paul's epistles, we find descriptions of the Christian community gathering to celebrate the Lord's Supper, the Eucharist. In the catacombs in Rome, the tombs of martyrs were used as altars for the celebration of the earliest forms of the Mass, making the tie between the sacrifice of Christ on the Cross, its re-presentation in the Mass, and the strengthening of the faith of Christians explicit.

The Catholic Church says all believers have an obligation to go to Mass every Sunday and it must be an obligation is done willingly, but many people don't understand why the Church requires this of them. In the Third Commandment, God tells us to "Remember to keep holy the Sabbath day." For the Jews, the Sabbath was Saturday; Christians, however, transferred the Sabbath to Sunday, the day of Jesus Christ's resurrection from the dead. In order to fulfil the Third Commandment believers must refrain from unnecessary work on Sundays and participated in the Mass which is their chief form of worship as believers.

Rituals

Sacraments

According to the Council of Trent, Christ instituted seven sacraments and entrusted them to the Church hence Catholicism is a faith that revolves around the seven sacraments. Sacraments are visible rituals that Catholics see as signs of God's presence and effective channels of God's grace to all those who receive them with the proper disposition. Christians regard a sacrament as an outward sign of an inward grace or as an enacted truth. The Catechism of the Catholic Church categorises the sacraments into three groups, the "sacraments of Christian initiation", "sacraments of healing" and "sacraments at the service of communion and the mission of the faithful". These groups broadly reflect the stages of people's natural and spiritual lives which each sacrament is intended to serve. The seven sacraments are:
- Baptism
- Reconciliation (Penance)
- Eucharist
- Confirmation
- Holy Matrimony (Marriage)

- Holy orders (joining the priesthood)
- Anointing of the sick (once called extreme unction or the last rites).

The sacraments of initiation: Baptism, Confirmation, and Holy Communion are the three primary sacraments on which the rest of the life of Catholic believers depends. Originally tied very closely together, the three sacraments are now, in the Western Church, celebrated at different milestones in one's spiritual life. (In the Eastern Church, both Catholic and Orthodox, all three sacraments are administered to infants at the same time.)

Baptism

The Sacrament of Baptism, the first of the three sacraments of initiation, is also the first of the seven sacraments in the Catholic Church.
Baptism in Catholicism remits all sins (both original sin and personal sin) and their temporal punishments. If one were to die immediately after Baptism, he would go straight to Heaven (assuming one presents no obstacles). Being baptized imprints an permanent mark on the soul of the baptized which marks him as God's and initiates them into the life of the Church thus allows them to receive the other Sacraments. It is through Baptism that they are born again, regenerated of water and Spirit and receives new life.
Baptism infuses sanctifying grace, supernatural gifts, and virtues. There is only one Baptism, therefore the Sacrament may be received only once (if one is unsure whether he/she was validly baptized, he is baptized conditionally). For those who have reached the age of reason, the Sacrament must also be

received in faith. If one does not have faith in Baptism but receives it anyway, he is still validly baptized, but the fruits of his Baptism will be delayed until he does have faith. In the case of infants, it is the faith of the parents that operates until the child himself reaches the age of reason.

There are a two ways to enter the Church through Baptism:

Private Baptism:

An emergency, bare-essentials baptism which can be performed anywhere, by anyone - Catholic, pagan, Jew, Protestant, who uses the proper matter and form and intends to do what the Church does when performing the baptism. Because of that last condition, Baptism by heretics or apostates should always be followed by a conditional Baptism. Baptism must only be administered to those who request it; Baptism must never, ever be against the will of the person to be baptized, or his parents' will if he is a child. Also those who, with contrite hearts, have expressed a true desire for Baptism and have vowed to receive the Sacrament, but die before receiving it are baptized "by desire." In any case, a person baptized in a private Baptism should participate in the Solemn Rite of Baptism if and when he is able.

Solemn Baptism:

Baptism by a priest, who is the usual minister of Baptism which includes ceremonies such as a formal renunciation of Satan and all his works, exorcism, the use of water blessed at the Easter Vigil or Pentecost, the imposition of blessed salt, an anointing with

Chrism, etc. One may be solemnly baptized as an infant; or by preparing oneself through catechesis and being baptized by a priest outside the Easter Vigil; or, as is most common, by being baptized at the Easter Vigil by a priest and after a period of official catechesis.

Sacrament of Reconciliation (Penance aka Confession)

The Sacrament of Penance is seen as a gift. Catholics believe that Christ, in His most Holy Wisdom, gave them this precious Sacrament to literally and truly bestow His grace upon believers through His priests as a means of forgiving them and assuring them of His mercy and love for all Catholics. This psychological benefit of "feeling assured" and "clean again" stems not only from the supernatural fruits of the Sacrament, but from human nature and the need to purge ones self of those things that plague ones consciences. When a Catholic comes from confession, he does truly, by definition, step out into that dawn of his own new beginning. Catholics believe that in and through this brief ritual God has remade them in His own image. If one has just been validly baptized, they don't need confession, because Baptism wipes away all guilt of sin (and the temporal effects of sin, by the way). If, however, they were validly baptized years ago and are just now coming to the Sacrament for the first time, they might want to make what's known as a "General Confession," which includes sins of one's entire life, since it might take a bit longer than usual. "General Confessions" are also often made before marriage or ordination.

Three things are required of a penitent in order to receive the sacrament worthily:
- ➢ He must be contrite or, in other words, sorry for his sins.
- ➢ He must confess those sins fully, in kind and in number.
- ➢ He must be willing to do penance and make amends for his sins.

Sacrament of Eucharist/Holy Communion

For Catholics, the Eucharist is the sacrament which completes Christian initiation. The sacrament commemorates the Last Supper, in which bread and wine are consecrated and consumed. The Eucharistic celebration, also called the Mass or Divine Liturgy includes prayers and scriptural readings leading to the consecration of the bread and wine. The ceremony in which a Catholic first receives the Eucharist is known as First Communion. Celebration of the Eucharist re-presents (makes present) the sacrifice of Jesus on the cross, and perpetuates it, as well as being a banquet of communion with Christ's body and blood in the consecrated bread and wine, and is "wholly directed toward the intimate union of the faithful with Christ". The prayers and readings in a Eucharistic service remind those taking part of that final meal and of the solemn words and actions of someone standing at the edge of death. The people taking part drink a sip of wine (or grape juice) and eat a tiny piece of some form of bread, both of which have been consecrated. Because the Church teaches that Christ is present in the Eucharist, there are strict rules about who may celebrate and who may receive the Eucharist in the Catholic Church. Those who are conscious of being in a state of mortal sin are forbidden to receive the sacrament until they have received absolution through the sacrament of Reconciliation (Penance). Catholics are normally obliged to abstain from eating for at least an hour before receiving the sacrament. Non-Catholics are ordinarily prohibited from receiving the Eucharist as well.

Holy Communion symbolises the new covenant given by God to his followers. The old covenant was the one given by God to Israel when he freed his people from slavery in Egypt. The new sacrament symbolises freedom from the slavery of sin and the promise of eternal life.

Roman Catholics believe that the bread and wine that is offered is the actual body and blood of Christ and another form of sacrifice. They believe that although the bread and wine physically remain the same, it is transformed beyond human comprehension into the body, blood soul and divinity of Jesus. This is called Transubstantiation and is celebrated in the festival of Corpus Christi.

For Roman Catholics, the Eucharist is the most important act of worship. All Roman Catholics are encouraged to receive communion at least once a week during Mass. Some practising Catholics may receive the Eucharist every day. The Catholic Church practises closed communion and only baptised members of the Church in a state of grace are ordinarily permitted to receive the Eucharist.

Sacrament of Confirmation

The Sacrament of Confirmation may only be received by one who is baptized, preferably while he is in a state of grace (i.e. not in a state of mortal sin). It is the perfection of Baptism. If it is received when the recipient is not in a state of grace, it is illicitly but still validly received; the fruits of the Sacrament will be delayed until he receives Penance. In addition, if the person has reached the age of reason, he should be well-catechized and know the Pater (Our Father), the Ave (Hail Mary), the Apostles' Creed, and the 10 Commandments.

Confirmation indelibly seals the person to the Holy Ghost, hence its name, "Sacrament of the Seal." Because this seal is indelible and leaves a permanent mark on the recipient's soul, the Sacrament, like Baptism and Holy Orders, may be received only once. It is believed that Confirmation imparts the 7 Gifts of the Holy Ghost, as in a "personal Pentecost":

- Wisdom
- Understanding
- Counsel
- Fortitude
- Knowledge
- Piety
- Fear of the Lord

Many people think of the laying on of hands, which signifies the descent of the Holy Spirit, as the central act in the Sacrament of Confirmation. The essential element, however, is the anointing of the the person being confirmed with chrism (an aromatic oil that has been consecrated by a bishop), accompanied by the words "Be sealed with the Gift of the Holy Spirit" (or, in the Eastern Catholic Churches, "The seal of the gift of the Holy Spirit"). This seal is a consecration, representing the safeguarding by the Holy Spirit of the graces conferred on the believer at Baptism.

Sacrament of Holy Orders

The Sacrament of Holy Orders is the continuation of Christ's priesthood, which He bestowed upon His Apostles; thus, the Catechism of the Catholic Church refers to the Sacrament of Holy Orders as "the sacrament of apostolic ministry."
"Ordination" comes from the Latin word ordinatio, which means to incorporate someone into an order. In the Sacrament of Holy Orders, a man is incorporated into the priesthood of Christ, at one of three levels: the episcopate, the priesthood, or the diaconate.

Holy Orders is the Sacrament by which men become priests and are given a sacred power (sacra potestas) to act in total sacramental identification with Christ (i.e., to act in persona Christi) in order confect Christ's Body and offer it up to the Father at the Mass for the remission of sins; to forgive sins through the Sacrament of Penance; to solemnly baptize; to preside during the Sacrament of Holy Matrimony; to offer Unction to the dying; to preach; and to otherwise teach, guide, and sanctify their sheep. With and only with the permission of his Bishop, he may be delegated to offer the Sacrament of Confirmation, but to the Bishop alone is reserved the power to ordain other priests (though a priest may be delegated to ordain men to the sub-diaconate and the minor orders).

The recipient of the Sacrament must be a baptized, healthy male, at least 25 years of age, who has a vocation from God, a strong Catholic faith, intelligence, a good moral character, and a life marked by sanctity. He must be committed to living a celibate and chaste life, and to prayer (especially the Divine Office, which he is obligated to pray), and must have been properly established in seminary. While the episcopate is reserved to unmarried men, the discipline regarding the priesthood varies in East and West. The Eastern Churches allow married men to be ordained priests, while the Western Church insists on celibacy. Once a man has received the Sacrament of Holy Orders, however, he cannot marry.

Sacrament of Anointing the Sick

The Sacrament "Extreme Unction," also called "Last Rites" or "Anointing of the Sick," is the anointing given to those who are gravely ill in body, especially those in danger of death from bodily illness or from violence already done to the body (i.e. a soldier about to go into battle is not a candidate for the Sacrament; one who has been shot and lies gravely wounded or, especially, dying, is).
The conditions for receiving Unction are that one must:

- have reached the age of reason (usually considered to be around the age of 7)
- be in a state of grace (Penance is part of the Rite)
- be sorrowful for past sins, trust in God and resign himself to His will, whether His positive will is to heal the sick person or His passive will is the person's death
- the effects of the Sacrament are the strengthening and comfort of the soul of the anointed one, the remission of sins and some of their temporal

punishments, and the possible restoration of bodily health.

The Rite in which the Sacrament is offered includes the Sacraments of Penance and the Eucharist (in that order), followed by the Sacrament of Unction itself. It may be received conditionally up to three or four hours after apparent death (we can't presume to know the moment the soul leaves the body and can only know with moral certainty that death has occurred after corruption has begun). If the sick one is unconscious, conditional absolution and Unction are offered, without the Eucharist (known at this time as "Viaticum," meaning "Food for the Journey").
The matter of the Sacrament is the Oil of the Sick ("Oleum Infirmorum"), which is olive oil blessed by the Bishop on Maundy Thursday (the Thursday of Holy Week the week before Easter). When in doubt, priests should err on the side of caution and provide the sacrament to the faithful who request it.

Catholic Funerals

Now, a person confronting death should receive the Sacrament of Unction for the possible restoration of body and, most importantly, soul. This is of prime importance and is never be neglected. Other ways to help prepare the sick person for death are to pray the Holy Rosary (focusing on the Sorrowful Mysteries), the Divine Mercy Chaplet, to St. Joseph (the Patron of the dying) for a holy death, etc. with the sick person, if possible, or in such a manner that sick person can hear the prayer. This includes audible prayer for the unconscious.

The sick person should have a Crucifix (a St. Benedict Medal Crucifix, if possible) in view, perhaps to hold if they can, and should be encouraged to offer up his sufferings and to trust in the love and mercy of the Lord Jesus Christ. A lit blessed candle, as a symbol of the sick person's Baptism, a symbol of sanctifying grace and the promise of eternal life is also placed nearby so they can see the flame where permissible. Throughout the dying person's time in their sick bed, short acclamations that encourage the focus on Christ and the prayers of the Saints are encouraged. As death approaches more closely, the sick person's soul is commended to God. After the soul has left the body, special prayers are prayed.

Funeral Proceedings

In Catholic funerals it is believed that the body of the dead one will be resurrected and reunited with the soul when Jesus comes again at the Last Judgement. In addition, if the deceased is saved, his body will be glorified. For this reason, the bodies of loved ones are treated with the utmost respect and, so, it is against Catholic custom to cremate the body, having been allowable in the past only during times of pestilence, for ex., when cremation was done for the common good. Now, however, the 1983 Code of Canon Law reads "The Church earnestly recommends that the pious custom of burial be retained; but it does not forbid cremation, unless this is chosen for reasons which are contrary to Christian teaching."
A traditional Catholic funeral consists of three main parts: the Vigil (sometimes called the "Wake"), the Requiem Mass, and the Burial and informal after-burial gatherings. This pertains to funerals for adults;

funerals for baptized children who've not yet reached the age of reason are quite different and joyful because they, without a doubt, go straight to Heaven, not having had the opportunity to commit a mortal sin. In childrens' funerals, the priest wears white, the Gloria Patri is not replaced with the Requiem aeternam, the Gloria in excelsis is said, etc. Their Mass is not a Requiem Mass, but a "Votive Mass of the Angels.

Vigil

Most often takes place in a funeral home though it could take place in a home, parish church or chapel, or other place, depending on the laws of the state and the practices of the parish or chapel. The Vigil is the time when family gathers around the dead one, first of all to pray for him/her, and also to remember their life, and console one another. If the wake takes place in a funeral home, funeral cards, a type of holy card, are usually present (ordered through the funeral home's funeral director), with a Catholic image on one side and, on the other, a prayer, and the name, birthdate, and Heavenly birthdate, of the dead. If the wake is not held at a funeral home, one can still order custom-made funeral cards or make one's own.

The Vigil, which may last from a few hours to two days, has the very specific purpose of attending to the soul of the dead one. At the Vigil, therefore, prayer for the dead is central, and one asks the priest to lead the mourners in the Rosary (Glorious Mysteries) for the soul of the departed. The "Eternal Rest" prayer, is prayed for the dead after each decade of the Rosary (where the Fatima Prayer is usually prayed).

During the Vigil, the casket is usually open, flanked by candles at both ends (one's Baptismal Candle can be used, if possible). In some Catholic cultures, mirrors are covered or turned toward the wall during this time. It is typical for Catholics to kiss their loved one goodbye, and in most cases keep a lock of hair or some other memento which is later placed, along with funeral cards and the like, on the family altar. This will help remind them to pray for their loved one.

Flowers are always present, though some might request that, aside from a few representative flowers from closest family members, donations be made to selected charities instead of additional bouquets being bought. A Crucifix is, of course, always present, too, and often a Rosary will be placed in the dead person's hands.

Requiem Mass

On the day following the Wake is the Requiem Mass where the body is taken from the place of the Vigil to the church or chapel as the "tenor bell" tolls, if possible. The body is taken toward the Altar, to just outside the sanctuary. It is placed feet toward the Altar if the body is that of a layman, and head toward the Altar if the body is that of a priest.
The priest, dressed in a black cape, will greet the coffin at the door of the Church, sprinkling it with Holy Water, and intoning the De Profundis (Psalm 129) and the Miserere (Psalm 50). The Introit asks that eternal rest be given to the departed, and the Collect asks that God deliver his or her soul. The Epistle will be a reading of I Thessalonians 4:13-18, in which St. Paul speaks of death. After the Gradual, a Tract asking

absolution from every bond of sin on the part of the deceased is intoned, followed by the glorious Sequence, the Dies Irae. The Gospel will be a reading of John 11:21-27, the story of St. Martha's profession of faith that her brother, Lazarus, will rise again. The Offertory prayer asks Jesus Christ, King of Glory, to deliver the souls of the faithful departed from Hell, and for St. Michael to lead them into the holy Light. The Secret asks pity on the soul of the departed. The Communion asks that light eternal shine on the departed, and the Post-communion asks that the Sacrifice of the Mass purify the departed.

Burial

After the Requiem Mass, the coffin is taken to the cemetery. The ground or mausoleum in which the body will be disposed should be blessed by a priest if the cemetery is not a proper Catholic cemetery (which is the ideal) or already blessed. This is done with specific words by the priest as the grave and body are sprinkled with holy water and incensed. Traditionally, in Catholic cemeteries, the body of a layman is buried such that the head faces East, symbolizing their awaiting bodily resurrection by Christ, Who is called "Orient." Priests are buried in the opposite direction of the laity, symbolizing their having to confront the effects of their pastoring on the souls entrusted to them by God.
After the funeral, it is typical to gather at the house of the one closest to the departed, to eat, drink, remember, console one another, and pray (these informal post-burial gatherings are also sometimes referred to as "wakes." This isn't strictly accurate, but common usage). This is when bringing food and drink

is especially appreciated, as it is in the days to come when the crowds go home but the survivors, still grieving, are beginning to confront the sad reality of their temporal loss. In fact, it tends to be the days after the funeral, when all the distractions of funeral arrangements and greeting people have vanished, that are most painful.

Festivals and Holidays

Unlike pagan religions which see time as an endless cycle, Christians see time as being linear; it has a beginning and will have an end. Within Christianity's linear, "big picture" sense of time, though, the passing of hours is experienced as cycles of meditations on holy things. Think of a spiral of a circle of time moving ever forward toward His Coming -- and you will have a sense of "Catholic time."

The Catholic year (the "liturgical year") is made special by cycles of celebrations commemorating the lives of Jesus and His mother, the angels, and the legion of Saints who modelled lives of sanctity. Below are 25 Feasts and times, in chronological order, that demonstrate how the liturgical year is a reliving of the life of Christ.

Advent	He is coming
Nativity	He comes
Circumcision	He follows Old Testament Law
Epiphany	He reveals Himself as God
Holy Family	He grows up in a human family

Candlemas	Simeon's prophecy
Septuagesima	We are in exile without Christ
Ash Wednesday	Without Christ, we are dust
Lent	Christ is in the Desert
Passion Sunday	Jews make plans to kill Jesus
7 Sorrows	Mary's suffers at what is to come
Palm Sunday	He triumphantly enters Jerusalem
Spy Wednesday	Jesus is betrayed by Judas
Maundy Thursday	He offers the first Holy Mass
Good Friday	He is put to death and fulfils Old Testament Law
Holy Saturday	He is in the tomb
Easter	He is risen
Ascension	He ascends into Heaven
Pentecost	He sends the Holy Ghost
Trinity Sunday	The Most Holy Trinity has been fully revealed
Assumption	Mary is assumed into Heaven & crowned Queen
Christ the King	We recognize Christ's Kingship now and forever
All Saints	We will triumph as have our heroic Saints
All Souls	We pray for those who are awaiting their triumph
Last Sunday in Time after Pentecost	Apocalypse. He will come to judge the world.

Every single year, Catholics "re-live" the Gospel, from Christ's Incarnation and Birth to His Ascension and Heavenly reign. In Spring He enters the world by coming to rest in Mary's immaculate womb; nine months later, He is born, circumcised, and given a Name. He is raised in the Holy Family, and meets His cousin, John. He goes into the Desert and the church go with Him during the Lenten Season. Then follow His Passion and Agony, which are soon vanquished by His Resurrection, His Ascension, and the Pentecost. Now He reigns forever and they await His Second Coming as they prepare to celebrate again His First Coming. Then the cycle begins again. The Catholic who celebrates the Feasts well and practices the traditions of the Church is believed to live intimately with Him.

All of the Church's Feasts fall into one of the 2 main "liturgical cycles" made of 7 "liturgical seasons." Each of the Seasons has an associated mood, its own "feeling in the air," its own scents and ornaments. There is even for each Season an associated colour which is reflected in the priests' vestments and liturgical art, church decoration, and so on (though on certain Holy Days within a particular season, that Day's colour will take precedence over the season's colour).

Here's an overview of the two liturgical cycles and their seven seasons, days that change from time to time.

Cycle 1: The Christmas Cycle

Season 1: Advent

The word "Advent" comes from the Latin "advenire" which means "arrival" and refers to our awaiting the arrival of the commemoration of Christ's birth, and His Second Coming. This penitential season of expectation lasts from the first Sunday of Advent ("Advent Sunday") to 24 December (22 - 28 calendar days). Its colour is violet.

Season 2: Christmastide

As it's the celebration of Christ's Incarnation, the mood of Christmastide is of humble, grateful, joyous celebration. This season lasts from Vespers of 24 December to 13 January (the Octave of the Epiphany) inclusive (19 calendar days in terms of liturgical calculations). The Feast of Christmas *itself* lasts 12 days ("The Twelve Days of Christmas"), but the spiritual focus of Christmas doesn't end truly until Candlemas on 2 February. Its colour is white or gold.

Season 3: Time After Epiphany

This season, which continues the Christmas focus on and the Divine Childhood and moves into focusing on Jesus' public ministry, lasts from 14 January to the vigil of Septuagesima Sunday (the ninth Sunday before Easter, which is the same as 3 Sundays before Ash Wednesday) inclusive (4 - 38 calendar days). Its colour is green.

Cycle 2: The Easter Cycle

Season 4: Septuagesima

This Season, whose name means "Seventy" and which recalls the Babylonian Exile, lasts from Septuagesima Sunday to Shrove Tuesday (the day before Ash Wednesday) inclusive (16 calendar days). Its color is violet.

Season 5: Lent (Quadragesima)

This season, also called "Quadraegesima," meaning "Forty," is a somber, penitential Season that recalls Christ's 40 days in the desert, prefigured by the Israelites' wandering in the desert for 40 years. "Passiontide" is the last two weeks of Lent, from Passion Sunday (the 5th Sunday of Lent) to the day before Palm Sunday. The second week of Passiontide is called "Holy Week." The last three days of Holy Week i.e., Maundy Thursday, Good Friday, and Holy Saturday are called the Sacred Triduum.

Lent lasts 40 days (but temporally includes six Sundays which aren't counted as "Lent" because Sundays are always about the Resurrection and are joyous), from Ash Wednesday to the Saturday before Easter, with the last three days -- the Sacred Triduum -- being treated separately liturgically speaking (46 calendar days). Its colour is violet.

Season 6: Paschaltide (Eastertide)

The joyous, victorious Easter season lasts from the Easter Vigil to the day before Trinity Sunday (56 calendar days, not counting Easter Vigil). Its color is white or gold.

Season 7: Time After Pentecost

This Season's focus is the Holy Spirit in the Millennium, the Church Age that we now live in, and Christ's Reign as King of Kings -- the time between the Age of the Apostles and the Age to Come. This season lasts from Trinity Sunday to the day before Advent Sunday (per the calendar, its length varies). Its colour is green.

Advent

The focus of Advent is preparation for the coming of the Lord, both in commemoration of His Nativity and His coming again at the end of time. Though far too many Catholics see this time of year as a part of the "Christmas Season," it isn't; the Christmas season does not begin until the first Mass at Christmas Eve, and doesn't end liturgically until the Octave of the Epiphany on January 14. It goes on in the spiritual sense until Candlemas on February 2, when all celebrations of Christ's Childhood give way to Septuagesima and Lent.

Advent is the time to make ready for Christ to live with the people. Lent is the time to make people ready to die with Christ. Advent makes Lent possible. Lent makes salvation possible. Advent is the time when eternity approaches earth. Lent is the time when time reaches consummation in Christ's eternal Sacrifice to the Father. Advent leads to Christ's life in time on earth. Lent leads to Christ's eternal Life in Heaven. The Cross through the Mass, penance, and mortification; is the bridge connecting Advent and Lent, Christ and His Church, man and God. Each of the Church's penitential seasons is a dying to the world with the goal of attaining new life in Christ.
On the first day of Advent, Catholic families will set up Advent wreath which is a wreath of greenery adorned by a set of four candles that is typically, three violet-coloured, and one rose-coloured to match the priest's vestments on each of the days the candles are lit. The wreath is either set upon a table (especially the dining room table), on the family altar, on pedestals, an end table, etc., or it can by suspended by ribbons from the ceiling, such as from a light fixture. The candles can be long, slim tapers, small votives, or fat pillars. There

can be pinecones and such adorning the greenery, but because Advent is a penitential season, it shouldn't be highly decorated with colourful ornaments.

The circular shape of the wreath is a symbol of eternity, and the greenery symbolizes hope and renewal. The colours of the typically-used violet and rose candles symbolize penance and joy, respectively. Each candle also represents one of the four weeks of Advent, and one thousand years of the four thousand years that (at least metaphorically) passed between Adam and Eve to Christ's coming. The first candle also recalls the Patriarchs; the second candle recalls the Prophets; the third candle recalls St. John the Baptist; and the final candle recalls the Virgin Mary. At midnight on Christmas Eve, the Advent wreath is replaced by a white "Christ candle" that is suitably adorned with holly, or by being carved with symbols of Christ, etc. This Christ Candle is used until the Ephiphany or Candlemas, depending on the family's particular Christmas customs. The greenery of the Advent wreath can now be decorated and turned into a Christmas wreath for use throughout the Christmas season.

Christmastide

This, not Advent, is the true Christmas Season. As most people in secular or countries are putting away "Christmas-y" things Catholics are just getting started. The cleaning and baking during penitential Advent pays off now, and the feasting and carolling begin. The entire Christmas Cycle is a crescendo of Christ manifesting Himself as God and King to the shepherds, to the Magi, at His Baptism, to Simeon and the prophetess, Anna. The days from the Feast of the

Nativity to the Epiphany are known as "The Twelve Days of Christmas," with Christmas itself being the first day, and Twelfth night i.e. 5 January, being the last of the twelve days. Christmastide liturgically ends on 13 January, the Octave of the Epiphany and the Baptism of Christ (at which time the season of Time After Epiphany begins). But Christmas doesn't end spiritually i.e. the celebration of the events of Christ's life as a child don't end, and the great Christmas Cycle doesn't end until Candlemas on 2 February and the beginning of the Season of Septuagesima.

If Advent preparations have been handled well, the house should be clean, work should be done, and things should be fresh and ready for 12 days of rejoicing! Once the sun goes down on Christmas Eve, the Yule log is lit in the fireplace. Back when homes had great fireplaces, fires were lit on Christmas Eve using logs that were so huge as to be able to burn for all the days of Christmas. 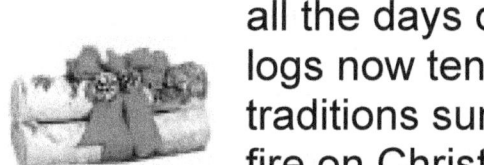 These Yule logs now tend to be much smaller, but the traditions surrounding them remain: the fire on Christmas Eve should be lit using a piece of last year's Yule Log which has been stored under the bed of the mistress of the house, which some say brings good fortune and prevents lightning strikes to the home.

The Christ candle which is a large white candle decorated with holly etc. is lit for Christmas Eve Supper, replacing the Advent wreath. It is re-lit each night until the Epiphany, to represent Christ's Light and in order to help guide the Magi to the manger. The greenery of the Advent wreath itself is now decorated and hung on the front door, remaining there throughout the Christmas season.

Christmas Eve (before the Vigil Mass) is a day of fasting and abstinence. The 1983 Code of Canon Law eliminated this fast altogether, but traditional Catholics still keep the fast, eating seafood (the Italians eat fish), noodles, other forms of pasta, etc. for the Christmas Eve Supper. Christmas Eve and Christmas Day foods vary from country to country, but Christmas Eve dinners are meatless, while Christmas Day is the day of unrestricted feasting, when Christmas candies, marzipan, oranges, apples, tangerines, nuts, and the cookies baked during Advent are all laid out.

Mass is obligatory on Christmas, and this can be fulfilled by going to any one of three Masses:

- Mass at Midnight, called the "Angels' Mass"
- the Mass on Christmas morning, called the "Shepherds' Mass"
- the Mass on Christmas day, called the "Mass of the Divine Word" or "Kings' Mass"

The Midnight Mass, though, is the one most Catholics do their best to attend. Gift giving is done differently by different Catholic households. Some families present gifts on December 6, the Feast of St. Nicholas, Bishop of Myra after whom "Santa Claus" was partly modelled. Many Catholics (such as Italian Catholics) present gifts on January 6, the Feast of the Epiphany, in imitation of the Magi. And some exchange them on Christmas Eve or on Christmas Day.

Traditionally, Catholics did not put up their Christmas trees until after noon on Christmas Eve. The same was true of all Christmas decorations. The purpose of the tree and the decorations is to celebrate the feast of Christmas.

Feast of Circumcision

The 1st day of January is the Octave Day of Christmas (i.e. from December 25 to January 1, inclusive, are 8 days). This is the Feast of the Circumcision, a day known in the Novus Ordo as "Mary, Mother of God"; either way, January 1 is a Holy Day of Obligation on which all Catholics must attend Mass. On this day, they recall the Lord's submitting to the Mosaic Law by getting circumcised on the 8th day of His human life in obedience to the Law. The Lord later fulfilled this part of Torah through the Sacrament of Baptism, an event which is focused on, on the Feast of the Epiphany in 5 days and again on the 13th of January at the Commemoration of the Baptism of the Lord. His Circumcision, though, has a deeper meaning in that it symbolizes and foreshadows the Blood He will shed for believers on Calvary.

Feast of the Holy Name of Jesus

This Feast is associated with the Feast of the Circumcision, for it is when a child was circumcised that he received a name and was accepted as a son of Abraham and a full member of his family. So honoured is His Holy Name that devout Catholics bow their heads (men removing their hats) at the sound of "Jesus", both inside and outside of the liturgy. To protect the sacredness and honour due to the Holy Name, that when hearing the Name of the Lord taken in vain, it is right to pray "Sit nomen Dómini benedíctum!" ("Blessed be the Name of the Lord"), to which the reply, if overheard, is "Ex hoc nunc, et usque in sæculum!" ("From this time forth for evermore!"). A full indulgence, under the usual conditions, may be received if one were to visit a church or chapel on this day.

Twelfth Night

The Eve of the Feast of the Epiphany is the twelfth day of Christmas and is known as "Twelfth Night". It begins the celebration of Christ revealing His Divinity in three ways:

- to the Magi who, guided by the great and mysterious Star of Bethlehem, came to visit Him when He was a Baby (Matthew 2:1-19)
- through His Baptism by St. John, when "the Spirit of God descending as a dove" came upon Him and there was heard a voice from Heaven saying, "This is my beloved Son, in whom I am well pleased" (Matthew 3, Mark 1, Luke 3, John 1)
- through His first public miracle -- that of the wedding at Cana when Jesus turned water into wine at the request of His Mother (John 2).

In many Catholic homes (especially Italian ones), it's not Christmas Day that is for giving presents to children, but the Feast of Epiphany, when the gifts are given in a way related to the Magi. After a candlelight feast the "Three Kings Cake" is eaten in honour of the three kings, one slice being set aside "for God."

Feast of Epiphany

Epiphany, the 12th day after Christmas, celebrates the visit of the three kings or wise men to the Christ Child, signifying the extension of salvation to the Gentiles. This feast is also known as the "Theophany" or "Three Kings Day". For families who practice traditions involving "the Magi" or "La Befana" leaving gifts for children, the day begins with the children discovering what was left for them while they slept on Twelfth Night.

At mass there is a blessing of gold, frankincense, myrrh, Epiphany Water, and after Communion, a blessing of chalk. Catholics take small special items of gold to have with them during the Mass, and they are blessed if they are exposed as they sit in their pew with them (e.g. wedding rings, rosaries, piece of gold jewellery etc.)

When Mass is over, they will take some of the blessed chalk, frankincense, myrrh, and Epiphany Water home. Upon arriving at home, they sprinkle some Epiphany water in the rooms of their homes to protect it and bring blessings. This Holy Water recalls the waters of the Jordan, and is a visible reminder of Christ's Divinity, of Jesus revealing Himself as God at His Baptism.

Time after Epiphany

The season of Time after Epiphany is more a season set up for liturgical reasons than spiritual ones, as it is spiritually a continuation of Christmas's devotion to the Divine Childhood. Because the date of Easter changes each year, two seasons have variable lengths in order to balance the calendar. The Season

of Time After Pentecost can have as few as 23 Sundays or as many as 28 Sundays depending on the date of Easter. This season can have anywhere from 4 to 38 days, depending on the date of Easter. If this season is short, then Time after Pentecost will be longer; and if this Season is long, Time after Pentecost will be shorter.
But the spiritual focus of the Season up until Candlemas is the continuation of Christmas and contemplation of the Divine Childhood. After Candlemas, the celebration of events of His young life gives way to a focus on His adult life.

Septuagesima

Septuagesima and Lent are both times of penance, Septuagesima being a time of voluntary fasting in preparation for the obligatory Great Fast of Lent. The theme is the Babylonian exile, the "mortal coil" that one must endure as they await the Heavenly Jerusalem. Sobriety and sombreness reign liturgically. The Sundays of Septugesima are named for their distance away from Easter.

➢ The first Sunday of Septuagesima gives its name to the entire season as it is known as "Septuagesima" which means "seventy," and Septuagesima Sunday occurs roughly seventy days before Easter. This seventy represents the seventy years of the Babylonian Captivity. It is on this Sunday that the alleluia is "put away," not to be said again until the Vigil of Easter.
➢ The second Sunday of Septuagesima is known as "Sexagesima, which means "sixty". Sexagesima Sunday comes roughly sixty days before Easter.

- The third Sunday of Septuagesima is known as "Quinquagesima," which means "fifty" and which comes roughly fifty days before Easter.
- Quadragesima means "forty," and this is the name of the first Sunday of Lent and the Latin name for the entire season of Lent.

Feast of St. Valentine

St. Valentine (Valentino) was a Roman priest who performed marriages in spite of Claudius II's law (Claudius believed that marriage was distracting to his soldiers, so outlawed it to them for a time). Valentine was martyred in A.D. 270 on the Flammian way, and at the site of his martyrdom, Julius I built a popular basilica. Other than this, little is known.

Because of his Nuptial Masses, he became the patron of lovers, the affianced, and married couples, and fortuitous to the priest's association with romance is the belief that halfway through the month of February, birds choose their mates, hence St. Valentine's association with birds, especially lovebirds and doves. Also fortuitous is the fact that red is both the colour of Martyrs and the colour associated with love. Red roses are also a symbol of both martyrdom and love, and had also always been associated with the Roman goddess of love, Venus.

Shrovetide

The Monday and Tuesday before Ash Wednesday are known as "Shrovetide," from an old English word "shrive," meaning "to confess," a name acquired from the tradition of going to Confession in the days before Lent started. Shrovetide is traditionally the time for "spring cleaning," and houses are cleaned in these days in preparation for Lent and through confession Catholics "clean their souls" so they can enter the penitential season afresh.

Shrovetide is the last two days of "Carnival," an unofficial period that began after the Epiphany and which takes its name from the Latin carnelevare, referring to the "taking away of flesh" (meat) during Lent which begins on Ash Wednesday, the day following Shrove Tuesday.

The Tuesday of Shrovetide is a particularly big party day known as "Mardi Gras" (French for "Fat Tuesday") or "Pancake Tuesday" because fats, eggs, and butter in the house had to be used up before Lent began, and making pancakes or waffles was a good way to do it.

Lent

Lent is a 40-day period of preparation for Easter Sunday and one of the major liturgical seasons of the Catholic Church. A penitential season marked by prayer, fasting and abstinence, and almsgiving. Lent begins on either Ash Wednesday (for Latin Rite Catholics and those Protestants who observe Lent) or Clean Monday (for Eastern Rite Catholics and Eastern Orthodox) and ends on either Holy Thursday or Holy Saturday. The last two weeks of Lent are known as "Passiontide," made up of Passion Week and Holy Week. The last three days of Holy Week -- Maundy Thursday, Good Friday, and Holy Saturday -- are known as the "Sacred Triduum."

The focus of this Season is the Cross and penance as Catholics imitate Christ's forty days of fasting and await the triumph of Easter. Catholics fast, abstain, mortify the flesh, give alms and think more of charitable works. Because of the focus on penance and reparation, it is traditional for Catholics to go to confession at least once during this Season to fulfil the precept of the Church that they go to Confession at least once a year, and receive the Eucharist at least once a year during Eastertide.

On those days of fasting and abstinence, meatless soup is traditional. Sundays are always free of fasting and abstinence; even in the heart of Lent, Sundays are about the glorious Resurrection. This pattern of fasting and abstinence ends after the Vigil Mass of Holy Saturday. Special Lenten foods include vegetables, sea foods, salads, pastas, and beans mark the Season, in addition to the meatless soups. The fasting of this time once even precluded the eating of eggs and fats, so the pretzel became the bread and symbol of the times. They had always been a Christian food, ever since Roman times, their very shape being the creation of monks. The three holes represent the Holy Trinity, and the twists of the dough represent the arms of someone praying.

Ash Wednesday

In the Roman Catholic Church, Ash Wednesday is the first day of Lent, the season of preparation for the resurrection of Jesus Christ on Easter Sunday. (In Eastern Rite Catholic churches, Lent begins two days earlier, on Clean Monday.) Ash Wednesday always falls 46 days before Easter. While Ash Wednesday is not a Holy Day of Obligation, all Roman Catholics are encouraged to attend Mass on this day in order to mark the beginning of the Lenten season.

During Mass, the ashes which give Ash Wednesday its name are distributed. The ashes are made by burning the blessed palms that were distributed the previous year on Palm Sunday; many churches ask their parishioners to return any palms that they took home so that they can be burned. After the priest blesses the ashes and sprinkles them with holy water, the faithful come forward to receive them. The priest dips his right thumb in the ashes and, making the Sign of the Cross on each person's forehead, says, "Remember, man, that thou art dust, and to dust thou shalt return" (or a variation on those words).

The distribution of ashes reminds them of their own mortality and calls them to repentance. In the early Church, Ash Wednesday was the day on which those who had sinned, and who wished to be readmitted to the Church, would begin their public penance. The ashes that are received are a reminder of ones own sinfulness, and many Catholics leave them on their foreheads all day as a sign of humility.

The Church emphasizes the penitential nature of Ash Wednesday by calling them to fast and abstain from meat. Catholics who are over the age of 18 and under the age of 60 are required to fast, which means that they can eat only one complete meal and two smaller ones during the day, with no food in between. Catholics who are over the age of 14 are required to refrain from eating any meat, or any food made with meat, on Ash Wednesday.

Palm Sunday

Palm Sunday commemorates the triumphal entrance of Christ into Jerusalem (Matthew 21:1-9), when palm branches were placed in His path, before His arrest on

Holy Thursday and His Crucifixion on Good Friday. It thus marks the beginning of Holy Week, the final week of Lent, and the week in which Christians celebrate the mystery of their salvation through Christ's Death and His Resurrection on Easter Sunday.

Before the Mass is the Blessing of the Palms, which includes an Antiphon, Psalms, and Gospel reading. Then comes the Procession with hymns, where the palms are carried either around the church or outside, weather permitting, and then the Mass, during which there is a very long reading sung in 3 parts by 3 deacons, a long recitation of the Passion.

The palms are blessed before the High Mass. Standing at the Epistle side of the Altar, the priest recites a short prayer, and then reads a lesson from the book of Exodus which tells of the children of Israel coming to Elim on their way to the Promised Land, where they found a fountain and seventy palm trees. It was at Elim that God sent manna. The palms are distributed to the people at the Communion rail. The priest will press the palm against follower's lips so they can kiss it, and then kiss the priests hand. Alternatively, the palms may be handed out by the altar boys. In any case, Scripture and prayers follow, and then a procession of clergy, servers, and people through the church or outside around the church.

Now, this day has in the past sometimes been called "Fig Sunday" because just after Christ's entry into Jerusalem, He cursed the fig tree. Because of the cursing of the fig tree, the eating of figs is customary.

Good Friday

Good Friday, the Friday before Easter Sunday, commemorates the Passion and Death of the Lord Jesus Christ on the Cross. Good Friday is the second of the three days of the Easter Triduum. Good Friday is also called "Great Friday" or "Holy Friday" and is the most sombre day of the entire year. A silence pervades, socializing is kept to a minimum, things are done quietly; it is a day of mourning; it is a funeral. The Temple of the Body of Christ is destroyed, capping the penitential seasons begun on Septuagesima

Sunday and becoming more intense throughout Lent. Traditional Catholics wear black, cover their mirrors, extinguish candles and any lamps burning before icons, keep amusements and distractions down, and go about the day in great solemnity. Though a sombre atmosphere will last until the Easter Vigil, after "The Hour" (3:00 PM) passes, it eases a bit, and life can go back to a "sombre normal." The phone can put back on the hook, etc., but candles and other symbols of Christ shouldn't be used, music shouldn't be played, raucous games should be eliminated, etc., while Christ is "in His Tomb" i.e., until after Vigil of Holy Saturday when Eastertide officially begins.

No true Mass is offered instead a liturgy called the "Mass of the Presanctified" is offered, which is not a true Mass because no consecration takes place. Vestment colours will be black, and the liturgy consists of lessons, prayer, St. John's version of the Passion, and ends with a long series of prayers for various intentions.

Then the Cross will be unveiled and elevated to be adored by kneeling three times before it at the words "Venite, adorémus" (come, let us adore). Kneeling is done thrice because He was mocked thrice: in the high priest's courtyard, in Pilate's house, and on Mt. Calvary. Then the priest lays the Cross on a cushion and covers it with a white veil to symbolize the Entombment. He takes off his shoes, like Moses before God, and kneels three times as the choir chants. He and his acolytes kneel and kiss the Cross. The Cross is held up for congregators who file past, men first, then women to kneel and kiss the Cross while the choir sings the Improperia (the Reproaches) of Christ. Because Christ spent 40 hours in His tomb (from 3 PM Good Friday until 7 AM Pascha morning, a span covering 3 separate Jewish days as even a part of one day is counted as "a day"), from the very earliest Christian times, it's been customary for some to fast and keep vigil during this entire period, which is known as "40 Hours' Devotion" (Quarant'ore).

As to foods, Hot Cross Buns are traditionally eaten for breakfast on this day, and are about the only luxury afforded in this time of mourning. Legend says that a priest at St. Alban's Abbey in Hertfordshire gave these to the poor on Good Friday beginning in A.D. 1361, and the tradition was born. Hot Cross buns are said to never corrupt and Catholics used to keep a few all year to grate some of it into water for the sick to consume.

Easter Sunday

Easter is the greatest feast in the Christian calendar. On this Sunday, Christians celebrate the resurrection of Jesus Christ from the dead. For Catholics, Easter Sunday comes at the end of 40 days of prayer, fasting, and almsgiving known as Lent. Through spiritual struggle and self-denial, Catholics have prepared themselves to die spiritually with Christ on Good Friday, the day of His Crucifixion, so that they can rise again with Him in new life on Easter. On this most beautiful of Feasts, the Easter table is adorned with the best of everything, the

most beautiful china, a pure, white tablecloth, the best possible wine, flowers (especially pussy willow, lilies, and spring bulb flowers), all with the colours white and gold symbolizing purity and glory and the traditional symbols of Easter predominating. The Paschal Candle representing the Light of Christ (Lumen Christi) is the centrepiece of the table and like the Paschal Candle at church is relit each day until the Feast of the Ascension in 40 days when the Light of the World leaves to ascend to His Father. The candle is usually large and white, and surrounded with flowers and the symbols of Easter. It was once believed that the flesh of the peacock never corrupts, so peacocks became the classic symbol of immortality. They are an ancient Christian symbol of the Resurrection, and representations of them are found on the tombs of ancient Christians as an expression of their hope to follow Christ in His defeat of death.

Another level of symbolism is that the egg represents birth, the Creation, the elements, and the world itself, with the shell representing the firmament, the vault of the sky where the fiery stars lie; the thin membrane symbolizing air; the white symbolizing the waters; and the yolk representing earth. Painted red, eggs are a demonstration that the salvation and re-birth of the world comes through Christ's Blood and Resurrection. Old legend has it that St. Mary Magdalene went to Rome and met with the Emperor Tiberius to tell him about the Resurrection of Jesus. She held out an egg to him as a symbol of this, and he scoffed, saying that a man could no more rise from the dead than that egg that she held could turn scarlet. The egg turned deep red in her hands, and this is the origin of Easter eggs, and the reason why Mary Magdalene is often portrayed holding a scarlet egg. Because of this legend and all of the egg's symbolism, and because eggs are special because they were once forbidden during Lent, Catholics make great use of them on this day, eating them, decorating them, and decorating with them. Red is the classic colour to use when dying eggs to be eaten, but other colours are more often used these days.

Because of the central importance of Easter to the Christian faith, the Catholic Church requires that all Catholics who have made their First Communion receive the Holy Eucharist sometime during the Easter season, which lasts through Pentecost, 50 days after Easter. This reception of the Eucharist is a visible sign of faith and participation in the Kingdom of God. Pentecost Sunday, which marks the end of the Easter season in the Christian calendar, celebrates the descent of the Holy Spirit on the Apostles.

Trinity Sunday

God's Triune Nature has been fully revealed, and now Catholics celebrate the Most Holy Trinity on this day. The Time After Pentecost, the season that represents the Church Age, begins.
Symbols for the day are the natural symbols of the Trinity, the shamrock used by St. Patrick to explain the Trinity to the ancient Irish, the pansy viola tricolour also called the "Trinity Flower," a candle with 3 flames, the triangle, the trefoil, 3 interlocking circles, etc.
There are no particular customs for the day. Whoever wishes to be saved must, above all, keep the Catholic faith. For unless a person keeps this faith whole and entire, he will undoubtedly be lost forever. This is what the catholic faith teaches: "we worship one God in the Trinity and the Trinity in unity. Neither confounding the Persons, nor dividing the substance. For there is one Person of the Father, another of the Son, another of the Holy Spirit."

Wedding Ceremonies

Marriage is a practice common to all cultures in all ages. It is, therefore, a natural institution, something common to all mankind. At its most basic level, marriage is a union between a man and a woman for the purpose of procreation and mutual support, or love. In the Catholic Church, marriage is more than a natural institution; it was elevated by Christ Himself, in

His participation in the wedding at Cana (John 2:1-11), to be one of the seven sacraments. A marriage between two Christians, therefore, has a supernatural element as well as a natural one. While few Christians outside of the Catholic and Orthodox Churches regard marriage as a sacrament, the Catholic Church insists that marriage between any two baptized Christians, as long as it is entered into with the intention to contract a true marriage, is a sacrament.

Marriages that take place between two unbaptized people or between a baptized and an unbaptized person are said to be non-sacramental "natural marriages" which do not bring forth sanctifying grace. Once one is sacramentally married, it is for life, but merely natural marriages, which are in and of themselves good, can sometimes be dissolved with what is known as the "Pauline Privilege" or the "Petrine Privilege."

The Pauline Privelege

The Pauline Privilege is exercised when: parties are unbaptized at the time of marriage, one of the parties becomes baptized, and the unbaptized party leaves. This is performed by the local Bishop.

The Petrine Privelege

The Petrine Privilege is exercised when: one of the parties was unbaptized at the time of the marriage, they separate without the baptized party being at fault (or plan to separate and the unbaptized party refuses Baptism and will not live peaceably with the baptized party), and the baptized party now wants to marry a Catholic. Unlike the Pauline Privilege which is handled by the local Bishop, this sort of case is sent to Rome to be adjudicated by the Pope himself.

Note that the exercise of the Petrine or Pauline Privileges is not a declaration of nullity (an "annulment"). A declaration of nullity is the finding that a marriage was merely putative and never existed at all; the Petrine and Pauline Privileges dissolve non-sacramental natural marriages. Truly sacramental marriages marriages joined together by God Himself that are ratified and consummated can be dissolved by no one. If both the parties are baptized and have never been married before, there should be no problem in having their marriage blessed. It is advised that one refrain from the Sacraments until they are sure about the status of their marriage.

Conditions for a valid Sacramental Marriage

The Catholic Church has requirements before Catholics can be considered validly married in the eyes of the Church. A valid Catholic marriage results from four elements:

- the spouses are free to marry;
- they freely exchange their consent;
- in consenting to marry, they have the intention to marry for life, to be faithful to one another and be open to children; and
- their consent is given in the canonical form, i.e., in the presence of two witnesses and before a properly authorized church minister.

Exceptions to the last requirement must be approved by church authority. The Church provides classes several months before marriage to help the participants inform their consent. During or before this time, the would-be spouses are confirmed if they have not previously received confirmation and it can be done without grave inconvenience (Canon 1065).

In addition to meeting these criteria, a Catholic must seek permission from the local bishop to marry a non-Catholic. If the person is a non-Catholic Christian, this permission is called a "permission to enter into a mixed marriage", and lack of it does not make a marriage invalid if the normal conditions are met. If the person is a non-Christian, the permission is called a "dispensation from disparity of cult" and is a condition for the validity of the marriage. Those helping to prepare the couple for marriage can assist with the permission process. In present-day circumstances, with communities no longer so homogenous religiously, authorization is more easily granted than in earlier centuries.

The Church prefers that marriages between Catholics, or between Catholics and other Christians, be celebrated in the parish church of one of the spouses.

Getting married in Church

If the couple are both baptized and in a state of grace (couples should make a general confession and receive Communion as soon before marriage as possible), the first thing they do is announce the betrothal to their priest, who will then publish the "banns of marriage." The banns are a public announcement of the upcoming marriage so that any impediments can be discovered. This "publication" is usually made on three consecutive Holy Days (including Sundays), during the Mass itself (before or after the sermon) and/or in the parish bulletin (for good reason, sometimes the banns may be dispensed with).

As far as wedding plans go, the bride's dress (and bridesmaids' dresses) must conform to the same rules of modesty and decorum that apply any time a woman enters a church, i.e. her head must be covered, the dress must cover the knees when standing or sitting, the neckline should be modest, etc. The Rite of Marriage itself can be offered with or without a Mass and Nuptial Blessing (traditionally, the Nuptial Mass and Blessing are only offered when the bride and groom are both Catholic, not in the case of mixed marriages).

If the couple wants a Mass and Nuptial Blessing, the form of the Mass will depend on the day of the wedding. The default Mass offered is the Nuptial Mass (colour white) but this Mass may not be said on certain days.

The Rite of Marriage

The bride and groom stand before the priest, just outside the sanctuary. The groom stands on the Joseph/Epistle side of the church (the right from the point of view of the congregation), and the bride stands on the Mary/Gospel side. Necessary marriage vows are committed where after the priest sprinkles the couple with Holy Water. Then he blesses the bride's ring. Then the priest sprinkles the ring (which is considered a sacramental) with holy water in the form of a cross; and the bridegroom, having received the ring from the hand of the priest, places it on the finger of the left hand of the bride. The priest performs a prayer and thus ends the Rite of Marriage. There is usually no applause for the couple afterwards in the church; save that for outside when they leave the church (i.e., at the typical "rice-throwing time" outdoors) and at the couple's entrance at their reception.

The Nuptial Mass and Nuptial Blessing are optional for the couple. If they are desired, they will follow the Marriage Rite above. The Nuptial Mass is like any other Mass except that the Gloria and Creed are omitted. The Nuptial Mass can't be offered on any of the following days: Feasts of the first or second class; on Sundays or holydays of obligation; within the octaves of the Epiphany, Easter, Pentecost, Corpus Christi; on Ash Wednesday; during Holy Week; on the vigils of Christmas, Epiphany or Pentecost; All Soul's Day.

After the Pater Noster, the priest goes to the Epistle side of the Altar. The Bride and Groom kneel before him. The priest folds his hands and, turning towards the bridegroom and bride, says over them two prayers. After the prayers, he continues the Mass, and the Bride and Groom resume their places. The couple receive Communion as usual, at the proper time. The priest continues the Mass as usual with the prayer Deliver us, we beseech Thee, O Lord.

It is a traditionally a custom for the bride to leave her bouquet (or another bundle of flowers) in front of the statue of Mary in the church, praying to Mary to help her in her duties as a wife and intercede in blessing her with children. This custom symbolizes the bride offering her virginity, as indicated by the flowers in return for her prayers to make her marriage fruitful. The groom might light a candle in front of the statue of St. Joseph and ask him to intercede for him as a husband.

After the wedding, a reception follows. Customs at these receptions vary from ethnic group to ethnic group. At some point during the reception, the groom will stomp on a glass that has been wrapped up in a white linen towel, the broken glass symbolizing the irrevocability of marriage, and the number of shards left behind representing the number of happy years they will have together. On the wedding night, it is an old custom for some couples to abstain from the marital act, dedicating the first night of marriage to St. Joseph (making the night "St. Joseph's Night"), and performing some devotion to the Saint.

Other

Purgatory

Purgatory, according to Catholic Church doctrine, is an intermediary state after physical death in which those destined for heaven "undergo purification, so as to achieve the holiness necessary to enter the joy of heaven". Only those who die in the state of grace but have not in life reached a sufficient level of holiness can be in Purgatory, and therefore no one in Purgatory will remain forever in that state or go to hell. This theological notion has ancient roots and is well-attested in early Christian literature, but the poetic conception of Purgatory as a geographically existing place is largely the creation of medieval Christian piety and imagination.

According to Catholic belief, immediately after death, a person undergoes judgment in which the soul's eternal destiny is specified. Some are eternally united with God in Heaven, envisioned as a paradise of eternal joy, where Theosis is completed and one experiences the beatific vision of God. Conversely, others (those who die in the state of mortal sin) reach a state called Hell, that is eternal separation from God often envisioned as an abode of never ending, fiery torment, a fire sometimes considered to bemetaphorical. Purgatory is commonly regarded as a cleansing by way of painful temporal punishment, which, like the eternal punishment of hell, is associated with the idea of fire. While "pain of the senses" (as opposed to "pain of longing" for the Beatific Vision) is not doctrinally defined as being a part of Purgatory, the overwhelming consensus of theologians has been that it does involve pain of the senses.

The envisioning of Heaven, Hell, and Purgatory as places in the physical universe was never a Church doctrine. Nonetheless, in antiquity and medieval times, Heaven and Hell were widely regarded as places existing within the physical universe: Heaven "above", in the sky; Hell "below", in or beneath the earth. Similarly, Purgatory has at times been thought of as a physical location.

Crucifixes and Crosses

Every Catholic home usually has a Crucifix hanging over the bed in each bedroom, and, most importantly, at least one in a common area, such as the Dining Room, Living Room, or Family Room. In addition, generally speaking, Catholics should wear Crucifixes not empty Crosses (aside from stylized ones of significance)

around their necks. Why Crucifixes instead of empty Crosses? Because Catholics preach Christ crucified and believe that they get to the Resurrection through the Cross, that they are called to pick up their own crosses and carry them, offering up their sufferings in imitation of Him.

You will see on some Crucifixes, a skull and crossbones at the foot of the Cross. Aside from symbolizing victory over death, this skull more specifically represents the skull of Adam, said in Jewish and Christian tradition to have been buried at Golgotha, where Jesus was crucified. The Blood of Christ, the New Adam, redeems man, as symbolized by the skull of the First Adam. Crucifixes should be blessed by a priest and treated with great veneration. Kissing a Crucifix is an indulgenced act.
There are a few Crucifixes and Crosses that stand out and should be mentioned individually.

Crucifixes and Crosses

The San Damiano Crucifix was written by an 11th or 12th century Umbrian artist, and it came to adorn the chapel of San Damiano in Assisi, Italy. It was before this Crucifix that Saint Francis of Assisi was converted and received word from the Lord to repair His Church. The Poor Clares, an Order of nuns founded by Clare of Assisi, a good friend of St. Francis, took the Crucifix with them to San Giorgio in 1257, and it now resides at San Giorgio's Chapel in the Basilica of St Clare of Assisi.

This Crucifix is full of the Gospel events of His Passion. At the top, we see the Lord ascending into Heaven, toward the hand of His Father.

The Blessed Virgin and John, who was appointed to be her caretaker, stand to Christ's right. To Christ's left are the Magdalen, Mary Cleophas (mother of James), and the Centurion. The little boy behind the Centurion is the Centurion's son whom Jesus healed. Also present are two other Roman soldiers, Longinus, who pierced Jesus' side with a lance, and Stephen, who gave Him vinegar to drink (some say this second figure is that of Pilate). The transverse arm of the Cross is actually a tomb, the empty tomb and at either end are Peter and John running toward it, being met by the two groups of two angels who let them know "He is not here." Beside His right leg is Adam, biting into the apple, and above Adam is the rooster as a symbol of Peter's denial. At the very bottom, under His feet, are 6 unknown Saints.

The Pardon Crucifix

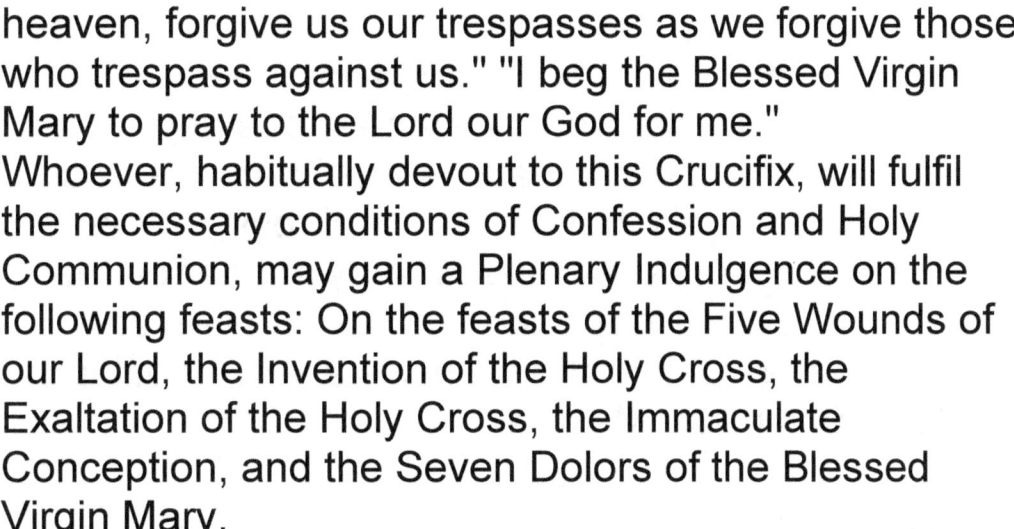

This Crucifix is ornate and is relevant to Pope St. Pius X. Whoever carries on his person the Pardon Crucifix, may thereby gain an indulgence. For devoutly kissing the Crucifix, an indulgence is gained.
Whoever says one of the following invocations before this crucifix may gain each time an indulgence: "Our Father who art in heaven, forgive us our trespasses as we forgive those who trespass against us." "I beg the Blessed Virgin Mary to pray to the Lord our God for me."
Whoever, habitually devout to this Crucifix, will fulfil the necessary conditions of Confession and Holy Communion, may gain a Plenary Indulgence on the following feasts: On the feasts of the Five Wounds of our Lord, the Invention of the Holy Cross, the Exaltation of the Holy Cross, the Immaculate Conception, and the Seven Dolors of the Blessed Virgin Mary.
Whoever at the moment of death, fortified with the Sacraments of the Church, or contrite of heart, in the supposition of being unable to receive them, will kiss this Crucifix and ask pardon of God for his sins, and pardon his neighbour, will gain a Plenary Indulgence. On the back of the Crucifix, on the transverse arms, are the words, "Father, forgive them." On the long part

of the Cross are the words, "Behold this heart which has so loved men." The Sacred Heart is shown where the two arms of the Cross meet.

Caravaca Cross or Crucifix

This Cross takes its name from Caravaca (now known as Caravaca de la Cruz), Spain, a town in the province of Murcia where, in A.D. 1231, a priest was imprisoned by the Moors. Out of curiosity, his captors' King, Abu Zeid, asked him to say Mass, but as the priest began, he realized he didn't have the necessary Crucifix. As his captors grew angry, the Patriarch of Jerusalem's pectoral cross was transported to the priest through an open window, borne by two angels. Seeing this, King Abu Zeid converted to the true religion.

The "Caravaca Cross," then, is the two-armed Lorraine Cross that is used by Archbishops and Patriarchs. Some representations are Crucifixes and may show the angels that carried the Cross, one on each side. The words "Caravaca" may appear on the second arm of the Cross such that "Cara" is on one side, and "vaca" on the other. This is a very popular Crucifix in Spain and Mexico.

Dagma Cross

The name of this Cross, which is pronounced "dowmer," is derived from the name of the Queen who wore it, Queen Dagmar of Denmark. She was born around A.D. 1189 in Bohemia, and

became the wife of the Danish king, Valdemar II ("Valdemar the Victorious"), who reigned from A.D. 1202-1241. When her grave was opened in 1690, this Cross was found around her neck. Though Dagmar was a 13th century personality, the Cross is believed to date to around A.D. 1000. At the centre of the Cross is the figure of Christ, and the four arms depict, starting at the top and moving clockwise, St. John Chrysostom, St. John the Evangelist, St. Basil, and Our Lady. The backside of the Cross is a Crucifix. It is especially prized by the Danish people (because of Dagmar's birthplace, the Cross was adopted by Lutherans as a symbol, too, sadly. It is, though, in fact, a Catholic Cross originally and now).

Symbols of Christmas

	Light is the pre-eminent symbol of Christmas. The Light Who is Christ was foreshadowed by the Advent candles, and is now symbolized by the Christ Candle that burns throughout the Twelve Days of Christmas. The Feasts of the Epiphany and Candlemas celebrate Christ as Light of the World in even more explicit ways.
	In the Middle Ages, mystery plays were held on Christmas Eve which featured a Paradise Tree, a tree representing both the Tree of the Knowledge of Good and Evil and the Tree of Life from the Garden of Eden. The tree was decorated with colourful apples representing the forbidden fruit, and with candies representing the Tree of Life. These Mystery plays

	were suppressed during the fifteenth century, but the faithful kept the "Paradise Tree" tradition.
	Laurel, often used in wreaths as in ancient Roman times, is a symbol of victory and accomplishment, and came to be seen as a symbol of Christ's victory. Laurel is often see, on tombstones and is the root of the word "laureate," meaning crowned with laurel, or accomplished.
	In Roman times wreaths (made of laurel) were used as symbols of victory. Christians adopted the practice, using wreaths (usually of pine nowadays) to represent the victory of the new born King. Some families turn their Advent wreaths into Christmas wreaths to be used starting on Christmas morning.
	Rosemary is a very old Christmas symbol. Legend has it that on the Flight to Egypt after the Magis' visit and St. Joseph's dream, the Virgin Mary washed Baby Jesus' clothes out and laid them across some rosemary bushes to dry. Since then, God blessed them with their lovely fragrance.
	Ivy was originally banned for Christian use because of its pagan associations, but after they were forgotten in the Middle Ages, ivy became seen as a symbol for human reliance on divine strength because of the way it clings to what it grows on.

	The prickly leaves and red berries of holly (*Ilex opaca*) represent the Crown of Thorns with Christ's Blood, a reminder that the Holy Infant was born on this night only to redeem with His Blood. Earlier symbolism associates holly with the burning thorn bush that Moses saw.
	Mistletoe is a poisonous parasite that grows on hardwood trees and was considered "sacred" by the Druids and Vikings. French tradition holds that the reason mistletoe is poisonous is because it was growing on a tree that was used to make the Cross that Jesus was crucified on.
	Poinsettia plants called "Nativity Flower," or "Flowers of Holy Night" in Mexico, is a New World Christmas tradition. The shape of the leaves symbolize the Star of Bethlehem, their red color represents the Blood of Christ and the burning love of God.
	The Christmas Rose is a Christmas tradition that springs from Germany. A legend surrounds it that is similar to that of the poinsettia: a humble shepherdess felt that anything she gave to Baby Jesus couldn't compare with what the Magi gave. As she sat weeping, an angel came and swept the snow away from around her feet, and lovely cup-shaped white blooms sprang up. This lovely flower can bloom all Winter long.

	In A.D. 63, St. Joseph of Arimathea (John 19) and 11 companions were sent to England by St. Philip the Apostle. Legend says that when he arrived at Somersetshire, he thrust into the ground his staff which was made of hawthorn a plant from the Mediterranean area. The Glastonbury Thorn sprouted from it a plant which has the odd ability, in Somerset, to bloom around Eastertime and at Christmas. The original plant was destroyed by Cromwell's Puritans (the soldier who cut it down is said to have been blinded by a large splinter from the tree), but many shoots had been taken from it and its progeny live in Glastonbury to this day, heralding Christmas with its blossoms. Since 1929, blossoms have been sent to grace the Queen's (or King's) table on Christmas Day.
	Rose of Jericho survives in a curled up, dormant, brown, desiccated state for years, and then opens up and turns green with a bit of water. After returning to a lovely green, it goes dormant again when its water source is removed. Because of this fascinating property, it is often kept dormant in the home and brought out at Christmas time to blossom and then close in order to symbolize the opening and closing of Mary's womb.

	The legend is that in the late 1800's a candy maker in Indiana wanted to express the holy meaning of Christmas through a symbol made of candy. He took white peppermint sticks and bent them to suggest both the shepherd's staff carried by the adoring shepherds, and the letter "J" for Jesus. He let the color white symbolize the purity and sinless nature of Jesus, but added the color red to represent His Blood. The three small stripes symbolize the stripes of His scourging, and that there are three of them represents the Holy Trinity; the bold stripe represents the Blood Jesus shed for mankind.
	The red-breasted robin is another symbol of Christmas. The story is told is that Joseph built a fire in the manger to keep Mary and Jesus warm, but the flames kept dying. A robin fanned them with its wings so that the fire wouldn't die, and his proximity to the fire turned his breast red. It's also said that a robin landed on the shoulder of Jesus as He carried the Cross on Good Friday. When the bird plucked thorns from His brow, the bird's breast was stained forever with His Blood.

The Papacy

History of the Papacy

The pre-eminence of the bishop of Rome over the entire Catholic church, an institution known as "the papacy," took centuries to develop. In the first few hundred years of the church, the term "pope," which means "father," was used for any important and respected bishop, and the bishop of Rome was one of several important bishops in Christendom.

Jesus is believed to have appointed Peter as the rock on which the church will be built; and Peter is believed to have been martyred in Rome. As the capital of the empire, Rome is also a natural centre for the growing church. Rome had always been honoured for her association with Peter and Paul and her position as the church in the Empire's capital but especially after Christianity was legalized under Emperor Constantine, the special status of that office grew even more with each passing Roman bishop. The doctrine of the supremacy of the pope finally reached its height in the late 13th century, when Pope Boniface VIII claimed full religious and secular authority over every human being.

Bishops in the Early Church

In the early history of Christianity, five cities emerged as important centres of Christianity: Rome, Jerusalem, Antioch, Alexandria, and Constantinople. Although the Roman church was always highly respected, the churches in the East generally had more numbers and more authority than those of the West. After the Edict of Milan granted Christianity legal status, the church adopted the same governmental structure as the Empire: geographical provinces ruled by bishops. These bishops of important cities therefore rose in power.

Rome was not the only city that could claim a special role in Christ's Church. Jerusalem had the prestige of being the city of Christ's death and resurrection, and an important church council was held there in the first century. Antioch was the place where Jesus' followers were first called "Christians" and, with Alexandria, was an important early centre of Christian thought. Constantinople became highly important after Constantine moved his capital there in 330 AD. By the fifth century, however, the bishop of Rome began to claim his supremacy over all other bishops, and some church fathers also made this claim for him.

Saint Malachy, was born in Northern Ireland and was appointed Archbishop of Armagh in 1132. Many of those who knew him best said he received the gift of prophecy and witnessed many miracles throughout his lifetime. He was even known to have predicted the day and hour of his death.

In 1139 he received a vision from the Lord which revealed a long list of popes who would rule the church until the end of time (112 Popes total). This vision eventually became known as the "prophecy of the succession of the Popes," which has resurfaced with the election of the new pope.

Malachy's predictions are contained in a list of 112 symbolic phrases supposedly representing a list of 112 popes in succession. Most likely, though, the prophecy was created as an attempt to influence the papal election of 1590 in favor of Cardinal Girolamo Simoncelli by having Malachy's prophecy identify him as the next pope. But Simoncelli was not elected, and

Niccolò Sfondrati, who took the name Gregory XIV, was.

Since the resignation of Pope Benedict there has been an upsurge of interest in the new pope, Jorge Mario Bergoglio (also known as Pope Francis) and his link to the Saint Malachy's prophecy.

Malachy's last ten Popes according to the *"Prophecies of the Succession of the Popes"*

Pope Pius X (1903-1914) received the title, *"The Burning Fire,"* from Malachy's prophecies. This Pope showed a burning passion for spiritual renewal in the Church.

Pope Benedict XV (1914-1922) received the title, *"Religion Laid Waste,"* from Malachy's prophecies. This pope made an attempt to bring peace during World War 1 but failed, which lead to the deaths of millions of Christians. He witnessed the rise of communism which brought an end to the Christian influence in Russia.

Pope Pius XI (1922-1939) received the title, *"Unshaken Faith,"* from Malachy's prophecies. This pope witnessed the rise of Nazi Germany, during which time; he was an outspoken critic of communism and fascism. He ruled when Christians were under persecution from the Europeans and stood faithful until his death.

Pope Pius XII (1939-1958) received the title, *"Angelic Shepherd."* This Pope had an affinity for the spiritual world and was known as an Angelic pastor to his flock.

Pope John XXIII (1958-1963) received the title, *"Pastor and Marine."* Prior to his election, he was the patriarch of Venice, which is a marine city.

Pope Paul VI (1963-1978), received the title, *"Flower of Flowers."* His personal arms displayed three lilies.

Pope John Paul I (1978-1978), received the title, *"Of the Half-Moon."* This pope was elected during a half-moon and ruled for only one month because he died unexpectedly during the next half-moon.

Pope John Paul II (1978-2005), received the title, *"Eclipse of the Sun, or Labour of the Sun."* This pope was born during a solar eclipse and was buried in Rome during another solar eclipse. He was from Poland and used the Solidarity Labour Union.

Joseph Ratzinger (2005-2013) received the title, *"The Glory of the Olive."* Joseph chose the name Pope Benedict XVI. Interestingly, the Order of the Benedictines refer to themselves as, *"The Olivetans."* Not only that, but the name Benedict means "blessing." If we were to put his name together it can literally mean, *"The Blessing of the Olive."* This pope resigned Feb. 2013, which now leads us to the current pope, and his prediction from Saint Malachy. The Vatican stressed that no specific medical condition prompted Benedict's decision to quit - the first pontiff to do so in 600 years. The move surprised even his closest aides, even though Benedict, 85, had made clear in the past he would step down if he became too old or infirm. In recent years, the Pope had slowed down significantly, cutting back his foreign travel and limiting his audiences.

This was the moment lightning struck the Vatican today - hours after Pope Benedict XVI's resignation. The lightning touched the dome of St. Peter's Basilica, one of the holiest

Catholic churches. Benedict said he would serve the church for the remainder of his days "through a life dedicated to prayer."

According to Malachy's prophecy, the 112th pope will be known as *"Peter the Roman,"* the last and final pope. Here is the prophecy...
"In the extreme persecution of the Holy Roman Church, there will sit... Peter the Roman, who will pasture his sheep in many tribulations: and when these things are finished, the city of seven hills will be destroyed, and the terrible judge will judge his people. The End."

The current pope is Jorge Mario Bergoglio, who chose for himself the name of, Pope Francis. No Pope has ever taken on the name of "Peter," so it is no surprise that Jorge did not either. The shock lies in the fact that Jorge picked the name, Pope Francis, whose real name is, Giovanni di Pietro [or Peter]. The word *"Roman"* implies that the pope must be of Italian decent. Jorge is a native of Buenos Aires, Argentina, and one of five children of Italian immigrants, thus making him of Italian decent and fulfilling the prophecy of *"Peter the Roman."* Pope Francis is the first Jesuit pope, the first pope from America, and the first pope from outside Europe since Pope Gregory III in the 8th century. Could this pope be the fulfilment of Malachy's final prophecy or is there a twist?

Election of Popes

A papal conclave is a meeting of the College of Cardinals convened to elect a new Bishop of Rome, also known as the Pope. The pope is considered by

Roman Catholics to be the apostolic successor of Saint Peter and earthly head of the Roman Catholic Church. The conclave has been the procedure for choosing the pope for more than half of the time the church has been in existence, and is the oldest on-going method for choosing the leader of an institution.

A history of political interference in papal selection and consequently long vacancies between popes, culminating in the interregnum of 1268–1271, prompted Pope Gregory X to decree during the Second Council of Lyons in 1274 that the cardinal electors should be locked in seclusion *cum clave* (Latin for "with a key") and not permitted to leave until a new Bishop of Rome had been elected. Conclaves are now held in the Sistine Chapel of the Apostolic Palace.

Since the Apostolic Age, the Bishop of Rome, like other bishops, was chosen by the consensus of the clergy and laity of the diocese. The body of electors was more precisely defined when, in 1059, the College of Cardinals was designated the sole body of electors. Since then, other details of the process have developed. In 1970, Pope Paul VI limited the electors to cardinals less than 80 years of age. The current procedures were established by Pope John Paul II in his apostolic constitution *Universi Dominici Gregis* as amended by Pope Benedict XVI dated 11 June 2007 and 25 February 2013. A two-thirds supermajority vote is required to elect the new pope, which also requires acceptance from the person elected.

Conclave

Voting for a new pope occurs in what is known as a "conclave," which literally means "with a key." The term stems from the fact that the voting cardinals have been traditionally locked up somewhere "with a key" for the entire period of their voting.

And they have been locked up pretty tight. For more modern elections, telephone wires were removed. Televisions were removed. As they entered, cardinals were searched for telephones, pagers, microphones, and communications devices of all kinds. Outside windows were sealed and shuttered. Traditionally, the facilities were to be improvised, which is to say that they weren't to be designed for housing so many people like that. This, in turn, meant that they were not to be very comfortable and that was the point. They are under pressure to elect the next pope and they have a tremendous responsibility to the Roman Catholic Church as a whole.

When the cardinals first enter the conclave they are required to take an oath that they will follow the rules set down by the previous popes for electing a new pope and that they will uphold absolute secrecy about everything that occurs during the voting and deliberations. No one is to know the details about the discussions, the deliberations, or the compromises being made. Should anyone violate this oath and reveal anything that happens during the voting and deliberation process, they suffer the penalty of automatic excommunication.

Voting itself takes place in the Sistine Chapel, so the cardinals will be bussed back and forth between there and the *Domus Sanctae Marthae*.

It should not be assumed that discussions in the conclaves are always congenial; on the contrary, there can be rancorous debates and even slanderous accusations levelled against this or that candidate. Electing a pope is as much a political task as it is religious. Nationalist aspirations mix with the defense of orthodoxy and progressive sentiments to create a very volatile mixture; keeping the electors isolated together for long periods of time only ensures that this mixture remains problematic.

Naturally, there is a real desire not only to prevent cheating and tampering, but also to prevent people from knowing who has voted for whom. Election can occur via acclamation (where everyone spontaneously agrees to the same man), compromise (where the choice is entrusted to a small group) or scrutiny, where everyone votes via secret ballot. The most common form of election is via scrutiny and it is very rare that the other forms take place.

When the cardinals vote together on who will be the next pope, everyone has a paper ballot labelled "Eligo in Summum Pontificem," which means "I elect as

Supreme Pontiff." Here they write the name of their first choice, but preferably in disguised handwriting. Each cardinal then goes to an altar, kneels for a silent prayer, and then states the oath: "I call to witness Christ the Lord who will be my judge that my vote is given to the one whom before God I consider should be elected." The ballot is held up high so that everyone can visually confirm that the cardinal has voted and the ballot is placed in a paten and then is tipped into a chalice that stands on the altar.

If any of the cardinals are too sick to be present, their votes are collected by three other cardinals (chosen by lots) who return from the temporary residence with the votes and place them into the chalice as well. After all the votes are there, the chalice is shaken and one of three cardinals chosen as "scrutineers" removes the ballots one by one, in view of everyone present, and places them in another container. This process ensures that the same number of ballots is removed as were put in, if the number is wrong, the entire vote is deemed invalid.

After everyone has finished this process, the Cardinal Camerlengo counts them in full view of the cardinal electors with the help of the three scrutineers. The presence of these three assistants is to ensure that there is no cheating and no errors: each assistant reads the name on a ballot, then reads it aloud, writes the name on a tally sheet, and passes the ballot to the next assistant for the process to continue.

Once the third assistant has gone through this with a ballot, he runs a threaded needle through the centre, eventually joining all of the ballots together. This ensures that all ballots are verified three times, but only counted once. Later all ballots, tally sheets, and notes will be burned. When, after a series of votes, no new pope is elected, the papers are mixed with straw when burned in order to give off a black smoke that lets people know that an unsuccessful vote has occurred. However, if a pope is elected, then papers are added to the fire that give off white smoke, telling everyone outside that there is a new pontiff for the Roman Catholic Church.

The Vatican

Vatican City, officially Vatican City State, is one of the last six remaining absolute monarchies whose territory consists of a walled enclave within the city of Rome. It has an area of approximately 44 hectares, and a population of around 1000. Vatican city (Citta del Vaticano) is the papal residence and was built over the tomb of Saint Peter. The Vatican's position as a sovereign state within a state was quarantined by the Lateran Treaty of 1929, marked by the building of a new road, the Via della Conciliazione. This leads from huge St Peter's basilica to Castel Sant' Angelo, a monument to a far grimmer past.

Vatican is the smallest state in the world, based in Rome in Italy. Inside the Vatican city there are 11 Vatican Museums with the restored Michelangelo's Sistine Chapel, and Vatican Gardens (a system of large and small gardens, fountain, fish pool and enclousure for rabbits). They date back to medieval times when vineyards and orchards extended to the north of the Apostolic Palace.

Vatican radio station broadcasts all over the world in 29 languages, it has its television station, the daily newspaper, post office with Vatican stamps, shops, offices and publishing house. All sign posted, in highly-sophisticated system of organisation. More than a thousand residents are responsible for the smooth, day-to-day running of this nerve centre of official Christianity, with of course the Pope at its head, all guarded by the Swiss guard.

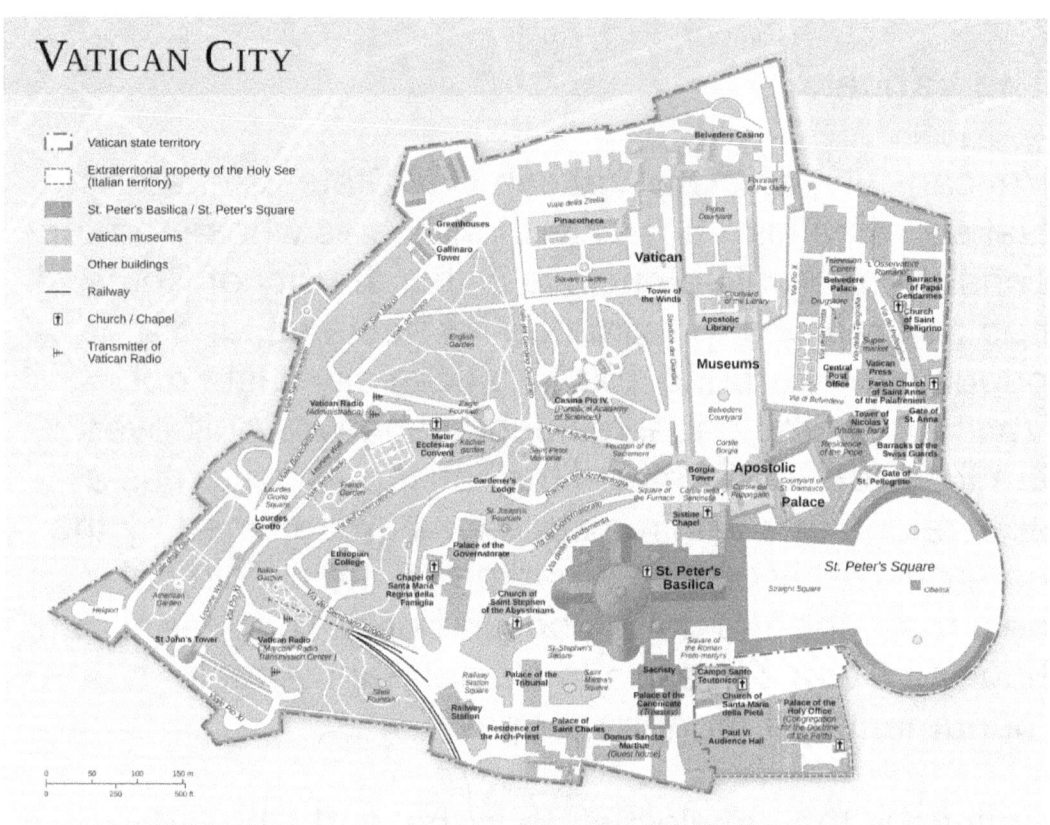

St Peter's Basilica (Basilica di San Pietro)

It's the world's largest Basilica of Christianity, nested into the heart of the Vatican city, with its 186 metres of length (218m if you consider the porch too), a height of 46 metres in the central aisle, a main dome 136 metre high and 42 metres large in diameter. The huge façade is 114 metres wide and 47 metres high. It has a surface of 22000 square metres and twenty thousand persons can pray in it.

The indigenous St Peter's Basilica, nowadays forgotten, was constructed by will of Emperor Constantine around 320AD in the area where Saint Peter had been martyrized (together with other Christians) close to the circus of Nero that, in fact, rose in the vicinity. For about thousand years the Basilica grew and got enriched. The first repair and enlargement intervention was ordered in the middle of the 15th century by pope Niccolo V, who entrusted Leon Battista Alberti and his helper Bernardo Rossellino. Later pope Giulio II charged Bramante who in 1506 demolished the old Saint Peter's Basilica planning a new one with a Greek cross plan. But at the time of the death of both pope and architect only the central pillars had been constructed.

Rafael (with the contribution of experts such as Fra Giocondo and Giuliano Da Sangallo) took over the guidance of the works, and proposed a Latin cross plan. Rafael was succeeded by Baldassarre Peruzzi first and Michelangelo later, who instead chose a return to the Greek cross. After the death of all contenders, pope Paolo V imposed the Latin cross structure, which was realized by Maderno who took care as well of the façade as we see it today.
The St Peter's Basilica was consecrated in 1626. The plan of the dome belongs to Michelangelo who managed to finish only the portion of the dome basement called Tamburo. It was Giacomo Dalla Porta who completed the dome according to Michelangelo's drawings in 1588-89. The positioning of most of the interior furnishing of the Basilica was

assigned to Bernini by his untiring pope Urbano VIII Barberini. Bernini worked in the St Peter's Basilica for twenty years and is responsible for the arrangement of the St Peter's square in front of the Basilica as well (1656-1667). Inside the Basilica is numerous and priceless art pieces kept in the forty five altars and eleven chapels. There are about ten thousand square metres of mosaics, Michelangelo's Pieta, the papal canopy and the monument to Urbano VIII both by Bernini, the monument to Cristina of Sweden by Carlo Fontana, the monument to the countess Matilda by Canossa (under drawing of Bernini), only to quote some of the most important pieces.

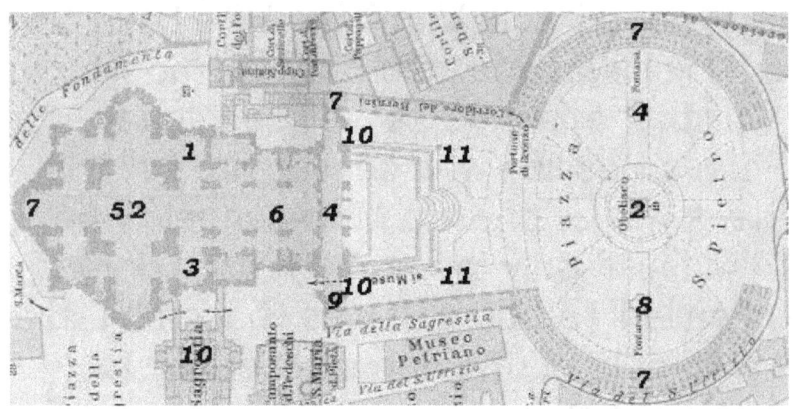

Castel Sant' Angelo (Castle of the Holy Angel)

The Mausoleum of Hadrian, usually known as Castel Sant'Angelo (*Castle of the Holy Angel*), is a towering cylindrical building in Parco Adriano, Rome, Italy. It was initially commissioned by the Roman Emperor Hadrian as a mausoleum for himself and his family. The building was later used by the popes as a fortress and castle, and is now a museum. The Castel was once the tallest building in Rome.
The tomb of the Roman emperor Hadrian, also called Hadrian's mole, was erected on the right bank of the Tiber, between 130 AD and 139 AD. Originally the mausoleum was a decorated cylinder, with a garden top and golden quadriga. Hadrian's ashes were placed here a year after his death in 138 AD, together with those of his wife Sabina, and his first adopted son, Lucius Aelius, who also died in 138 AD. Following this, the remains of succeeding emperors were also placed here, the last recorded deposition being Caracalla in 217 AD. The urns containing these ashes were probably placed in what is now known as

the Treasury room deep within the building. Hadrian also built the Pons Aelius facing straight onto the mausoleum – it still provides a scenic approach from the center of Rome and the right bank of the Tiber, and is renowned for the Baroque additions of statues of angels holding aloft elements of the Passion of Christ. The popes converted the structure into a castle, beginning in the 14th century; Pope Nicholas III connected the castle to St Peter's Basilica by a covered fortified corridor called the *Passetto di Borgo.* The fortress was the refuge of Pope Clement VII from the siege of Charles V's Landsknechte during the Sack of Rome (1527), in which Benvenuto Cellini describes strolling the ramparts and shooting enemy soldiers.

The Sistine Chapel

The Sistine Chapel (Latin: *Sacellum Sixtinum*; Italian: *Cappella Sistina*) is a large and renowned chapel of the Apostolic Palace, the official residence of the Pope in the Vatican City. Originally known as the *Cappella Magna*, the chapel takes its name from Pope Sixtus IV, who restored it between 1477 and 1480. Since that time, the chapel has served as a place of both religious and functionary papal activity. Today it is the site of the Papal conclave, the process by which a new Pope is selected. The fame of the Sistine Chapel lies mainly in the frescos that decorate the interior, and most particularly the Sistine Chapel ceiling and *The Last Judgment* by Michelangelo.

During the reign of Sixtus IV, a team of Renaissance painters that included Sandro Botticelli, Pietro Perugino, Pinturicchio, Domenico Ghirlandaio and Cosimo Roselli, created a series of frescos depicting the *Life of Moses* and the *Life of Christ*, offset by papal portraits above and trompe l'oeil drapery below. These paintings were completed in 1482, and on 15 August 1483. Sixtus IV celebrated the first mass in the Sistine Chapel for the Feast of the Assumption, at which ceremony the chapel was consecrated and dedicated to the Virgin Mary. Between 1508 and 1512, under the patronage of Pope Julius II, Michelangelo painted the *Sistine Chapel ceiling*, a masterpiece without precedent that was to change the course of Western art. In a different climate after the Sack of Rome, he returned and between 1535 and 1541, painted *The Last Judgement* for Popes Clement VII and Paul III. The fame of Michelangelo's paintings has drawn multitudes of visitors to the chapel, ever since they were revealed five hundred years ago.

The Catholic Church proclaims itself to be the church that Jesus Christ died for, the church that was established and built by the apostles. Is that the true origin of the Catholic Church? Even a cursory reading of the New Testament will reveal that the Catholic Church does not have its origin in the teachings of Jesus or His apostles. In the New Testament, there is no mention of the papacy, worship/adoration of Mary (or the immaculate conception of Mary, the perpetual virginity of Mary, the assumption of Mary, or Mary as co-redemptrix and mediatrix), petitioning saints in heaven for their prayers, apostolic succession, the ordinances of the church functioning as sacraments, infant baptism, confession of sin to a priest, purgatory, indulgences, or the equal authority of church tradition and Scripture. So, if the origin of the Catholic Church is not in the teachings of Jesus and His apostles, as recorded in the New Testament, one has to question what the true origin of the Catholic Church is.

Chapter 14: Father and Father's day

Call no man your father on earth, for you have one Father, who is in heaven

Matthew 23:9

I will be a Father to you, and you will be my sons and daughters, says the Lord Almighty.

2 Corinthians 6:18

Yes, these can easily be taken out of context, and like many other passages from the Holy Book can be deadly when spoken by the conniving tongue and heard (and yes spoken) by the none knowledgeable child of God.

In this world we live in we are surrounded with a lot of 'fathers', we have Father Christmas (a.k.a. Santa Clause), spiritual fathers, religious father figures and Father's Day.

Within this chapter, we will discuss the above ideas not with intentions to harm, but with hopes to invoke more thought and interest on the subject. And with hope to draw ourselves nearer to our Creator and seek even more wisdom and more revelation knowledge from Him. However superficial some topics may seem on face value, it is important that we engrave at the back of our minds warnings from the Bible:

My people perish from a lack of knowledge

Hosea 4: 6

So children of God lets soldier on and do as Paul suggests in Ephesians 6:13 and equip ourselves and put on the full armour of God.

Before we look at a lot of things, let's first place focus on this word "father". Let's study its meaning and full understanding of what this word actually means.

Especially since Jesus warns us about it and that we are not to use it carelessly.

Definition of Father:

- A male ancestor, whether immediate or distant.
- A man who creates, originates, or founds something.
- In Christianity:
    - God.
    - The first person of the Godhead.
- An elderly or vulnerable man. Used as a title of respect.
- A protector, provider.
- Authority, eminence, superiority, a right to command, and a claim to particular respect.
- Someone with the power to give and take life.

Figurative and derived uses of the word "father" in biblical and (still applicable in) today times:

- **A father is a spiritual ancestor who has infused his own spirit into others**, whether good, as Abraham, "the father of the faithful" (Romans 4:11); or bad "Ye are of your father the devil." (John 8:44).

- Indicating closest resemblance, kinship, affinity: "If I have said to corruption, Thou art my father." (Job 17:14).

From the Old Testament times, it is witnessed that the following powers are bestowed upon the person who is called 'father':

- The father in the Hebrew family, as in the Roman, had supreme rights over his children,
- He could dispose of his daughter in marriage (Genesis 29),
- He can arrange his son's marriage (Genesis 24),
- He can sell his children (Exodus 21:7), but not his daughter to a stranger (Nehemiah 5:5),
- He had power of life and death, as in the case of Isaac (Genesis 22), Jephthah's daughter (Judges 11:34), the sacrificing of his children to Molech (Leviticus 18:21; 20:3-5), etc.

The following are some of the duties and characteristics of a "father" from looking at the bible:

- He loves (Genesis 37:4);
- commands (Genesis 50:16; Proverbs 6:20);
- instructs (Proverbs 1:8, etc.);
- guides, encourages, warns (Jeremiah 3:4; 1 Thessalonians 2:11);
- trains (Hosea 11:3);
- rebukes (Genesis 34:30);
- restrains (Eli, by contrast, 1 Samuel 3:13);
- punishes (Deuteronomy 21:18);
- chastens (Proverbs 3:12; Deuteronomy 8:5);
- nourishes (Isaiah 1:2);

- ➤ delights in his son (Proverbs 3:12), and in his son's wisdom (Proverbs 10:1);
- ➤ is deeply pained by his folly (Proverbs 17:25);
- ➤ he is considerate of his children's needs and requests (Matthew 7:10);
- ➤ considerate of their burdens, or sins (Malachi 3:17);
- ➤ tenderly familiar (Luke 11:7);
- ➤ considerately self-restrained (Ephesians 6:4);
- ➤ having in view the highest ends;
- ➤ pitiful (Psalms 103:13);
- ➤ the last human friend to desert the child. "When my father and my mother forsake me, then Yahweh will take me up" (Psalms 27:10).

Father Christmas (a.k.a. Santa Clause)

Father Christmas is a figure that is celebrated worldwide by some Christians and non-Christians on the day that we ought to remember the birth of our Lord and Saviour, Jesus Christ. Now a lot of stories are associated with this character, and some of which link him to Christianity. Thus creating a perception and making him an acceptable analogy to the Christian domain.

Joshua 23:7 says:

"Do not associate with these nations that remain among you; do not invoke the names of their gods or swear by them. You must not serve them or bow down to them.".

Joshua 23:7

It is critical that as Christians we always keep at the front of our minds the living knowledge that yes we are in the world but we are not of the world as affirmed by Jesus in John 17.

It is for a number of reasons that we as Christians should shy away from figures such as these. The devil is not sleeping and he has the patience and the fore-vision to plan thousands of years ahead. Now if we do not guard ourselves and our souls, it won't be long before we forget the real significance of Christmas and start idolising this Santa Clause character who we so affectionately call him 'father'.

Based on the following we know for a fact that this character is not of God and is a spirit that we ought to be weary and steer clear of:

- Usage of the name 'father'
  With regards to this, the devil has gone head on with God and defies the very instruction given to us by Jesus that ***we must not call a man 'father' except for the Father who is our God and is in heaven***.
- Usage of the name Christmas
  Christmas is made up of two words. Christ and Mass. The name Christ means the anointed one. And Mass is a Catholic word which means "death sacrifice". Christ-Mass would therefore bear the meaning "death of Christ".
  With that highlighted, one can only imagine the dangers that we expose ourselves to. Dangers we expose our children to. Dangers we expose our children's children to. From earlier we now know that **a 'father' is a spiritual ancestor who has infused his own spirit into others, whether good or bad.**

Father Christmas is a jolly old satan whom we as Christians often speak of with so much affection and we allow our children to entertain the idea of Father Christmas or Santa Clause. Don't be deceived, the name switching from Father Christmas to Santa Clause is nothing but a ploy from the devil to shift the focus on one thing whilst still his plan to separate us from the Father is in motion.

Spiritual fathers

Looking at Matthew 23 1:12, God forbids us from calling ourselves teacher and or instructor. The bible further tells us not to call any man on the earth by the name of 'father'. By the blessing of Jesus, we are able to call ourselves the sons and daughters of God. And because of that we should therefore refer to each other as brother and sister.

Father's Day

It wasn't long ago when it felt as though the world was crying out for a special day to honour fathers, and that day we have come to know as Father's Day. What harm is done in this one may ask. But like with most things evil, they all started out innocent.
Who knows maybe there is no course for concern, as there is no section in the bible that says we may not honour our fathers. In fact the ten commandments specifically tells us to honour our fathers and mothers but from a bird's eye point of view, ALL the warning signs of looming danger ahead are there. And it is only fair that we take heed and prepare ourselves should we find ourselves giving honour to anyone other than God more especially on the Lord's day.

A quick history lesson on Father's day:

Sonora Smart Dodd (February 18, 1882 – March 22, 1978) can be said to be the founder of Father's Day. She was a Christian woman, a daughter to American Civil War veteran William Jackson Smart (1842-1919). At the age of 16 years Sonora's mother, Ellen Victoria Cheek Smart (1851-1898), died in childbirth with her sixth child. Sonora was the only girl child and she helped her father in raising her younger brothers including her new infant brother.

Due to the high esteem with which Sonora held her father, she proposed to the Spokane Ministerial Alliance that fathers be honoured. She suggested the 5th of June to be the day to commemorate fathers, and this was the same day as her father's birthday. The Alliance settled for the third Sunday (in Christianity Sunday is the Lord's day) in June. Father's Day has Methodist ties. For more on this false religion please read Part 3 of this book.

The world saw the first Father's Day being celebrated on the 19th of June 1910 in Spokane, Washington.

I am convinced that Father's Day is strategically placed on the Lord's Day by the principalities that rule this world. Although it may seem thoughtful, loving and caring for now it won't be long before the actual plan is revealed. As Christians it is important that we be still and allows God to open our eyes so that we are able to identify potential danger even long before it takes over our lives.

[28]The two holidays, mother's day and father's day share one common theme: observance on the day of veneration of the Sun - Sunday. This commonality betrays their connection with solar worship. The fact that it is held on or near the summer solstice, is a key to unlocking the mystery that leads to its Pagan source.

Most agronomic civilizations since ancient times, have commemorated the summer solstice with celebrations and worship of the sun.

Also known in some English speaking countries as Midsummer, it was often was celebrated with bonfires, sometimes referred to as "setting the watch."
It was believed that this fire would prevent evil spirits from entering a village. This Pagan ritual was in celebration of the power of the sun god, overcoming the darkness.

Sometimes called the Great Sky-Father's Day, it is associated with the Pagan ritual Litha, dedicated to the Celtic god, Lugh. This day, also known as the celebration of the "Holly King," is associated with solar veneration in many cultures including Alban Hefin, Birkat Hachama, Feill-Sheathain , and Thing-tide. Like all Pagan rituals, it was "Christianized" by the Roman Catholic church, after the time of Constantine. It is now referred to in the Catholic church as St. John's Day.

Sunwheels were often employed mark the occasion. A wheel would be set alight and then and rolled from a

---

[28] Craig Portwood - http://www.examiner.com/article/should-christians-celebrate-father-s-day

hill into a river. Some believed that if the fire went out before the wheel landed in the river, a good harvest would be ensured.

It is a sad fact that many professing believers will defend the practice of clinging to rituals and traditions that are rooted in pagan practice. They will protest that their indulgence in these customs are not against God's ordinances and will even try and quote scripture to support their desire. Some believe that God's commandments were abrogated by Christ's death on the cross, despite the fact that God's Word says otherwise.

When thou art come into the land which the LORD thy God giveth thee, thou shalt not learn to do after the abominations of those nations.

Deuteronomy 18:9

Hear ye the word which the LORD speaketh unto you, O house of Israel: Thus saith the LORD, Learn not the way of the heathen, and be not dismayed at the signs of heaven; for the heathen are dismayed at them.

Jeremiah 10:1-2

And why call ye me, Lord, Lord, and do not the things which I say? Whosoever cometh to me, and heareth my sayings, and doeth them, I will shew you to whom he is like: He is like a man which built an house, and digged deep, and laid the foundation on a rock: and when the flood arose, the stream beat vehemently upon that house, and could not shake it: for it was founded upon a rock. But he that heareth, and doeth not, is like a man that without a foundation built an house upon the earth; against which the stream did beat vehemently, and immediately it fell; and the ruin of that house was great.

Luke 6:46-49

The modern day believer can call Christ his Lord, but if he refuses to hear and do his commandments, they may have a rude awakening on judgment day.

[29]Mother's Day dates back to ancient cultures in Greece and Rome. In both cultures, mother goddesses *(Queen of Heaven).* were worshipped during the springtime with religious festivals. The ancient Greeks paid tribute to the powerful goddess Rhea, the wife of Cronus, known as the Mother of the Gods *(Queen of Heaven).* Similarly, evidence of a three-day Roman festival in Mid-March called Hilaria, to honor the Roman goddess Magna Mater, or Great Mother, dates back to 250 BCE.

As Christianity spread throughout Europe, the celebration of the "Mother Church" replaced the pagan tradition of honoring mythological goddesses. The fourth Sunday in Lent *(Weeping for Tammuz)*, a 40-day fasting period before Easter, became known as Mothering Sunday. To show appreciation for their mothers, they often brought gifts or a "mothering cake" *(Jeremiah 7:18)* and over time, it began to coincide with the celebration of the Mother Church. Mother's Day always falls on the second Sun-day of May, and like so many other holidays rooted in pagan sun-worship including Father's Day which always falls on the third Sun-day of June, usually fall on the day named in honor of their most powerful god -- The Sun!

---

[29] http://www.nazarite.net/evil-holidays.html

Annexure A - Babylon

Written By: Daniel Phaladi

In the last days the Bible talks about a dominant city that is a major center of commerce
that will be destroyed in one hour. Mystery Babylon The Great. The churches will tell
you it is referring to the Vatican in Rome.
To hold the view that this Babylon is referring to the Vatican, you basically ignore
98% of the Scriptures referring to it and hold to one verse that can be easily discredited
because a misunderstanding of one term in one verse that can easily be clarified. That
is how warped the whole Vatican theory is that most churches and prophecy 'gurus'
preach today when it comes to Revelation chapters 17 and 18. Why? Why do they want
the focus on somewhere else instead of where the Bible is really speaking of?
Consider this: The former prophets all warned of this coming Great Babylon. Let's
look at what each one said about it:
Isaiah said:
1. Babylon would be noted for its architecture, buildings and skyline (Isaiah 13:22)
2. Is the lone super power of the world (Isaiah 47:5,8)
3. Is the most respected and envied around the world and yet at the same time is hated
by the world. (Isaiah 18:2)
4. Has a unique and remarkable beginning, different from other nations and has been
awe-inspiring from it's conception. (Isaiah 18:2).

5. Babylon would the QUEEN AMONG THE NATIONS (Isa 47:5,7)
6. Babylon would be an END TIME GREAT NATION (Rev 17,18; Isa 13:6)
7. Babylon is called a lady, and has the symbol of the Lady (Isa 47:7-9). "LIBERTY" on
our money, and sits in the New York Harbor.
8. Babylon is nation "peeled", or timbered, a land of open fields (Isa 18:2).
9. Babylon is land quartered by mighty rivers (Isa 18:2).
10. Babylon is a land that is measured out, and populated throughout (Isa 18:2).
11. Babylon destroys her own land, with pollution and waste (Isa 14:20, 18:2, 7).
12. Babylon is the leading INDUSTRIAL NATION OF THE WORLD
13. Babylon has a huge aviation program (Isa 14:13-14;
14. Babylon is a REPUBLIC or a DEMOCRACY, it is ruled by many counsels (Isa
47:13).
15. Babylon's governmental system breaks down (Isa 47:13).
16. Babylon is bogged down with deliberations and cannot govern properly (Isa 47:13).
17. Babylon's leaders use astrology, seers and mystics for guidance (Isa 47:13; Rev
18:2).
18. Babylon labored in the occult from her very inception (Isa 47:12).
19. Babylon is a nation of religious confusion (Isa 47:12-13).
20. THE KING OF BABYLON is called LUCIFER, the ANTICHRIST (Isa 14:4-6).
21. The King of Babylon will rule from THE GREAT CITY BABYLON (Isa 14:4-6; Rev
17: 18).

22. A world government entity will rise up to rule the world from BABYLON THE CITY

23. This entity will rise up and use the military power of Babylon the nation to RULE
THE WORLD (Isa 14:4-6;

24. Babylon is a nation of higher education and learning (Isa47:10, implied throughout).

25. Babylon is a VIRGIN NATION, her lands untouched by major war (Isa 47:1).9.
Babylon's enemy will lie on the opposite side of the world,over the poles (Isa 13:5)

26. The enemy of Babylon will be noted for her cruelty (Isa 13,14, Jer 50, 51, Rev 17,
18).

27. The people of Babylon would think they are God's elect and eternal (Isa 47:7-8,

28. The nation Babylon dwells carelessly before the Lord (Isa 47:8).

29. Babylon becomes proud, haughty, and does not consider her end (Isa 47:7-8).

30. Babylon deals in the occult, in sorceries and drugs (Isa 47:9, 12; Rev 18:23)

31. The people of Babylon are deep into astrology and spiritism (Isa 47:12; Rev 18:2).

32. Babylon's enemy will lie on the opposite side of the world,over the poles (Isa 13:5)

Jeremiah prophesied:

1. Babylon would be the center of a one world Luciferian religious movement (Jer 51:44)

2. Babylon would be the youngest and greatest of the end time nations (Jer 50:12). USA

3. Babylon would be the most powerful nation in the world (Isa 47, Jer 50, 51, Rev 18).
USA

4. Babylon would be the HAMMER OF THE WHOLE EARTH (Jer 50:23; Rev 18:23).
USA
5. Babylon would be the praise of the WHOLE EARTH (Jer 51:41). USA
6. Babylon is a land rich in mineral wealth (Jer 51:13).
7. Babylon is a the leading agricultural nation of the world (Jer 50, 51; Rev 18).
8. Babylon is the leading exporting nation in the world (Jer 51:13; Rev 18).
9. Babylon is the leading importing nation of the entire world.(Jer 50, 51; Rev 18).
10. Babylon is a nation filled with warehouses and granaries (Jer 50:26).
11. Babylon is the leading INDUSTRIAL NATION OF THE WORLD (Isa 13, 47, Jer 50,
51; Rev 18).
12. Babylon is noted for her horses (Jer 50:37). Think Kentucky
13. Babylon is noted for her cattle, sheep and other livestock (Jer 50:26, 27; Rev 18:13).
14. Babylon is noted for her fine flour and mill operations (Rev 18:13)
15. Babylon is a nation of farmers and harvests huge crops (Jer 50:16, 26, 27).28.
Babylon has a huge aviation program (Isa 14:13-14; Jer 51:53; Hab 1:6-10).
16. Babylon's skies are filled with the whisper of aircraft wings (Isa 18:1; Jer 51:53).
17. Babylon has a huge space industry, has "mounted up to the heavens"
(Jer 51:53).
18. Babylon fortifies her skies with a huge military aviation program (Jer 51:53).
19. Babylon is portrayed as a leading in high tech weapons and abilities (Jer 51:53; Hab

1:6-10; implied throughout).

20. Babylon is a coastal nation and sits upon MANY WATERS (Jer 51:13).

21. Babylon is nation filled with a "mingled" people (Jer 50:37).

22. Babylon is a SINGULAR NATION founded upon OUT OF MANY, ONE (Isa 13, 47, Jer 50, 51, Hab 1).

23. Babylon was born as a CHRISTIAN NATION (Jer 50:12).

24. Babylon turns upon its heritage and destroys it all in the end (Jer 50:11).

25. Babylon's Christian leaders lead their flock astray in prophecy and salvation (Jer 50:6; implied Rev 18:2).

26. Babylon's Christian leaders are "strangers" in the Lord Houses of Worship (Jer 51:51).

27. Babylon sets of detention centers for Jews and Christians and rounds them up for extermination (Jer 50:7, 33; 51:35, 49; Rev 17:6; 18:24).

28. Babylon has a mother nation that remains in existence from her birth to death (Jer 50: 12). (ENGLAND)

29. The mother of Babylon has the symbol of the LION (Dan7:4; Eze 38:13; Jer 51:38; Psalms 17:12).

30. The mother of Babylon will rule over her daughter her entire life (Dan 7:4; Jer 50:12). Follow the money, we are under total control of England's Banks, and have been since 1914

31. The mother of Babylon will be a state of major decline as the end nears (Jer 50:12).

32. Babylon is considered to be a lion's whelp (Eze 38:13; Jer 51:38).58.

33. Babylon will have the symbol of the EAGLE and builds her nest in the stars (Dan 7:4
EAGLE WINGS; Isa 14:13-14; Jer 51:53). Who else has a space program as we do?

34. Babylon is a huge producer and exporter of automobiles (Jer 50:37; Rev 18:13).

35. Babylon is a nation of CRAFTSMEN, experts in their trade (Jer 50, 51, Rev 18:22).

36. Babylon is a nation with a GREAT VOICE in world affairs (Jer 51:55)

37 .Babylon will be instrumental in the setting up of Israel in the Middle East, and is the
home of God's people (Jer 50:47;51:45).

38. Babylon will have a major enemy to her north (Jer 50:3, 9, 41).

39. The enemy of Babylon will also have a huge aviation military machine (Jer 50:9, 14,
Rev 18:8, 18 implied throughout).

40. Babylon will have all of her borders cut off, and there will be no way of escape (Jer
50:28; 51:32).

41. Babylon is land vast land with huge cities, towns and villages throughout (Implied
throughout).

42. Babylon will have been a huge missionary nation for Jesus Christ (Jer 50:11; 51:7).

43. Babylon would be a home to multitudes of Jews who leave (Jer 50:4-6, 8; 51:6, 45)

44. The people of Babylon would not know their true identity(Jer 50:6, implied
throughout).

45. The people of Babylon would grow mad upon their idols (Jer 50:2, 38; Hab 2:18).

46. How is the hammer of the whole earth cut asunder and broken! how is Babylon
become a desolation among the nations! -Jeremiah 50:23

47. O thou that dwellest upon many waters, abundant in treasures, thine end is come,
and the measure of thy covetousness. The LORD of hosts hath sworn by himself,
saying, Surely I will fill thee with men, as with caterpillars; and they shall lift up a shout
against thee. -Jeremiah 51:12-14

48. Plays a leadership role in Outer Space Exploration (Jer. 51:3)

49. Is where the world's leaders meet and assemble (Jer. 51:44)

50. Incorporated many aspects of the old Babylonian religion (Jer. 50:2).

The Apostle John said in the Book of Revelation:

1. Babylon deals in the occult, in sorceries and drugs (Isa 47:9, 12; Rev 18:23)

2. The people of Babylon would go into deep sins of all kinds (Rev 18:5).

3. The people of Babylon would think they are God's elect and eternal (Isa 47:7-8, Rev 18:7).

4. The people of Babylon would enjoy the highest standard of living in the world (Rev 18:7).

5. Babylon will be destroyed by nuclear fire (Implied throughout)

6. Babylon is land vast land with huge cities, towns and villages throughout (Implied
throughout).

7. The enemy of Babylon will be noted for her cruelty (Isa 13,14, Jer 50, 51, Rev 17, 18).

8. The enemy of Babylon will also have a huge aviation military machine (Jer 50:9, 14,
Rev 18:8, 18 implied throughout).

9. Babylon has a vast military machine (Jer 50:36; 51:30; Hab 1 & 2, Rev 13:4).

10. This entity will rise up and use the military power of Babylon the nation to RULE
THE WORLD (Isa 14:4-6; Hab 1 & 2, Rev 13, 17).
11. Babylon is a huge producer and exporter of automobiles (Jer 50:37; Rev 18:13).
12. Babylon is a nation of CRAFTSMEN, experts in their trade (Jer 50, 51, Rev 18:22).
13. Babylon is noted for her jewelry of gold and silver (Rev 18:22).
14. Babylon is a huge importer and exporter of spices (Rev 18:13).
15. Babylon is a huge exporter of fine marble products (Rev 18:22).
16. Babylon is noted for her iron and steel production (Rev 18:12).
17. Babylon has huge corporations that have bases around the world (Rev 18:23,
implied throughout)
18. A world government entity will rise up to rule the world from BABYLON THE CITY
(Isa 14; Hab 2, Rev 13, 17, 18).
19. Babylon turns totally antichrist and is the leading antichrist power at the end (Rev
18:2; Isa 14:4-6).
20. The King of Babylon will rule from THE GREAT CITY BABYLON (Isa 14:4-6; Rev
17: 18).
21. Babylon turns upon its own people and imprisons and slays them by millions (Jer
50:7,33; 51:35; 39; Dan 7:25; Rev 13:7;17:6; 18:24).
22. Babylon sets of detention centers for Jews and Christians and rounds them up for
extermination (Jer 50:7, 33; 51:35, 49; Rev 17:6; 18:24).
23. The people of Babylon are deep into astrology and spiritism (Isa 47:12; Rev 18:2).
24. Babylon becomes the home of all antichrist religions in the world (Rev 18:2).

25. Babylon's Christian leaders lead their flock astray in prophecy and salvation (Jer 50:6; implied Rev 18:2).
26. Babylon falls to the occult just before her end by nuclear fire (Rev 18:2)
27. Babylon's leaders use astrology, seers and mystics for guidance (Isa 47:13; Rev 18:2).
28. Babylon trades with all who have ships in the sea year round(Rev 18:17-18).
29. Babylon is a nation filled with warm water seaports (Rev 18:17-19).
30. Babylon is a huge exporter of MUSIC (Rev 18:22).
31. Babylon's musicians are known around the world (Rev 18:22)
32. Babylon is noted for her cattle, sheep and other livestock (Jer 50:26, 27; Rev 18:13).
33. Babylon is noted for her fine flour and mill operations (Rev 18:13)
34. Babylon is the leading INDUSTRIAL NATION OF THE WORLD (Isa 13, 47, Jer 50, 51; Rev 18).
35. Babylon is a the leading agricultural nation of the world (Jer 50, 51; Rev 18).
36. Babylon is the leading exporting nation in the world (Jer 51:13; Rev 18).
37. Babylon is the leading importing nation of the entire world.(Jer 50, 51; Rev 18).
38. Babylon is center of world trade (Jer 51:44; Rev 17:18; 18:19).USA
39. Babylon would grow to be the richest nation in the world (Rev 18:3, 7, 19, 23). USA
40. All nations that traded with Babylon would grow rich (Rev 18:3). USA
41. The merchants of Babylon were the GREAT MEN OF THE EARTH (Rev 18:23).

USA, all one need to do is look at the huge multi-national corporations that exist.

American companies (merchants) the greatest on Earth.

42. Babylon would the QUEEN AMONG THE NATIONS (Isa 47:5,7; Rev 18:7). USA

43. Babylon would be the most powerful nation in the world (Isa 47, Jer 50, 51, Rev 18).
USA

44. Babylon would be the HAMMER OF THE WHOLE EARTH (Jer 50:23; Rev 18:23).
USA

45. Babylon would be the center for the move to a global economic order (Rev 13:16).

46. The Great City Babylon would be the economic nerve center of the world (Rev
18:3). New York is the Financial Capital of the World.

47. Babylon would be an END TIME GREAT NATION (Rev 17,18; Isa 13:6).

48. Babylon would have a huge seaport city within its borders (Rev 18:17). New York
harbor is the biggest in theWorld.

49. The Great City Babylon is the home of a world government attempt (Rev 17:18).
This can only be NEW YORK, where the United Nations sits.

50. Is considered intoxicating for it's high society lifestyle (Rev. 17:2, 18:3,23)

51. Is noted for its elegant and extravagant lifestyle (Rev. 18:14).

52. Is noted for being a city/nation of immigrants from all over the world (Rev. 18:15).

53. Is noted for a massive population (Rev. 18:15).

54. Is noted for its importation of drugs (Rev. 18:23).

55.Is the leading center of Commerce (Rev. 17:2)

56. Is the leading center of imports and consumption (Rev. 18:11)

57.Is a leading center of manufacturing (Rev. 18:22)

58. Is the center for world trade in gold, silver, copper, oil, precious gems, cloth, clothing, fashions, lumber, containers, household items, furniture, wine, livestock, transportation, health products, cosmetics, spices, marble, irony, and iron. (Rev. 18:11-13)

There is no other city or nation on earth that could fulfill these requirements other than the United States of America. There are some who hold to the view this passage is referring only to New York City. In fact, it refers to both NYC and the entire nation. The term "city" translated from the Greek means city or nation. In this instance, it refers to a nation led by its chief city, which is New York City. So in some instances it is talking about New York City, and in others the nation itself. And if you're not convinced, go back and read all these prophecies again about the last great nation on earth.

The Bible confirms that America is Babylon, and that the beasts coming will rule here, will be here, and will take over and destroy this country. Isn't it amazing that there are over 100 prophecies that only one super power nation in the last days could fulfill and the churches tell you today that America isn't mentioned in last days prophecies?

Neither does the Vatican fulfill these prophecies, Europe, or anyone else. The Lone Super Power now is the United States, and in the last days, which we are in, the lone super power of the world remains the United States. There isn't enough time for another nation to rise and fulfill all these requirements and become the lone super power of the world. Many churches (SDA in the forefront) claim that the Roman Catholic Church is Mystery Babylon based on one verse in Revelation Chapter 17 that has been misunderstood. Mystery Babylon is the United States. And once you realize this, you soon learn how dominant America is in last days prophecies and what the truth is in regards to them.

Let's look at Revelation Chapter 17:
And there came one of the seven angels which had the seven vials and talked with me saying unto me, 'Come hither; and I will shew unto thee the judgment of the great whore that sitteth upon many waters: (verse 1)

The Apostle John is told by one of the seven angels holding the seven vials (known as the 7 bowl judgments) that he is going to show him the judgment of the great whore that sitteth upon many waters. The term whore is in reference to the Greek word "porne" which in English we use for pornography. In Greek it is also used for improper sexual relations which could mean anything sexual that occurs outside of marriage. To the Jews who consider their relationship with God as a marriage, then the term could also be used worshiping another god or deity. In other words, idol worship.

Another thought is the fact that this nation has gone outside God and has aligned itself with someone or something else. In America, Satanism and witchcraft have become dominant, not to mention their alignment with Aliens and the forces of Satan in exchange for technology. America has over 129 deep underground military bases. How many of them are being used as joint military-alien bases?

The sentence "sitteth upon many waters" in Strongs it's #5204 which is figurative for many peoples. America is the melting pot of the world as far as immigration. The term 'waters' in relation to symbolism and Bible prophecy usually relates to people.

With whom the kings of the earth have commmitted fornication and the inhabitants of the earth have been made drunk with the wine of her fornication (verse 2).

This verse coincides with what Jeremiah said in 51:7 "Babylon has been a golden cup in the Lord's hand, that made all the earth drunken: the nations have drunken her wine; therefore the nations are mad."

America has influenced the other nations of the earth to partake in her fornication. They are drunk with the wine of her fornication. They are filled with God's wrath as they partake in America's fornication which is adultery, fornication, homosexuality, lesbianism, intercourse with animals etc. and also idol worship. Worshiping things outside and contrary to the Lord.

America is steeped in its masonic heritage with its masonic and satanic idols and symbols all over the land from the statue of Liberty to the dollar bill.

Not only are the many perversions here spreading across the world, but the kings of

other nations have also been negotiating their own treaties with the aliens and Satan's
forces to gain technology from them.
The Christian nations, or what were considered at one time to be Christian nations,
have turned their backs on God and have climbed in bed with the devil. This gives him
access and authority to rule over these nations and he's overtaken them all as he
prepares to come to earth as the Antichrist. Even the Gentile nations have secretly
gotten involved with the greed of having their own UFO technology.
So he carried me away in the spirit into the
wildernesss: and I saw a woman sit upon a scarlet
colored beast, full of names of blasphemy, having
seven heads and ten horns (verse 3).
The woman is sitting on the beast. She's dominating the red colored beast that is
full of names of blasphemy and has seven heads and ten horns.
The seven heads are seven mountains on which the woman sitteth as revealed
further down in verse 9. The term mountains in symbolism can refer to a land mass or a
political authority. In this instance, she sits in authority over 7 mountains, or land
masses. The Seven continents. The final "Rome", the final great empire of the earth, will
rule the earth, literally. The last great empire on earth will rule over all the continents on
it. How? Economics, refer to Revelation 13 where the entire world must join the beast
economic policy that originates from Babylon. Or, the United Nations that dominates
and rules over the continents of the earth.

Still yet, Babylon sits on top of the UN and dominates her. Babylon the whore,
dominates the beast and his 7 heads and 10 horns.
And the woman was arrayed in purple, and
scarlet, and decked with gold and precious stones
and pearls, having a golden cup in her hand full of
abominations and filthiness of her fornication (verse 4).
The woman is dressed in purple and scarlet. In symbolic term purple represents
royalty and in the last days, red represents the false Jews, the Edomites, and/or the
isms such as communism, socialism, fascism, etc..
Gold and jewelry signifies her wealth. The woman is seen as royalty. What does
royalty have? Wealth, power, and authority and she contains Edomites and/or one of
the isms. John even describes "having a golden cup in her hand" which is a trademark
of the Statue of Liberty which was originally designed to hold a cup, but was changed to
hold a torch instead to be a light in the harbor for ships for navigation. Cup is also used
as a term for judgment. The term abominations means moral or physical pollutions. It is
also just another term for sin. Abominations are sins. Fornication means impurity
and/or idolatry. Idolatry in her unholy relationship with Satan, secret societies, aliens
and fallen angels. America has many idolatries. She is filled with them.
A nation holding a cup. She is holding judgment (perhaps meting out judgment on

others as policeman of the world) filled with her many idolatries not to mention treaties
with unholy Satanic alien beings.
And upon her forehead was a name written,
MYSTERY, BABYLON THE GREAT, THE
MOTHER OF HARLOTS AND ABOMINATIONS
OF THE EARTH" (verse 5).
I view this verse a bit differently than most. The term Mystery always seems to
have an occultic connotation to it. Or it can mean a secret. In this instance I think we can let
it speak for itself since it is in regards to unholy Satanic ridden Babylon in that it is a
mystery is in regards to the occult. Or even that it operates, secretly (although getting more
out in the open) through satanic secret societies that worship the devil. Not to mention the
shadow government that operates behind the scenes in alliance with Lucifer and his alien
forces.
In other words, Mystery, or Occultic Babylon the Great. The term harlots is another
term used for prostitutes. These kinds of terms are almost used in regards to religious
termsIt has a religious and sexual meaning. But in this instance, I am led to believe it is
the religious one. Mixing Christianity with the occult!! (three high words?, UFO, Pyramids)
America, the Mother of Prostitutes. The Mother of all those who prostitute the Word of God,
or Him. Some of you cannot fathom the idea that America is this evil. You hold this country
in high esteem with all its pastors and religious leaders, its churches, radio and television

networks that seemingly teach and preach His Word and about Him to the world. But once
you get away from the religious programming and start seeking Him for the truth you realize
how evil our religious system is and how these false doctrines that most of our religious
leaders and churches teach today are leading people to hell and not to HIM. And until you
do that you will not understand the
significance of this verse.
These prostitutes are the false prophets and false shepherds leading this country, and
going out into the world, evangelizing and leading people to the pit of hell instead of to
Him. They are preaching a false gospel and a different Jesus than the one He came
here as. "They proclaim My Name, but they know Me not!" It is that horrifying and that
simple.
And if this isn't enough to prove to you that this entire passage of Scripture is talking
about America, read the book America, The Babylon by R.A. Coombes as he goes into
an indepth study on our masonic Statue of Liberty (a representation of the goddess
Ishtar) that alone fulfills all the identifying characteristics of this Babylon of the future. It
will shock you to learn that the founding of this country from the start had its roots in
occultic origins. Not to mention the layout of Washington D.C. and the capital-temple of
D.C. dedicated to the goddess Ishtar when constructed.
And I saw the woman drunken with the blood
of the saints, and with the blood of the martyrs
of Jesus: and when I saw her, I wondered with

great admiration" (verse 6).
Through martial law and the targeting of the saints through Patriot Acts 1 and 2,
tens of thousands, even millions will be killed and become martyrs for the Lord.
Since the 1980s under Operation Rex US government has built internment camps
across the country to hold 'resistors of the New World Order." All those it deems,
through their massive profiling over the years, who will resist the rule of the NWO. This
fulfills Jeremiah's prophecies about the last nation building internment camps and
slaughtering millions of its own people.
When disasters start to strike this country and cities start going under martial law,
they will implement their plans of eliminating Saints and Patriots who they have profiled
and listed as being likely resistors of the New World Order. How did they compile their
lists? various other ways, simply put, they spy on people. They spy on what you read,
what websites you visit, what groups you belong to, etc.. They even record your phone
conversations and read your emails. Over the years the NSA and FBI have compiled
records on just about every person in the United States. And from these records they
have compiled extermination lists and have you targeted by your social security
number.
Now do you realize the real reason for road blocks? When they want to target those
on red lists (immediate extermination) they will set up road blocks to find them. When

they stop your car they will run your SSN# to see if you are on the list. There are 3 lists, red, blue and green (some say it's yellow). Those on the red list are to be arrested and taken to an extermination facility immediately, no questions asked. Those on the blue list are taken to holding camps where they will be processed for extermination. Those on the green list are considered to be NWO friendly and not a threat.

The Satanic New World Order crowd fully intends on killing up to 60 million Americans to establish their control here in America without the hassles from possible resistors. And they have the facilities and capability to do so. And they did it all with taxpayer money and under the noses of the people.

When it says John wondered at her "with great admiration" it is not that he was impressed, he was flabbergasted! In the literal Greek translation it reads, "I was astonished beyond astonishment." He is disgusted at the ability, scope, and depth to which the saints will be murdered in America.

And the angel said unto me, Wherefore didst thou Marvel? I will tell thee the mystery of the woman, and of the beast that carrieth her, which hath the seven heads and ten horns" (verse 7).

In the previous verse it said the woman sits on the beast. In this one it says the beast carries her. Pretty much it means the same thing. Picture a horse and it's rider.

The beast that thou sawest was, and is not; and shall ascend out of the bottomless pit, and go into perdition: and they that dwell on the earth

shall wonder, whose names are not written into the book of life from the foundation of the world, when they behold the beast that was, and is not, and yet is" (verse 8).
and here is the mind which hath wisdom. The seven heads are seven mountains, on which the woman sitteth (verse 9).
Ok so we already know this from the previous verse. The seven head of the beast are seven mountains. This one verse is what throws most people off into thinking it is referring to the Vatican. The area of the Vatican is surrounded by 7 hills, not mountains. There are no mountains in Rome, if you were to take the term literal. In this instance, it is symbolic because we are being told that the woman sitting on the beast has authority over the entire world, all 7 continents. Something no previous empire had ever accomplished. Also, the term beast is masculine. It is referring to a person.
The woman rides the beast. Her power is unchallenged. She's in control of this beast. The woman is a nation. What kind of power? In economics, military, and influence. She is a lone super power.
And there are seven kings: five are fallen, and one is, and the other is not yet come: and when he cometh he must continue a short space.
And the beast that was, and is not, even he is an eighth, and is of the seven, and goeth into perdition (verses 10 and 11).
These seven kings represent the 7 empires of the past and the "present" as in

relating to John's time, which is approximately 90 A.D. or sometime towards the end of
that century. Some put John's book anywhere from 78 to 98 A.D. The ruling empires of the past were Egypt, Assyria, Babylon, Persia, and Greece.
At John's time, the ruling empire was Rome.
So what is the seventh ruling empire? The beast is from the seventh and becomes
the eighth himself. I believe the New World Order is the seventh and the NWO is being
dominated and run by America. The beast comes out of the 7th great ruling empire.
America is the lone super power today. There is no other empire since ancient Rome
that has dominated the earth as America has. Notice the beast is a king. It is the
Antichrist that comes from the last great ruling empire on earth, America.
And the ten horns which you sawest are ten
kings, which have received no kingdom as yet; but
receive power as kings for one hour with the beast.
These shall have one mind, and shall give their
power and strength to the beast.
These shall make war with the Lamb, and the
Lamb shall overcome them for He is Lord of lords,
and King of Kings: and they that are with him are
called, and chosen, and faithful (verses 12-14).
The 10 horns are 10 kings who receive power as kings for a short time with the
beast. The Greek word used, "basileis" doesn't always refer to kings in particular, but to
leaders. They have no kingdom as of yet. In other words, they are representatives or
ambassadors from other countries who become appointed by the beast as those

countries "kings."
The passage says these kings all have one mind and give their power to the beast.
This means they are all in agreement with each other and give their power and strength
to the beast. They form an alliance. They give him control or full support of their
militaries and financial backing.
So we have 10 people, who are awarded control of 10 countries, and then they give
that countries military and full support to the Antichrist beast. Doesn't make sense does
it? But that is what happens.
And what do all these geniuses decide to do? To make war with the Lamb, the real
Messiah Jesus Christ, Yahushua. They proclaim war on the Son of God.
Not too bright are they?
And he saith unto me, The waters which thou sawest, where the whore sitteth, are peoples,
and multitudes, and nations, and tongues (verse 15)..
The angel is telling John that the waters where the whore sits contains people of all
nations, races and languages. These people are in her land. In other words, where the
whore rules from, contains people of all races and languages. It contains immigrants
from around the world. America is the only nation in the world ever referred to as the
melting pot for exiles and immigrants.
And the ten horns which thou sawest upon the beast, these shall hate the whore, and
shall make her desolate and naked. And shall eat her flesh and burn her with fire.

For God hath put in their hearts to fulfill
his will, and to agree, and give their kingdom
unto the beast, until the words of God shall
be fulfilled (verses 16-17).
Ok, now remember the beast is a person, masculine tense, the whore is a nation.
The Beast comes OUT of the nation. He's from the nation itself. He goes and makes a
10 nation alliance, to destroy his own nation.
Why? Because he's a traitor? Well yes, but also because he subverted it to begin
with as a leader/president so he could do exactly what he's going to do, turn around and
destroy it.
He rises to political authority through America, as the President of the United States
no doubt, then makes an agreement and an alliance with the heads of 10 other
countries to destroy his own country.
Remember, the woman (nation) rides the beast. She controls him. He hates her,
(the nation) and so burns with her fire.
Doesn't make sense does it? But that is exactly what happens. As president he
makes her desolate and naked. He makes her desolate through the murder of
thousands, perhaps millions of the saints, then pulls her defenses down so she can be
attacked and destroyed.
The theatrics involved with bringing the former president of the USA back to
earth as God would warrant an Oscar nomination. It involves technology from a
gramophone at the space station to announce his arrival to theatrical light and image

effects from H.A.R.P. This whole charade is known as the Blue Beam Project and they have been working on perfecting it for years.

All of this stuff has been well planned in advance. In fact, it is American taxpayer money and the illegal sale of drugs and child pornography that has funded not only the preparation and the coming war on the saints, but the arrival of Satan as God in a spectacular display of technology with light and sound affects all the way from space to the earth.

And the woman which thou sawest is that great city which reigneth over the kings of the earth (verse 18).

Remember the term city also means nation. So it can be a literal city, or the chief city inside of a nation, or the nation itself. In this instance it's back to New York City itself and speaking of the United Nations, **which by now it already in ruling over the nations of the earth.**

Annexure B - Testimony of Daniel M Phaladi

Written By: Daniel Phaladi

The Number 27

The year was 1994. I was doing my standard 9 (Grade 11) and was 16 years old. I had not been baptized yet, and I did not really have much understanding about being born again. Sometimes, when my family went to church, I would go and play tennis. There was however something unusual, even though I never studied much of the Bible, I knew there was a character in the Bible called Jacob. And I knew how God loved Jacob. And so, although my name is Daniel, I just always referred to myself in my heart as Jacob. So I grew up believing in my heart that I was Jacob in the Bible.

On 27 November 1994 I was studying for my final examination. I had decided on this particular day to go and study at the National Library instead of my usual studying place which was my room at home. As I was busy studying, I realized I needed stationery from the CNA bookstore, so I went to the bookstore to get some pencils and some stationery.

When I was in the CNA, for the first time in my life I heard a "soft voice", speak to me. At first I thought it was me thinking, but then I soon realized, this "voice" was "thinking" different from what I would normally think. The voice said I should go to the shelves and look at the newspapers. I then reluctantly went over to the shelves, and looked over where there were many newspapers and magazines. As soon as I laid my eyes on the papers, something caught my attention. Each newspaper had a face of a lion on the first page. In other words different newspapers and magazines were reporting different stories about lions. I found that remarkable. The stories were not even related to each other. So I wondered to myself "Why do newspapers have faces of lions?". Then as if I was answering myself back inside my head, but I knew it couldn't have been me because the answer did not make any sense to me, this "soft voice" said, "you are seeing lions because today it's the 27th, 27 is a number of the Lion". Indeed, it was the 27th of November 1994. So I asked myself but what does it mean that 27 is a number of the Lion? Which Lion? And what does that have to do with me?

I went to the till to pay whatever I had with me with a puzzled look and a question in my head. I was only 16 years old and so you can imagine how puzzled I was at the happenings at CNA. So I went to the Library and I sat down. This voice in my came again.., it is not an audible voice, in fact it is like I'm the one thinking, but I know it is not my thoughts because the things I "think" do not make any sense to me. But for this testimony I will call it "the Voice". So the voice came again and said, why do you look puzzled that I said 27 is a number of a Lion.,, so I thought.. to myself.. well because it doesn't make sense to me. Then the voice asked me questions which I had to answer. The first question was;

1) "Who is the Time man of the year, Icon of peace and hope. The world's Superman". It was easy for me to answer, it was 1994, so I said Nelson Mandela. "Correct" the voice continued.
2) How long was Nelson Mandel in jail for? I said 27 years. The voice continued...the He asked...
3) Mandela when did he give you people your freedom, when is your freedom day, I said our freedom day is on the 27th of April. And finally he asked me one final question..,
4) What is the code of your country. I didn't know and started searching in the library and found out that the code for South Africa is +27.

So the head of a poor 16 year old boy started spinning. I left the library and headed straight home. Ok, I could see there was definitely something about 27 concerning this country, but what does that have to do with me? So I got home and something led me to count all the books of the Bible. So I counted all the Books, 66 books in total. 39 books in the Old Testament. And 27 books in the New Testament. So, then I somehow got the feeling that this 27 was not only related to South Africa, but had a Biblical application as well.

So I went to bed that night, feeling quite confused. My question was what does that 27 have to do with me? I could definitely see that there is definitely a spiritual implication to this, but what was it? But so far, I was glad that it had nothing to do with me. So days when by, and I did my matric. It appeared that the 27 had stopped and I forgot completely about it. Then in 1996 I was doing first year at university and went to do my first I.D book. The ID book was issued the following year 27 January 1997. I was amazed to see the date it was issued. Because I wondered, then why am I getting this 27?

So I studied and completed my studies, then I had to do my articles with an accounting firm in Johannesburg. The first thing when I got to Johannesburg was to apply for a Post Box. The computer gave me P.O box 127. I was further surprised by this. In the year 2003 I met my wife and got engaged to her.

We then both looked for a date in March 2004 to get married, because I wanted to use the Pretoria City Hall due to the number of people I anticipated to attend my wedding. The date that was available was Saturday 27 March 2004. So, I got married on that date.

We then started looking for a house. We looked everywhere in Johannesburg, North, East south and one day a friend of mine at work gave me a Pamphlet of houses that were sold in Midrand. I took my wife during lunchtime to see these houses. When we got to the developer's place, she told us we were late and all the places had been sold. So, we told her, "thank you ma'am" and we turned to walk away. She then stopped us and said, wait guys.., there is one unit in this complex, although the owner has already paid deposit for it, we wish you guys could buy the unit. This guy is bothering us and we don't want to sell to him anymore. So I asked her what is the number of the unit, she said UNIT 27. That is the unit I'm currently staying at.

At this point I decided that this was too much to be a coincident so I decided to call my father and tell him this phenomenon. I do not normally talk about it. So, after I told him he said, "Son, remember that my birthday is on the 27th of December". I also later learned that he was 27 years when I was born. My Dad then continued to say something, he said, since you were born, me and your mother know that you have a special gift, but just like the Bible says about Mary in Luke 2:19 "But Mary kept all these things and pondered them in her heart" we also have kept everything in our hearts".

One day I was driving back home after work, and I started having these questions to myself. What if these 27's that are appearing everywhere in my life are just random pure co-incidences. What if I'm seeing them because I want to see them. At that moment, that voice spoke to me again and said to me, what is your name so I said "Daniel". He continued asking, "Where did I place the book of Daniel in the Bible". I didn't know, so I parked my car and started counting the books of the Bible, starting with Genesis. I couldn't believe what I found! The book of Daniel was number 27 in the Bible. Then he said, count the letters of your names and what do you come up with, so I added the letters of my name, DANIEL MOTLHAWABOFELO PHALADI. The letters added up to 27 exactly. At this moment I started crying and I said "Lord what does this mean". But no answer came.

In the year 2010 April, I was sleeping and I heard in my sleep the same voice saying I am the Alpha and the Omega, wake up. So I woke up. Then I went and sat in the sitting room in the midst of the night

At that point scriptures started to flood my mind and I took my Bible quickly. As scriptures came to my mind, I had to read them, in order to gain understanding of what the number 27 means, and its relevance to my life.

The first scripture was Genesis 1:27. Where Go creates man in his own image. I still didn't understand what this meant. Then the next one was Genesis 27:27, because I've always referred to myself as Jacob. And in Gen 27:27, Jacob is receiving a blessing for the first time, from his blind prophet father after deceiving him into believing he was Esau. Then I went to Colossians 1:27, The mystery which is a "Christ in you, the Hope of Glory" I still didn't understand, then He led me to Matthew 1. In Matthew one he told me to count all the sons of David. So I started Solomon number 1, Roboam number 2, just like that. And I realized that Jesus Christ was the 27th from David.

I then got to understand the meaning of the 27. According to my understanding, God will have a people in the end-time who Christ will live in. Who their lives will only represents the Love that Christ has for the people. This will be a people in "Image" of God. Nothing can ever separate them from the Love of God, neither famine, persecution not hunger.

Encounter with the UFO's

One night, while lying in the bed around 2am, I saw as if my son, who was only a year old then, was approaching my bed. He seemed to come straight to the side where I was sleeping. As he got very close to me, he tried to climb the bed onto me. Somehow I stretched forth my hand to stop him from coming to me.

He then pressed harder against my hand, but I kept it stretched out. And then he pressed with a lot of power, which I knew it cannot come for a 1 year old, it was at this point that I noticed his eyes and features beginning to change. In no time at all, there was what looked like an alien in front of me, at that point I also noticed 8 to 10 other aliens in the room. This thing had 'changed his appearance" to look like my son. Through my curtains I could see many colours and a strange noise coming from the outside, giving the impression that it was their "space ship" They were all staring at me, and they started to do something as if to try and lift me up from my bed. I then said softly, Lord Jesus please come. What happened next was unexpected. The minute I called Jesus' name, these Aliens looked like they were being tormented and they disappeared, and their "Space Ship" disappeared too. I then said aloud "Aliens are demons", and immediately I woke up and did a bit of research on them. And I found out exactly that they are inter-dimensional demons. Fallen angels. I don't know what they were going to try to do to me, but I'm glad, Jesus Christ is Lord of All.

God bless you

Daniel

Annexure C - Sevenfold Glory of His Person

Written By: Daniel Phaladi

Larkin, Clarence (1919) – *Book of Revelation* from Page 11:

1. HIS "HEAD AND HIS HAIR."

His "**Head**" and "**Hair**" were "**WHITE LIKE WOOL**," as "**WHITE AS SNOW**." Here there is a correspondence to the "Snow White Wig" worn by English judges. This description of Christ reminds us of Daniel's vision of the "**ANCIENT OF DAYS**," "whose garment was white as snow, and the **hair of his head** like the **PURE WOOL**." Daniel 7:9. Daniel refers three times to the "Ancient Of Days." In Chap. 7:13, he distinguishes between the "Son of Man" and the "Ancient of Days," but in verses 9 and 22 he associates the "Ancient of Days" with a "Throne of Judgment," and as God the Father has committed all judgment to the Son (John 5:22), and the Father and the Son are one, the title "Ancient Of Days" is used interchangeably. And as the title "Ancient of Days" is applied to the "Son of Man" (Christ) at the time He assumes the Judgeship (Dan. 7:9-10), which is not until after the Rapture of the Church, we have here additional corroborative proof that John's Vision belongs to the "Day of the Lord." The "White Hair" of the Son of Man refers to His **ANTIQUITY**, to His patriarchal dignity, not that His hair was made white by age, for the Eternal never grows old, but it bespeaks wisdom and experience, and the venerableness of His character.

2. **HIS EYES**

"His **Eyes** were a **FLAME OF FIRE**." Those eyes that had often been dimmed with human tears, and that wept at the grave of Lazarus, are here pictured as burning with an "**OMNISCIENT FLAME**." How often when on the earth those eyes read the inner-most thoughts of men, and even soldiers quailed before His soul penetrating gaze, so when He sits as the Judge of men all things will be **NAKED** and **OPEN** before Him.

3. **HIS FEET.**

"His **Feet** like unto fine **BRASS**, as if they **BURNED IN A FURNACE**." In that day those feet that trod the Via Dolorosa of suffering will be like unto **INCANDESCENT BRASS**, that shall tread and crush Antichrist and Satan when He comes to "Tread the **WINE-PRESS** of the **fierceness** and **wrath** of Almighty God." Rev. 19:15.

4. **HIS VOICE.**

"His **Voice** as the **SOUND OF MANY WATERS**." There is nothing more melodious or musical than the babbling brook, or more thunderous than the rush of the cataract over the falls, and there is nothing more fearful to the criminal than the words of the Judge as he passes sentence; but how terrifying will be the sentence when with a strong voice the Son of Man shall say in the Judgment Day, "Depart from me, ye cursed, into everlasting fire, prepared for the Devil and his angels." Matt. 25:41.

5. HIS HAND.

"In His **Right Hand SEVEN STARS**." We are told in verse 20, that the "**Seven Stars**" stand for the "**ANGELS**" of the "Seven Churches." These "Angels" are not angelic beings but the Messengers or Ministers of the churches. What a beautiful and solemn lesson is taught here. It is that the ministers of Christ derive their power and office from Him, and that He holds them in His hand. If they are false to Him, no one can deliver them from His power, and if they are true and loyal, no one can touch or molest, or do them harm.

6. HIS MOUTH.

"Out of His **Mouth** went a **SHARP TWO-EDGED SWORD**." While the "Sword of the Spirit" is the "Word of God" (Eph. 6:17), and the "Word of God" is quick, and powerful, and sharper than any **TWO-EDGED SWORD**, piercing even to the dividing asunder of soul and spirit, and of the joints and marrow (the body), (Heb. 4:12), that is not the sword meant here. The "Sword of the Spirit" is the **Holy Spirit's SWORD**, and He alone wields it. The sword meant here is the **Sword** of the Son of Man (Christ), and it is the "**SWORD OF JUSTICE**," for the Son of Man, out of whose mouth this sword comes, is the "White Horse Rider" of Rev. 19:11-15, "out of whose mouth goeth a **SHARP SWORD**, that with it He should smite the nations." And that sword, like the "Sword of the Spirit" will be **TWO-EDGED** also, for the protection of His people, and the destruction of His enemies. This is still further proof that John's vision of Christ was as He shall appear in the "**DAY OF THE LORD**."

7. HIS COUNTENANCE.

"His Countenance was as the **SUN SHINETH IN HIS STRENGTH**." This recalls to our memory His appearance on the Mount of Transfiguration when "His **Face** did shine **AS THE SUN**," Matt. 17:2. And we read of the New Jerusalem that the inhabitants thereof have no need of the **SUN**, for the **LAMB is the Light thereof**. Rev. 21:23. And when we recall that the Prophet Malachi tells us that when Jesus comes back He will be the **SUN OF RIGHTEOUSNESS** (Malachi 4:2), we see that John's vision of the Son of Man was as He shall appear at the Second Stage of His Return, the "Revelation." Thus we have in John's "Seven-Fold" description of the **person** of the "Glorified Son of Man" circumstantial or indirect evidence that John saw his vision of the Son of Man, not on a Sabbath Day (or the "Lord's Day" as we now call it), but was projected by the Holy Spirit forward into the "**Day of the Lord**" and saw Him as He will appear then as the **Judge**, and the coming "**SUN OF RIGHTEOUSNESS**." (Clarence Larkin).

Below if the explanation from Branham, William (1964) – *An Exposition of the Seven Church Ages*, Chapter Two:

THE SEVENFOLD GLORY OF HIS PERSON
Revelation 1:14-16, "His head and His hairs were white like wool, as white as snow; and His eyes were as a flame of fire. And His feet like unto fine brass, as if they burned in a furnace; and His voice as the sound of many waters. And He had in His right hand seven

stars: and out of His mouth went a sharp two-edged sword: and His countenance was as the sun shineth in his strength." How deeply moving and inspiring was the appearing of Jesus to John, who was in exile for the cause of the Word, and behold, the Living WORD now stands before him. What an illuminating vision, for every descriptive attribute has a significance. What a revelation of His glorious Being.

1. His Hair as White as Snow.

John first notices and mentions the whiteness of His hair. It was white, and as bright as snow. This was not because of His age. Oh, no. The brilliantly white hair does not signify age but experience, maturity, and wisdom. The Eternal One does not age. What is time to God? Time means little to God, but wisdom means much. It is as when Solomon called to God for wisdom to judge the people of Israel. Now He is coming, the Judge of all the earth. He will be crowned with wisdom. That is what the white and glistening hair signifies. See this in Daniel 7:9-14, "I beheld till the thrones were cast down, and the Ancient of Days did sit, Whose garment was white as snow, and the hair of His head like the pure wool: His throne was like the fiery flame, and His wheels as burning fire… …Even the world understands this symbology, for in ancient times the judge would appear and convene court, dressed in a white wig and a long robe that signified his complete authority (head to foot robe) to mete out justice.

2. His Eyes as Fire.

Think of it. Those eyes that were once dimmed with tears of sorrow and pity. Those eyes that wept with compassion at the grave of Lazarus. Those eyes that saw not the evil of the murderers who hanged Him on a cross but in sorrow cried, "Father forgive them." Now those eyes are a flame of fire, the eyes of the Judge Who will recompence those who rejected Him…

…Those fiery flaming eyes of the Judge are even now recording the lives of all flesh. Running to and fro throughout the earth, there is nothing He does not know. He knows the desires of the heart and what each one intends to do. There is nothing hidden that shall not be revealed, for all things are naked before Him with Whom we have to do. Think of it, He knows even now what you are thinking…

3. The Feet of Brass.
…Those feet of brass will crush the enemy. They will destroy the anti-christ, the beast and the image and all that is vile in His sight. He will destroy the church systems that have taken His Name only to corrupt its brilliance and crush them along with the antichrist. All the wicked, the atheists, the agnostics, the modernists, the liberals, will all be there…

4. His Voice Was as the Sound of Many Waters.
…Have you ever thought how terrifying it is to a man drifting helplessly toward a cataract? Think now of that roar as he approaches his sure and certain doom. And just exactly like that is coming the day of judgment when the roar of the multitude of voices condemns you for not having paid heed ere it was too late. Take heed this very hour. For at this moment your thoughts are being recorded in heaven. There your thoughts speak louder than your words. Like the Pharisee who claimed so much with his mouth, but not listening to the Lord, his heart became corrupt and evil until it was

too late, even now this could be your last call to hear the Word and receive it unto eternal life. It will be too late when you approach the roar of the many voices of judgment and doom…

5. In His Right Hand Were Seven Stars.
"And He had in His right hand seven stars." Now of course we already know from verse twenty what the seven stars actually are. "And the mystery of the seven stars are the angels (messengers) of the seven churches." Now we couldn't make a mistake here on any account, as He interprets it for us. These seven stars are the messengers to the seven successive church ages. They are not called by name. They are just set forth as seven, one to each age…

6. The Two-edged Sword.
"And out of His mouth went a sharp two-edged sword." In Hebrews 4:12, "For the Word of God is quick, and powerful and sharper than any two-edged sword, piercing even to the dividing asunder of soul and spirit, and of the joints and marrow, and is a discerner of the thoughts and intents of the heart." Out of His mouth went the sharp two-edged sword which is the WORD OF GOD. Revelation 19:11-16, "And I saw heaven opened, and behold a white horse; and He that sat upon him was called Faithful and True, and in righteousness He doth judge and make war…

7. His Face Like The Sun.

"And His countenance was as the sun shineth in its strength." Matthew 17:1-13, "And after six days Jesus taketh Peter, James, and John his brother, and bringeth them up into an high mountain apart. And was transfigured before them: and His face did shine as the sun, and His raiment was white as the light…
…In Revelation 21:23, "And the city had no need of the sun, neither of the moon, to shine in it: for the glory of God did lighten it, and the Lamb is the light thereof." This is the New Jerusalem. The Lamb will be in that city, and because of His presence, there will be no light needed. The sun won't rise and shine there, for He is the Sun and Light thereof, Himself. The nations that come into it will walk in His light. Aren't you happy that day is upon us? John saw that day coming…‖
…He's the Lily of the Valley, the Bright and Morning Star. He's the fairest of ten thousand to my soul. Yes, that great day is ready to break and the Sun of Righteousness will arise with healing in His wings.

Stratospheric Cloud over Northern Arizona

Abstract. *An unusual ring-shaped cloud was widely observed over northern Arizona near sunset on 28 February 1963. From a large number of observers' reports it is known to have appeared overhead near Flagstaff, Arizona. From initial computations based on four photos taken in Tucson, 190 miles south of the cloud, its altitude was approximately 35 kilometers. The most distant observation reported was made 280 miles from the cloud. The cloud remained sunlit for 28 minutes after local sunset. Iridescence was noted by many observers. Tentatively, the cloud may be regarded as similar to a nacreous cloud; but its unusually great height and unusually low latitude, plus its remarkable shape, suggest that it was a cloud of previously unrecorded type.*

Fig. 1. Stratospheric cloud over Flagstaff, Arizona, from a point about 160 miles east-southeast, after sunset. The dark clouds in the west are cirrus clouds on which the sun has already set. [I. E. Daniels, Springerville, Arizona]

Near sunset, on 28 February 1963, a cloud of unusual configuration and coloration was observed in widely scattered localities in Arizona and some surrounding states. The cloud took the form of a large oval ring (clear in the middle) with the long axis running north and south (Fig. 1 and cover photograph, this issue). It remained brightly illuminated well after the sun had set on high cirrus clouds to the west. From Tucson, 190 miles to the south, its angular elevation appeared to be about 6 degrees. A rough computation of its height, based on sunset geometry (*1*), made immediately after the cloud entered the earth's shadow, led me to appeal by press and radio for confirmatory reports in order to establish the approximate location and to secure descriptions from the largest possible number of other observers.

From approximately 150 reports, many communicated by persons well aware that they had seen a type of cloud unprecedented in years of sky-watching, it was quickly established that the cloud lay overhead in the vicinity of Flagstaff, Arizona, that it exhibited iridescence of the sort associated with stratospheric nacreous clouds in the arctic (*2*, *3*), and that its internal structure was very peculiar. To observers nearly underneath, the colors green and blue were visible, and a pinkish cast was noted at times. A fibrous texture, described by several independent observers as resembling a "wood grain" appearance, was present over much of its northern extent, but its southern end was denser and more cumuliform. Its overall shape was compared by some (ranchers) to a horseshoe or a horsecollar if it was viewed from the south; from the north it appeared as a closed loop with a long thin trail that could be seen extending northward, from the oval, and several observers in that sector compared its shape with that of a "hangman's noose." The cloud was seen from distances as great as 280 miles (near Douglas, Arizona, and Albuquerque, New Mexico, respectively).

Many observers reported a second cloud off to the northwest of the main cloud, with shape very much like that of the main cloud, but only about a quarter as large. Correctness of these reports has been established from some of the first photographs that have come in from northern Arizona. The cloud was evidently moving generally southeastward, though visual reports are in some conflict on this point; this point can only be resolved from further studies by triangulation.

By fortunate coincidence, the cloud appeared within a few tens of miles of the U.S. Weather Bureau radiosonde station at Winslow, Arizona, and a high-altitude sounding had been completed there only an hour before the appearance of the cloud. A jet stream lay almost directly under the cloud and over Flagstaff, and there were peak winds of 98 knots from the northwest occurring over Winslow at an altitude of about 11 kilometers. The radiosonde run terminated at the 13-millibar level of atmospheric pressure (about 29 km), where the temperature was $-46°C$. There was very little direction shear in the Winslow wind sounding, a condition known to favor formation of mountain waves and believed to be conducive to nacreous clouds, at least in Scandinavia (*2*). It is possible, therefore, that the San Francisco Peaks just north of Flagstaff disturbed the flow so that wave motion was set up in the stratosphere, but this remains a conjecture, pending further study of reports of first appearance. Whereas some recent studies (*4*) suggest strong local stratospheric cooling as a prerequisite for the formation of nacreous clouds, the sounding at Winslow showed little departure from average temperature conditions in the lower and middle stratosphere.

Photogrammetric analysis of the four photographs known to have been taken in the Tucson area have yielded elevation angles of the near point ranging from 5.9 to 6.2 degrees. Because the exact range to the nearest point of the cloud is not yet known to better than about 10 or 15 miles in 190 miles, the exact height cannot yet be determined. However, the cited elevation angles plus allowance for earth curvature give

Dr. James E. McDonald

Supplement

May 31, 1963

Institute of Atmospheric Physics,

University of Arizona

Tucson, Arizona

STATUS OF INVESTIGATION OF THE NORTHERN ARIZONA

STRATOSPHERIC CLOUD OF FEBRUARY 28, 1963

James E. McDonald

<u>V. A possible explanation - a Vandenberg AFB rocket explosion.</u>

<u>A. Thor booster explosion.</u> A search of West Coast newspapers for the 28th disclosed a brief note on a intentional destruction of a military-satellite launch booster sometime on the 28th. Further information was found in the March 11, 1963, issue of Missiles and Rockets, which contained the following item: The Air Force deliberately destroyed a secret satellite, believed to be of the Discoverer series, after launching it aboard the souped up Thor Feb. 28 from Vandenberg AFB. All four motors were ignited at launch, but deviation from the programmed trajectory

forced safety officials to destroy the booster before payload separation. The thrust-augmented Thor (TAT) is a liquid-fueled Thor with three Thiokol solid rockets spaced around the Thor case.

This was the combinations first test. It became essential to find the time of this detonation and to explore further details bearing on the cloud, so both by direct inquiry and by inquiry through the Office of

Naval Research in Pasadena, further information was sought. Mr. E. E. Clary, Chief Scientist at Vandenberg, has very kindly provided unclassified information on this flight. The booster was destroyed at an altitude of 146,000 ft, almost directly overhead (but a bit south) of Vandenberg AFB at 1352 PST. As soon as this information was received, it appeared to offer the first solid clue as to the Flagstaff clouds origin. The altitude at detonation was close to the photogram metrically estimated cloud altitude, and the time of detonation made it necessary to consider very seriously the possibility that the Flagstaff cloud was some aftermath of the detonation. A crucial question was whether the time interval between the detonation over Vandenberg and the passage of the cloud over Flagstaff would match photogram metrically estimated cloud-drift speed and/or other independent wind-speed observations. Taking 1840 MST as the time of passage over Flagstaff, the 1452 MST (= 1352 PST) detonation time implies a hypothetical drift-time of 3 hours and 48 minutes. The airline distance to Vandenberg from Flagstaff is 510 miles, so the minimum mean drift speed required to associate these two events is very nearly 135 mph. This required drift speed is substantially larger than Schleys roughly estimated 110 mph, and even further from the 77-95 mph estimated from the Lordsburg photos.

Thus the agreement with respect to drift speed seemed rather poor, even though the height agreement between detonation and cloud seemed very encouraging. It was clearly necessary to seek further wind data, so inquiry was made concerning possible observational data from the Meteorological Rocket Network.

B. Rocket wind-data. The two nearest rocket-wind observation points happen to be rather well located to indicate winds along the trajectory that might have carried some explosion aftermath from Vandenberg to Flagstaff: One station is at Pt. Mugu, Calif., and the next nearest one is at White Sands, N. M. Queries were sent to both stations. White Sands sent a Judi sounding rocket up at 0800MST on 28 February, about 10 hours before the Flagstaff passage. At 140,000 ft. the winds were 109 mph from WSW; at 150,000 ft. the winds were 97 mph from WSW. The following day, March 1, at 1215 MST, White Sands launched a Loki II sounding rocket that indicated winds of just over 90 mph from WSW at both 140,000 and 150,000 ft. No sounding was available from Pt. Mugu on the 28th; but an Arcas launched at 0800 PST on March 1 indicated winds of 127 mph from the west at 140,000 ft. and 112 mph from the west at 150,000 at that time.

The rocket-sounding winds come tantalizingly close to fitting the hypothesis that the Flagstaff cloud was some byproduct of the Vandenberg detonation; yet the agreement is not quite close enough to be conclusive. The White Sands winds of the morning of the 28th seem significantly too low to match the required drift speed of 135 mph; but they agree rather well with the maximum cloud-drift speed estimated from the

Lordsburg photos. It is regrettable that no Pt. Mugu winds were measured on the 28th. They would have shown whether the winds at that upwind location were enough higher than those at White Sands to imply a mean drift speed of around 135 mph. (A

West Coast speed of something like 160 mph would be needed to yield the required mean of 135 mph, if we take the White Sands 0800 speed of 109 mph as typical of the stratosphere over Flagstaff near 140,000 to 150,000 ft. at 1840 MST on the 28th.)

Although Mr. Willis Webb of the White Sands missile Range emphasized, in phone conversation on the problem, that variations above or below measured winds at times between observations might well approach 20 per cent of the measured values at these levels, it remains uncertain whether one may concluded that the Flagstaff cloud was due to the detonation at Vandenberg. It is necessary to seek still further crosschecks.

Annexure D

From *Gifts And Callings Are Without Repentance* preached in Carlsbad, New Mexico in March, 1950:

After while, I met up with the Full Gospel people. And I… Just before then, I received the baptism of the Holy Ghost. And then look like it just kept coming more and more. And then it, He appeared on the river, one time when I was baptizing before probably ten thousand people, like a great morning star came down where I was standing. Thousands seen It. He went back right into the heavens.

From *God Revealing Himself To His People* preached in Cleveland, Ohio on August 13, 1950:

But It appeared down there on the Ohio River before nearly ten thousand people while I was baptizing in August. I was baptizing some fi–five hundred, I guess, that afternoon. Hundreds of them was standing, and the choir singing, On Jordan's Stormy Banks I Stand. Was about two o'clock. We hadn't had rain for about two weeks. I had my seventeenth candidate I was taking out in the water. And I raised up, and I asked him if he believed. He had. He would been repented at the meeting? Yes. I raised up my hand, I said, "Father, as I baptize this boy with water, may You baptize him with the Holy Spirit." And as I started, Something went, whew Brother Branham illustrates–Ed. I looked up. I heard a Voice. Said, "Look up." Thousands standing all over the bank on the Ohio River facing Louisville. Paper carried a big article of it. And I looked, coming right down out of the heavens, out of a place about as big as this platform, where the blue skies churning like waters… Coming right down out of there came a big thing, like a star, whirling around, going, whew [Brother Branham illustrates–Ed.], coming right down visibly before the eyes. Moved right down, looked like a star at a distance. When it got close, It looked like a milling fire of Light, moving right down and stood over where I was. Then went right back up into the heavens again. The waters let up. I've often wondered if that wasn't the Angel that was on the waters (See?) in Bethesda, you know. Went away… And papers carried a big article, "Mysterious Star Appears Over Minister While Baptizing." And on down, It kept coming.

From *Believe Ye That I Am Able To Do This* preached in Cleveland, Ohio on August 20, 1950:

When I was baptizing hundreds down at the Ohio River at the foot of Spring Street in Jeffersonville, where thousands were blacked on the bank… At right at two o'clock in the afternoon, I was baptizing the seventeenth person. I started to pray, and thousands standing there looking. And down from the heavens came that green, whirling down like a big star in the distance. When It got close, It was that Light, a Pillar of Fire. I think It's the same One that led the children of Israel in the days that went before Moses. And It's in the church today. It's here tonight, the same Pillar of Fire. When He told me, He said, "As Moses was given two signs to vindicate his ministry, so will you be given two signs. And by these signs, that people will believe." And there It is. I believe It's the same Angel of the covenant. And He came down when hundreds and hundreds standing there, people fainted, and fell, and everything. The papers carried a great article, "Mystic star appears over minister at two o'clock in the afternoon while baptizing." There It was.

From *My Commission* preached in Los Angeles, California on May 5, 1951:

About twelve years ago, I was baptizing my first group after my–one of my revivals at Jeffersonville, Indiana, where I lived at this time–my home is, rather. And standing on the banks of the Ohio River where Blank.spot.on.tape–Ed. had gathered out. And while I was baptizing… It was two o'clock in the evening, on June. And the seventeenth candidate, I was baptizing in water at the Ohio River at the foot of Spring Street. And I heard Something speak, and I felt Something take a hold of me. And I looked up. And when I did, coming down from glory came this whirl coming down where I was at. "Courier Journal Newspaper" packed an article of it, said, "A mystic star appears over a local Baptist pastor while baptizing in the river." They couldn't make out. Oh, up to probably ten thousand people saw It as It moved down where I was at, and went back up in the skies. Come right where I was and went back up into the sky. Well I… Many asked me what It meant. And I said, "I do not know."

From *Do You Now Believe* preached in Battle Creek, Michigan on August 17, 1952:

Recently when I was baptizing on the river at Jeffersonville, when all the local newspapers packed It, two o'clock in the afternoon when I was praying, here It come right down out of the heavens, right at two o'clock in the evening, June, or in the afternoon, rather, in June, about the middle of June, hung right over where I was, and a Voice from It, saying, "As John the Baptist was sent to warn the people of the first coming of Christ, so is this Message to warn the people of the second coming." Right back up into the heavens, when people screamed, fainted. What is it? God, getting the Church ready. You don't need no new doctrine. You don't need no new theories. You need real true hearts to Almighty God, to believe on God, and His Son, Christ Jesus. Have fellowship with everybody, all the Christians, by the Holy Spirit. Amen.

From *The Pillar Of Fire* preached in Jonesboro, Arkansas preached on May 9, 1953:

And He… When I was–I was a young Baptist preacher baptizing my first converts, five hundred of them down on the river , my first revival… I had about three thousand attend at the revival. And my education was so poor, till my girlfriend read the Bible while I preached.

From *The Angel Of The Covenant* preached in Phoenix, Arizona on March 1, 1954:

It was seen on the river there when I was just a boy, baptizing my first group in the Baptist church: Five hundred, one afternoon, at the foot of Spring Street in Jeffersonville. The newspapers packed an article of it: A Mystic Light Appears Over Local Baptist Minister

While Baptizing At The River .

From *Why I'm Praying For The Sick* preached in Columbus, Ohio on March 14, 1954:

One night while in prayer, away, there was a Man come walking to me on the floor. And I seen Him; this was not a vision. It was the Man. I'd heard His voice many times, saw Him when I baptized at the river , and I was first ordained a Baptist minister. Had my revival, baptized five hundred, my converts, after a two weeks meeting at the foot of Spring Street. And right there all the local papers packed the article of it: "Mystic Light Hangs Over Minister While Baptizing." And It can't… It was like a Pillar of Fire. And It hung down there and they… And then, the people asked me about It, and they got me scared, and told me It was the devil. And one night while I was in prayer… Many years later, just before coming to the Full Gospel people, I was praying, "God, take this thing away from me." I said, "Lord, You know I love You, and I don't want It no more, please." I went to pray all night about it. And I heard someone walking. I looked coming over to this side; there come a tall Man, big, long hair. Now, it didn't look like the picture of Jesus. I believe, I say this reverently. I believe, by vision, I seen Jesus twice. I–I–I… It was a little Man, but it doesn't look much like the artist paints Him. But I–I fainted when He–looked at Him, so I… it was… He was standing off to my side.

From *Sirs We Would See Jesus* preached in Louisville, Kentucky on March 28, 1954:

So then, I–I–I have never feared. I've just went humbly to preach the Gospel. As God sent me to do this. And the things that I speak of right here… Even in one of your papers here not long ago, the old "Louisville Herald," I believe it was, or something like that, declared the article when it was down here on the river, and that Light come down and hung over where I was at, when I was baptizing, a young minister many years ago out across the country.

From *Questions and Answers* preached in Jeffersonville, Indiana on May 15, 1954:

Just the same thing He said when I baptized right down here on the Ohio River, many of you was standing there, twenty-three years ago, right on the Ohio River that Light, Angel, come right down to where we was at, and said, "As John the Baptist was sent for a forerunner of the first coming of Jesus Christ, your Message will bring the second coming of Jesus Christ." And it's done it. It's… He hasn't come yet, but look what it's done; it's swept the world around. See? And today now, just thinking, the–the effort that's went forth, there's been literally millions…

From *The Deep Calleth To The Deep* preached in Washington, DC on June 24, 1954:

And now, they–you look in there, and you'll see another picture of It where It settled down, and a newspaper photographer caught that one at Camden Arkansas. But it wasn't authentic like this American Association. And they–they got it, and it was–then it became authentic. So we–and many thousands of people… I was standing on the river here some time ago baptizing five hundred after a revival, and It come right down where I was standing. And people fainted and–just there where It was. And It was just like a roaring noise, a whipping fire. I pray that God will come visible before the audience tonight in that manner here at the capital once more, if I can find favor with God…

From *Everlasting Life And How To Receive It* preached in Jeffersonville, Indiana on December 31, 1954:

Sometime ago, as a young minister, when my first revival come, I had it over here on the corner, where this housing project in a tent. I was baptizing a group down at the river that Sunday afternoon, when the Angel of the Lord made His first appearance in public in a vindication of the Message that I was to speak. And It was a Light came down from heaven and stood there. People are perhaps in the tabernacle tonight, who stood and seen that Light. And I started forth, telling it, and so forth. And all you know how the story goes, and on and on. And people sometime would walk away, and say, "That's just imagination." They'd leave a meeting where people would see It, and walk away, say, "I saw It." Others say, "Well, I didn't see It." Now, of course, God lets see who He wants to see.

From *How The Anger Came To Me and His Commission* preached in Chicago, Illinois on January 17, 1955:

So then I–then I was getting too critical on speaking with tongues, you see. But one day, then, how God vindicated that to me! I was baptizing down on the river, my first converts, at the Ohio River, and the seventeenth person I was baptizing, as I started to baptize him, I said, "Father, as I baptize him with water, You baptize him with the Holy Spirit." I started to–to put him under the water. And just then a whirl come from the heavens above, and here come that Light, shining down. Hundreds and hundreds of people on the bank, right at two o'clock in the afternoon, in June. And It hung right over where I was at. A Voice spoke from there, and said, "As John the

Baptist was sent for the forerunner of the first coming of Christ, you've got a… have a Message that will bring forth the forerunning of the Second Coming of Christ." And it liked to scared me to death. And I went back, and all the people there, the–the foundry men and all them, the druggist, and all of them on the bank. I had baptized about two or three hundred that afternoon. And when they taken me out, pulled me out of the water, the deacons and so forth went up, they asked me, said, "What did that Light mean?" A big group of colored people from the–the Gilt Edge Baptist church and the Lone Star church down there, and many of those was down there, they begin screaming when they saw that happen, people fainted.

From The Approach To God preached in Chicago, Illinois on January 23, 1955:
We were singing that when the Morning Star, the Angel of the Lord made Its first appearance over where I was standing in public, for the first time in my life, at the foot of Spring Street in the Ohio river in June '33, as a young Baptist minister, there baptizing.

From The Healing of Jairus' Daughter preached in Phoenix, Arizona on February 27, 1955:
I was baptizing them down at the end of Spring Street in Jeffersonville, Indiana, in the Ohio River, when… nearly seven or eight thousand people standing on the bank, bear witness, that two o'clock in the evening, June, 1933, how that a Pillar of Fire come down out of heaven, and hung over where I was standing. The "Courier Journal," and "The Times News"… no, it was the… [Brother Branham snaps his fingers–Ed.] Oh, I'll get the name of the paper just in a minute, He snaps his fingers again–Ed. if I could think of it, the Louisville

paper: great article: Mystic Light Appears Over Local Baptist Evangelist While Baptizing At River. Very mystic thing, people could not understand. Many fainted at the Presence of It. The Angel of the Lord come right down and hung over where I was. The "Louisville Herald" is what it was, "Louisville Herald, Herald Post" of Louisville, Kentucky.

From Blind Bartimaeus preached in Alberta, Canada in April, 1955:

And then on the river, when I was first ordained in the Baptist church (twenty-three-year-old boy, or, man), God come down that day when I was baptizing five hundred at the river, and appeared in that same Light. The papers packed articles of it. And then later on, they said, "Oh, well, it might have been psychology." When It come into the meetings and people, some people so close to God, or, may it not been that, may it was for them. Some people can see things and some doesn't see things.

From Enticing Spirits preached in Jeffersonville, Indiana on July 24, 1955:

Won't you come and go along? I remember when about five hundred of us standing yonder when I was baptizing a hundred and twenty, about this time of year, down here on the banks of the river, when that great Morning Star come shining there on the river. Hallelujah! A voice speaking from It, said, "Someday you'll spread the Gospel throughout the world." I said, "A poor, little, ignorant farm boy will never do that. It's the grace of God." Amen. Oh, who will come and go? Get rid of, lay aside every weight now. Don't listen to those enticing spirits. Come, listen to the Word of God, THUS SAITH THE LORD. "Blessed are they that hunger and thirst for righteousness, for they shall be filled."

From The True And False Vines preached in Shreveport, Louisiana on March 11, 1956:
I'd just been ordained in the Baptist church, about–about two weeks and had a revival there in the city, lasted for two weeks. And we was baptizing five hundred converts on the river that afternoon when the Angel of the Lord come visible. The newspapers and things picked it up, and so forth: twenty-three years ago. And the voice that He spoke from there, it has done just exactly what He said He would do.

From Witnesses preached in Chicago, Illinois on September 30, 1956:
Not only that, but I say this: I'm looking down here at the audience now. Here not long ago standing yonder on the Ohio River…?… gone and such unqualified, a poor…?… boy trying to do what thought was right for the Lord Jesus. There before thousands of people, the Pillar of Fire moved from the sky, come down there and said, "As John was sent for a witness before the first coming, this message you'll take will be a witness to the whole world for the second coming. That'll be proven," He said.

From God Keeps His Word preached in Sturgis, Michigan on January 15, 1957:
About ten years before that, about–about fifteen, nearly ten or fifteen years before that, when I was just a young Baptist preacher, no more than a boy, baptizing out there in the river, hundreds of people that afternoon, my first revival; and that Light come down from heaven and stood there before thousands of people. They fainted and everything, years ago when I was baptizing. And a Voice spoke from there and said that I would take a message around the world, which would start a revival just like that it did in the days of John the Baptist before the second coming

of Christ. I knowed a bit more about it than nothing. I wrote it down and kept it. They kept it. The newspapers had it, and everything. "Mystic Light Appears Over Local Baptist Boy, Pastor, While He's A Baptizing In The Water," and all about it.

From Questions And Answers On Hebrews 2 preached in Jeffersonville, Indiana on October 2, 1957:

How many remembers the Star hanging down here at the Ohio River, many years ago, when He said… Here's a picture of It here yet, when He come down. Said, "Your Message will go forth as a forerunner for the second coming, just like John went forth as a forerunner for the first coming." And look, around the world has swept a revival. Tens of thousands times thousands and thousands, and a great revival…

From Faith preached in Jeffersonville, Indiana on December 29, 1957:

And right yonder on the river , many, many, many years ago, when we was baptizing from my first little revival, there where this Angel of the Lord here, come down and hung over where we was at, and He said to me this message will go around the world, and would start a revival that'll sweep around the world, and it'll be just before the coming of Christ the second time. And when the–Brother Davis, Doctor Roy Davis, many of you know him, who ordained me into the church, into the Baptist Church, when he said I had a nightmare, how would I, with a seventh grade education go and preach to kings and potentates and monarchs around the world.

From God Called Man preached in Jeffersonville, Indiana on October 5, 1958:

How many's still living, when It first appeared before mankind down here on the river when I was baptizing them hundreds down there that day, in the building, raise up your hand. There's three or four hands: still living from years ago down here on the river when It come down, and the message of the Lord came: still just the same. Did It do just what It said there, that the ministry I would be preaching would start a revival around the world just before the second coming of Christ? Look what it's done. See?

From What Was The Holy Ghost Given For preached in Jeffersonville, Indiana on December 17, 1959:

I can hear the water splash yonder on the Ohio River. When I was a little old boy preacher about twenty-two years old, singing that there, and I heard… Looked up above me and heard a Voice, said, "Look up." Here comes that big Light hanging right yonder, come moving down over me and said, "As John the Baptist was sent to forerun the first coming of Christ, you'll have a Message that'll forerun the second coming of Christ." Oh, how could I believe it? But it happened just the same. And tonight revival fires are burning around and around the world. The great ransomed Church of God lifted Herself out of that place. And great campaigns of healing, and signs, and wonders, and miracles, showing forth the coming.

From The Revelation That Was Given To Me preached in San Juan, Puerto Rico on February 10, 1960:

Then when I was converted, I joined the Baptist church, started preaching the Gospel, right away. The Lord blessed greatly, and I had my first revival, a two weeks revival, five hundred came to the Lord. I taken them down at the river to baptize them. And while they was around ten thousand on the bank, watching… It was real dry, no rain for two or three weeks. People were praying for rain. And when I was baptizing the seventeenth convert, I heard a Voice, said, "Look up." It scared me. I was just a young boy.

The girl that I later married, was taking pictures on the bank. I heard It again; said, "Look up." And I was afraid to look up. Everyone on the bank was wondering what I was hesitating about. All–many peoples up and down the banks of the river … Newspaper photographers… And then It said again, "Look up." And I looked up, and as I looked up, here come that Light coming down. People begin fainting, falling, and a Voice came that shook all around the place there, said, "As John, the Baptist, was sent to forerun the first coming of Christ, the Message that is given you will be a forerunning of the second coming of Christ." Not that I would be a forerunner, but the Message was the forerunning. I'm no more than no one else. It's the Christ we're speaking of. Then I– them visions started coming to me more than ever. E-9 Now, that newspaper went on to Associated Press. It went all the way into Canada, and all through… We have the clippings of it yet. Said, "A mystic Light appears over a local Baptist minister while…"

From Elijah And The Meal Offering preached in Phoenix, Arizona on March 10, 1960:

But one thing that I'm happy about tonight, my wife… As much as we have been together, and she's seen the great visions of God manifested and come to pass. She was down at the river that day at Jeffersonville when the Angel of the Lord made His first appearance; it was packed on the Associated Press across the nation. Been a… It was 1933. She was standing there, but she heard the Voice but didn't see the Light. Where, even the newspaper photographers saw the Light. But she was quite young then, and about twelve years old, and she never seen the Light. She was

watching the people, many were fainting. And It just stayed there just about one minute and then It went right straight back up into the skies again. And the newspapers put a great article, "Mystic light appears over–over a local Baptist minister while baptizing." Went all the way into Canada, got on the Canada press.
From the message From That Time preached in Klamath Falls, Oregon on July 16, 1960:
Look at Elijah. What did he call? He couldn't help it. He's cried out against that Jezebel, did he? How… Here come John the Baptist with his same spirit. How could he have helped crying out about it: "It's not lawful for you to have your brother's wife." It cost him his head. See? God takes His man, but never His spirit. See? It keeps moving on down. The forerunning of the coming of the Lord Jesus, as You spoke down there at the river in the–in 1933 when I was baptizing there, and you see what happened to it. See? It's just exactly what He said it would take place. So you can't help it. And a few paragraph's later in the same message:
My wife, about six months ago, saw It for her first time. She was on the river that day when it appeared down there. When the article went all over the–the English speaking world on the Associated Press: "Mystic Light Appears Over Local Baptist Minister While Baptizing." Stood there… It talked; people heard It talking back and forth. Thousands of people standing there watching me baptize from my first revival–five hundred converts–in the Ohio River… It was in the paper, newspaper clippings; we have it. Got on the Associated Press, Canada got it, all around over the country. "Mystic Light…"

From The Signs Of His Coming preached in Cleveland, Tennessee on April 7, 1962:
You remember when that Angel come down on the river (which you have the picture of it, and you know about), when it said here about–in 1933, when I was baptizing my first group, that the message would sweep the world? And every nation they've got a revival going. They've had it everywhere. See? Sure. Pulling the elected out. That's right. "This Gospel shall be preached."

From A Greater Than Solomon Is Here preached in Bloomington, Illinois on April 12, 1961:
And the papers packed it, "Mystic Light appearing over local Baptist minister," a boy, while baptizing five hundred at the Ohio River. And He said, "As John the Baptist was sent to forerun the first coming of Christ, this message shall forerun the second." Here we are.

From Questions And Answers preached in Jeffersonville, Indiana on May 27, 1962:
Then I think about the river in 1936, I think what He said. What happened there? Many of you know. I was just a boy, and of baptizing my first baptism when that Angel of the Lord came down and stood over where I was at. Some people said, "You didn't see it." Then science proved that it was so. See, see? Now, what did He say there? "As it was, as John the Baptist was sent forth to forerun the first coming of Christ, your message will forerun the second coming."

From Perseverant preached in South Gate, California on June 23, 1962:
Years ago, as a little boy, when I was baptizing down on the river that day, just my first message in the Missionary Baptist church… I was baptizing five hundred. And that afternoon, on June, 1933, on June, about the 15th, here come that Pillar of Fire whirling

out of the skies, like the pretty, sunshiny afternoon, and go right down in that Voice and shook the whole country round there, said, "As John the Baptist was sent to forerun the first coming of Christ, your Message will forerun the second coming." Now, it's started a revival immediately after that. And there it's went across the nation, around the world, Pentecost reviving. And that's what has taken place, the second coming of Christ. And now, the newspapers packed it way up in Canada. It was on articles, and so forth, and went on the Associated Press. I kept telling people. Then finally the eye of the camera begin to catch it. And now they've got it back there.

From A Testimony Upon The Sea preached in Port Alberni, British Columbia, Canada on July 26, 1962: It's all down through the records. The first time that was ever taken, the Canadian newspaper packed it thirty-one years ago, across the whole province of Canada, all the provinces, the Dominion of Canada. Said, "A mystic Light appears over a minister while baptizing in the river ." That was in 1930, at the foot of Spring Street at Jeffersonville, Indiana, when around ten thousand people was standing there. And I was baptizing my seventeenth person. I said, "Heavenly Father…" And I was a young Baptist preacher, and I said, "Heavenly Father, I can only baptize him with water unto the fellowship of this church. But I pray that You'll baptize him with the Holy Spirit." And I said that, Something said, "Look up." I heard it a third time said, "Look up." And I turned and looked, and a great roar shook around over the crowd, and here come that Light milling itself down, and stood right over me where I was standing. And a Voice came from it, said, "As John the Baptist was sent to forerun the first coming of Christ, your message will forerun the second coming." Look at it today. A revival broke after that, and around the world it's went, a Pentecostal, Holy Ghost revival. Now, Lutherans, Baptists, Presbyterian, Catholics and all's receiving the Holy Ghost, everywhere, and the church making ready to go in. The message is coming to the end. See? There you are.

From Is This The Sign Of The End Sir preached in Jeffersonville, Indiana on December 30, 1962:

When that Angel there… And I suppose, besides my wife, there's people here tonight, from thirty years ago, that was standing close when That come down. Is there anybody in the audience now that was there when the Angel of the Lord, that come down on the river the first time, before people? Raise up your hands. Yes, there they are. See? Now, I see Mrs. Wilson raise up her hand. She was standing there. My wife, there, she was there. And I don't know who some of the rest of them is, that was standing on the bank here, before many, many people, when I was baptizing at two o'clock in the afternoon. And right out of a brassy sky, where there hadn't been rain for weeks, here He come with a roar, and said, "As John the Baptist was sent forth, to forerun the first coming of Christ, you're sent forth with a Message, to forerun the second Coming of Christ."

From An Absolute preached in Phoenix, Arizona on January 27, 1963:

Now, if I've got the wrong thing, then God will never confirm it. But if you have got the right thing, God is obligated to confirm it. There you are. And that's the proof of it. See? If it's right, God is obligated to prove it's right. If it's wrong, He will have nothing to do with it. So, I remember, after my first revival. I was down on the river, baptizing. I took the seventeenth person out. My wife, a little girl standing on the bank at that time. (I had never been married to my first wife that's dead.) And there she was, on the bank. And they was all standing there, hundreds and hundreds of people, yes, four or five thousand, maybe more, up-and-down the riverbank, a real hot afternoon in June. I walked out in the water, and I took a candidate, about the seventeenth person, to baptize him. I had around five hundred, after my revival, to be baptized. And I walked out in the water with this person. I started to raise my hand. I said, "Heavenly Father, as I..." And about that time, Something shook me. I thought, "Where is it?" I looked around. Everybody had their heads bowed, oh, as far as I could see. Way back up on the banks, there was, oh, cars and people piled all over the walls, and things. I looked again. I heard a Voice say, "Look up." And I was afraid to look up. I was just a kid. We got the picture of It. I said, "Father..." Something said, "Look up." I put my hand down. This young fellow, I was to baptize, looked at me in the face. He said, "Well, Brother Bill?" I said, "Did you hear That?" He said, "No." I said, "Heavenly Father..." He said, "Look up." I looked up, like this. And coming down from the skies come a Pillar of Light whirling around, a Voice coming from It, roaring, coming down. Said, "As John the Baptist was sent to forerun the first coming of Jesus Christ, so are you sent." O God! I watched that Light. I had seen It, since a little boy. I tried to tell people. They said, "You're out of your mind."

From The Second Seal preached in Jeffersonville, Indiana on March 19, 1963:

When He appeared down there on the river thirty-three years ago this coming June in the form of a

Light, you old-timers remember that I told you since a little boy that voice and that Light, and people thought you was kind of a little bit off at the head; of course, I would've probably thought the same thing somebody said it. But now, you don't have to wonder about it now, and the church hasn't wondered since 1933. Down on the river that day where I was baptizing hundreds of people, I remember that Mayer boy told me, said, "You're going down to duck those people, Billy." Little Jim Mayer down here, I think he's dead now. I think he got killed out there; some woman shot him. But he–he asked me, "Are you going down to duck those people?" I said, "No, sir, I'm going to baptize them in the Name of our Lord Jesus." And there was a woman going along in the group. She said to another woman; she said–made a remark, something about it. She said, "Well, I wouldn't mind to be ducked"; said, "that's all right; I don't care…" I said, "Go back and repent. You're not fit to be baptized in the Name of Jesus Christ." This is not nothing to play with. It's the Gospel of Christ, revealed by a commission, the Word. Just, now… You saying, "Nonsense," and "Foolishness," you could've placed it somewhere else; but remember, it's promised in the Word that this would happen, and just exactly what it would be, and here it is. See? Then down there that day, when they were standing at the river, and the Angel of the Lord that I had told you that It looked like a–a star or something in the distant, and then It got close, and told you how the emerald Light looked, and there It come right down on the river where I was baptizing, when businessmen down here in the city said, "What does that mean?" I said, "That wasn't for me; that was for you; I believe. That was for your sake that God did that to let you know that I'm telling you the Truth." By being a kid, a boy like, and about 21 years old, they–they wouldn't believe that (You see?), because it's too much for a kid.

From Humble Thyself preached in Jeffersonville, Indiana on July 17, 1963:

Do you know what brought these things to pass, when I first started and the Lord appeared to me down on the river and told me that? And Brother Vayle saw that, I believe, in a paper in Canada, many years ago, where that Angel of the Lord appeared on the river down there, it was on Associated Press, "Mystic Light over local minister, while baptizing ." And–and you know what did that? When we had the tent meeting just across the street, a tent that seated about, oh, twenty-five hundred people, ministers come from everywhere, and said, "Brother, come here a minute." I was just a boy, like, oh, just a kid. And they said, "How do you keep those people in one accord? They love one another till… I haven't seen people love one another."

From Go Awake Jesus preached in Shreveport, Louisiana on November 30, 1963:

That day down there, about thirty-three years ago, or thirty-four, standing on the banks of the Ohio River there, at the bridge, and about five thousand people or more gathered on the banks. I was just about twenty years old, twenty-three, twenty-two or twenty-three years old, my first revival. I was baptizing five hundred people, that afternoon. And the deacons had led me out in the water. About the seventeenth person, when I was baptizing, I heard a Voice say, "Look up." And I turned to look up. Billy's mother, we wasn't even married then, just going together. Here come that Pillar of Fire, circling out of the bright blue skies, at two o'clock on June the 15th, coming right down out of the skies, like that. And a Voice roared out, all over the place there, and said, "As John the Baptist was sent forth to forerun the first coming of Christ, you have the Message that'll now forerun the second Coming of Christ." Photographers taking the picture. How could we believe that, with just barely a grammar school education, and so forth? But I believed it. That afternoon, when I was so tired when I got finished baptizing , they had to come get me out of the water. I couldn't hardly stand no more of the current of the river . And It went, come down, and they took the pictures of It. It was on the Associated Press, went world-wide almost, up into Canada. Brother Lee Vayle has a copy of it yet, I think, from on the Associated Press, "A mystery Light hangs over a local Baptist minister while baptizing at the foot of Spring Street in Jeffersonville, Indiana." The Louisville Herald picked it up, took the pictures, and went off, and away it went across on the Associated Press.

From A Trial preached in Louisville, Mississippi on April 5, 1964:

I went down then to baptize a bunch of people on the river. When I was baptizing there, where about five thousand people standing on the bank; right in the middle of the day, two o'clock in the afternoon; hot, they hadn't

had a rain for a week or two; and standing on the bank. Here come that Pillar of Fire whirling out of the air, coming down where I was standing, and the Voice saying, "As John the Baptist was sent, and to forerun the first coming of Christ, your Message will forerun the Second Coming of Christ." The newspapers packed it, and it swept into Canada on the Associated Press, around the world, "A local minister, Baptist minister, baptizing , and," said, "a mystic Light appears over him." The very One that they caught the picture of here, and done it in Germany and–and everywhere. And it's done. My pastor said to me, he said, "Billy, what kind of a dream did you have? Why, you know you didn't see…" I said, "There were hundreds standing there, witnessed It." And they'd come down, said, "Oh, that's a mental delusion." Trying his best, that's old man Unbelief and Mr. Skeptic.

From A Court Trial preached in Birmingham, Alabama on April 12, 1964:

I remember down there, when I was a little boy. You've read my life story, and you know the story. I remember, on the river down there, when I was a young Baptist preacher, and was baptizing there. About ten thousand people standing on the bank, when one afternoon… My first great revival, somewhat around a thousand converts, and I was baptizing them out there in the water. The seventeenth person, I was leading out into the water. And I heard a noise, and I looked around. It was hot. It was on June, 1933, at the foot of Spring Street at Jeffersonville, Indiana. I was leading them out there. And the banks, all up-and-down, was just crowded with people. I walked out with this little boy. I had seen him at the altar. I said, "Son, have you accepted Jesus Christ to be your personal Saviour?" He said, "I have." His name was Edward Colvin. And I said, "Edward, do you know what I'm doing now?" He said, "I do, Brother Branham." I said, "I am baptizing you, showing to this audience out here, that you've accepted Christ as your personal Saviour. When I baptize you in the Name of Jesus Christ, you take on His Name. You rise for a new life. And when you leave here, you're to walk a new life. Do you understand that, Edward?" He said, "I do." I said, "Bow your head." I said, "Heavenly Father, as this young

man has confessed his faith in You. And as Thou hast commissioned us to 'go into all the world and preach the Gospel, baptizing them into the Name of the Father, Son, and Holy Ghost,' commissioning them to believe all things which You have taught." "I therefore baptize thee, my beloved brother, in the Name of the Lord Jesus Christ." And as I laid him into the water, I come up, I heard something going, "Whooosh!" I looked at the crowd, and it… I heard a Voice say, "Look up!" I thought, "What is that? Billy here, his mother, two or three years before we was married, she was standing there. I seen her face, white. She had a camera in her hand. "Look up!" I heard it the second time. I was scared. I looked around, the people standing there just looking, just dumbfounded. I heard it say again, "Look up!" And when I looked, here come that same Pillar of Fire that led Israel through the wilderness. Thousands of eyes looking at It coming right down over where I was standing. And said, "As John the Baptist was sent forth to forerun the first coming of Christ, your Message shall cover the earth and forerun the Second Coming of Christ." That went into the newspaper, on the Associated Press. Doctor Lee Vayle, here this afternoon, picked it up, plumb in Canada and around, "Local Baptist preacher, while baptizing, a mystic Light appears over him."
From The Trial preached in Tampa, Florida on April 19, 1964:

One day at the river , I was baptizing five hundred people at the river , when, all of a sudden, this same Light that come in when I was a little boy. And I had told the people I had been seeing It. They said I was dreaming and it was some kind of a mental conception that I had. But before better than five thousand people, at two o'clock in the afternoon, in 1933, out of the skies come this Cloud coming down, speaking these Words, "As John the Baptist was commissioned to forerun the first coming of Christ, your ministry will forerun the second coming of Christ," where thousands times thousands of people heard it, and newspapers give witness of it.

From A Trial preached in Tucson, Arizona on April 27, 1964:

And I had a baptismal service down on the river , on 1933, on the middle of June, about sixteenth or eighteenth of June. And standing out there, it had been so hot, for weeks. Hadn't had no rain for two or three weeks, and the country was burning up, nearly. And there was, I guess, around seven or eight thousand people on the bank. And I walked out in the water, with my seventeenth candidate, to baptize. And when I baptized, started to baptize, I said, "As I baptize thee with water, may the Lord Jesus…" When I said that, Something struck me and said, "Look up." And as I turned to look, after the third time It said it, a place about fifteen-feetsquare was churning up-and-down in them brassy skies. And down from there came that same Pillar of Light that come in when I was a little baby, that spoke to me in the burning bush, or the bush back there that day, and come into that bush, and come hung over where thousands of people. Newspapers packed it all across the nation, plumb into Canada. We got the clippings. "Mystic Light appears over local Baptist minister while preaching, or baptizing." And that Voice came down and said, "As John the Baptist was sent forth, to forerun the first coming of Christ, so will your Message forerun the second Coming of Christ."

From Questions and Answers 4 preached in Jeffersonville, Indiana on August 30, 1964:

I remember Sister Wilson there when I was called to her bedside dying with TB, hemorrhaging, till the sheets and pillow slips was laying bloody in the corner. I remember the Holy Spirit stopping the blood. A few days afterwards I baptized her in the Ohio River in icy water in the Name of Jesus Christ, and set her in the back of my open car, a little old roadster, and rode her from Utica… Wasn't that right? From… [Sister Wilson speaks to Brother Branham–Ed.] Yeah. Sister Hope, my wife, Sister there, was in the front seat of a little roadster, and my mother and Sister Snelling in the back. I got their picture, Sister Snelling, mom, and all, Mrs. Weber, Mrs.–my mother-in-law, all of them standing there, and Meda, just a little bitty girl standing out there, and now, gray-headed woman. [A sister speaks to Brother Branham–Ed.]

From This Day This Scripture Is Fulfilled preached in Jeffersonville, Indiana on
February 19, 1965:

Then, consider now, I ask you at this hour, you people here of Jeffersonville. In 1933, the supernatural Light that fell down yonder on the river , that day when I was baptizing five hundred in the Name of Jesus Christ, as about a twenty-year-old boy. What did It say, Jeffersonville? What was It at the foot of Spring Street there, when the Courier Journal, I believe it was the Louisville Herald, packed the article of It? It went plumb across the Associated Press, plumb into Canada. Doctor Lee Vayle cut it out of the paper, way up in Canada, in 1933. When I was baptizing my seventeenth person, under this Witness; and you know the rest of the story. And when I was standing there, baptizing the seventeenth person, a Light come down from Heaven, shining down above there, like a Star falling from the Heaven. A Voice said, "As John the Baptist was sent to forerun the first coming of Christ, your Message shall forerun His second Coming, into all the world." This day this Scripture is fulfilled.

References

http://www.iloveulove.com/spirituality/hindu/goddess.htm
www.patheos.com
http://www.ancient.eu.com/hinduism/
http://www.hinduwebsite.com/idols.asp
http://en.wikibooks.org/wiki/Wikijunior:Ancient_Civilizations/Vedic
http://hinduismfacts.org/hindu-customs-and-traditions/
wiki.answers.com › ... › Categories › Religion & Spirituality › Hinduism
http://www.mahavidya.ca/
http://hinduism.iskcon.org/lifestyle/811.htm
http://hinduism.about.com/
http://www.mailerindia.com/
http://en.wikipedia.org/wiki/Hindu_temple
http://bharathkidilse.blogspot.com/
http://www.beliefnet.com/Faiths/Hinduism/
http://www.aryabhatt.com/
http://hinduonline.co/HinduCulture/ListOfFestivals.html
http://www.raksha-bandhan.com/
http://www.weddingdetails.com/lore-tradition/hindu/
http://www.thecultureist.com/
http://www.culturalindia.net/weddings/regional-weddings/hindu-wedding.html
http://www.sahistory.org.za/hinduism
http://www.religionfacts.com/hinduism/symbols.htm
http://bibleresources.org/yoga/
www.sprint.net.au
David Steward
Jesus is Savior
Heritage Academy.

Encyclopaedia of Witches, Witchcraft and Wicca by Rosemary Guiley

"traditional witchcraft and occultism" African folklore, encyclopaedia

Traditional Witchcraft Sarah Ann Lawless and Spirit Walk Ministry

Author: Luna Silverwings Wicca or Traditional Witchcraft: Some Differences Posted: February 23rd. 2014

www.paganspace.net/profiles/blogs/traditional-witchcraft#sthash.MQIrZ7eG.dpufn Anglfire.com

Heritage Witchcraft Tradition and Academy Author: Grayson Magnus

blue-moon-manor.com

Topic of discussion - "What witchcraft do or do not believe in: Student "Flowing River": - study hall: - witchcraft 101 "Lucifer in witchcraft" from "Heritage witchcraft Academy"

www.inplainsite.org/html/paganism.html#sthash.LvW5sWC0.dpuf

American folkloric Witchcraft.

www.afwcraft.blogspot.com

alcohol and drug initiation; www.mylife4jesus.co.za

Wikipedia, the free encyclopedia

Manx Wytch www.manxwytch.wordpress.com

alcohol and drug initiation; www.mylife4jesus.co.za

Africa Traditional religion in Biblical Perception by Richard. J. Gehman.

www. ithonga.co.za

Dr David L. Cooper

wwwmysticmooncrow.wordpress.com

encyclopaedia of witches, witchcraft and wicca.

Kanaan ministries and Arthur Burk's article of August 2008

Kannaan ministries Journey to Freedom Giants and Strongholds
Kanaan ministries End-Time Battle plans:DID/SRA Soul Care Advance Training B3
Kanaan ministries Africa come forth out of Bondage
Kanaan ministries-Expecting-Welcoming our next Generation
Witchcraft: Harvestime Books: Vance Ferrell
www.mysticmooncrow.wordpress.com
Altered Dimensions www.altereddimensions.net
Alternative Medicine superstition by Sharon Hill October 7, 2013; www.livescience.com article by Benjamin Rodford;
witchcraft. www.mylife4jesus.co.za
Eagle spirit ministry www.eaglespiritministry.com
By Benjamin Radford, LiveScience's Bad Science Columnist October 11, 2013 www.livescience.com
Wikipedia
www.southafrica.com
website www.altereddimensions.net
www.paganlore.com
Mistress of Magic misstressofmagic.com
Know the classification of the magic
www.coventina.net
Evil defined From a Christian Perspective by Roger Boehm.
Demon busters.com
THE FETICH--WITCHCRAFT--A BLACK ART—DEMONOLOGY www.sacred-text.com
"Prepare for War" Rebecca Brown
Encyclopaedia of Wicca and witchcraft by Raven Grimassi; a Treatise on Astral Projection by Robert Bruce. www.bibliotecapleyades.net
 Kanaan Ministries

www.paganspace.net/profiles/blogs/traditional witchcraft#sthash.MQIrZ7eG.dpuf
National Geographic
Controverscial.Com
midwifes and witches-wondersandmarvels.com
Gemma Garry Traditional Witches observe Moon phases.
www.paganlore.com
Moonsmuses.com
www.oocities.org and traditional witchcraft by echo witch www.oocities.organd
The Bible and the moon; www.geocentricity.com
www.spiritedenterprise.com
www.ahayahyashiyaisraelitesunite.wordpress.com
Manx Wytch www.manxwytch.wordpress.com
The old ways The temple by Doug and Sandy Kopf also Traditional Witch website.
www.tradionalwitch.net
www.cyberwith.com; witches guide to life, Kala Trobe; www.controverscial.com/Murder%20by%20Witchcraft.htm
Charles Walton (murder victim) From Wikipedia, the free encyclopaedia
The EIGHT SABBATS OF WITCHCRAFT by Mike Nichols, copyright by Micro Muse Press
www.underthewaningmoon.tumblt.com/post/25318009234/widdershins-or-deosil
"The Monastery:"- Traditional Witch and "Forbidden Rites; Your complete introduction to traditional witchcraft Jeanette Ellis.
Ibid
About.com
www.christianinformation.org
Harry Potter: From Wikipedia, the free encyclopaedia

Harry Potter and International relations. Edited by Daniel H. Nexon, Iver B. Leumann.

www.jesus-savior.com/False%20Religions/Wicca%20&%20Witchcraft/harry_potter-real_names.htm

www.jesus-is-avior.com/False%20Religions/Wicca%20&%20Witchcraft/psychics_are_satanic.htm

www.sciforums.com

"The Harlot Demon unveiled, the death angel" Maxine Malcolm

www.freemasonryesotericatumblr.com

Alan, Brill. Dwelling with Kabbalah: Meditation, Ritual, and study

http://ebookbrowsee.net/gdoc.php?id=41848810&url=8e4cfd93f8bc80a37f3e4240ce67fa2b

Bible Gateway, King James Version & New King James Version

http://www.biblegateway.com

See chapter 5, "Sacred Rituals," in Donald B. Kraybill, Karen M. Johnson-Weiner, and Steven M. Nolt, *The Amish*. (Baltimore: Johns Hopkins University Press, 2013).

See chapter 5, "Rites of Redemption and Purification," in Donald B. Kraybill, *The Riddle of Amish Culture*, 2nd ed. (Baltimore: Johns Hopkins University Press, 2001).

See chapter 9, "The Practice of Forgiveness," in Donald B. Kraybill, Steven M. Nolt, and David L. Weaver-Zercher, *Amish Grace: How Forgiveness Transcended Tragedy* (San Francisco: Jossey-Bass, 2007)

Jamie Frater

Wikipedia

Refer to
http://www.vatican.va/archive/ENG1104/_INDEX.HTM for all Canon Laws
http://www.catholic.com/quickquestions/when-did-the-term-roman-catholic-church-first-come-into-being
http://www.gotquestions.org/origin-Catholic-church.html#ixzz36PGtaEKr
http://www.evidenceforchristianity.org/where-and-when-did-the-catholicism-begin/
http://www.religionfacts.com/christianity/denominations/catholicism.htm
http://global.britannica.com/EBchecked/topic/507284/Roman-Catholicism
http://www.infoplease.com/encyclopedia/society/roman-catholic-church-beliefs-doctrines-practices.html
http://en.wikipedia.org/wiki/Catholic_Church
http://www.catholicculture.org/culture
http://diocese-tribunal.org/canonlaw.php
http://catholicism.about.com
http://www.historyworld.net/wrldhis/plaintexthistories.asp?historyid=ac65
http://www.religionfacts.com/christianity/history/papacy.htm
http://atheism.about.com/od/papalelections/
http://www.rome.info/vatican/

www.ingramcontent.com/pod-product-compliance
Lightning Source LLC
Chambersburg PA
CBHW080527300426
44111CB00017B/2638